D0866527

a Trumpet to Arms

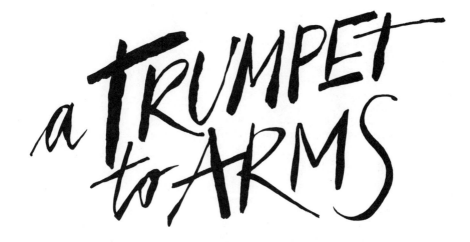

Alternative Media in America

David Armstrong
Foreword by Ben H. Bagdikian

Published by
J. P. Tarcher, Inc., Los Angeles
Distributed by
Houghton Mifflin Company, Boston

Library of Congress Cataloging in Publication Data

Armstrong, David, 1945-
  A trumpet to arms.

  Bibliography: p. 376
  Includes index.
  1. Mass media—United States. 2. United States—
Popular culture. I. Title.
P92.U5A68 302.2'3 79-66690
ISBN 0-87477-158-7 AACR2

J. P. Tarcher, Inc.
9110 Sunset Blvd.
Los Angeles, CA 90069

Library of Congress Catalog Card No.: 79–66690

Design by Cynthia Eyring

Manufactured in the United States of America

10 9 8 7 6 5 4 3 2 1
First Edition

For my parents, Richard Armstrong and Christine Pelton Armstrong

Contents

Acknowledgments

The solitary author's name on the spine of a book is deceptive, for bookmaking is a collaborative act—this book especially so. For their advice, encouragement, and support I thank my friends Arnie Passman, Steve Ranieri, Gar Smith, Dave and Leslie Whitehead, Carl Mellor, and Lionel and Henrietta Haines; my agents, Michael Larsen and Elizabeth Pomada, who gave the work form and direction in its gestation period; Vicki Pasternack, who brought the book to J. P. Tarcher and believed in it from the beginning; Peggy Kimball, who copy-edited the manuscript with an unerring eye; John Brogna and Cynthia Eyring, who designed the book inside and out; and my editor, Kirsten Grimstad, whose erudition, humor, and patience through many months of work were immeasurably helpful. I also thank the nearly two hundred alternative media workers who told me about their lives and work. While I can't cite everyone by name, each person deepened my understanding of a rich and complex subject.

That's too many people to fit into a garret anywhere in the world.

From the east to the west blow the
    trumpet to arms!
Through the land let the sound of it
    flee;
Let the far and the near all unite, with
    a cheer,
In defense of our Liberty Tree.

Thomas Paine
"The Liberty Tree"
July 1775

Foreword

Americans love heroes. We thrive on legends of lonely fighters for people's justice—the ragged kids at Concord breaking up the King's contingent or Andy Jackson and his backwoods boys destroying the most magnificent army ever to land in North America at the Battle of New Orleans. David-and-Goliath used to be our national parable.

But if our historical heroes are Davids, why is our vision dominated by Goliaths? One reason is that whatever the campaigns of our Davids may be, it is the Goliaths who write the histories, publish the newspapers, operate the broadcasting stations, and make the movies. They organize the world according to the Goliaths' needs. In the modern world, that means high technology and bureaucracy, which means orthodoxy and predictability, and, above all, preservation of a status quo favorable to giants.

Historically, our culture's treatment of its Davids has not been kind. The politicians, writers, and artists who have broken through barriers to change have not had an easy lot. This was as true during the American Revolution as in that extraordinary period we call "the sixties."

Tom Paine is considered a mythic revolutionary hero. Schoolchildren today are taught about his brave polemic pamphlets for freedom and that George Washington said the Revolution could not have been won without him. But we seldom hear of his most powerful revolutionary message or his ultimate fate. Paine's most telling argument was economic—that beyond the politics and legalities of the conflict, the colonies were sources of profit the crown would never relinquish. This simple message clarified the revolution for thousands of confused rebels who had been debating points of law with London.

Paine was contemptuous of elite power and preached that the only legitimate government was one controlled by common people and that served the common people. His insulting depictions of King George III shocked proper Americans, but in the end it helped destroy the residual belief in the divine right of kings. There was an echo 190 years later when activists heaped indignities upon Lyndon Johnson and Richard Nixon in the attempt to demystify imperial presidencies.

After the Revolution, Paine went back to England to sow the seeds of "power to the people" (echo again) abroad. He criticized the British government and supported the French Revolution. Indicted for treason, he escaped to France with the help of William Blake. In France, Paine again got into trouble by denouncing the Terror in favor of constitutional government. Paine was condemned to die but escaped the guillotine only because the terrorists were careless.

Nothing deterred Paine from his ideals. He criticized his old compatriate, George Washington, for excessive militarism. The proper Bostonian, John Adams, one of the few Harvard graduates to support the Revolution, called him "the filthy Paine." Fashionable young men of London had their cobblers form the initials "T. P." with nails on their bootheels so they could grind Paine into the dirt with every step. Paine returned to the United States where he died poor, sick and abandoned.

Paine was the first in a distinguished line of speakers of disturbing ideas and taunters of authority who do not fade into the golden sunset in warm glory and beatification. They are usually crushed or co-opted, or they destroy themselves. Truth—usually in the form of the truth-tellers—gets dashed to earth. It does rise again but only at considerable cost to those who resurrect it. So it was in the beginning of the Republic and so it was 190 years later.

The incredibly creative and chaotic period labeled "the 1960s" was not the American Revolution, though some of its activists thought it was. Nor was it a coherent campaign against a simple target, though some rebels thought that unseating Lyndon Johnson would have the same liberating impact as bouncing King George. But it was an important rebellion against the accumulated rigidities of oppressive puritanism, commercialized culture, corporate power, warmaking, and race, class and sex prejudice. It was a conglomeration of passions with a multitude of forms, some violent, most not. Most of it was the work of a new generation sufficiently educated and informed to see intolerable conflicts within their society who chose not to die for those conflicts in Vietnam. Most of them had the boldness of Tom Paine—though they lacked generals on their side—and shared Paine's contempt for the authorities. But the centuries had made a difference.

Like Tom Paine, the new dissidents began to speak in stark and impolite terms calculated to shake and enrage a smug and proper society.

An early manifestation was appropriately called The Free Speech Movement. Thousands marched, made speeches, lay down on the tracks of troop trains. Some threw stones; a few threw bombs. The authorities beat them, gassed them, infiltrated them, and, sometimes, as we know now from official records, murdered them in cold blood. In a passion of liberation and anger the protestors and rebels wrote, played music and acted political dramas on stages. But they faced a problem Tom Paine did not.

It was not hard for Paine, with a little bit of help from his well-placed friends, to find presses that would run off multiple editions of his revolutionary pamphlet, *Common Sense*. In Paine's time, most Americans lived in small towns and villages. A personal speech, a handbill posted in the tavern, a few dozen pamphlets reached most of the population.

By 1960 things had changed. The population had increased from 4 million to 180 million. Small towns and villages were replaced by urban agglomerations of millions of people. You reached an audience through large, technologically complex and expensive systems of communication—metropolitan newspapers, commercial broadcasting stations, national magazines, and Hollywood movies. Most of these systems carried standardized, conventional information and ideas with a little novelty thrown in to grab attention. The youth culture of the 1960s played to this media pendant for novelty, creating events and sensations to break into the news. Too late they found that it either corrputed them, or placed them in the short half-life of all media sensations—reporters and cameras turned away when the talk became serious.

The alternative was to invent their own media. And they did. They learned how to print newspapers in ways the Goliaths had never thought of. They published magazines that ran sophisticated investigation of corruption in high places. They learned how to make movies with handheld cameras and to project them on bedsheets. Eventually they developed polished skills that produced political satires and documentaries that played in standard movie houses. A whole culture was held together by music, including records and tapes distributed nationally outside conventional commercial channels.

In the massive outpouring there was some silliness, self-indulgence and corruption as there is in any culture, especially a spontaneous new one. But the net result was the birth of a new family of American media, without which much of the message of the 1960s would have been lost.

"The 1960s" was a period poignant in its ill-fated optimism, but it was the most creative decade we have yet experienced in this tragic century.

Out of the experience of the sixties has come a new class of weekly newspapers, citizen-supported broadcasters, unorthodox magazines, books and movies, small and sometimes ephemeral creatures that live between the cracks of an economy dominated by giants.

The alternative media are not always noble or unselfish or thoughtful. Most need profits to stay alive and some exist solely to make as much money as possible. But as a class they represent a greater possibility for introducing new ideas that in turn is a measure of society's ability to find its malfunctions, to discover new needs, and thus to survive. The alternative media are a crucial balance to the power of the giants whose computers tell them that there is less profit in new writers, new thinkers, new artists than in old formulas and slick stereotypes.

David Armstrong has written a superb account of a whole generation's invention of its own culture and communications. It describes the results, the new family of smaller communications that now seem to be a fixture in the American scene. But it is more than that. It is important social history of a period in danger of being trivialized by an old adversary, the media giants.

Ben H. Bagdikian
Berkeley, California

COMMON SENSE;

ADDRESSED TO THE

INHABITANTS

OF

AMERICA,

On the following interesting

SUBJECTS.

I. Of the Origin and Design of Government in general, with concise Remarks on the English Constitution.

II. Of Monarchy and Hereditary Succession.

III. Thoughts on the present State of American Affairs.

IV. Of the present Ability of America, with some miscellaneous Reflections.

Man knows no Master save creating HEAVEN,
Or those whom choice and common good ordain.

THOMSON.

PHILADELPHIA;

Printed, and Sold, by R. BELL, in Third-Street.

MDCCLXXVI.

one

Catalysts of Change

IN 1776, A CERTAIN RADICAL journalist—who had recently violated convention by attacking slavery in the Philadelphia papers—wrote a pamphlet exhorting the American colonies to declare their independence from England. The journalist was Thomas Paine, and his pamphlet was *Common Sense*. It sold a phenomenal 150,000 copies in sparsely populated colonial America and lit a fire under the timorous American independence movement. After independence was won, Paine set sail for Europe, where his writing helped fuel the French Revolution.

Paine's uncompromising journalism was the most dramatically successful use of media to spark social change in American history. Social and political activists in today's alternative media claim Paine as an honored predecessor, together with the abolitionists, suffragists, Transcendentalists, muckrakers, socialists, and others who have made extensive use of media to promote their visions of a better world.

This book is about Paine's heirs in the alternative media, particularly the activist media of the 1960s and 1970s, which sounded the trumpet to

Paine set standards of polemic writing that have yet to be surpassed in American letters. (Paine portrait and cover of Common Sense *courtesy of the American Philosophical Society.)*

arms on many fronts. The antiwar movement, the counterculture, the resurgence of American feminism, and the ecology movement, among others, owe much to independent media, often operated by activists themselves. These media—the alternative media and their predecessors, the underground media—serve as the central nervous system in the body politic of the adversary culture. Through that culture's media are transmitted the ideas, values, and visions that make up the shared language that radicals and dissidents use to communicate with each other and engage the dominant culture in dialogue.

Thomas Paine had only the printing press and the spoken word with which to help give form to America in embryo. Contemporary cultural and political radicals use those media, and others besides (video, radio, cinema, and some access to computers and cable television), to inform Americans that there are radical alternatives available to the way we live now—radical in the broadest, deepest sense, from the Latin radix, or root. Alternative media, in their most authentic forms, dig to the roots of issues as a means of clarifying problems and offering choices.

This book is itself the result of choices made by the author more than a decade ago. In the spring of 1967, I was an undergraduate at Syracuse University, and, like a lot of students at the time, uncertain about a good many things: the Vietnam war and my attitude toward it, the draft, drugs, the black power movement that was challenging comfortable notions of equality. I didn't see those realities expressed in the media with anything approaching the intensity and urgency that my friends and myself were experiencing them until I came across a bookstore copy of a thin weekly newspaper published on the West Coast called the *Berkeley Barb*.

The *Barb* was unlike any paper I had ever seen. In contrast to the mass media, which gave equivocal support to responsible Negro leaders who bided their time and worked for reform through established channels, the *Barb* backed the black power movement, insisting that liberation, not just legalistic civil rights, was the proper goal of people of all races. The *Barb* also strongly opposed the war. Articles were written about, even by, draft resisters and soldiers in the ranks opposed to the fighting, in contrast to the gentle dissents of liberal clerics on the op-ed pages of major daily newspapers. The paper did not neglect the cultural front either. One issue announced the upcoming Monterey Pop Festival, where tens of thousands of young people would gather for the first time to listen to music seldom played on commercial radio and never taken seriously by the mass media.

Reading the *Barb* and papers like it over the next few years confirmed that many people felt the way my friends and I did. They validated our existence in a media-saturated society in which, for many, the significance of movements and ideas is measured in column inches and seconds on television news. Since the mass media portrayed cultural and political radicals in an unflattering light, the underground media arose to fill a steadily expanding journalistic credibility gap. America was changing, seemingly irresistibly, and the new media were catalysts of that change.

Shortly thereafter, I began writing for—as well as reading—the underground press. In 1975–1976, I served as editor of the *Berkeley Barb*. By then, changing America no longer seemed as easy as it once did, although it seemed equally important. After having experienced the day-to-day realities at the paper which helped shape my values, I learned that what had come to be called the alternative media had many short-comings. Conviction could harden into dogma. The rude vitality that originally attracted me to the *Barb* and papers like it sometimes spelled a disregard for accuracy and analysis.

And yet I felt that alternative media were important. In the *Barb* and media outlets like it were heard voices of persons who were seldom permitted to speak for themselves: minorities, women, the poor, the working class, the politically unconventional, the artistic avant-garde. Nonjournalists who had something to say could say it in the alternative media along with hard-working, underpaid journalists who were no less talented for being unknown. Moreover, I noticed that important news reports broken in the alternative media frequently surfaced later— sometimes years later—in the mainstream media, often without attribution. I saw ideas and trends debuted, debated, and developed in the alternative media and then adapted by the mass media and passed on to the general public. I concluded that the alternative media, indirectly at least, affect the lives of everyone in America.

With this in mind, I felt it imperative to explore the role of alternative media in America—and thereby, I hoped, examine the social fabric of the nation itself through the lens of those media. I talked to people who work in the alternative media, and I read books and watched films by and about alternative media activists. Some of the latter were superb but they all dealt with only one medium—independent film, say, or the underground press. Since the media, alternative and otherwise, function simultaneously in real life, I concluded that a book about the alternative media must consider them together.

As Marshall McLuhan pointed out in the sixties, media combine to form an information environment within which we live much of our lives. As such, the media have much to do with how we perceive reality: the one-step-at-a-time logic of conventional prose corresponds to the workings of linear thought; songs resonating on the radio evoke the immediacy and ritual magic of preliterate society.

In the seventies, journalists such as David Halberstam and sociologists such as Herbert Gans and Todd Gitlin showed that media color what we believe about what we perceive. Protests of corporate media executives to the contrary, media convey, implicitly or explicitly, the political values of the people who own and operate them. They are not neutral conveyors of information.

In an age when media are so pervasive, their political coloration has far-reaching consequences. In his treatment of Henry Luce's *Time* in *The Powers That Be*, Halberstam cites Luce's suppression of Theodore White's critical dispatches from China in favor of hosannas for the despised Chiang Kai-shek as a leading cause of myopia about Asian communism. That myopia, Halberstam argues, helped lead to the paranoic vision of McCarthyism a few years later.

The conservative bias that Luce's *Time* carried to an extreme is not an aberration. According to Gans, all American mainstream media are conservative in varying degrees. In his study of bias in the mass media, *Deciding What's News*, Gans identified eight "enduring values" of American journalism: ethnocentrism, altruistic democracy (the belief that politics should be rooted in public service and that American-style government does this best), responsible capitalism, small-town pastoralism, individualism, moderatism, order, and leadership (essentially an extension of individualism). Observing that "journalists are not much interested in ideology or aware that they, too, promote ideology," Gans concluded that the American mass media are essentially right-wing in their news reportage, although their conservatism is tempered by a respect for liberal-minded reform. The enduring values that Gans identified in the mass media are, not coincidentally, the values infusing mainstream American culture.

In addition to upholding mainstream values in their content, the mass media uphold them in their form. They turn information into a commodity, with the unstated premise that access to information is a privilege for which media consumers must pay. Deadly serious newscasts are routinely interrupted by commercial messages, a form of everyday surrealism that media consumers have come to take for granted. Mass-media journalists refer to their field, without irony or apology, as "the news business."

The executives who oversee the news business have much in common with other captains of industry. They lunch with bank officers and corporation presidents as a matter of course, join the same clubs, send their children to the same schools, frequently sit on one another's boards of directors. Officials of the Times-Mirror Corporation, owners of the *Los Angeles Times* and *Newsday*, hold directorships of Pan-American World Airways, Rohr Corporation, Bank of America, Ford Motor Company, American Airlines, Colgate-Palmolive, Mutual Life Insurance, Security Pacific National Bank, Southern California Edison, Levi Strauss, and Kaiser Steel, among others. Referring generally to executives of major American newspapers, the authors of a special report on interlocking directorships for the *Columbia Journalism Review* wrote, in 1979, "The directors are overwhelmingly white and male, and drawn from among the most privileged members of society."

Within the mass media themselves, power is highly concentrated. Time, Inc., controls several national magazines (including *Time*, *Fortune*, and *People*); a metropolitan daily newspaper (the *Washington Star*); book publishing houses (Time-Life Books and Little, Brown); the Book-of-the-Month Club; a cable television franchise operator (American Television and Communication, the second largest in the field); and a film production company (Time-Life Films). Those diversified holdings give Time, Inc., tremendous power in acquiring, developing, and selling information packages. In 1979, *Time* excerpted passages from Henry Kissinger's *The White House Years* just prior to publication of the book by Little, Brown and selection of the volume by the Book-of-the-Month Club. It is difficult to imagine a more clear-cut example of information as product.

And information is an increasingly important product. Today, half of the United States Gross National Product is generated by the production, dissemination, and consumption of information in its various forms: the press, books, movies, records and tapes, government and corporate documents, legal briefs, computer printouts, radio, video discs and tapes, broadcast and cable television. Together, they comprise what the German critic and poet Hans Magnus Enzensberger calls "the consciousness industry."

The consciousness industry does more than entertain and inform. It furnishes many of our values and ideas and helps shape our behavior. People rely on the media, in Todd Gitlin's words, "for bearings in an obscure and shifting world." In his book *The Whole World Is Watching*, Gitlin writes: "The media bring a manufactured public world into private space. From within their private crevices, people find themselves relying on the media for concepts, for images of their heroes, for guiding information, for emotional charges, for a recognition of public values, for symbols in general, even for language. Of all the institutions of everyday life, the media specialize in orchestrating everyday consciousness."

It's not surprising, therefore, that consciousness itself has become a battleground. Revolutionaries and guardians of the status quo alike understand the importance of controlling the means of producing consciousness. The Ayatollah Khomeini smoothed his road to power in Iran by telephoning tape-recorded messages to sympathetic workers in the state telephone company, who reproduced his talks on tape cassettes and circulated them throughout Iran in a matter of days. In the Soviet Union, photocopying machines are few, and access to them is severely restricted; the rulers of that country keenly appreciate their potential as instruments of social change.

Realizing the centrality of media to modern life, social and political activists in the United States made fitful attempts to gain access to commercial mass media, even as they developed media of their own. For the most part, activists' efforts to secure a large national audience through the mass media were self-defeating. Martin Luther King, Jr., received a fair amount of generally balanced coverage in the national media, but more militant black leaders such as Malcolm X and Stokely Carmichael were portrayed as firebrands whose names became synonymous with violence. Observed Gans, "When, years ago, the news reported that Stokely Carmichael had 'turned up' somewhere, while the president had, on the same day, 'arrived' somewhere else . . . the appropriate values were not difficult to discern. . . ." Youthful war protestors fared little better, generally being portrayed as violence-prone, vulgar people whose unorthodox lifestyles warranted more attention than their politics—which, in any case, were presented as impractical at best, dangerously extremist at worst.

With conventional avenues of expression closed to them, radicals and dissidents started media of their own to express values and visions of a cooperative, peaceful, egalitarian society. It all began with the underground—that broad variety of media efforts that flourished roughly between 1966 and 1972 and were united chiefly in their opposition to the Vietnam war and their advocacy of drugs, rock music, and sex. Some underground media were reform-minded, dedicated to redeeming the American system, and some were radical, committed to replacing it.

The generation that created underground—and later alternative—

media was an affluent generation, the progeny of the prosperous Pax Eisenhower. It was the generation of the Baby Boom, beginning to sense its strength in numbers. And it was a generation at home with technology, children of The Bomb and the cathode-ray tube, primed to make imaginative use of the communications media to convey its message of change.

The underground's early expressions bore the imprints of the backgrounds, values, and personalities of their founders—middle-class white men in their thirties and forties who were themselves shaped by the libertarianism and hedonism of the Beats. Men like Art Kunkin and Max Scherr, who founded the *Los Angeles Free Press* and the *Berkeley Barb*, respectively (the first sixties underground newspapers); Bob Fass, who pioneered the freeform radio mix of talk, poetry, politics, and music on New York's WBAI; Stewart Brand, the creator of the *Whole Earth Catalog*; Paul Krassner, editor and publisher of *The Realist*; and Warren Hinckle, the editor of *Ramparts* in its muckraking heyday, were archetypal underground media personalities. Often flamboyant, always audacious, they were individualists who advocated new forms of community, mixing satire and seriousness in almost equal proportions, with a touch of apocalyptic rhetoric to spice the sauce.

By the end of the sixties, the activists these men trained and inspired launched media enterprises of their own in which collegial decision-making sometimes replaced the early patriarchal forms and new issues replaced sex, drugs, rock, and Vietnam as editorial preoccupations. Issues first explored in the underground media—chiefly feminism, gay liberation, and environmentalism—grew to full-fledged movements with media of their own, part of the expanded notion of what came to be called alternative media. In the early seventies, alternative media, witnesses to the governmental repression of underground media and movements, backed away from the confrontational style of the underground. They examined the commercial exploitation of drugs, sex, and rock more fully and critically than did the underground, and they explored the confluence of the personal and political. Many rooted their environmental activism in local communities.

Today's alternative media include activist newspapers and magazines, small-press publishers, independent film and video, community access to cable TV, comics, news services, user-controlled computer networks—even, in two notable instances, quiltmaking and breadbaking-with-a-message. Regardless of the medium employed, alternative media share several characteristics.

First and foremost, they are used as tools for community action and organizing. They have an activist rather than passive relationship with their constituents. They seek to create change rather than affirming things as they are.

Alternative media are not neutral. They are, instead, highly partisan media enterprises that make no attempt to disguise their partisanship. Alternative media activists frequently participate in the stories they cover. Sometimes they even help instigate those stories. In 1980, for example, worried about the threat of war, staffers at Berkeley's alternative KPFA radio looked for a revival of the sixties tradition of antiwar teach-ins to broadcast. Finding none, the station organized its own teach-in and aired the two days of activity live in a California-wide hookup with other community stations.

Organizing such an event would be anathema to mainstream journalists, who consider themselves neutral observers above the fray, whose ethics do not allow them to participate in the movements they cover. Such partisanship would be less than objective, they reason, and, therefore, unprofessional. But for alternative media activists, participation in the news is all in a day's work.

Most of the volunteer KPFA staff who put on the antiwar teach-in were not paid professionals. They were inspired amateurs, community people who decided to get involved with media whose goals and values were similar to their own. Because alternative media are set up to facilitate just such grassroots involvement, the participation of community people was welcomed, not merely tolerated. By providing access, alternative media empower constituencies that are usually shut out of the mass media, rather than penetrating markets with prepackaged information as the conventional media do.

Alternative media activists take seriously A. J. Leibling's observation that "Freedom of the press is guaranteed only to those whose own one." Outside of the alternative media, control of the media is restricted to a handful of people (media producers) who transmit material of their choosing to everyone else (media consumers). Visionaries such as Hans Magnus Enzensberger advocate "emancipatory" media—decentralized, controlled by the users, with a built-in, two-way capacity in which every receiver is a potential transmitter. In such a media democracy, the process of communicating would be more important than consumption of media products. The communications media would be deserving of the name, rather than serving mainly as a means of delivering customers to advertisers.

That kind of media democracy exists in embryonic form in the alternative media, although they are still small and few in comparison with the mainstream media. There is only one alternative television station (KBDI, near Denver, Colorado) out of some 1,000 American TV stations; two radical daily newspapers (the Communist Party's *Daily World* and the Yiddish-language socialist paper *Morning Freiheit*) out of 1,750 dailies; roughly a hundred weekly newspapers out of a total of 8,000 weeklies; and approximately sixty noncommercial community radio stations out of 9,000 radio outlets. The combined yearly budget of the five alternative Pacifica Foundation stations is $2 million—just over three percent of the $58 million budgeted for 1980 by the conservative Christian Broadcasting Network. Alternative media are minority media, attempting to grow in a cultural climate that is, by and large, inimical to their visions and values.

This inevitably leads to compromises, some of them serious enough to blunt the alternative thrust of the media enterprises that make them. Most compromises are struck over money. It is very difficult for media that do not carry compromising advertising and editorial fluff designed for maximum return to survive in a market economy. Most alternative media get by with marginal budgets raised from supporters who are themselves often insolvent. Thus, the temptation is always there to "sell out" or "go commercial." The result is a tension between ideals and needs, between developing constituencies and penetrating markets, which courses throughout the history of the alternative and underground media.

Alternative journalists have tackled the problem of survival in a variety of ways, ranging from the conventional heavy reliance on advertising of early underground papers such as the *Los Angeles Free Press* to the staunchly noncommercial stance of the listener-sponsored Pacifica radio stations (which do, however, accept government funds). Some alternative media outlets are supported by political parties, othes by environmental and other special-interest organizations. Still others subsist largely on private donations, such as the socialist newsweekly *In These Times*. Very few alternative media enterprises are self-supporting. Somewhere, a compromise nearly always is made, a dependency relationship accepted.

The alternative media's varied ways of handling (and getting) mney are paralleled by their diverse ways of handling power. The early underground papers usually had patriarchal, top-down management structures; Art Kunkin ran the *Free Press*, Max Scherr ran the *Barb*. This traditional setup was modified, and in some cases abandoned altogether in the seventies by alternative activists who tried to develop structures that combined democracy and efficiency. Instead of mimicking traditional structures, alternative media activists tried to live the egalitarian ideals they espoused.

Their experimentation took (and still takes) many forms. At *Mother Jones*, the business staff elects the magazine's publisher. At Boston's weekly *Real Paper*, there is a strong in-house union and a traditional management structure, while some feminist and anarchist media use consensus decision-making. Indeed, there are almost as many ways of dealing with the dilemma of power—who has it, how they got it, how they use it—as there are alternative media outlets. Deciding how to handle power is still very much in the process of being worked out in the alternative media, as it is in the social and political movements they serve.

The alternative media play a crucial role within the movements for social change in America. They are heralds that announce new ideas; mirrors that permit activists to see the forms their work takes in society; party lines on which members of alternative social movements exchange information and impressions; critics that provide perspectives on grassroots political efforts.

In 1968, for example, a prolonged and heated debate in the underground media about the wisdom of demonstrating at the Democratic national convention in Chicago had much to do with the form the world-famous demonstrations ultimately took. Ten years later, when an alternative press reporter revealed that a New Age tea company was preparing to do business with racist South Africa, the outcry from customers who read the story caused cancellation of the deal. In both cases, the movement's own media served as vehicles for debating strategy and ethics.

As *Village Voice* press critic Alexander Cockburn has accurately observed, "Without an alternative culture, there can be no alternative press." The reverse is equally true. Without media of their own to convey messages that radicals and dissidents themselves select and shape, activists become isolated and weak. If activists supply alternative media with a constituency, alternative media provide activists with a sense of identity and collective purpose. There is a symbiosis between alternative media and alternative culture—an exchange of vital energy that is critical to the health of both.

Social activists are keenly aware of this, often displaying a sense of commitment to their media that goes well beyond consumer brand-name loyalty. In 1978, a spontaneous outpouring of donations and volunteer labor saved the Wyoming-based environmental newspaper *High Country*

News after an automobile accident that killed a member of the paper's small staff and badly hurt three others threatened its survival. The *High Country News* pulled through, thanks to readers who felt that the continuing flow of information from the paper was of vital importance to their lives.

Within society as a whole, the alternative media are catalytic, introducing new concepts and values which society then accepts (usually with modifications) or rejects. Over time, the alternative media and their culture progressively modify society with humanistic reforms. This is consistent with the historic role of radicals in America, to whom can be traced once-extremist ideas such as the abolition of slavery; the progressive income tax; the initiative, referendum, and recall; direct election of United States Senators; the eight-hour work day; child-labor laws; workers' compensation; social security; unemployment insurance; women's suffrage; racially integrated schools; pure-food-and-drug laws; and many more. In short, radicals and their media play an essential role in American life—that of creative critics from whom come many of our culture's humanistic features.

The relationship of alternative media to the dominant society is, of course, two-way. Not only do ideas introduced by alternative media modify society, they are also themselves modified in the course of being absorbed by mainstream culture. In effect, the mass media, through which the public is introduced directly to those ideas, use the alternative media for research and development.

Typically, a new idea or cultural value—a belief in the health-giving qualities of natural yogurt, for example—first appears in the alternative media—the monthly magazine *New Age*, let's say. From there, the notion that yogurt-is-good-for-you might be picked up by *Rolling Stone* or the *Village Voice*, periodicals that draw much of their material from alternative cultural and political movements of which they are not quite a part themselves. Once having gained fairly wide exposure in the *Voice* or *Rolling Stone*, yogurt graduates to the lifestyle pages of a trend-conscious daily newspaper—say, the *Washington Post* or the *Los Angeles Times*. Yogurt is now legitimate. No longer a fringe food associated with health faddists, the brave new food becomes the subject of favorable stories in *Time* and *Newsweek*. From there, it's a short step to that final certification of popular acceptance, network television.

Of course, something happens to the yogurt along the way. It is dosed with preservatives and artificial colors and flavors and laced with sweeteners to mask its original tart taste. And instead of coming in a modest container with a handwritten list of ingredients, it is squeezed out of a custard machine as a frozen confection. In the process of making inroads on the American diet, the brave new food has itself been changed.

Something similar happens to all ideas, trends, and styles that emerge from the alternative media. Taken from their original context and sweetened by the merchandisers of mass culture, alternative values and concepts are changed even as they change society. Thus, once far-out expressions of cultural radicalism—rock music, unisex fashions, recreational drug paraphernalia—which received early and exhaustive attention in the underground media have been thoroughly absorbed into mainstream culture, stripped of their challenging context, and marketed as accoutrements of the good life.

In addition to serving as sources of trends, serious and otherwise, for mass culture, alternative and underground media have influenced the formats and style of mass media. Bald imitations of Robert Crumb's underground comics were, for several years, staples of mass media advertising, as were the flashing colors and astrological symbols popularized by Peter Max. Mainstream periodicals adapted and refined the graphic boldness of the underground press in the seventies, when even the *New York Times* jettisoned its column-rules and made increased use of white space and imaginative graphics—and hired a former art director of the underground *East Village Other* to redesign its op-ed page.

Moreover, the notion that journalists must be objective chroniclers of events, standing wholly apart from the stories they covered, was weakened by the combined impact of underground writers and New Journalists on mainstream reporters, as well as by the more cataclysmic events themselves—the Vietnam war, domestic riots, Watergate—which demanded more flexible coverage than that permitted by the strictures of objective newswriting. The result, on many daily newspapers, was an increase in the number and prominence of interpretive features and news analyses. Objective journalism has not been toppled as a shibboleth of the mainstream media, but it has been shaken; the aggressiveness of alternative media activists is partly responsible for that.

Champions of hardnosed reporting such as Warren Hinckle and Robert Scheer, who served as editors of the muckraking monthly *Ramparts*, now write for daily newspapers (the *San Francisco Chronicle* and the *Los Angeles Times*, respectively). Other alternative media activists and veterans have been honored with top awards: a Pulitzer Prize for editorial cartooning for the *Philadelphia Inquirer*'s Tony Auth, who formerly drew for the underground press; an Academy Award for best documentary for

Barbara Kopple's film, *Harlan County USA*; and several George Foster Peabody Awards (radio's Pulitzer) to KPFA for public-affairs programming.

Like other people, alternative media activists appreciate recognition and payment for their efforts. For most, however, awards are secondary to the real purpose of their work: stimulating social change. And while some popular products of the alternative and underground media have been trivialized in their absorption by mainstream culture, many others have contributed materially to changing the ways we live.

Underground media were the first to openly oppose the war in Vietnam—not an inconsiderable act amid the patriotic fervor of the middle and late sixties. As the only consistent sources of antiwar news and views in the early days of the war, underground media were of fundamental importance to the peace movement. In time they helped expand a minority movement of students and radicals into a groundswell that eventually enlisted (with varying degrees of commitment) a majority of the American people.

Alternative and underground media also addressed the female majority with ideas—some of them dormant for a generation, many never before articulated—which challenged age-old conventions. From mimeographed memos and hand-stapled journals of opinion, feminist media evolved into artistically rendered national magazines and related media enterprises that submitted the most persistent and perceptive examinations of sexual politics. As a consequence of the radical feminist analysis of inherited sex roles, movements for gay and lesbian liberation—each with its own catalytic media—shook the supposedly quiescent seventies with public pronouncements of ideas that had to be whispered only a decade earlier.

At the same time that alternative media were attempting to chart new directions for the future, countercultural media looked to the past, to Eastern and American Indian spiritual traditions, as sources of lessons for the present. "Hip" media rediscovered the mystical traditions of mind expansion that lie at the core of most religions and—unlike the mass media, which were filled with scare stories—regarded drug-taking as a potentially enriching, if necessarily risky, activity. From the religious revival heralded in alternative media came a resurgence of interest in diets of whole, natural foods and a spurt of growth in the popularity of yoga, holistic health, and humanistic psychologies that came to be known under the rubric of the "New Age."

Alternative media also gave early and empathetic coverage to ecology and back-to-the-land lifestyles, helping to generate a historic return to farms and small towns in the seventies. Many such media warned of the dangers of nuclear power for nearly a decade before the attention of the world turned to a previously obscure spot in Pennsylvania called Three Mile Island.

America today looks very different than it did when underground media activists, building on the advocacy tradition of journalism, cranked up their printing presses, cameras, and tape recorders in the middle sixties, intent upon reinventing America. What follows is an immersion in the richness and complexity of that largely untold story.

two

Rise of the Underground Press

IT WAS A MAY DAY in 1964. Lyndon Johnson had recently become president, and the police action in Indochina was commanding ever more of his attention. The Beatles topped the pop music charts. Miniskirts were in. LSD was legal. And Art Kunkin, 36, an unemployed tool-and-die maker, was standing at KPFK radio's Renaissance Faire in a Robin Hood costume, a four-foot feather in his cap, hawking copies of a new newspaper to passersby. The paper was an arts and politics tabloid, only eight pages long, that Kunkin called the *Los Angeles Free Press*. It was the first underground newspaper of the 1960s.

A little over a year later, on a sunny August morning in 1965, reporter Bob Randolph squinted down the tracks at the Berkeley railway station at an approaching troop train. As he watched, dozens of antiwar pro-

Art Kunkin, in Robin Hood costume, gave away the first issue of the Los Angeles Free Press. The Masses *effusion of art and politics anticipated the underground by fifty years. (Photo courtesy of Art Kunkin.)*

testers stood on the tracks—hoping to halt the train—only to quickly scatter when it became obvious that the train wasn't stopping. As the troop train whipped by, Randolph spotted signs in the windows, put there by draftees. "We don't want to go!" read one hand-lettered sign. "Hang in there, we're with you!" read another. Many local and national reporters covered the action that day, but only Randolph conveyed the passion of the demonstrators and the antiwar fervor of some of the soldiers. Randolph's story did not appear in a recognized, respectable newspaper, but in the first issue of a tabloid created to cover the demonstration, the *Berkeley Barb.* The shared anguish of protesters, troops, and reporter was the counterpoint to the whimsy of Art Kunkin's Robin Hood costume. Anguish and whimsy remained the hallmarks of the underground press throughout its short, spectacular existence.

As its beginnings show, the underground press was a participatory medium. It was an unabashedly partisan press, given to the glories of subjectivity and outright propaganda, an advocacy press that reveled in its biases and invited the reader to join in. The objective was nothing less than changing the world.

Technological change helped open the floodgates of this new wave of media activism. Prior to the 1960s, newspaper copy had to be set laboriously in hot type on a Linotype machine. That required technical training as well as money. But the widespread introduction of offset printing in the early years of the decade made papers cheap, easy, and quick to produce. In offset printing, a competent typist can use a standard typewriter to prepare copy, which is then pasted down on flat sheets, photographed, and duplicated. The offset revolution made it possible for virtually anyone so inclined to produce a newspaper. In the middle sixties, with a few dollars, a pot of glue, a typewriter, and a handful of volunteers to write and lay out stories, several thousand copies of an offset tabloid newspaper could be printed.

Kunkin started the *Free Press* with a budget of $15 and 5,000 copies of his new paper—4,000 of which he gave away to drum up interest. By 1969, only five years later, Kunkin was turning out 64-page issues and claiming a paid circulation of 100,000, the highest in the underground. From that single paper in 1964, the underground rose to an estimated 400 publications (many of them issued irregularly) by the end of the sixties. Their readers were overwhelmingly young (in their late teens to early thirties), white, and middle class. It was to them that the underground directed its coverage of the unholy trinity of revolution, sex, and drugs.

Despite their romantic, beyond-the-law aura, underground papers were never illegal. Underground publishers used the word underground metaphorically. They meant to both call attention to a continuing radical presence in American life and invoke the image of a vast conspiracy of hirsute, zealous revolutionaries—seemingly materialized from nowhere and everywhere—poised to take over.

The conspirators of the underground press claim a distinguished heritage. Thomas Paine was only one of many revolutionary ancestors in the late eighteenth century. In the 1760s and 1770s, Sam and John Adams, among others, divided their time between the libations of the Green Dragon tavern and the office of a renegade weekly newspaper called the *Boston Gazette*. The *Gazette*, which published from 1719 to 1798, campaigned effectively for repeal of portions of the hated Stamp Act pertaining to printers and published confidential letters written by the colonial governor of Massachusetts that led to the governor's recall. Legend has it that the perpetrators of the Boston Tea Party donned their Indian costumes in the *Gazette* office. During the Revolutionary War, the *Gazette* was forced to publish outside British-occupied Boston, as was another well-known radical paper, the *Massachusetts Spy*. John Adams, the future president, gleefully described the work of the *Gazette* as "cooking up paragraphs, articles, & occurances [*sic*], &c., working the political engine!"

Even the fiery radical journalists of the revolutionary era were generally faint-hearted when it came to advocating the freedom of any but property-holding white males, however. Thus arose an independent abolitionist press inspired and operated by free blacks and their white allies in the early nineteenth century. Some two dozen abolitionist papers were issued before the Civil War.

Freedom's Journal, published from 1827 to 1829, was the first black-owned, black-run newspaper. It was launched to counter editorial broadsides against blacks by white newspapers and to agitate for the end of slavery. Similarly, the *Ram's Horn* was sounded in 1847 when the *New York Sun* refused Willis A. Hodges, a black man, the right to make an uncensored reply—even in a paid advertisement—to a *Sun* attack on black rights. "The *Sun* shines for all white men and not for colored men," Hodges was told by a *Sun* staffer. That same year, Frederick Douglass, the famed black abolitionist, started his *North Star* (later renamed *Frederick Douglass' Paper*) to agitate for the end of slavery.

Because most blacks of their day were kept poor, illiterate, and politically powerless, most early black periodicals aimed their efforts at white readers they hoped to influence. Many other abolitionist papers were, for similar reasons, issued by and for whites. One such paper was the *National Era*, which serialized, in 1851–1852, one of the most influential books in American history—Harriet Beecher Stowe's *Uncle Tom's Cabin*—before it was published in book form. *Uncle Tom's Cabin* crystallized antislavery emotions with its sentimental but powerful story line. Wrote Van Dyke Brooks, "If this book was not the cause of the Civil War, as Lincoln said later, it was at least one of the major causes, for it blocked the operation of the Fugitive Slave Act."

The surge of antislavery feeling sparked by *Uncle Tom's Cabin* was the result of persistent agitation by the abolitionist movement and its press in the years before the Civil War. Often their work was done at great peril. In 1835, William Lloyd Garrison, the young white editor of *The Liberator*, was dragged through the streets of Boston and nearly killed by a proslavery mob. Even free blacks in Georgetown, the District of Columbia, were forbidden by law to pick up *The Liberator* at the post office under threat of fine or imprisonment. Convicted black readers who failed to pay the fine could be sold into slavery for up to four months.

Such obstacles made the fiery Garrison all the more determined. He condemned slavery and advocated peace and temperance in language rich with religious metaphor. At its founding in 1831, *The Liberator* shocked even the abolitionist movement by declaring that the slaves should be freed immediately instead of gradually. Garrison put aside his pacifist principles to back the Union effort in the Civil War. When Lincoln issued the Emancipation Proclamation in 1862, *The Liberator* published an editorial headlined "Glory Hallelujah!"

Its work done, *The Liberator* folded at the end of 1865. *The Nation*, itself then newly founded, eulogized *The Liberator* by observing, "There was a stern monotony in its issues that was like the pressure of fate. It was an unvarying soliloquy thirty-five years long. It is perhaps the most remarkable instance on record of single-hearted devotion to a cause."

Devoted Garrison was, but his interests ranged widely. Garrison came out in favor of women's rights in 1837. He also subscribed to the pacifism and utopian communist principles of John H. Noyes, founder of the Oneida community. Like many of the radical press activists of his time, Garrison was influenced by the broad sweep of utopian ideas and values. In this he foreshadowed the determinedly eclectic media activists of the 1960s and 1970s who embraced communal living, feminism, environmentalism, pacifism, and racial equality.

The utopian communities—over two hundred of them, by some

counts—that took root throughout the United States in the nineteenth century were often heralded and explained in periodicals. Noyes' Oneida communards and free-love advocates had their *Oneida Circular* (published from 1851 to 1876); Robert Owen's New Harmony settlement published the *New Harmony Gazette* (1825–1835); and the Fourierists on the famous Brook Farm issued *The Harbinger* (1845–1849) and enlisted Horace Greeley, Charles A. Dana, and Arthur Brisbane as contributors. In the pages of such publications can be seen the germination of twentieth-century alternative periodicals such as *Communities, Utopian Eyes,* and *Green Revolution.*

The most influential utopian periodical did not originate in a geographical community, however, but in a community of interest. It was *The Dial* (1840–1844), the quarterly journal of the Transcendentalists, edited first by Margaret Fuller, then by Ralph Waldo Emerson. Henry David Thoreau was first published in *The Dial.* Although it never had more than three hundred paying subscribers, the magazine was read by influential American and European thinkers and writers. Dedicated mainly to the contemplation of mystical nature worship, *The Dial* was called to task for being too airy by Thomas Carlyle, a regular reader:

> Alas, it is so easy to screw one's self up into high and ever higher altitudes of Transcendentalism and see nothing under one but the snow of Himmalayeh . . . easy . . . but where does it lead? Well, I do believe, for one thing, a man has no right to say to his own generation, turning quite away from it: "Be damned!" It is the whole Past and the whole Future, this same cotton-spinning, dollar-hunting, canting, and shrieking, very wretched generation of ours. Come back to it, I tell you.

The Dial kept on with its esthetic concerns, but, like New Age spiritual seekers who were criticized for narcissism more than a hundred years later, the precursors of our century's counterculture occasionally lowered their eyes to earth. In *The Dial's* July 1843 issue, Margaret Fuller contributed an essay entitled "The Great Lawsuit," a high-minded polemic that called for the removal of all barriers to women in society. Revised and expanded, the work was published in book form in 1845 as *Woman in the Nineteenth Century,* and it is credited with preparing much of the intellectual groundwork for the first women's rights convention in Seneca Falls three years later.

Modern feminists had forebears in the activist women's press of the nineteenth century. Like today's feminists, many of whom cut their political teeth in the civil rights and antiwar movements, early women's rights advocates were often first active in other movements, particularly the abolitionist movement. And, like later feminists who found their freedom was not respected by either mainstream society or activist media and movements, the women's rights advocates of the previous century started their own press.

Amelia Bloomer, who gave her name to the baggy pantaloons—the first radical departure from constricting female garb—first made her mark as publisher of a feminist magazine (the *Lily*, 1849–1859), as did Elizabeth Cady Stanton and Susan B. Anthony, editor and business manager, respectively, of a newspaper boldly entitled *The Revolution*. Veterans of the abolitionist movement, Stanton and Anthony were angered when the Fourteenth and Fifteenth Amendments, enacted after the Civil War, gave black men—but not women of any race—the right to vote.

Launched in January 1868, *The Revolution* advocated not only female suffrage, but the eight-hour day, prison reform, the abolition of standing armies, and improved conditions for working women as part of an all-embracing social critique. "We declare war to the death on the idea that woman was made for man . . ." Stanton wrote. "We proclaim the higher truth that, like man, she was created by God for Individual Moral Responsibility and progress here and forever. . . ." For her trouble, the *New York Sunday Times* suggested that Stanton "attend a little more to her domestic duties and a little less to those of the great public."

Plagued by underfinancing, a small number of subscribers (3,000), and competition from the well-financed, more conservative *Woman's Journal* (1870–1917), *The Revolution* folded in 1872. Although it published only briefly, *The Revolution* was remarkably prophetic, raising issues that would be taken up again a century later. The causes of its demise would also be repeated in the histories of other radical media.

Like many of her radical contemporaries, Susan B. Anthony was influenced by the remarkably eclectic utopian ideas of her day. Besides being a feminist and abolitionist, Anthony was a spiritualist. Communication with the spirit world was all the rage in the middle of the nineteenth century. About twenty spiritualist publications sprang up in response to this eager market. One such publication, the *Mountain Cove Journal and Spiritual Harbinger*, published in 1852–1853 in Virginia, was—announced its earthly proprietors—"dictated by Spirits out of the flesh, and by them edited, superintended, and controlled."

Though often ridiculed by the mainstream press, spiritualist periodicals found a ready audience for their message through the end of the century. Esoteric books sometimes attracted wide readerships as well. H. P. Blavatsky's *Isis Unveiled* (1877) and *The Secret Doctrine* (1888), both published by her own Theosophist Society, were widely read volumes of Eastern and occultist lore. Blavatsky also started such magazines as *The Theosophist* (1879) and *Lucifer* (1887), which she described as a periodical "to bring to light the hidden things of darkness."

Partly through her writings, Blavatsky converted the respected editor and writer Annie Besant, who had previously come to notice as a feminist and socialist. Besant, in turn, recruited J. Krishnamurti, whose teachings enjoyed popularity in the spiritual and occultist renaissance of the 1960s. Periodicals such as the Krishna Consciousness Society's *Back to Godhead* and the publications of Transcendental Meditation and Guru Maharaj Ji have their roots in the occultist magazines of the nineteenth century, as did countercultural underground papers such as *Astral Projection*. Present-day New Age media derive part of their journalistic heritage from those same sources as well.

In the left-wing press, political activists advocated more down-to-earth solutions to personal and collective problems. Leftist periodicals, most of them published in the early twentieth century, espoused a scientific socialism rooted in Marxian thought. As such, they were more analytically inclined, and preoccupied with the industrial class struggle, than were the earlier utopian publications.

Karl Marx himself served a curious stint as European correspondent for Horace Greeley's *New York Tribune* from 1851 to 1862, but Marx didn't enjoy the experience. In a letter to Friedrich Engels, Marx complained that "Grinding bones and making soup out of them like the paupers in the workhouse, that is what political work for such a paper amounts to. . . ."

Unfortunately for Marx, he didn't write for a radical newspaper. Many other leftists, seeing the difficulty of expressing radical values in the conventional press, started periodicals of their own. According to Joseph R. Conlin, editor of *The American Radical Press, 1880–1960*, "At least 600 distinct periodicals were published during the Socialist Party's happiest days. In 1912 alone there were 323 avowedly Socialist periodical publications issued in the United States, including 5 English-language dailies and 8 dailies in foreign languages; 262 English weeklies and 36 in other languages; and 10 English and 2 foreign language monthly magazines."

Radical leftists took the task of establishing their own press seriously. Writes Conlin:

From Daniel DeLeon, who devoted most of his time to the Socialist Labor Party's *People*, through Big Bill Haywood, who gruffly complained of the desk work but nevertheless put in a stint editing the *Miner's Magazine*, there have been few active radicals who have not directed a large share of their labor on behalf of the new society to journalism. No other facet of radical political activity in the United States—not strike, not subversion, not demonstration, not terrorism, not oratory—has claimed more attention or time.

The most popular radical publication of any kind in American history was a weekly newspaper published in Girard, Kansas called *Appeal to Reason*. Issued from 1895 to 1917, the *Appeal* survived without subsidy from wealthy backers, heavy advertising, or support from a political party (though it generally championed the Socialist Party) by offering a lively, easy-to-read editorial mix. Edited by J. A. Wayland, who wrote most of the early numbers himself, the *Appeal* combined folksy sermons on self-improvement with fire-breathing blasts at the "ghoulish plutocrats": "Work, you slaves, so your master will make enough money out of you to buy a titled husband for his daughter, so she can live in Yurrup among decent people. . . . Will they learn better? O! Maybe."

The *Appeal* published frequent contributions from Eugene V. Debs and from Upton Sinclair, who called the paper "the refuge of suppressed muckrakers." In 1905, the *Appeal* serialized Sinclair's classic, *The Jungle*, a year before it was published in book form. In 1912, the *Appeal* actively backed Debs' run for the White House and was a major factor in mustering voters for his relatively strong showing: six percent of the popular vote, the best ever by a leftist candidate. However, Wayland's suicide that same year took some of the fight out of the paper. The *Appeal*'s circulation peaked at 760,000 in late 1912, giving the paper the highest circulation of any radical publication before or since. Interestingly, Frank Luther Mott's *American Journalism*, a 901-page standard text of media history, does not mention the *Appeal*.

The Masses, a monthly magazine published in New York, was a sophisticated urban contemporary of the *Appeal*. Published from 1911 to 1917, in the heady avant-garde atmosphere of pre-World War I Greenwich Village, *The Masses* attempted to fuse politics with art and was surprisingly successful. The magazine's ambitious philosophy was spelled out on its masthead:

A revolutionary and not a reform magazine: a magazine with no dividends to pay: a free magazine: frank, arrogant, searching for the true causes: a magazine directed against rigidity and dogma whenever it is found: printing what is too naked or true for a moneymaking press: a magazine whose final policy is to do as it pleases and conciliate nobody, not even its readers—there is room for this publication in America.

Brilliantly edited by Max Eastman, *The Masses* drew upon first-rate contributors such as Sherwood Anderson, Floyd Dell, and John Reed, author of the classic history of the Russian Revolution, *Ten Days That Shook the World*. Publishing superb labor reportage and forceful antiwar views, the magazine also gave extensive space to what was then considered a dangerously libertine attitude toward sex. *The Masses* backed Margaret Sanger's birth-control crusades, printed stories on official harassment of prostitutes, and shocked Victorian sensibilities by carrying ads for sex manuals.

The Masses also published enormous cartoons in its large (10½″ × 13½″) format. Radical cartoonists such as Art Young and Robert Minor savaged middle-class values and ruling-class control. Their drawing styles, if not their political values, visibly influenced mainstream periodicals such as *Harper's Weekly*. No subject was off limits. The magazine delighted in depicting Christ as the proletarian son of a carpenter. One likeness of Christ was captioned, "Comrade Jesus: He Stirreth Up the Masses."

The Masses strongly opposed World War I as a rich man's war and, in one cartoon, depicted Christ being shot as a deserter. In a devastating article entitled "One Solid Month of Liberty," John Reed detailed the violation of domestic civil liberties that occurred immediately after America entered the war: radicals jailed, suffragists mobbed in Washington, D.C., socialist marchers beaten in Boston—and revolutionary magazines suppressed.

Such work ensured that *The Masses'* own liberties would be curtailed in that time of nationalistic frenzy. *The Masses'* second-class mailing privileges were revoked along with those of fifty other radical periodicals, including *Appeal to Reason*; the Industrial Workers of the World's *Industrial Worker*; and Emma Goldman's anarchist magazine, *Mother Earth*. *The Masses'* editors were tried twice under the Espionage Act for allegedly harming recruiting efforts with their antiwar propaganda. They were acquitted both times, but the wave of repression finally swamped *The Masses*. With the demise of *The Masses* came the end of a free-wheeling era of press eclecticism that would not return until the underground media explosion of the sixties—an explosion that engendered its own wave of repression.

In the twenties and thirties the bold mood of the prewar years gave way to the ideological struggles of the Stalin era and the survival struggles of the Depression. Periodicals such as the Communist Party's *Daily Worker* (1924–1958) reflected the somber mood of those years. Founded at the behest of Lenin, the *Worker* covered strikes, councils of the unemployed, and hunger marches. During the "popular front" years, the paper had a lively entertainment section to which Woody Guthrie and Mike Gold contributed columns. The *Worker* also advocated the racial integration of sports long before it occurred. *Worker* sports editor Lester Rodney is credited with influencing the Brooklyn Dodgers' Branch Rickey to sign Jackie Robinson.

In the McCarthy deepfreeze of the late forties and early fifties, the *Worker* lost many of its readers to a new paper, the *National Guardian*. Founded in 1948 to back the Progressive Party presidential bid of Henry Wallace, the *Guardian* offered comprehensive, professionally written news from a left-liberal perspective. Editor James Aronson had worked for the *New York Times*, and his cofounders, Cecil Belfridge and James McManus, were also long-time pros. The paper published stories on race relations by W. E. B. DuBois and foreign affairs by correspondents Anna Louise Strong and Wilfred Burchett. The *National Guardian* also spearheaded the doomed international campaign to save the Rosenbergs in the early fifties.

Not all of the left-leaning papers were communist, like the *Daily Worker*, or socialist, like the *National Guardian*. Christened on May Day, 1933, as a religious alternative to the *Daily Worker*, the *Catholic Worker* promoted pacifism, the dignity of labor, and the glory of God. The paper was edited by Dorothy Day, a Greenwich Village leftist who dramatically converted to Catholicism in the twenties. One of the young managing editors who served under Day, Michael Harrington, went on to write *The Other America*, a wrenching exposé of poverty in America that helped convince John Kennedy and Lyndon Johnson to launch the federal social welfare programs in the sixties. *The Worker*'s program of civil disobedience and nonviolent moral witnessing provided a model of behavior for antiwar activists in the sixties. The *Catholic Worker* was edited by Dorothy Day until just before her death in 1980, at the age of 83. The paper claims a circulation of 90,000 and sells for a penny.

The nonviolent direct action of the *Catholic Worker* was complemented by the intellectual anarchism of *Liberation* (1956–1977), a monthly mag-

azine founded by pacifist luminary A. J. Muste. Drawing on work by
Paul Goodman, Bertrand Russell, and Dave Dellinger, a World War II
draft resister who became a leader of the antiwar movement of the sixties,
Liberation preached an essentially religious activism that inspired draft-
card burners and conscientious objectors to challenge government
authority.

If *Liberation* and the *Catholic Worker* supplied sixties activists with
moral guidelines, *I. F. Stone's Weekly* (1953–1971) provided them with a
model of conscientious reporting. A defrocked daily journalist who had
worked for *The Nation* and several defunct liberal dailies, Stone wrote
and researched well-documented reports of official duplicity, drawn
directly from published government documents. A libertarian in the
classic mold, Stone strongly criticized Joseph McCarthy at a time when
the nation's broadcasters and major newspapers seemed mesmerized by
the red-baiting senator from Wisconsin.

In later years, Stone scolded J. Edgar Hoover's then-sacrosanct FBI
for failing to protect the civil rights of blacks, chipped away at Cold War
foreign policy, and supplied intellectual ammunition to the antiwar
movement. Almost alone among the nation's Washington reporters,
Stone criticized the 1964 Gulf of Tonkin resolution as a fraud and a sly
maneuver to commit U.S. military forces to Vietnam. His meticulous
research came to be used by peace activists as a useful supplement to war
reportage in the *New York Times* and *Le Monde*.

In 1955, two yers after Stone started his *Weekly*, the triumvirate of Dan
Wolf, Ed Fancher, and Norman Mailer started New York's weekly
Village Voice. Launched as a vehicle for stylish personal writing and
Democratic Party reform politics, the *Voice* quickly attracted a following
for its coverage of the Greenwich Village arts scene. In its first year, the
Voice also led a fight to stop a freeway aimed at the heart of historic
Washington Square Park by New York power broker Robert Moses. It
was one of the first successful instances of resistance to insensitive urban
renewal and gave the new paper a reputation as a giant-killer.

But it wasn't chiefly for its political stands that the *Voice* became
known. Rather, it was the paper's tone—cool, literate, witty, "with-
it"—and its scope—coverage of off-Broadway theatre, poetry, avant-
garde cinema, and the day-to-day experiences of living in the historic
heart of American bohemia—that gave the *Voice* its character. The *Voice*
also gained renown as a writer's paper; editor Dan Wolf recruited
gifted contributors and gave them the space and editorial freedom they
needed to develop their ideas. At times Wolf's "hands-off" editing re-

sulted in rambling, egocentric writing. But at its best, the *Voice* published in-depth, informed writing unmatched by any weekly in the country. Cofounder Norman Mailer penned a column in the early days of the paper, as did the distinguished critic Gilbert Seldes. Wolf brought in jazz critic Nat Hentoff to write about education and the First Amendment and gave an inexperienced young artist named Jules Feiffer a weekly comic strip.

When the existentialist angst of the fifties was shoved aside by the social upheavals of the sixties, the *Voice* turned its attention to the new radical movements. Jack Newfield, a cofounder of Students for a Democratic Society (SDS), wrote about the Vietnam war and the New Left and about the doomed liberal hope of the sixties, Bobby Kennedy, whom Newfield adored. Jill Johnston, the paper's dance critic, turned in increasingly personal columns on lesbian-feminist activism, her experimental prose style unbroken by capital letters and nearly devoid of punctuation. But while the *Voice* opened its pages to partisans of the radical movements, Wolf carefully refrained from committing the *Voice* to the movements themselves. In the early seventies, the paper grew increasingly critical of the New Left, giving prominent display to neoconservative writers such as Lucian Truscott IV and Clark Whelton, who pinned part of the blame for the Attica massacre on radical negotiators William Kunstler and Bobby Seale.

Much of the *Voice*'s increasing skepticism about the New Left and the counterculture was attributable to Wolf himself. Wolf had helped start the *Voice* as an outlet for nonconformity and personal self-expression. In *The Great American Newspaper,* Kevin McAuliffe's history of the *Voice*, McAuliffe wrote of Wolf, "With him, the big thing had been to keep your individuality. Now the thing was to be part of something bigger than yourself, to join some movement, some collective, some commune, some committee, to be a member of some overwhelming 'we.' That was not his sensibility, he knew. . . ." Cofounder Ed Fancher was similarly uninvolved politically. Mailer had not written or helped put out the paper since the early days.

The *Voice*—liberal rather than radical, always traditionally owned and operated—was a problematic model for the underground press. But it was an influential one nevertheless. Its style and wit were much admired by underground press pioneers such as Art Kunkin, who modeled the *Los Angeles Free Press* on the *Voice*. The *Free Press* never matched the *Voice*'s literary quality, but, with its extensive coverage of radical politics and the Los Angeles cultural scene, it echoed the *Voice*'s conscious appeal to a community of interest.

The final element of the underground press' editorial makeup—its bombast and sense of calculated outrage—was largely provided by another New York publication, Paul Krassner's satirical magazine *The Realist*, which used ridicule to deflate political opponents. Krassner, a former comedian and freelance writer for *Mad*, started *The Realist* in 1958 and published it until 1974. *The Realist*'s early issues contained conventional libertarian/atheist stuff, but before long Krassner was kicking over the traces, fusing fact and fiction and often using real people as characters in his fantasies:

> *John Foster Dulles:* . . . and so in the interest of maintaining friendly Anglo-American relations, I've come to ask you to stop harping about H-bomb tests. You're only aiding the communist cause.
>
> *Bertrand Russell:* Nonsense, I'm opposed to all forms of totalitarianism.
>
> *John Foster Dulles:* But suppose the communists come out in favor of deep breathing . . .

Krassner reached his high point—or low, depending on one's point of view—in 1967, when he depicted Lyndon Johnson performing a sex act upon the corpse of John Kennedy during Air Force One's return from Dallas. The story, supposedly a suppressed passage from William Manchester's *The Death of a President*, was fictitious, but a number of Krassner's readers believed it. "The truth," shrugged Krassner by way of explanation, "is silly putty." He intended the story as a metaphor for what Johnson allegedly did to his predecessor and was then doing to the country. For many people, the metaphor worked.

The underground press borrowed ingredients from its journalistic precursors to concoct an editorial mix all its own. The satirical edge of *The Realist*; the personal reportage of the *Village Voice*; the fusion of art and radical politics of *The Masses*; the political advocacy of *Appeal to Reason*; the mysticism of the spiritualist periodicals; and the primitive communism of the utopian publications were all incorporated into the underground press of the 1960s, marking a return to the diversity that characterized the radical press before World War I.

Those qualities did not, of course, find expression to the same extent in every publication. Countercultural papers, such as the *San Francisco*

Paul Krasssner, trickster extraordinaire, fused fact and fiction in his magazine The Realist, *inspiring the calculated outrage of the underground press. (Photo by Dave Patrick.)*

Max Scherr (below) started the Berkeley Barb *to give empathetic coverage to an antiwar demonstration, not knowing if the paper would publish a second issue. The* Barb *lasted fifteen years, praising sex, drugs, and revolution and damning racism, repression, and the Vietnam war. (Photo by Janet Fries.)*

Oracle, were preoccupied with mysticism and drugs, while political periodicals, such as the SDS organ, *New Left Notes*, gave more space to analyses of the economic and social system. In the middle of the spectrum, however—and far more numerous than periodicals devoted to politics *or* religion—were publications devoted to *both*. Papers such as the *Los Angeles Free Press* were likely to position a first-person account of taking LSD at a love-in on the same page with a meditation on the nature of imperialism.

Eclecticism was the underground press' stock in trade. Traditional leftists denounced the underground's journalistic grab bag as mere confusion. Underground editors, in turn, regarded the Old Left and its press as hopelessly square and outdated. Remembering the beginnings of the *Free Press*, Kunkin said, "I was involved with the Socialist Party at that point, and was very fed up with the way all the radical papers were very European-oriented. So I had this idea of starting something that would listen to people here—listen to minorities, listen to young people. I wasn't locked in theoretically to just being for workers. The other movements were equally valid to me."

Kunkin's interest in reaching beyond the working class—the historic base of revolutionary Marxism as it was formulated in Europe—was shared by most underground editors. It was a sharp departure from the traditional leftist press. Most underground journalists believed that the American working class had been brought off with split-level homes and color TVs, transforming the lean proletarian advance guard of the revolution into corpulent guardians of the system that Marx had predicted they would overthrow.

Underground journalists rejected the empty, monotonous life they associated with bourgeois comforts. Their papers were, accordingly, published chiefly by and for the alienated. As people who noisily derided middle-class values, underground journalists concerned themselves with liberating the body, mind, and spirit in "uptight, plastic" America. A 1966 issue of *The Digger Papers*, an occasional publication of politicized hippies in San Francisco's Haight-Ashbury district, charged that "Middle class living rooms are funeral parlors and only undertakers will stay in them. Our fight is with those who would kill us through dumb work, insane war, dull money morality."

As part of its rejection of middle-class life, the underground press rejected the authority of the political system that sustained it. There was a strong anarchist strain in the underground, manifested as a celebration of spontaneity and all things "natural." This impulse led not only to a rejection of duly constituted authority but to a challenge of revolutionary authority, as well—at least revolutionary authority as the *Daily Worker* would have defined it. In her "Revolutionary Letter #48," Diane DiPrima, whose poetry was published throughout the underground press, wrote:

Be careful.
With what relief do we fall back on
the tale, so often told in revolutions
that *now* we must
organize, obey the rules, so that *later*
we can be free.
It is the point
at which revolution stops. To be carried forward
later and in another country, this is
the pattern, but we can
break the pattern.

Shattering received cultural patterns—in love and war, in work, in matters of the mind and spirit—was the announced purpose of the underground press. In keeping with the tradition of activist journalism, *Berkeley Barb* founder Max Scherr saw the *Barb* as a propaganda vehicle and organizing tool fully as much as he did a newspaper of record. (He originally planned to call the paper the *Berkeley Bias*.) "We'd plant small articles in the paper saying, 'There's a rumor going around that something is going to happen on Telegraph Avenue Friday at two o'clock,'" Scherr recalled. "So people would show up on Friday at two to see what would happen, someone would say, 'Hey, let's close off the street,' and something *would* happen."

The *Barb* covered most of the happenings of the middle and late sixties from the instigators' points of view: the Human Be-In in Golden Gate Park, where San Francisco acidheads and Berkeley politicos formed an ecstatic but short-lived alliance; the exorcism of the Pentagon in 1967; the first big rock (they called it "pop") festival in Monterey that same year; the street actions at the Chicago Democratic convention; the student strikes at San Francisco State and Berkeley; and, finally, People's Park.

The *Barb* moved—or, rather, ran—to stage center when Berkeley activists, including several *Barb* reporters, seized a muddy, rutted vacant lot owned by the University of California and transformed it into a "people's park," complete with transplanted turf, flowers, and a pond. The plan to take the land was announced in the *Barb*'s April 13, 1969, issue: "A park will be built this Sunday between Telegraph and Haste," the announcement read. "Bring shovels, hoes, chains, grass, paints, flowers, trees, bulldozers, top soil, colorful smiles, laughter, and lots of sweat. . . . 'Nobody supervises and the trip belongs to whoever dreams.'" The short article was signed "Robin Hood's Park Commissioner."

Over the next several weeks, *Barb* reporters wrote about the park the paper had helped start. "We were building a park last Sunday," Stew Albert wrote. "There were no speeches or long debates. Several hundred Berkeley Freemen showed up for work . . . For the first time in my life, I enjoyed working . . . What we were creating was our own desires, so we worked like madmen and loved it."

But before long People's Park was to become a paradise lost for Berkeley radicals. After the predawn police raid that retook the park, one person was killed and another was blinded, setting off street fighting that lasted for days and resulted in martial law. Public interest in People's Park was enormous, and *Barb* reporters were in the streets with notebooks and cameras, recording what went down with telling visceral accuracy:

> Blue clouds of tear gas strangle Sproul Plaza as this is being phoned in. Hundreds of choking students pour, half-blinded, off the campus. Pigs wearing gas masks rush to club those who fall. Terrified thousands are driven into the streets. The canisters of tear gas keep coming down Telegraph Avenue.
>
> Bancroft and Telly is like an open-air gas chamber.
>
> A black youth cries out, "We're all niggers now!"

The *Barb*'s brand of journalism proved compelling reading, especially after California Governor Ronald Reagan singled out the paper by name for helping to sabotage law and order. The *Barb*'s circulation peaked at 93,000 in mid-1969, soon after People's Park. The creation and destruction of People's Park was a classic example of how underground papers created as well as reported news of social change. "The role of the *Barb*," said Max Scherr, "was to remind people that their lives were at stake all the time."

Other periodicals strained to keep the pace. Local papers around the country served as vehicles, each in its own way, for political organizing. Underground papers blossomed in the American heartland as well as in the East and West Coast media centers. There was *Kaleidoscope* in Milwaukee; the *Fifth Estate* in Detroit; the *Seed* in Chicago; *Kudzu* in Jackson, Mississippi; the *Great Speckled Bird* in Atlanta; *Chinook* in Denver; *The Rag* in Austin, Texas; *Nola Express* in New Orleans. Beyond the United States, Montreal had *Logos* and Vancouver the *Georgia Straight;* London hosted *Oz* and *International Times*; Amsterdam's hippie anarchists published *Om*. Underground papers arose in Italy, France, Finland, Japan, Australia, South America—each sparked by the determination to create the news they reported.

One of the most dramatically successful activist papers, for a time, was *Rat*, a New York City biweekly founded by Jeff Shero, a veteran of the civil rights movement and SDS. *Rat* provided a fascinating counterweight to the *New York Times'* coverage of the student revolt at Columbia University in 1968, ignited by Columbia's plan to displace low-income tenants to build a gymnasium. The *Times* expressed shock at the rowdy behavior of demonstrators who occupied campus buildings and smoked President Grayson Kirk's cigars, drank his sherry, overturned desks for barricades, and scattered books on the floor. *Rat*, in its turn, showed outrage over the brutal beatings of nonviolent students by police and charged that *Times* publisher Arthur Sulzberger's seat on the Columbia board of trustees influenced his newspaper's coverage.

Rat mobilized its small staff to cover the rebellion, placing reporters and photographers inside the occupied buildings. Except for their New Left colleagues from Liberation News Service and the radical filmmaking collective, Newsreel, there were no other journalists inside with the demonstrators. In a special "Heil Columbia" issue, *Rat* published photos of police pouring through the windows of occupied buildings, statements of students who had been hospitalized from beatings, and reproductions of purloined university documents that showed the frustrations of the university's neighborhood tenants in dealing with the campus bureaucracy.

In his piece on the occupation, Jeff Shero captured the drama of the moment:

> Segmented time lost its normal meaning, sleepless hours blurred into sleepless days. While events crashed, racing through the minds of the participants, changing more swiftly than months of arguments ever would, certain moments, sometimes inconsequential, stand out like rays of clarity in the jumbled joy and strain of the time. . . . A Negro sergeant, supposedly guarding the ledge outside the Presidential suite, made friends with the window-watchers and when he got too cold,

Rat showed that the groves of Academe were not oases of pure reason in its inside coverage of the Columbia rebellion.

RAT
SUBTERRANEAN NEWS

LIBERATED
DOCUMENTS
PAGE 8

may 3-16, 1968
n.y.c. 15¢ outside 25¢

HEIL COLUMBIA

gladly took a glass of the President's imported sherry. . . . Sir Stephen
Spender, the elderly British poet, climbed through the second story
window to greet the students. Some, unaware of their guest's fame,
demanded forcefully to know if he was a reporter. Reporters aren't
allowed.

That last sentence says it all. *Rat* staffers were not considered "reporters" (outsiders), like the journalists from the *Times* or the networks;
they were paticipants (insiders), helping to foster the action by their
presence as well as by their partisan coverage.

Third World journalists, like white media activists, participated in the
events they covered. *El Malcriado*, founded in 1964 in Fresno, California,
was the voice of the largely Mexican-American United Farmworkers
Union, whose organizing drives in the fields of the Southwest attracted
much support from white liberals and radicals. *El Grito Del Norte*, a
militant Chicano paper in New Mexico, helped fuel the Mexican-
American rights movement by publishing polemics against the Anglo
power structure and urging independence for the heavily Mexican areas
of the Southwest.

Perhaps the best known Third World paper, *The Black Panther*, was
founded by Black Panther Party leaders Huey Newton and Bobby Seale
in Oakland in 1967. Newton and Seale both contributed to the paper, as
did Eldridge Cleaver, the party's minister of information and the author
of the widely read *Soul on Ice*. Articles decrying the police presence in
black communities and boosting the Black Panther program for black
self-determination filled the paper's pages together with crude cartoons
of police "pigs" with tusks and squiggly tails. Drawings of angry black
people carrying firearms were much in evidence, and a famous photograph of Newton—in black beret and leather jacket, and clutching a
gun—appeared frequently. Back issues of *The Black Panther*, with their
emotional calls to arms, are period pieces now. But, as we shall see in
chapter six, the paper experienced direct physical repression by an
establishment bent on silencing it. This context of often real, imminent
threat fostered the emotional and seemingly paranoid tone that characterized the publication.

American Indian periodicals, while not numerous, played an important role in the resurgence of Native American cultural identity in the
late sixties and throughout the seventies. The largest Indian paper,
Akwesasne Notes, was (and is) loosely associated with the American Indian
Movement (AIM), the leading militant Indian organization. *Notes* re-

porters helped occupy the Bureau of Indian Affairs (BIA) building in Washington, D.C., in 1972 along with other demonstrators protesting years of broken treaties. *Notes* correspondents were also on the scene in 1973, when AIM members occupied Wounded Knee, South Dakota, and were besieged by government troops. *Akwesasne Notes* later published inside accounts in book form of both the BIA and Wounded Knee takeovers, giving readers detailed explanations of the events from an activist Indian point of view.

Readers comparing the coverage of Wounded Knee in *Akwesasne Notes* with that of virtually any daily newspaper could be excused for thinking that the two papers were published on different planets. The daily reporters cleaved to the tenets of "objective" journalism—reporting which, as Herbert Gans and others have pointed out, has its own hidden biases. *Notes* writers, by way of contrast, were openly partisan, befitting their open participation in the occupation. This put them in the tradition of advocacy reporting established by *The Liberator* and the *Boston Gazette*. It is this participatory quality that makes *Akwesasne Notes* and other radical papers a social force and directly challenges the ideology of conventional journalism.

Of the compelling issues that fueled the forces of the underground media, a libertine attitude toward sex was a crucial ingredient. Underground papers celebrated sex and believed, after Whilhelm Reich, that unrepressed sexuality is radical by definition. If sexual repression caused a "muscular armoring," as Reich believed—a physical tightening that corresponds to the psychological constriction that underlies political repression—then the underground press would help America loosen up. The nudity and four-letter words frequently found in underground papers were intended not as mindless vulgarity, but as deliberate challenges to what media activists saw as the Puritanical taboos and laws of a literally uptight America.

In the middle and late sixties, underground publishers faced frequent legal harassment for violating those taboos. Far from feeling intimidated, the underground responded by upping the ante. Busted in Boston for the liberal use of four-letter words, the *Avatar* responded by publishing the same words over and over, in large, bold type, throughout its next issue. Hauled into court in San Francisco for selling Lenore Kendel's collection of erotic poems, *The Love Book*, in his City Lights bookstore, poet Lawrence Ferlinghetti fought the law and won. Sales of *The Love Book* soared from a dozen or so a week before the arrest to thousands after-

w,ards. "Censorship always backfires," Ferlinghetti observed with satisfaction.

The underground press both benefited from changing attitudes to sex
and helped hurry them along. Underground papers championed birth
control and abortion rights, helping to establish do-it-yourself sex education as a legitimate option for young people whose sexuality was
repressed in the schools, the church, and the home. But more than
illuminating the mechanics of sex, the underground celebrated sexual
esthetics.

Sex was natural, thus desirable—even revolutionary—to most underground journalists. Said Paul Krassner, "I think that the arousal of
prurient interest is, in and of itself, a socially redeeming act." Casual sex
was equated with feeling free and unashamed of one's body. If practiced
outside the bourgeois conventions of monogamy, some underground
papers maintained, sex could undermine the psychic authoritarianism
that underlies the status quo. It was this freewheeling advocacy of sex
that gave underground papers much of their reputation for radicalism.

Papers such as the *Los Angeles Free Press* gained reputations as sex
papers, even though they covered many othesubjects. The *Freep*, as it
was called by readers, published detailed accountings of the Watts riots
and police beatings of demonstrators during President Johnson's appearance in Century City and regularly ran Sam Kushner's informed reporting on the United Farmworkers. The paper also boasted the underground's most powerful editorial cartoonist in Ron Cobb and two of its
most expressive cultural pundits in Harlan Ellison, the *Freep*'s TV critic,
and Gene Youngblood, a frequent contributor on cinema. Jerry Farber's
essay, "The Student as Nigger," one of the most widely read polemics on
education in the sixties, was first printed in the *Free Press*. Yet, despite the
paper's long list of accomplishments, there is no question that the *Freep*'s
tight embrace of sex is what attracted many of its readers.

Beginning with its first issue—which carried an account of the closure,
for alleged obscenity, of the Kenneth Anger film *Scorpio Rising*—the *Free
Press* covered the sex beat. Whenever a writer or artist was harassed for
the sexual explicitness of his or her work, the *Free Press* was there on the
side of the artist. And as the news pages in the front of the paper filled up
with accounts of fights for artistic freedom, the back pages filled up with
the "swingers'" classified ads for which the paper became notorious:

COUPLE WANTS TO SWING. Novices mid 40s want to learn gdlkg cpl want
to meet same white he 6'2, 190, she 5'7" 125 prf/bkgd. discreet only.
no kooks.

YNG ATTRACTIVE MALE 5'7" 140 Greek style culture passive needs daily contact all details 1st letter answered in kind Buddy

It wasn't the first time that American newspapers had carried sex advertising. According to Gore Vidal's *1876*, James Gordon Bennett's famed *New York Herald* did the same. "Good folk complain about the *Herald*'s advertisements," confided Vidal's fictional character, a journalist, "but everyone reads them." Everyone read the *Freep*'s sex ads, too. And similar ads in the *Berkeley Barb* and New York's *East Village Other*, the incendiary *Rat*, and later even the highbrow *New York Review of Books*. For many otherwise conventional readers who wouldn't dream of embracing the underground's radical politics, the sex ads made the hottest reading in town.

To hear the underground press founders tell it, the ads started innocently enough. "In the beginning," remembered Art Kunkin, "those ads where people were meeting one another were really groovy. I mean, it was part of the community." Max Scherr recalled that he accepted his paper's first sex classified from friends he met while peddling the *Barb* one day on the streets of Berkeley. Scherr's friends, a man and a woman who wanted to meet other couples for sex, had no other way to contact like-minded people, and, as a libertarian, Scherr thought it was their right to do just that if they wished.

Pleased to have the income the sex classifieds generated, and convinced that by helping people to express themselves sexually they were performing a revolutionary service, underground papers such as the *Barb* emphasized sex all the more. The *Barb* adopted the Sexual Freedom League as its own, running numerous, usually rapturous, accounts of the League's self-conscious parties. The paper also highlighted, and assisted, the growing popularity of nude beaches along the California coast, printing travel directions and accounts of arrests at the illegal enclaves of sun worshipers. And no report of a be-in was complete without a photograph of a nude hippie woman, usually heading the page.

Some of the *Barb*'s enthusiastic coverage of sex was informed with humor and genuine usefulness. "Dr. HiPpocrates," a medical advice column that dealt mostly with readers' questions about sex and drugs, was introduced in early 1967 and quickly became one of the *Barb*'s—and the underground's—most popular features. Written by Eugene Schoenfeld, a Berkeley medical doctor, the column aired "information your family doctor never told you" and served as a reliable and entertaining guide for the perplexed:

Q: A friend of mine has been forbidden by his doctor to indulge in intercourse until a nasty bit of the clap is entirely cleaned up. If any of his girlfriends should decide to employ digital manipulation of his primary sex organ to achieve orgasm and release on his part would this result in a case of the "hand-clap?"

A: I applaud the concern you have for your friend and his friends. Gonorrhea of the hand is unknown because the gonococci bacteria favors a warm, moist airless environment. . . . Most physicians believe all sexual activity should be avoided while treatment for gonorrhea is continuing. [Schoenfeld then detailed the symptoms of the disease.]

The good doctor's quips aside, Dr. Hip was the first source of accurate, nonjudgmental information about sex for young readers. After several years of syndication in the underground press, Schoenfeld's column became so popular it was picked up for syndication in mainstream dailies. Schoenfeld's uninhibited humor and often-explicit language were dampened considerably there, however, and the column seemed tame compared to its halcyon days in the underground. Nevertheless, Dr. Hip had a noticeable effect on conventional newspapers, opening up the way for straightforward advice about sex and drugs, subjects most had previously ignored.

But while Dr. Hip drew readers starved for hard information, it was the sex classifieds—and proliferating display ads for hardcore pornography, massage parlors, and "marital aids"—that paid the bills. Unlike the first personal classified ads, the influx of ads from prostitutes and professional pornographers was not innocent. No longer was sex being presented as the free medium of exchange that radicals had envisioned, but as a commodity being sold for the profit of a few.

For the two senior underground papers, the *Barb* and the *Free Press*, the sex ads did more than keep the wolf from the door; they enriched the papers and their proprietors. Max Scherr maintained that estimates that the *Barb* was pulling in $5,000 a week from the sex ads were exaggerated, but he admitted that the actual sum was substantial. Art Kunkin found it necessary to install a telephone in his car to keep up with the burgeoning business of the *Free Press*. By the late sixties, the two tiny radical papers weren't so little anymore, and critical readers were beginning to notice that when it came to portraying sex roles, the papers weren't so radical either.

In a letter to the *Barb* in 1968, alluding to the then-fledgling women's movement and outlining America's sexual malaise, SDS cofounder Tom Hayden wrote: "The *Barb* only appears to make a break with those repressive sexual patterns. There's a sexual attitude in the *Barb* that seems to suppose that whatever is taboo should be celebrated by radicals. . . . The *Barb* repeats a hip version of the Dirty Old Man, rather than exploring any real alternatives to America's sexual neurosis." The *Barb* ran Hayden's letter above a series of photographs of a bare female breast, sans the woman's face and plus Scherr's barbed response: "*Barb* must commend Tom Hayden for . . . his ability to rise above all others on 'the woman question.' . . ."

At the *Free Press*, Kunkin replied to criticism more politely, but with similar results: "Well, when the people from the women's movement came to me, I said, 'Find me another way of financing the paper on this scale, and I'll drop the ads'," Kunkin recalled. "And, meanwhile, my attitude was—and I told this to the women's movement—'This [the sex ads] may be in the back pages, but in the front, I'm going to give you all the space that's possible to counterbalance this force.'" Kunkin added that taking money from people he didn't agree with, such as pornographers, was a type of "financial jujitsu" that would "further the editorial causes of the paper."

Kunkin kept his word by giving space to the women's movement and other causes, but the jujitsu he mentioned flattened the *Freep* as a credible alternative in the eyes of many. Appearing amid pages of advertising that perpetuated stereotypes of women as pliant, pleasure-giving machines, the reports and polemics in support of women's rights in the editorial columns didn't have much bite. No longer were the *Free Press*, the *Barb*, and other underground papers radical alternatives that assaulted received notions of sexuality. By commodifying sex, they merely duplicated the cultural patterns the underground press had set out so boldly to break.

If selling sex was a short-term financial bonanza for the underground press, it was a long-term political failure—one that led directly to the founding of feminist media as alternatives to the underground press itself.

Like sex and revolution, drugs intensely preoccupied underground press activists. In this they were unique; no earlier papers had heralded drugs as means to liberation. To the underground, drugs—especially marijuana and LSD—were revolutionary tools for expanding one's consciousness. More prosaically, they were also useful for having a good

time: for making love, listening to music, or just getting stoned and
eating. Sometimes spiritual, sometimes hedonistic, the drug culture heralded by the underground press was a contradictory but colorful beat.

Until the middle sixties, accounts of drug experimentation were confined to medical journals and the occasional popular book, such as
Aldous Huxley's *The Doors of Perception*, published in 1954. By the
midpoint of the decade, however, drugs were discussed as serious tools
for personal growth in a small, modest-looking journal called the *Psychedelic Review*. The difference between the *Review* and other journals is
that, in the *Review*, mystical language had replaced medical terminology
and articles were written not by impartial researchers, but by defrocked
scientists such as Timothy Leary, Richard Alpert, and Ralph Metzger,
who used the drugs they were writing about.

By 1966–1967, the underground press began reaching large numbers
of people, most of them in their teens and twenties, with popularly
written articles on drugs. Certainly mass-media exposure, such as a *Life*
cover story on LSD in 1966, increased Americans' awareness of drugs
too; but the underground press gave sustained attention to drugs, treat-
ing drug use as a beat: detailing what drugs did to one, how they did it,
how to take them, and what dangers to watch out for. It was the
underground press' sustained, detailed, usually positive treatment of
drugs that legitimized marijuana and LSD for millions of young people.
Tim Leary recognized the intimate relationship between the rise of drug
usage and the underground press when he intoned, "There are three
groups who are bringing about the great revolution of the new age. . . .
They are the DOPE DEALERS, the ROCK MUSICIANS, and
the UNDERGROUND ARTISTS AND WRITERS" (original emphasis).

Leary propagated his philosophy of better living through chemistry in
a column he wrote for the *East Village Other (EVO)*, entitled "Turn On,
Tune In, and Drop Out." The column was widely reprinted in newspapers that subscribed to cultural radicalism. In 1969, Leary extolled the
saintly providers of revolutionary tools, the dope dealers:

> I remember talking recently to a group of clear-eyed, smiling, beauti-
> ful dealers. . . . Their life situation was close to perfect. They were
> living together with their families in nature and there was no reason for
> them to leave the country on one of those thrilling missions. They
> were planning another scam. I asked them, "Why are you doing it?
> You know that at this particular time, with the Nixon administration

waging an all-out war on turned-on kids, with the aid of border guards, secret agents, it's just not a cool time to do it. You have got all the land and dope you need to center your own lives. Why take chances?" They thought for a moment and their answer was interesting. "We believe that dope is the hope of the human race, it is a way to make people free and happy. We couldn't feel good just sitting here smoking the dope we have and saving our souls knowing that there are thirty million kids that need dope to center themselves. . . .Our brothers and sisters out there should be as liberated and as loving as we are." There was no way for me to argue with that point of view and they took off for the Middle East with my blessings.

Leary ended the column by adding, "Don't ever buy grass or acid from a dealer who doesn't lay a prayer on you while he takes your money."

At about the same time that he wrote that column, Leary made a move to enter the underground newspaper field himself. *Barb* writer George Kaufman recalled Leary, in a meeting with the staff, producing a chart with a triangle labeled "LSD" at the top. Kaufman also got the distinct impression that a starring role was planned for Leary in the new *Barb*. Though the *Barb* ultimately rejected Leary's offer, it hardly mattered. Leary had plenty of followers, throughout the underground press, promoting Leary's message that drugs are the path to enlightenment. The *Barb* was prodrug, but it also published numerous articles by and about political radicals. Across the bay in San Francisco, the hippies of the Haight-Ashbury opted for flower power over the more concretely political. The *San Francisco Oracle* was their newspaper.

The *Oracle* published only about a dozen irregular issues in its first incarnation (hip businesspeople later used the name for a porno sheet), but every issue was an event. Spirituality through drugs and yoga was the inspiration for every article and lovingly reproduced illustration. The *Oracle*'s esoterica caught on surprisingly well. The paper was selling 100,000 copies when it ceased publication in 1969, three years after it began.

Like other underground papers, the *Oracle* was an activist, advocacy paper. The first Human Be-In, the colorful gathering of hippie tribes in Golden Gate Park on January 14, 1967, was sponsored by the *Oracle*. The paper proclaimed the Be-In on its front page, together with an illustration of a Christ-like being, his two earthly eyes closed in meditation, his spiritual third eye open, the better to see the approach of the Age of Aquarius.

The *Oracle* considered itself an alchemists' journal, changing the lead of modern life into the gold of the New Age. The paper did all it could to bring this New Age into being, including providing its readers with spiritual guidance appropriate to lifting their eyes from the streets to the heavens. The lead article in its February 1967 issue was a 23,000-word, tape-recorded conversation between Leary, Alan Watts, Allen Ginsberg, and Gary Snyder, the upshot of which was that spiritual seekers need to find gurus to ground their search.

The year 1967 was a big one for the *Oracle*, for the much-publicized Summer of Love arrived that year. Thousands of long-haired gypsies from all over North America poured into the Haight-Ashbury, pushing the neighborhood's improvised community services to the breaking point. The *Oracle* helped make sense of it all, as did another hippie media venture called the Communications Company.

The Communications Company—the collective name of a group of utopian visionaries who believed that information, like everything else, should be free—issued daily mimeographed newssheets which were passed around the neighborhood. Mostly they conveyed functional messages: where to "score" food, what number to call in case of a bad trip, where to stay the night, how to avoid unwanted police attention, when the next free rock concert in Golden Gate Park would be held. Mixed with the functional stuff was an occasional hippie aphorism: "Standing on a street corner waiting for no one is power."

Such nuts-and-bolts information became a fixture of underground papers across the country. Underground papers consciously helped stitch together new communities of transients who had nothing and no one but each other. In return, their constituencies helped provide the underground papers with news. "In the early days, I used to sell the *Barb* myself," recalled Max Scherr, "and people on the street would stop and talk and tell me what was going on with them. Then the paper would write it up. I got a lot of stories that way."

Much of the information circulated through hip communities by the underground press was about drugs. Most of the information was accurate. Nearly all of it was material that young readers were unable to find anywhere else. Dr. Hip again came in handy with medical advice and unsentimental perspectives on hard drugs. Some papers carried reports on soft drug prices, availability, and quality. Nearly all of them carried headline news of drug arrests. In 1969, the *Los Angeles Free Press* got in trouble with the law—not for selling drugs, but for publishing the names, home addresses, and phone numbers of eighty narcotics agents, in the belief, according to Art Kunkin, that "there should be no secret police."

In addition to detailing hard information on drugs and criticizing restrictive drug laws, underground papers floated an occasional hoax about the miraculous powers of imaginary hallucinogens. A short item in the *Barb* in 1967 started a rumor (which received national attention when it was picked up by the wire services) that smoking banana peels produced a powerful high. It didn't, but *Barb* staffers had fun watching how far and fast a drug rumor could spread.

The underground's coverage of both the funny and the serious aspects of drug use made the papers indispensable to young readers, who otherwise got only stories of chromosome damage and heroin addiction from the mass media. Spiritual teachers used the underground press to address young seekers who formed the core of New Age religious movements in the seventies. Drug-enhanced hedonism also led, paradoxically, to a new wave of consumerism, with records, clothes, drug paraphernalia, and gourmet drugs such as cocaine becoming commodity fetishes. As the leading source of information, whether spiritual or material, about drugs, the underground press grew quickly in popularity. By the late sixties, underground papers began popping up around the country like mushroom clusters on a wet lawn.

Sensing their growing numbers and influence, underground papers banded together in June 1966 in a loosely constituted organization called the Underground Press Syndicate (UPS). UPS was formed to pursue national advertisers, give the underground papers a collective identity, and allow members to reprint each other's material free of charge. The five founding members of this underground Associated Press—*East Village Other*, *San Francisco Oracle*, *Los Angeles Free Press*, *Berkeley Barb*, and *The Paper* of Lansing, Michigan—were quickly joined by other papers here and abroad. With the birth of UPS, the underground press became a true network, growing synergistically instead of in fits and starts.

Accounts differ on how UPS got its name. The most whimsical story had *EVO* editor Walter Bowart on the phone with a reporter from *Time* who was quizzing Bowart on the new organization. "What is it called?" the *Time* reporter asked. At that moment, Bowart spied a United Parcel Service truck passing by outside. "Uh, UPS," Bowart is said to have replied. "What does that mean?" "Underground Press Syndicate."

Whatever the circumstances of its christening, the new organization was formed with an eye toward convincing the outside world that the underground press not only existed but flourished—and was unstoppable. With the half serious, half tongue-in-cheek bombast characteristic of the underground, the organization's founding statement claimed that UPS' purpose was "To warn the civilized world of it impending collapse. . . . To offer as many alternatives to current problems as the mind can bear. . . . To consciously lay the foundations for the 21st century." The five newspapers that issued that ambitious proclamation had a combined paid circulation of fifty thousand at the time. By the end of the sixties, the four hundred American underground publications had a combined paid circulation of five million and an estimated total readership (based on a high pass-along readership of six persons per copy) of thirty million.

"The underground press," UPS coordinator Tom Forcade wrote, "is crouched like a Panther, dollars and days away from daily publication and thus total domination in the print media. After the underground press goes daily, they'll die like flies."

SATURDAY · JANUARY 14, 1967 · 1–5 PM
A GATHERING OF THE TRIBES FOR A HUMAN · BE · IN

ALLEN GINSBERG   TIMOTHY LEARY
RICHARD ALPERT MICHAEL JERRY RUBIN
DICK GREGORY McCLURE GARY SNYDER
JACK WEINBURG   LENORE KANDEL
FREE
ALL S.F. ROCK GROUPS
AT THE POLO FIELD · GOLDEN GATE PARK

three

The New Media Environment

IN EARLY 1966, KEN KESEY, the novelist, and Stewart Brand, later the editor of the *Whole Earth Catalog,* helped organize a multimedia event in San Francisco called the Trips Festival. Bands played, films and light shows throbbed on the walls, and microphones were placed around the room for impromptu use by guests. The celebrants—they numbered in the hundreds and gathered in a cavernous union hall—took LSD and, with the help of the enveloping, highly charged media environment, attempted to obliterate the separate "I" of rational Western culture in a state of mystic union. Kesey did not return to book-writing after the Trips Festival; he went to work on a movie of his psychedelic adventures instead. When Stewart Brand began the *Whole Earth Catalog* in 1968, he turned not to a standard periodical format, but to the nonlinear, random access of a catalog—the better to duplicate the free-association qualities of drugs and media sensoriums.

The San Francisco Oracle *heralded and sponsored the first Be-In. (Above) Technology and mysticism were joined in the videotape "Union." (Photo synthesized by Stephen Beck and Katy McGuire.)*

Kesey and Brand's leap into the Trips Festival epitomized the multi-media sensibility of the sixties. Historically, most media activism had been confined to the world of print. The generation of activists who came of age in the sixties, however, had grown up in a media environment that transcended the linear, rational properties of print. Young activists were intimately acquainted with the nuances and texture of film, the immediacy of TV and radio, and were at ease with the way media blended to form an environment of sensory information.

It seemed as logical and inevitable to media activists of the sixties to embrace electronic media and film to convey their messages of change as it must have been for Thomas Paine to pick up his quill pen. Underground media activists did not abandon print, but those that remained in the print medium did their best to explode print's linear quality—to infuse their publications with the immediacy of electronic media. In the process, they pioneered innovations in graphic design that gave underground publications a distinctive look and feel and prompted conventional media to modify the stodgy designs they had inherited from an earlier age when print reigned unchallenged.

Underground media activists were heavily influenced by Marshall McLuhan, who maintained that the encompassing "allatonceness" of the electronic media broke down the individual ego that stands apart from the universe and, often, tries to conquer fear by conquering nature or assaulting other individuals. By transcending what they saw as the rigidity of print, underground media activists believed they were transforming the physiological, psychological, and spiritual basis of Western culture.

McLuhan viewed TV and radio as extensions of the human brain and nervous system and likened the electronic circuitry that linked people around the globe in shared experiences—the televised funeral of John F. Kennedy, say—to the participatory rituals of preliterate times. In a world where such experiences were shared instantaneously by millions, McLuhan argued, the fragmented, abstract patterns of perception created by print were becoming increasingly outmoded. "Electronic media circuitry is Orientalizing the West," McLuhan wrote, referring to Eastern mystical traditions. "The contained, the distinct, the separate—our Western legacy—are being replaced by the flowing, the unified, the fused."

To underground media activists—children of electronic media who used the flowing, unifying, fusing properties of psychedelic drugs as a rite of passage—such a conception of media came easily. As they used psychedelics to explore their inner selves, they would use media to reach out to the world, championing qualities considered subversive of the social order: spontaneity over delayed gratification; mystical union over rugged individualism; participation over passivity. Moreover, activists decided that their media would not only advocate those values, but exemplify them. Underground media would practice the journalism of consciousness in video and radio, in periodical and book publishing, in film.

Film, the oldest rival of print, produced revolutionaries who challenged conventional concepts of cinematic form and content as early as the 1920s. Sergei Eisenstein, the great Soviet filmmaker, dispensed with standard narrative form in films such as *October*, his symbolic reenactment of the Russian Revolution, released in 1927. Eisenstein developed a montage style of editing in which distinct, heterogeneous images were juxtaposed to make a thematic statement—the opulence of a church, say, framed in a shot of a peasant praying, to illustrate his point that religion is a tool of the rich. Eisenstein used montage not as mere technique, but as a cinematic expression of dialectical materialism, in which an idea (thesis) is paired with its opposite (antithesis) to produce a third, higher state (synthesis). Eisenstein thus challenged orthodoxy not only in the content of his films (they favored the revolution without reservation), but in their form.

Eisenstein and other leading Soviet filmmakers were greatly admired by American radical filmmakers, who often screened their own efforts together with Soviet films at public showings. Unlike Soviet filmmakers, whose productions were funded by their government, American radicals made do with shoestring budgets and dilapidated equipment.

Revolutionary filmmaking groups like the Workers Film and Photo League (WFPL), now nearly forgotten, produced newsreels of the strikes, hunger marches, and other conflicts of the Depression. Like many other radical media efforts, the WFPL, founded in 1930, was a partisan response to what its supporters saw as slanted and incomplete coverage of labor and minorities in the established media—particularly in Henry Luce's "March of Time" newsreels. The WFPL films had a rough vitality imparted to them by the filmmakers' obvious political engagement. The WFPL's hand-held cameras jiggled, jumped, and swooped, literally showing the action from the demonstrators' point of view.

The WFPL films were not made primarily for the theatrical showings, but for screenings in churches, union halls, community centers, and canteens as consciousness-raising and organizing tools. League news-reels were used in organizing drives by the militant National Mineworkers Union in Appalachia and the Cannery and Agricultural Workers Union on the West Coast. Political and artistic differences between members who wanted to make fiction films and feature-length historical reenactments, in the Soviet style, and those who wanted to continue producing short, agitational newsreels helped finish the group in 1936.

Even the Cold War didn't stop dissident filmmaking entirely. In 1956, blacklisted film industry people made—entirely under wraps—one of the most powerful political films to come out of America, *Salt of the Earth*, which paired professional actors such as Will Geer with amateurs from the New Mexico mines. A dramatic reenactment of a strike of Chicano zinc miners, *Salt of the Earth* not only depicted the determination of male miners to earn a living wage and improved working conditions, but it also highlighted the militance of Chicana women who threw over traditional sex roles to pick up picket signs and plan strategies. The footage was secretly processed after hours by sympathetic lab technicians after How-ard Hughes, then a power in the motion picture industry, labeled *Salt of the Earth* communist propaganda and exhorted film processors to refuse to handle the film. Most of them complied. When it was finally com-pleted, *Salt of the Earth* was shown in only thirteen commercial theaters in America, though it was very successful abroad, where its unusual blend of labor militancy and feminism found a sympathetic response.

Salt of the Earth was an anomaly in the fifties, however, as political films nearly disappeared from the American scene. Independent pro-ductions of the era were mostly personal art films. Like the Soviet revolutionaries several decades earlier, American independent filmmak-ers of the fifties and early sixties experimented with both form and content. In the case of American independents, however, content was not leftist politics, but the stuff of cultural radicalism—sex, drugs, magic.

Underground art films took their inspiration from the surrealistic avant-garde of the twenties and the experimental films of the forties by the likes of Kenneth Anger and Maya Deren. The term *underground* came into use in the late fifties and was a metaphorical rather than legal term. Wrote Sheldon Renan in *An Introduction to the American Underground Film*, "The underground film . . . is a film conceived and made essen-tially by one person. It is a film that dissents radically in form, or in technique, or in content, or perhaps in all three. It is usually made for very little money . . . and its exhibition is outside commercial film channels."

The types of film used by underground filmmakers were different too. The 35mm film favored by the major studios was too elaborate and expensive for individual filmmakers, so they turned to 16mm and 8mm, the film of choice for home movies, giving underground films a home-made quality similar to that of the underground press. The films were screened in lofts, in storefronts, by campus film societies, and, in the case of showings at Canyon Cinematheque in Berkeley, on white sheets hung up in filmmaker Bruce Baille's backyard.

Underground art films were considered, first and foremost, as vehicles of personal expression. As such, they were seldom explicitly political. They were, however, implicitly political in that they dealt directly with sensitive subjects such as drugs and sex. Parallels to the drug experience were invoked by unorthodox techniques such as kaleidoscopic images, bold colors, and stroboscobic effects. Many underground films, including several of Andy Warhol's highly publicized movies, took the use of drugs for granted, depicting characters lighting a joint of marijuana, taking LSD, popping heroin. Kenneth Anger's films, such as *Invocation of My Demon Brother* and *Scorpio Rising*, joined sex with occultism and, in their deliberate repetition of images and sounds, were intended as magical rituals.

Underground cinema's preoccupation with drugs and magic linked them to the underground press, as did their frank depiction of nudity and sex. Sexual explicitness accounted for the notoriety of otherwise quiet art films such as Carolee Schneemann's *Fuses*. A sensitively photographed cycle of lovemaking, pregnancy, and childbirth, *Fuses* was regarded in some circles as pornographic because of its explicit lovemaking scenes. Showings of underground films were raided by police from time to time, and the films were confiscated. Writers and critics in the underground press were invariably among the first to defend impounded films on grounds of artistic freedom.

The commercial press, by and large, ignored underground film, but their ambitious rivals in the underground press did not. Gene Youngblood wrote knowledgeably about film in the *Los Angeles Free Press*, and Lenny Lipton, himself a filmmaker, contributed a column on movies to the *Berkeley Barb*—and later the *Berkeley Tribe*—which gave frequent attention to underground films. The *Village Voice* also devoted ample coverage to underground cinema, most of it written by Jonas Mekas, who made and exhibited films as well as writing about them. A symbiotic relationship between underground film and underground print media grew up in the late sixties, before the work of filmmakers like Stan Brakhage, Mike and George Kuchar, Ken Jacobs, Carolee Schneemann, and Michael Snow were accepted as fit subjects for comment in major media.

As the combined assault of underground media and movements began to crack the conservative heritage of the fifties, some independent filmmakers returned to political movies, especially documentaries. The first notable new radical documentary was *Point of Order*, an anti-McCarthy film made in 1963 by Emile de Antonio, a middle-aged New Yorker who had long been on the fringes of both the left and the artistic avant-garde. Although he had never made a movie before, in *Point of Order* de Antonio boldly departed from the American documentary tradition. Using old kinescopes of the Army–McCarthy hearings, de Antonio blended a rapid-fire array of images and snippets of speeches— quite without a voice-over narrator to serve as a linear point of reference. Like Eisenstein, de Antonio established his radical point of view by skillful editing.

In 1965, de Antonio released *Rush to Judgment*, a critical look at the Warren Commission report, based on Mark Lane's book of the same name. The following year, he filmed *The Year of the Pig*, a powerful antiwar statement constructed by crosscutting personal interviews with prowar and antiwar spokespeople to illustrate inconsistencies in the prowar tradition. Then, in 1972, de Antonio weighed in with *Millhouse: A White Comedy*.

Millhouse was an attempt to use Richard Nixon's words and body language to reveal his character. As with *Point of Order*, de Antonio used tightly edited TV and newsreel footage to establish his highly critical view of the subject. "Since Nixon's fall, there have been numerous books by shrinks trying to psychoanalyze the former president. But they are lesser in every detail to *Millhouse*," the filmmaker opined, "because the doctors *explain* what's wrong with the man, whereas the film *shows* what's wrong."

De Antonio's work was radical in the sense that the filmmaker attempted to penetrate to the roots of a situation. But it was not revolutionary; de Antonio did not explicitly advocate the dismemberment of the political order. Jean Luc Godard, the French New Wave director who began his career as a critic, took a more pointed political stance. A Maoist at the height of the Cultural Revolution, Godard saw art as a revolutionary tool. In the midst of depicting bourgeois society as hopelessly decadent, fated to go nowhere (his metaphor for that society in *Weekend* was a traffic jam in the countryside), Godard thought nothing of subverting the narrative flow of his films by having characters stop to read selections from Mao's Little Red Book or deliver long, didactic soliloquies on why art should be employed as a weapon in the class struggle—"cinema as a gun," in Godard's memorable phrase.

If de Antonio reclaimed American politics as a subject for politically radical filmmakers, Godard provided a sense of urgency and a sharpened sense of struggle. Godard's gun metaphor was adapted in America by Newsreel, a documentary filmmaking group whose trademark logo was a machine gun. A collective of New Left filmmakers with branches in New York, Boston, San Francisco, and other cities, Newsreel came together in early 1968 to make the kind of agit-prop documentaries that the Workers Film and Photo League had done more than thirty years earlier. Newsreel used students and minorities instead of workers as sympathetic subjects as well as the prime audience for their films. No campus rally of the late sixties or early seventies was quite complete without a stirring documentary from Newsreel.

The Newsreel collectives turned out short films on student strikes at San Francisco State and Columbia, People's Park, the exorcism of the Pentagon, the Black Panthers, and, of course, the war and the rising tide of world revolution that activists believed would soon cleanse the United States. Like WFPL's before them, Newsreel's films were unpolished, but they had undeniable force—imparted to the films both by the filmmakers' commitment and by the politically charged atmosphere in which they were shown.

In *Black Panther*, the filmmakers relate the history of the Black Panther Party, detailing the party's rationale for carrying arms and outlining the Panthers' proposals for community control of police and free breakfasts for poor children. Then, in a scene that captures perfectly the militancy and theatricality of sixties politics, the film records several hundred Panthers—each in a black leather jacket and black beret and wearing a single earring—going through a military drill, then massing outside the county courthouse in Oakland, chanting, "The Revolution has come! Off the pig! Time to pick up the gun! Off the pig!"

In *Columbia Revolt*, Newsreel's most popular early film, the corporate liberalism of Columbia President Grayson Kirk is portrayed as bankrupt, while the student rebels assume the roles of heroic guerrillas. Writing in the *Village Voice*, Jim Hoberman described the look and feel of *Columbia Revolt*:

> . . . the film opens with a low-angled shot designed to turn Columbia's towers into the Tombs, as the soundtrack provides a litany of the trustees' corporate connections. The subsequent depiction of the occupied buildings (featuring Mark Rudd and cameos by Rap Brown and Tom Hayden) is a virtual how-to-do-it for constructing barricades and setting up communications networks and front lines. The high spirited commune is enlivened by a wedding, impromptu dancing, and draft card burning, then brutally liquidated when the administration calls in the police.

Columbia Revolt, as its construction and tone indicate, was not intended as entertainment. It was usually shown on college campuses with a veteran of the Columbia commune in attendance to lead a political discussion after the screening. To Newsreel, film was a tool for changing society, and revolution dominated their coming attractions.

Not all the guerrillas with cameras saw a violent revolution through their viewfinders. Cultural revolutionaries dominated the brand-new field of independent video. Unlike cinema, which was introduced at the turn of the century, video had the glamorous appeal of new technology. Lacking a politically radical tradition—indeed, lacking *any* tradition—video attracted mostly media activists who followed McLuhan rather than Eisenstein or Godard. Instead of viewing media as tools with which one class would overthrow another, video activists saw media as means of bringing people together. That was consistent with McLuhan's belief that media are their own messages, that one does not presume to send a didactic message through the media. Instead, one joins in the communion induced by the flowing, unifying, fusing nature of the electronic media themselves.

Like McLuhan, the leading alternative videomakers of the late sixties assumed that the economic prosperity of Western civilization would continue indefinitely, replacing the industrial age of scarcity with a leisure-time society presided over by machines of loving grace. And like McLuhan, underground videomakers saw distinct similarities between the electronic circuitry of the media—including computer technology—and the functions of the human brain and nervous system. Through application of the principles of cybernetics, McLuhan and his disciples hoped to direct the growing interdependence of human beings and their electronic extensions into beneficent channels.

Observing the accelerating growth of the electronic media, McLuhan and company concluded that we were becoming a cybernetic society in which the old paradigms based on muscle and blood no longer applied. New patterns of learning, of transportation, of communication were emerging to replace the Newtonian world of levers and pulleys and print. Control the evolution of the electronic media, they reasoned, and the cultural evolution of the human race could be directed. "In a cybernetic culture," wrote Michael Shamberg in his book *Guerrilla Television*, "power grows from computer printouts, not the power of a gun."

Videotape was introduced for use in broadcast television in 1956, but it wasn't until 1968, when the Sony Corporation marketed a portable video camera and recorder (known as a portapak), that video came within the reach of artists and social activists. The impact of portapaks on video art and activism was comparable to the effect of offset printing on the print media. All of a sudden, access to complex, expensive broadcasting studios was unnecessary; virtually anyone could make and show a tape.

Early video art, as practiced by the New York artist Nam June Paik and others, frequently employed random feeds of imagery that duplicated the nonlinear, free-associative qualities of psychedelic drugs. Such work was designed to liberate television from the conceptual straightjackets imposed by standards of commercial broadcasting. Viewed mostly in galleries and over public television, however, video art attracted limited audiences.

Social activists employed video directly, in local communities, to achieve political goals. While the pioneering efforts of video activists were also viewed by limited numbers of people, the relationship of community people who saw the tapes was an intimate one, since they often helped produce the work.

The first stirrings of community television occurred in small, spare studios and on city streets. In Montreal in 1968, a group of residents of a slum area talked Canada's National Film Board into lending them a portapak, microphones, and videotapes, which they took into the streets to interview their neighbors. The local people they taped spoke their minds with eloquent intensity about what they saw as neglect by landlords and government, and over the course of time a collectively made neighborhood documentary evolved. It was shown to authorities as a true sample of public opinion and was credited by neighborhood people with helping to restore a sense of community spirit in the area. The

Montreal project was especially notable for having been initiated by the community itself rather than by outside activists or professionals.

Most community videotapes were initiated by video activists and made with the cooperation of local people. One such tape by People's Video Theatre (PVT), a New York City group, recorded conflicting opinions about what should be done with a public park. The tape was screened for city officials, whose responses were added to the tape, and then played back for the neighborhood in the park; PVT called this "media-tion." By the end of the sixties, the group was making other, similar tapes, as purposeful as Nam June Paik's art tapes were purposeless. The Young Lords, a radical Puerto Rican group, were shown on one PVT tape protesting the killing of one of their members by police. Indians demonstrating on Thanksgiving Day at Plymouth Rock were the subjects of another tape, which, like the Young Lords piece, included interviews and speeches in which the demonstrators explained their actions in detail.

Video activists believed strongly in the power of the new technology to create a video democracy. Organizations such as Raindance Corporation, Videofreex, Media Access Center, and Global Village formed to spread the gospel of video. Of these, the most influential was Raindance. Headed by former *Time-Life* staffer Michael Shamberg, Raindance Corporation was established in late 1969 as a video production team and a think tank for devising media strategies for the counterculture—an underground RAND Corporation. Before long the group also began publication of a magazine called *Radical Software*, which was a forum for both discussing the potential of video and exchanging information on the actual production of tapes.

Shamberg and the Raindance Corporation quickly emerged as spokespeople for a type of technological radicalism inspired by McLuhan. Techno-radicals believed that social problems were solved not by boorish behavior in the streets, but by redesigning the technological means by which people communicate. Wrote Shamberg: "It's nostalgia to think that . . . balance can be restored politically when politics are a function of Media-America, not vice versa. Only through a radical redesign of the information structure to incorporate two-way, decentralized inputs can Media-America optimize the feedback it needs to come back to its senses."

This line of thinking, which Shamberg optimistically labeled "post-political," was derived from McLuhan's view that political problems are caused primarily by communications breakdowns—not by the conscious clash of political interests. McLuhan attributed the clash between young and old—the much-debated generation gap—not to a conflict of political opinions per se, but to a difference in patterns of perception induced by the media, which was then expressed in political terms.

In *The Medium Is the Message*, McLuhan asserted that "Youth instinctively understands the present environment, the electric drama. It lives mythically and in depth. This is the reason for the great alienation between the generations." Young people, in other words, demanded involvement and harmony because they were retribalized by TV and radio, while their elders remained remote because they persisted in seeing the world in the fragmented patterns induced by print. The way to resolve conflict, then, was not to directly assault the political and economic system, as in a political revolution, but to extend the unifying properties of the most sophisticated electronic media to everyone. That would change people's basic patterns of perception and thus their politics.

Michael Shamberg and other video activists, while placing great store in the new technologies, were not as reductionist as McLuhan. By attempting to use television to convey the messages of the Young Lords, American Indians, and other disenfranchised minorities, video activists showed that they didn't believe the medium was the entire message— otherwise, why choose one subject over another? Unlike political radicals, however, video visionaries believed that the importance of strikes, sit-ins, marches, and the like was chiefly as raw material for the cameras. To video activists, political actions had little value in and of themselves; their greatest worth was as symbols for transmission through the media—as electric drama, in McLuhan's terms.

Video visionaries such as Shamberg differed from McLuhan in another important respect. Unlike McLuhan, who accepted commercial mass media more or less as he found them, Shamberg felt that the mass media were conditioning agents that numbed rather than enlightened and depended for success on accumulating mass audiences, which he viewed as antithetical to democracy. "A standard of success that demands thirty to fifty million people can only trend to homogeneity," Shamberg wrote. "Yet homogeneity is entropic. Information survival demands a diversity of options and they're just not possible within the broadcast technology or context."

Shamberg proposed a new context: "guerrilla television"—low-cost, decentralized TV made by the citizenry itself for its own purposes. Guerrilla television was intended to coexist with commercial broadcasting as a means of restoring balance to the "media ecology" of America. The government could have one channel on the new forty-channel cable TV systems then envisioned, Shamberg suggested; advertisers could have another channel, and the commercial networks still another. The people would have the remaining thirty-seven channels. Perhaps the Young Lords would have a channel in New York; then they wouldn't need to take to the streets at all.

It was a concept that many media activists of the late sixties found appealing. Video groups popped up around the country to augment the work of the original activists, determined to provide alternatives to conventional television. With their roots in local communities and their nonconfrontational styles, most young video makers stood between McLuhan and the New Left filmmakers of Newsreel in the political spectrum and foreshadowed the ascendance of alternative media in the seventies.

Not all the media visionaries were in the visual media. Although it didn't offer the novelty and extravagant promise of video technology, underground radio was an exciting medium in the 1960s, giving voice to New Left politics, countercultural values, and innovative rock music at a time when mainstream radio was off limits to political and cultural radicals. In the process, underground radio affirmed the growing sense of community among young listeners, becoming what McLuhan termed their "tribal drum."

The roots of sixties underground radio can be traced to 1949, when a small group of pacifists and libertarians founded KPFA-FM in Berkeley as the nation's first noncommercial, listener-sponsored radio station. The birth was not without complications. FM receivers were so rare at the time that the station had to sell sets to potential listeners. With only $15,000 in the bank, KPFA was also undercapitalized—so much so that the station was forced to shut down for lack of funds after only a year on the air. In desperation, KPFA turned to its listeners for additional support, and, in a matter of months, the station was back on the air—still with a shoestring budget, but back on the air. In 1951, KPFA's survival was ensured when the fledgling station was awarded a $150,000 grant from the Ford Foundation for a three-year study of listener-sponsored radio.

Station KPFA and its parent Pacifica Foundation were the creations of Lew Hill, a World War II conscientious objector and former American Civil Liberties Union official. Hill and his cofounders had a fierce dedication to the First Amendment and the exercise of free speech. This was generally unpopular in the conservative early fifties, but it was a rallying point for beleaguered liberals and leftwingers whose movements had otherwise lost momentum. Many of KPFA's early supporters and programmers were professors at the nearby University of California. Their collective knowledge gave the new station quality programming unmatched by many wealthier commercial stations and even by much network programming.

KPFA was a horn of plenty, offering classical and popular music from around the world, live drama, and other cultural programming to go with in-depth documentaries and news broadcasts that were notable for their even-handedness and depth. The station was always broke and rent with internal strife among its talented, ambitious, egotistical, underpaid staff, but it produced unique and exciting radio. The station survived Hill's suicide in 1957, won a coveted Peabody Award in 1958 for public service, and continued to attract topnotch talent. Alan Watts and Kenneth Rexroth appeared as commentators; Paul Robeson and Pete Seeger sang out; and the young Pauline Kael served as film critic.

KPFA also had a unique ability to take and defend unpopular stands at a time when most of its commercial competitors remained discreetly silent. In 1954, several anonymous marijuana smokers defended the evil weed in a remarkable live program. Although it was never clear whether the smokers had actually lit up while on the air, many listeners believed they had, bringing the station unwanted attention from the Federal Communications Commission over an idea whose time had not yet come.

Years later, assessing the early years of KPFA in an interview with *City Miner* magazine, Lawrence Ferlinghetti remembered:

KPFA had a large influence in the fifties. This was before everyone had a TV. KPFA was really a focal point for a lot of the underground . . . When I arrived [in San Francisco] in 1951, it was in full force. It was the center of the intellectual community right up on through the early sixties. There were regular commentators and programs that gave me a complete education that was much better than anything I got out of college. I mean, I used to listen to Alan Watts and Kenneth Rexroth regularly. Kenneth didn't just review poetry books, he reviewed everything and generally from an anarchist, libertarian, populist perspective.

For ten years, KPFA was the only listener-sponsored radio station in America. It accepted no advertising, although it did take federal and foundation grants when it could get them. The backbone of the station, however, was its listenership, its electronic community. They paid most of the bills, provided unpaid volunteers, and gave the embattled broadcasters needed moral support. In 1959, this lonely crowd got a bit bigger when Pacifica started KPFK in Los Angeles. That same year, an eccentric millionaire named Louis Schweitzer called Pacifica's general manager and offered the astonished executive his radio station, WBA, in New York, simply because he admired Pacifica's programming; WBAI signed on the air as Pacifica's third station in 1960. (In the 1970s, Pacifica added FM stations in Houston and Washington, D.C., to become a five-station mini-network.)

WBAI became one of the most important, innovative stations in American radio. In 1962, the station aired an interview with ex-FBI special agent Jack Levine, who accused the agency of conducting illegal telephone taps, mail surveillance, and break-ins. Levine also blasted the FBI for failing to vigorously investigate violations of the civil rights of blacks and for deliberately exaggerating the "communist menace" to fatten the agency's budget. It was the first time the American electronic media had taken the FBI seriously to task—a risky business, since radio was closely regulated by the federal government. WBAI also gave early and empathetic coverage to the civil rights movement, for which it won several broadcasting awards, and collaborated with KPFA and KPFK to produce an antiwar teach-in, in 1965, which many colleges in the stations' signal areas used as a focal point for their discussions in classrooms and organizational meetings.

WBAI's contributions to the sixties sensibility was not limited to the content of its programming, but extended to the innovative formats of key programs. Bob Fass's "Radio Unnameable," a Saturday-night special of music, poetry, and talk, was an exciting and unpredictable audio collage—radio's equivalent of a multimedia sensorium or the visual collage style of the underground press. Fass's show wasn't the first Pacifica program to make use of the collage format. John Leonard (now a *New York Times* columnist and a former editor of the *Book Review*) had aired an earlier program called "NightSounds" on KPFA. While Leonard's program was carefully sculpted in advance, Fass didn't know what he would play or say from one moment to the next.

"Radio Unnameable" was the radio of consciousness, an intimate, shared experience that elicited immense loyalty among Fass's listeners. When, in the middle sixties, Fass began identifying openly with the counterculture and the antiwar movement, a large part of his audience identified with those movements too. Fass began taking his microphones to demonstrations and inviting New Left leaders to discuss their plans and problems on the air. Among them were leaders of the Columbia rebellion, who spoke over WBAI while the occupation was in progress. Moreover, listeners began to call Fass with *their* plans and problems—so much so that Fass employed a full-time worker to take calls, make referrals to free clinics, give phone numbers for bum-trip counseling, or just talk to someone who was down. By 1965, Fass was joined in what was becoming known as "freeform" radio by Larry Josephson and Steve Post, who hosted similar shows.

"Fass used to say that what he was doing was running a giant switchboard," remembered Post. "Fass would use his program and the telephone lines to put people in touch with one another. In essence, you could experience what was happening and listen to a commentary on it at the same time. But not just a cold, abstracted commentary, because the station was actually involved in what was happening."

The greatly increased participation of listeners in Pacifica's programming marked a major difference between listener-sponsored radio, operated chiefly for the benefit of the listeners, and commercial radio, operated mainly for the profit of its owners. The difference was duly noted by other would-be radio activists. In 1964, a former KPFA volunteer named Lorenzo Milam founded KRAB-FM, a noncommercial station in Seattle, with his $450,000 inheritance. Like Lew Hill and Bob Fass, Lorenzo Milam was an audio visionary. Milam was passionately committed to an anarchistic media democracy in which things would be run as much as possible by the listeners themselves, and he eagerly provided community people with the air time, the training, and even the stations to do it.

Milam explained his radio philosophy in his self-published book, *Sex and Broadcasting: A Handbook on Starting a Radio Station for the Community*:

> The people who come to volunteer at the station will be graduates from the Columbia School of Broadcasting who want to be Boss Jocks, and listeners who love the station and want to be part of it.
>
> The Boss Jocks should be discouraged. Because they don't really care for community radio. . . . Their time at the Columbia School of Broadcasting has been a brainwash time. . . .
>
> You are better off with people who have never been on the air before: people who have no slickness, who have never run a control room, never been heard ten miles away. You are better off with people who love the radio station—who have heard it, and listen to it regu-

larly, and heard your plea over the air for volunteers, and answer because of that dark worm inside all our minds which screams COM-MUNICATE!

Milam's passion for community radio—and $1.1 million from the sale of a second station, KDNA-St. Louis, to commercial broadcasters in 1973—led him to become a veritable Johnny Appleseed of community radio. With his partner, Jeremy Lansman, Milam helped start fourteen noncommercial FM stations around the country, most of which endure as listener-sponsored outlets. When his philosophy was tested by a group of critical minority broadcasters at KPOO in San Francisco, also in 1973, Milam and the board of directors responded by giving them the station, which still broadcasts, still under the control of minority journalists.

With their humor, spontaneity, and intimate links to their listeners, Lorenzo Milam and Bob Fass exemplified the community radio that took root in the sixties. Even Milam-inspired stations and the Pacifica outlets didn't play much rock-and-roll, favoring international folk and classical music. Except for tightly formatted AM Top Forty stations, rock was just not played on American radio. By the middle sixties, however, a sizable audience had developed that wanted to hear on the radio the longer songs, more sophisticated instrumentation, drug-inspired sounds, and socially conscious lyrics they were hearing on records at home.

Such an obvious vacuum could not remain for long. In the spring of 1967, Tom Donahue, a former AM disc jockey, record producer, and concert promoter, walked into KMPX, a little FM station in San Francisco that aired mostly foreign-language programs and was only marginally profitable. A disc jockey named Larry Miller was already on the station in the all-night slot, playing rock and folk, and had attracted a devoted but small audience, Donahue proposed to employ his pro-moter's skills to multiply that audience. A commanding presence who weighed over three hundred pounds and had a deep bass voice, Donahue talked the station management into giving him four hours of time every evening, with the understanding that if his show took off, he, Donahue, would be made the station's program director.

Tom Donahue went on the air in April of 1967. By June, KMPX was playing rock-and-roll twenty-four hours a day. Donahue's success at ballyhooing the new format had been swift, with listeners sending incense and flowers and a Viet Cong pennant to decorate the station's small studio. "All of a sudden, people were hearing albums that they'd never heard on the radio before," recalled ex-KMPX disc jockey Bob McClay. "It was astounding to be able to hear that kind of music and it was so important." Risk-taking songs by psychedelic bands and protest singers were the electronic drumbeat to which the extended community of hip, young whites danced, made love, got high, and marched. With KMPX laying down the soundtrack to their lives, that community became more conscious of itself, more confident of its ability to remake society.

Although it was a commercial station, KMPX was considered "underground." As with the underground press and the underground cinema, the word *underground* was a metaphor. It described an attitude, a gestalt of rebellious music and countercultural values, rather than illegal status. Unlike their counterparts on AM Top Forty stations, KMPX disc jockeys selected their own records from a wide range of choices, played lengthy album cuts instead of being restricted to blandly compressed singles, and aired experimental records and records with controversial drugs-revolution-and-sex lyrics.

Like the freeform pioneers on Pacifica stations, KMPX personalities free-associated and talked to their audience between selections in a normal tone of voice. KMPX jocks programmed a higher ratio of music to talk than Bob Fass, however, and were less likely to interview New Left leaders or talk about movement issues as integral parts of their shows. Rock jocks were more inclined to believe that revolution should be fun. With on-air monikers like Dusty Street, Reno Nevada, and Travus T. Hipp, and stoned, "mellow" personalities, they attracted increasing numbers of listeners who shared their premise that parties were for dancing, not for formulating political lines.

When a sizable audience tuned in KMPX's unique brand of radio, advertisers showed an interest in the new station. Head shops, boutiques, restaurants, and, most importantly, record companies financed the station. It soon dawned on the owner of KMPX, one Leon Crosby, that there was a market, as well as a constituency, for this type of programming. Crosby decided he wanted more commercials, not all of them from counterculture businesses. Why not go after the Bank of America, he suggested. And, uh, could the disc jockeys sound a little snappier, a little more professional, when they read ad copy?

They couldn't, it appeared, not at first. Donahue and the staff—organized as the Amalgamated American Federation of International

FM Workers of the World, Ltd., North Beach Local No. 1—walked off the job as soon as the staff astrologer assured them the aspects were favorable. Two months later, in May 1968, the staff migrated en masse to a classical music station called KSFR, owned by the New York-based Metromedia Corporation. The station's call letters were changed to KSAN, and the revamped outlet signed on the air as San Francisco's second freeform rock station.

KSAN was supposed to be above money-making concerns, but as a commercial outlet of a private corporation, there was no way an attitude of purity could be maintained for long. KSAN didn't make the mistake of chasing big corporations for ads (unless they were record companies), and the resident jocks were allowed to read ad copy in their accustomed slow-and-easy way. KSAN even engaged a satirical group called the Congress of Wonders to do funny commercials for real clients, such as *Rolling Stone*, and imaginary ones as well: "Folks, this is Bob Crud of Tower of Crud stores, reminding you, don't forget."

The mix of music and humor, pitched to hippies and would-be hippies, proved profitable. Soon similar stations went on the air in New York, Los Angeles, and Boston. "Top Forty is dead," Donahue announced, "and its rotting corpse is stinking up the airwaves."

Music was the common denominator of FM rock radio, but a you-and-me-brother-against-the-Man attitude in public affairs did much to make underground rock radio an integral part of the youth community too. Rock stations hired newscasters who were much like their listeners: opinionated, skeptical of anything smacking of the establishment, attuned to a "now" multimedia sensibility.

Shortly after the KMPX staff went to KSAN, Wes "Scoop" Nisker, a satirical songwriter, showed up at KSAN to do audio collage newscasts. Splicing together tapes of songs, speeches, interviews, and undefinable sound effects, Nisker used the news as raw material to create a highly partisan but artistic and informative show.

Nisker's sense of fun did not preclude involvement in politics. He ended each show with the activist tagline: "If you don't like the news, go out and make some of your own." Sometimes Nisker helped his listeners make the news as well. "In 1970," remembered Nisker, "after the guilty verdicts in the Chicago Conspiracy Trial were announced [and radicals took to the streets in Berkeley in protest], the *San Francisco Examiner* had an article saying that the rioters were listening to the KSAN news to find out where to go. And they were, of course, because we were giving them directions." KSAN's nervous management told Nisker to do his newscasts without the sound effects, which they felt whipped up listeners' emotions. Nisker went to India instead. He was succeeded by former *Ramparts* managing editor Larry Bensky, who did the news without sound effects, but was not a whit less radical otherwise.

Listeners used rock radio stations in much the same way that readers used underground newspapers: as sources of information, entertainment, and opinion. One difference was that radio stations allowed their audiences more immediate participation than papers were able to give with letters to the editor and occasional solicited articles. When a spectator was stabbed to death at the Altamont rock festival in 1969, KSAN disc jockey Tony Pigg threw the telephone lines open for several hours so that the rock community could commiserate and debate what went wrong.

Yet despite the affirmative role that underground rock stations played among countercultural listeners, they were short-lived alternatives to the mainstream media. The walkout at KMPX was only a finger-in-the-dike tactic against the commercialism that eventually overwhelmed rock radio. The market for rock was simply too profitable to let rock radio stations remain idealistic for long.

This came in sharp contrast to the noncommercial quality and fractious democracy at the listener-sponsored stations of the Pacifica network and elsewhere. Because they were not designed for profit, the noncommercial stations never faced the temptation to package and sell their constituencies to advertisers. As a result, they endured as true alternatives to the mass media—and to the rock stations, whose very popularity doomed them to irrelevance as authentic alternatives.

Underground newspapers were quicker than most conventional newssheets to realize that they were competing with electronic media for public attention. No longer did newspapers have a monopoly on hard news or on advertisers' budgets, and their prestige had fallen accordingly. "I'm only in the underground press because I don't have the money to get into television," *Rat* editor Jeff Shero cheerfully confided. Since they couldn't afford to break into TV, underground publishers developed graphic design techniques that enabled them to approximate the flowing and fused visual effects of the electronic media.

The first underground newspaper to depart radically from conventional newspaper design was the *East Village Other*. *EVO*'s cofounder, Walter Bowart, a painter, and Allen Katzman, a poet, aimed to make their progeny the first "electric" newspaper—a newssheet with the

immediacy and flash of TV. As such, they thought nothing of changing
the format from week to week, in imitation of the flux Bowart and
Katzman associated with electronic media. *EVO* ran unjustified copy
around illustrations, reversed type to run white letters on black backgrounds, increased the size of dots in screens over illustrations to get a
pop-art effect, eliminated the halftones in photographs to get a stark
black-and-white look—all in an attempt to escape the confining qualities
of print.

EVO's illustrations were often collages—many both politically and
artistically crude, but unmistakable in their meaning: Lyndon Johnson's
face grafted onto a Nazi stormtrooper's body; an American general
seated atop an airplane whose bomb-bay doors swung open to drop
dollar bills. *EVO*'s headlines were also collages, with words cut out of
other newspapers or taken from supermarket ads—anything, just so it
jarred the sensibilities of readers and drew their eyes to the page. The
standard newspaper page, with its crazyquilt of body type, headlines,
and illustrations, is essentially a collage anyway; *EVO* underscored and
exaggerated this by adding elements of dada and surrealism. The result
was the visual equivalent of *EVO* contributor Tuli Kupferberg's war cry,
"Total assault on the culture!"

EVO layout artist Charlie Frick attributed the paper's bizarre appearance to the inspired amateurism of its art staff—many of them unpaid
volunteers—as much as to Bowart and Katzman's direction. "Since
many of the people didn't know what was really going on, they didn't
know what could not be done. . . . Some of the best tricks were lucky
accidents or art department fuck-ups."

Although *EVO* was innovative, it was not pretty to look at. Some of the
grime and sharp edges of life in the hip ghettos of New York found its
way into the paper, and some of its experiments were simply artless.

It was left to the *San Francisco Oracle* to bring beauty to the underground form and to influence pop artists like Peter Max. The *Oracle*
stretched the use of color to its limits—the result of the imaginative use of
split-fountain printing, in which metal dividers were placed in the ink
containers atop the press to allow primary colors to "bleed" into one
another and form additional colors. Two, four, eight colors would adorn
the paper, all sharply in register and in dazzling profusion. Articles were
arranged in the circular form of mandalas or shaped like pyramids—
whatever the spirit of the moment seemed to call for, and whatever the
layout artist thought would shake readers free of their habitual ways of
reading newspapers. The *Oracle*'s fluid, almost three-dimensional design

recalled the drug experience. Indeed, the paper's editors saw the *Oracle* as an agent of mind expansion, not only because the paper reported on and advocated spirituality, but because reading the paper was designed to be a "trip" in itself. Many of the *Oracle*'s best designs were blown up into posters that quickly became collectors' items. "When," asked underground publisher Richard Neville sarcastically, "did you last frame a page of the *Times*?"

The graphic innovations of the underground were watched with interest by publishers of slick magazines such as *Avant-Garde* and particularly by advertising agencies, which adapted some of the same techniques, refined and printed on glossy paper, in their ads in mainstream periodicals. "Whenever you see the use of ragged right text," said Charlie Frick, "of photo montage and collage, of crazy borders . . . of wacked-out cartoons and shimmering fountains of color, remember the hirsute dropout with a headful of acid who probably invented the style . . . in a dirty office on the mean side of town ten years ago."

Illustrations from the underground press were often used on posters, an especially popular art form during the sixties. The swirling, colorful psychedelic posters for hippie ballrooms such as the Avalon and the Fillmore effectively evoked the multimedia experience of the shows they advertised. Some psychedelic artwork found its way onto the covers of record albums, where it jostled for space with pictures of increasingly strange-looking bands and the funny, funky work of underground cartoonists such as Robert Crumb, who drew the cover for Big Brother and the Holding Company's album *Cheap Thrills*, one of the top records of 1968.

The underground comics of the 1960s ("comix," as they were known) drew upon numerous aspects of popular culture and synthesized them in a crude but often powerfully expressive form. Drugs, sex, politics, pollution, television, and the foibles of the counterculture and the New Left themselves were all fair game for freewheeling underground satirists, who didn't hesitate to violate the rules of newspaper cartooning by drawing upside down, by breaking out of panels, or by drawing backwards so one had to hold a drawing up to a mirror to decipher it.

Jules Feiffer's brilliant strips in the *Village Voice* on existential angst and atomic brinksmanship had long been popular, of course. However, Feiffer's work was more intellectual, more fifties, than that of the young cartoonists who began plying their trade in the underground press.

The pay for underground cartoonists was virtually nil, but underground papers gave the artists all-important artistic freedom and the rights to their work, plus an empathetic readership before whom they could make beginners' mistakes. Having grown up with the cute animals of Walt Disney and the pervasive skepticism of *Mad*, the new generation of cartoonists suddenly had the freedom to go far beyond Disney and *Mad* in their depiction of society. Underground cartoonists proceeded to push every taboo to the limit, depicting all known varieties of sexual experience explicitly and enthusiastically and portraying characters who ingested drugs in huge quantities and exotic combinations for the amusement of readers who were taking drugs in real life.

The leading vehicle for the new breed of cartoonists in the middle and late sixties was the *East Village Other*, itself a cartoon of a conventional newspaper and, by all accounts, a memorable place to work. "*EVO*," observed Bill Griffith, a comic artist who got his start there, "was the kind of place where you'd go to paste up a page and find pot seeds in the rubber cement."

EVO quickly attracted a pool of comic talent that included Griffith, Art Spiegelman, Kim Deitch, Vaughn Bode, Spain Rodriguez (formerly of a Buffalo, New York, motorcycle gang), Trina Robbins (one of the few women admitted to the boys' club of underground cartooning), and Robert Crumb. All proved popular with readers, especially Crumb, whose work was reprinted in Underground Press Syndicate newspapers throughout North America, Europe, Australia, and Japan.

Crumb created characters that readers easily recognized as comic representations of their neighbors and themselves: Fritz the Cat, a shallow college dropout who fancies himself a ladies' man and an existentialist king-of-the-road; Flakey Foont, a befuddled Everyman who can't quite figure out what life is all about; Mr. Natural, a white-bearded guru and Aquarian Age con artist who survives very nicely by fleecing the likes of Flakey Foont. Crumb's criticisms of the counterculture were especially keen because he knew it so well. They were insiders' criticisms, made palatable by the fact that Crumb was funny as well a perceptive.

Crumb had an immediately noticeable impact on mainstream media culture. His revival of the thirties hipsters' saying, "Keep on truckin'," was quickly and often illegally expropriated by mass-media advertising, along with his finger-popping, big-footed characters "trucking" comically down the sidewalk. (In the 1970s, Crumb made his living in part by out-of-court settlements of copyright infringement suits.) An establishment publisher issued Crumb's Fritz the Cat in a deluxe hardcover edition, and a mainstream filmmaker used the character in an X-rated feature-length animated movie that did well at the box office but lacked Crumb's insight and wit.

The dean of underground political cartoonists was Ron Cobb, whose strikingly powerful work appeared weekly in the *Los Angeles Free Press* between 1966 and 1970. Unlike the comic artists who drew strips and books that told stories and featured repeating characters, Cobb was an editorial cartoonist in the newspaper tradition. An excellent draftsman who posed his human protagonists—cops and hippies, businesspeople and Indians—against grim backgrounds of ruined natural landscapes and windowless totalitarian cityscapes, Cobb was unmatched at portraying the confrontational style and apocalyptic mood of the late sixties. "I'm fascinated with man in stress situations," said Cobb, "I'm fascinated with man at a crisis. So I love to create artificial crisis, because I think that rather than a cartoon making a timid, harmless point I would much prefer to draw someone into a situation where they have to say . . . 'Yeah! That could happen!' or 'Yeah! . . . what would I say if that did happen?' Where they have to react." Cobb was the most widely reprinted of the underground editorialists, his work appearing in several book-length collections and on several continents.

The do-it-yourself spirit that animated all underground media inspired underground newspaper cartoonists to produce comic books, some of them reprints of their newspaper work, most of them original art. *Zap #1*, published by Crumb in 1967, was the first full-length underground comic book. Carrying a "For Adult Intellectuals Only" warning and filled with drugs-and-sex fantasies, successive issues of *Zap* both showed the way and set the tone for other underground comic books.

Independent comic-book publishers such as Denis Kitchen's Krupp Comic Works in Milwaukee; Jay Lynch and Skip Williamson's Bijou Publishing Empire in Chicago; and the Print Mint, Last Gasp Eco-Funnies, Apex Novelties, San Francisco Comic Book Company, and Rip-Off Press in the San Francisco area sprang up to provide alternatives to the corporate comics giants—D.C., Dell, and Marvel—and freedom from the Comics Code Authority, which banned explicit sex and violence from comics. Sales of underground comic books in the late sixties and early seventies averaged about 20,000 per book, but bestsellers could go much higher. The first book in the *Young Lust* series, a satire of teenage romance comics edited by Bill Griffith and Jay Kinney, sold nearly

Robert Crumb, part-time banjo player and full-time comic genius, satirized "straight" society and the radical counterculture alike in strips for underground newspapers and comic books like Zap, *which he first published in 1967. (Photo by Dave Patrick.)*

"WELL...AT LEAST WE DON'T HAVE TO WORRY ABOUT ANARCHY ANYMORE...."

Ron Cobb was the underground press' foremost editorial cartoonist. Cobb went for the jugular of modern society in drawings depicting a technological police state and ecological disaster made inevitable by technology run amok. (Courtesy of Sawyer Press.)

200,000 copies; several of the early *Zap* comics sold 300,000 to 400,000, and Gilbert Shelton's *Fabulous Furry Freak Brothers* series has amassed nearly a million international sales.

Although they were hits with young readers, many underground comics were poorly executed. Drawings were rough, and the artists were frequently self-indulgent, filling up page after page with private fantasies—produced mostly, it seemed, for their shock value. Some of their fantasies reproduced the worst racial and sexual stereotypes. Crumb's black characters were jiving street hustlers with bulging eyes and loads of natural rhythm, and the female characters of many male cartoonists were beautiful-but-dumb hippie "chicks." Angered by the portrayal of women in the comics and determined to try their wings as artists, female cartoonists started comics of their own in the early seventies. (The growth of women's comics is examined in Chapter Ten.)

Despite the frequent lapses into stereotypes by underground cartoonists, the better artists produced socially conscious work that stands as perceptive statements years after publication. Justin Green's comic book, *Binky Brown Meets the Holy Virgin Mary* was an insightful and hilarious treatment of the guilt and fear of a pubescent Catholic schoolboy. In *Manning*, a satire of the popular TV police drama, *Mannix*, Spain Rodriguez reversed convention by making Manning a brutal cop who beat addicts and shook down helpless victims only to speed away into the night, muttering "Just a man doin' his job."

The development of underground comics had a strong effect on the sixties generation, who grew up with cartoons as part of the media environment and responded with enthusiasm to comics about themselves. The underground's unabashed treatment of sex, violence, and drugs helped lead to a loosening of the Comics Code in 1972. Underground artists and publishers also frequently fought and won against obscenity charges, strengthening the climate of freedom in publishing in the late sixties. Perhaps equally important, the reentry of imaginative artists and entrepreneurs into comics restored cartooning to the status of folk art it has traditionally enjoyed.

The self-starting spirit that moved media activists in the sixties infused the world of book publishing, where small, independent presses experienced an unprecedented explosion in growth. Like their counterparts in other underground media, independent press publishers were eager to experiment with both form and content. Sometimes it seemed that small presses were trying to explode the book form and get outside it, the better to provide alternatives to traditional notions of what a book is. Oversized books, books in odd shapes, books written in calligraphy, and books about unusual subjects—geodesic domes, indoor gardening, natural foods, making-your-own clothing/home/solar heater, holistic health, backpacking, Eastern religion—all were primarily the province of independent publishers working to present alternatives to the corporate conglomerates that were, by the middle sixties, gobbling up mainstream publishing houses.

Not all small-press books encompassed cultural trends or explored new regions of experience. Many, in fact, were published in the traditional domains of literature—serious poetry and fiction and dissident political opinions that large houses largely scorned—unless they came from the pens of well-known writers. Independent publishers, many of them on the West Coast and in other regions of the country removed from the center of commercial publishing in New York, decided that if innovative books were to be published, small-press publishers would have to publish them. The result was a surge in do-it-yourself publishing, some of it art for art's sake, some of it polemical writing that dovetailed with sixties political movements and helped clarify and strengthen them, nearly all of it useful in nurturing the growth of the alternative culture.

Like all underground media except independent video, small-press publishing has a history that predates its expansion in the sixties and seventies. Paine, Blake, Whitman, Poe, Joyce, Stephen Crane, and Anaïs Nin published some of their most important work themselves or with independent publishers. Lawrence's *Lady Chatterley's Lover* was self-published, and Upton Sinclair footed the printing bill for his critical study of the American press, *The Brass Check*.

The more recent roots of the independent publishing movement lie in the fifties and early sixties. In 1953, Lawrence Ferlinghetti opened the City Lights bookstore in San Francisco to give readers a broad selection of inexpensive paperback books. Two years later City Lights Press published its first book, Ferlinghetti's *Pictures of the Gone World*, and in 1958 introduced, to a firestorm of controversy, Allen Ginsberg's *Howl*. After City Lights beat the subsequent obscenity charges, *Howl* sold 800,000 copies, loosening restrictions on realistic language and sensitive subject matter—drugs, sex, madness—in the process. Most of the City Lights circle of writers bridged the gap between the Beat era and the hippie epoch, providing the sixties counterculture with a direct link to American bohemias of the past.

New York poet Ed Sanders launched his own frontal attack on censorship in the early sixties, titling his underground literary magazine *Fuck You: A Magazine of the Arts*. *Village Voice* columnist John Wilcock caused a minor stir simply by printing the title. Sanders also ran a bookstore, the Peace Eye, that became a hangout for radical writers and artists in the early days of the New York underground, much as City Lights did for dissident intellectuals in San Francisco.

Received notions of propriety and political legitimacy got yet another jolt from the underground in 1965, when Barbara Garson self-published her play *MacBird*, a satirical treatment of Lyndon Johnson loosely based on *MacBeth*. Garson's own Grassy Knoll Press sold 105,000 copies of the book before turning it over to Grove Press, which sold 300,000 more. Financed in part with money from Paul Krassner's *Realist*, *MacBird* became an off-Broadway hit. Unlike the prevailing polite criticism o Johnson's war policies in liberal circles, *MacBird* depicted the president as a madman and an object of ridicule. By doing so, Garson violated the conventions of good taste and what was known at the time as "responsible dissent." Most of the underground media would soon follow her example.

By the middle sixties, several hundred small presses had sprung up to publish the work of unknown writers, many of them outside the artistic and political mainstream. The literary world had long had its small presses and little magazines, of course, but never before had there been so many of them, especially presses that took cues as much from political involvement as the literary tradition. Commented Len Fulton, a novelist and small-press publisher:

> Journalism was in the streets in the underground newspapers, and there were little magazines starting up everywhere. In some electric way we saw that Godot would not come and save us if we only clowned and waited for *we* were Godot and it was out of our primal reality—movement—that saving had any meaning at all. The small press movement, freed from academic subsidy and principle, was a phenomenon pushed directly out of this awakening of the sound of the self.

In May of 1968, Jerry Burns, Fulton, and other politically engaged publishers met in Berkeley to talk things over. The group selected Fulton to chair a new organization, the Cooperative (later the Committee) of Small Magazine Editors and Publishers. COSMEP was started to get small-press magazines and books into libraries, to promote reviews in underground and mainstream media, and to put isolated editors and publishers in touch with one another.

At about the same time, Fulton started *Small Press Review*, an occasional magazine of reviews and information on the small-press scene. "I found it terribly agreeable to be in touch with other small pressmen, to know what they were doing," Fulton recalled. In 1972, the energetic Fulton started yearly publication of a *Small Press Record of Books in Print*. He had already published the *International Directory of Little Magazines and Small Presses* since 1965, when that annual publication debuted as a slim, forty-page volume with approximately 250 listings. (It now runs to nearly 500 pages, with over 2,500 entries.) Why this passion for documentation? Explained Fulton's associate Ellen Ferber in 1979, "The chronicling of any movement tends to encourage its expansion. The awareness of the existence of small publishers led others to try publishing themselves."

By the late sixties, the trickle of small-press publishers was turning into, if not a flood, at least a swift-running stream. The most successful independent effort, the *Whole Earth Catalog*, edited by Stewart Brand and published by the Portola Institute, first appeared in late 1968. The *Catalog*, a periodical published in an oversized book format, was prompted by the exodus of young people from the cities to the countryside. "A lot of my friends were moving to the boondocks and they needed to learn how to do things," said Brand. "The idea behind publishing the *Catalog* was to serve them and anyone else who was interested."

A lot of people were interested. Brand's nuts-and-bolts primer on survival in the margins of society sold a combined total of two million copies and won a National Book Award in 1972. "A member of the selection committee [Garry Wills] resigned, saying the *Catalog* was a non-book," laughed Brand. In a sense, it was. With its random-access format and open invitation to readers to experience and report on the topics covered in its pages, the *Catalog* reflected the multimedia sensibility that Brand and Ken Kesey experienced in the Trips Festival more accurately than it did a standard one-way, linear book format.

The success of the *Whole Earth Catalog* also ensured the survival of a small hippie distribution outfit in Berkeley called Book People. Book People hadn't done much business before the *Catalog* took off. After it did, the small company couldn't keep up with demand. Distribution of the *Catalog* was finally turned over to Random House, but not before the revenue had bought Book People a warehouse from which the company distributed an expanding line of small-press titles on countercultural pastimes: gardening, diet, yoga, backpacking, holistic health, and handi-crafts among them.

Many of those pastimes have since become popular throughout soci-ety. The small presses helped make them so, sometimes—as with the *Whole Earth Catalog*—by reaching people directly, other times by developing books that were later distributed or copublished by main-stream publishers, such as *The Well Body Book*, by Hal Bennett and Mike Samuels, M.D., a holistic health workbook copublished by Booksworks and Random House. In this way the sixties counterculture, amplified and exemplified by underground media, seeded the seventies lifestyles of millions.

While the various developments in the underground media are treated in discrete chapters in this book, in actuality they existed simul-taneously and were often complementary. Activists in one medium dove freely into other media to convey political messages or simply to express themselves. The Portola Institute not only published the *Whole Earth Catalog*, it operated the Media Access Center, a video information nexus. After *The Realist* helped fund the production of Barbara Garson's *Mac-Bird*, proceeds from the play were used as seed money for the *San Francisco Express Times*, which her husband, Marvin Garson, edited. When one underground enterprise succeeded, all the others were strengthened.

This did not only benefit activists. The public benefited, too, from the much greater availability of new visions and values, which broadened the political, cultural, and spiritual options of millions. By the end of the 1960s, in dozens of major cities and college towns, one could buy a radical newspaper, take in an underground film, watch experimental video, read small-press poetry, laugh at taboo-defying comics, or tune in the new psychedelic sounds on freeform radio. The many strands of the underground, each with a unique history, had come together in a way that none but the most driven media visionary would have predicted to form a new media environment. Without it, the counterculture and the New Left would not have taken root and flourished.

The whole thing was a lie!" *by a Special Forces He*

Ramparts

February 1966   Seventy-five

"I quit!"

four

What Rough Beast

IT WAS THE VIETNAM ERA, the center did not hold, and Yeats' "rough beast" slouched past Bethlehem to Southeast Asia to be born. The underground media attended the birth, breaking many of the biggest stories of the war, the bombing of civilians in North Vietnam and the slaughter of unarmed villagers at My Lai in the south. Their efforts helped shatter American consensus with the force of a fragmentation bomb, leaving slivers of guilt and rage embedded in the American body politic long after the events the underground uncovered had passed into history.

The underground media did more than supply the American public with much-needed facts, however; they conveyed an attitude, a perspective for understanding the thousands of fragmentary reports about the war. In pacifist magazines such as *Liberation* and *Win*, the basis for opposing the war was staunchly moral. In the leftist media, exemplified by *Ramparts* and the *National Guardian*, the war was condemned as imperialistic. Regardless of their respective analyses, passionate opposition to the Vietnam war was the common denominator of underground media.

Ramparts *and the* National Guardian's *ace correspondent, Wilfred Burchett, broke reports of American brutality that challenged the political justification of the Vietnam war years before mainstream media followed suit. (Burchett photo by Neal Cassidy.)*

The *National Guardian* began covering Indochina in the early fifties
when the Viet Minh, led by Ho Chi Minh, defeated the French colo-
nialists and forced the partition of Vietnam into northern and southern
regions. By the dawn of the sixties, the *Guardian* was expert in covering
Vietnam. In the May 22, 1961, *Guardian*, correspondent Anna Louise
Strong, a veteran of several decades of leftist journalism, published an
interview with Ho Chi Minh in which the Vietnamese leader warned,
"Your American imperialism spends so much money to keep Ngo Dinh
Diem in power. . . . In history, when people are oppressed too hard,
they make a revolution. Our people in the South are oppressed too hard
by Diem. So Diem will fall, as did Chiang Kai-shek and Syngman Rhee
and Batista. . . . All the money America spends on Diem is lost money."

A year or so later, America was expending ever more money and
materiel in a vain attempt to crush the National Liberation Front
(NLF)—described in United States press reports as the Viet Cong—and
the few American correspondents then on the scene were increasingly
critical of the war effort. U.S. officials lied to them about enemy body
counts, lied about the morale and fighting trim of the Saigon troops, and
blasted reporters for declining, as one high-ranking officer put it, to "get
on the team." Independent-minded mainstream reporters—journalists
such as David Halberstam of the *New York Times* and Peter Arnett of the
Associated Press, both future Pulitzer Prize winners—could, and did,
criticize U.S. conduct of the war in their dispatches. Yet neither they nor
the other mainstream reporters in Vietnam went beyond criticism of the
course of the war to criticism of its premises. In 1965, in his book *The
Making of a Quagmire*, Halberstam wrote, "The lesson to be learned from
Vietnam is that we must get in earlier, be shrewder, and force the other
side to practice the self-deception."

To radical journalists, the lesson of Vietnam was quite different.
Maintaining that the U.S. should not have gotten involved in Vietnam's
civil war in the first place, underground media called for the total
withdrawal of American forces, not victory for the U.S. One prominent
radical reporter, the prolific Wilfred Burchett, not only declined to get
on the American team, but openly supported the other side.

Burchett was an Australian-born communist journalist who had devoted a lifetime to leftist causes. As a young man in the thirties, Burchett
helped organize the escape of Jews from Hitler's Germany. In World
War II, covering the conflict for the *London Daily Express*, Burchett defied
orders from the U.S. occupation forces in Japan to become the first
Western correspondent to enter devastated Hiroshima. There he re-

ported the prevalence among the survivors of radiation sickness, a disease that the U.S. military insisted did not exist.

Burchett went on to cover the Korean war from the communist side, publishing provocative reports of U.S. "germ warfare" that were never confirmed. While in Korea, Burchett was charged with interrogating Western prisoners of war (he retorted that he was merely interviewing them for his stories), which prompted the Australian government to lift his passport in retaliation. In the sixties, Burchett traveled with a Cuban passport, covering the Indochina war for a variety of communist periodicals as well as noncommunist publications such as the *National Guardian*.

Burchett was the only full-time correspondent in Vietnam for the American radical media. Invariably short on experienced reporters and cash, underground media usually relied on judicious reading of establishment and foreign news reports for news of the war or on interviews with peace activists about what they saw on their infrequent trips to Vietnam. *Liberation* editors A. J. Muste, Dave Dellinger, and Barbara Deming were among the activist journalists who visited North Vietnam in defiance of a U.S. State Department travel ban.

As the war intensified in the wake of the Gulf of Tonkin resolution of August 7, 1964, which gave President Johnson greatly expanded war powers, the need for alternative reporting was never more apparent. Although the alleged attack on U.S. destroyers by North Vietnamese torpedo boats that prompted the resolution was later shown to be unconfirmed and possibly imaginary, the *New York Times* wrote of the incident as "the beginning of a mad adventure by the North Vietnamese communists."

In the months just after the Gulf of Tonkin resolution, Wilfred Burchett became the first Western correspondent to travel extensively with the NLF. In the first weeks of 1965, Burchett cabled a remarkable series of articles, datelined "From the liberated areas of South Vietnam," to the *National Guardian*. The articles detailed his travels with the guerrillas along jungle paths, over rickety bridges, and through elaborate tunnels extended by the Viet Cong to within several miles of Saigon. In his analyses of NLF military strategy, Burchett included fascinating touches of color: "Hunting teams attached to every unit ensured that there was always something to go with the rice. The 'something' varied from elephant steaks—the Americans bombed and strafed them from the air as 'supply vehicles'—to jungle rats, with monkey, wild pig, porcupine, civets, and other wild creatures in between."

Burchett also accurately described a successful NLF attack on the

U.S. airbase at Bien Hoa as a significant Viet Cong victory—early U.S. press reports pooh-poohed the raid—and reported that most of the guerrillas were natives of the south, not infiltrators from North Vietnam, as official U.S. policy maintained. Burchett concluded that the Americans were losing to the popular guerrillas, despite superior U.S. firepower, and would continue to lose. It was an accurate forecast of the next ten years of the war, but galley proofs of the series, offered to the wire services and major New York dailies by *National Guardian* editor James Aronson, were ignored in the belief that accurate information could only come from U.S. government sources or establishment reporters in Vietnam.

According to Aronson, *New York Times* editors expressed initial interest in the Burchett series and then abruptly changed their minds. On February 7, 1965, while the series was running in the *Guardian*, Lyndon Johnson ordered U.S. warplanes to bomb North Vietnam. In his book *Something to Guard* (published by Columbia University Press in 1978), Aronson speculated that had a paper with the prestige of the *Times* printed Burchett's reports, it "would have pulled the rug out from under Washington's justification for the bombings"—e.g., that the staging area for NLF activity was in North, not South, Vietnam.

Almost immediately, the foreign radical press began reporting that civilians were maimed and killed in the bombing of the north. The March 27, 1965, issue of the *Guardian* carried an article entitled "A Strange War Against Children and Patients." Reprinted from the February 16, 1965, issue of *L'Humanité*, a French communist paper, the article detailed the alleged bombing of a hospital and a school in North Vietnam by U.S. planes. "This is a strange war," the report read, "in which schools and hospitals are destroyed, children are killed and straw huts burned in operations that cannot possibly have any military significance."

On August 28, 1965, the *Guardian* published another atrocity story, this one a piece by British journalist Freda Cook, in which Cook charged that American planes leveled a North Vietnamese sanitarium for lepers. Commented Cook, "Does the American high command . . . really believe that such acts will bring the North Vietnamese to their knees, or give them more confidence in the sincerity of President Johnson's peace proposals, or make the common people compare the American way of life favorably with their own?"

A month later, in its September 28 issue, the *Guardian* published an interview with Michael Myerson, one of four Americans who defied

State Department regulations to go to North Vietnam in order to inspect bombing damage there. Myerson reported viewing "bombed hospitals, . . . farms, markets, and dams." The Americans also reported seeing a residential district in Danming, the North's third largest city, "flattened by bombs."

Despite the deadly rain of bombs, the American activists said that well-defended bridges attacked by U.S. planes remained intact and most of the few that were destroyed were quickly rebuilt, sometimes with portable pontoon bridges assembled at night. Morale in the north was high, they said, and the bombing didn't appear to seriously hamper transportation or the Vietnamese military effort. Mostly, it hit homes and hospitals. Said Myerson, "They [the North Vietnamese] are convinced that the hospitals are being blown up on purpose to terrorize the people."

One of Myerson's companions on the trip to North Vietnam was Chris Koch, the program director at WBAI radio in New York. Koch was so moved by what he saw in the north that when he got home he put together a series of four programs highly favorable to the revolutionaries. After the first two programs were aired, Louis Schweitzer, the man who had given WBAI to the Pacifica Foundation, was incensed by what he considered Koch's one-sidedness. Although Schweitzer no longer owned WBAI, he was its largest financial contributor. WBAI's nervous management held up the rebroadcast of one of Koch's programs and ordered the producer to delete portions of his upcoming shows. Koch walked out instead, taking much of the staff—and a third of the station's subscribers—with him as a protest against censorship. (Koch is now producer of National Public Radio's respected news program "All Things Considered.")

In the *National Guardian*'s October 9, 1965, issue, Wilfred Burchett wrote that "during August and September there has been systematic bombing of irrigation dams and flood control dikes in an attempt to produce famine and even disastrous flooding of the Red River, which could cost literally millions of lives." North Vietnam complained to the International Red Cross about the attacks, while U.S. officials denied harming any civilians.

Clearly, the war in Vietnam was rapidly escalating and the U.S. was becoming ever more deeply involved in that country. Yet the roots of the conflict were buried, all but invisible to the American public. It would take a determined scholar to unearth them. That's where Robert Scheer and *Ramparts* magazine entered the picture.

In early 1965, Robert Scheer was engaged in researching the history of American involvement in Southeast Asia for the Center for the Study of Democratic Institutions in Santa Barbara, California. The center planned to publish Scheer's findings in a scholarly report, but the study was unlikely to have wide circulation, and besides, Scheer complained, the Center's editors were cutting out "a lot of the good stuff." One of the people Scheer confided to was Warren Hinckle, the young editor of *Ramparts*, an intellectual Catholic magazine Hinckle was in the process of transforming into a muckraking journal. Hinckle jumped at the chance to publish the juicy parts of Scheer's research in *Ramparts*. The result was a devastating critique of what the magazine dubbed "the Vietnam Lobby."

Scheer and Hinckle, collaborating in the July 1965 issue of *Ramparts*, described the Vietnam Lobby as "a small but enthusiastic group of people—including a Cardinal, an ex-Austrian Socialist leader, and a CIA agent who maneuvered the Eisenhower administration and the American press into supporting the rootless, unpopular, and hopeless regime of a despot and believed it actually was all an exercise in democracy."

The *Ramparts* story detailed, among other things, how conservative Cardinal Francis Spellman groomed the future dictator of South Vietnam, Ngo Dinh Diem, at a seminary in New York in the early 1950s and lined up support for him in U.S. government and intellectual circles. The *Ramparts* piece also targeted press puffery such as a 1959 *New Leader* story about Diem, revealingly entitled "Democratic One Man Rule," which assured Americans that Diem's corrupt regime was an Asian "miracle" and a model of democracy. "Diem's authoritarian tactics were not explicitly reported in the American press until . . . he fell from power," *Ramparts* reported. *(Pushed from power* would be more to the point; Diem was assassinated, on CIA orders, in November 1963.)

Scheer and Hinckle's piece was the first detailed reporting in a popular periodical showing that U.S. involvement in Vietnam was early, extensive, and deliberate—not, as most press reports of the period had it, a haphazard and reluctant response to communist aggression. Not content to merely write about the war, Scheer ran a vigorous antiwar campaign for the Democratic nomination from California's Eighth Congressional District in 1966. He drew an impressive 45 percent of the vote—boosted, no doubt, by the sense of betrayal his research had engendered in voters who had heretofore taken their government's pleas of innocence at face value. Scheer—and the antiwar movement—had come a long way from the lean days of the early sixties, when *The Realist* financed a trip by

Scheer to Vietnam with the proceeds from a red, white, and blue "Fuck Communism!" poster that Paul Krassner had printed to show his true colors.

As the war intensified, *Ramparts* joined the *National Guardian* as a leading antiwar journal. The main source of *Ramparts'* appeal was its first-rate investigative reporting. The magazine added spice to its investigations by recruiting people to expose themselves in its pages. This they proceeded to do with a certain glee and considerable skill. There was no shortage of individuals with guilty consciences who wanted to atone by telling all in a widely read radical magazine. *Ramparts* became the confessor for defecting establishmentarians and, in an odd sort of way, continued to carry out its Catholic mandate.

The first big, first-person *Ramparts* exposé appeared in the February 1966 issue. Featured on the cover was a photograph of a formidable-looking Green Beret awash in a sea of medals and ribbons. A story blasting the military awaited within, obviously. But this was not a predictable putdown by an outsider. It was a comprehensive condemnation of the U.S. Army's conduct in Vietnam by former Master Sergeant Donald Duncan, who had left the Army only six months previously and was eager to talk.

What he had to say was bloodcurdling and enlightening: The U.S. frequently tortured and killed captured Viet Cong and people suspected of being Viet Cong. The U.S. had planned illegal assassination teams to bump off leaders in North Vietnam and neutral Cambodia. White U.S. soldiers consistently downgraded the character and courage of their Saigon allies and their black comrades-in-arms. And, as Wilfred Burchett had reported the previous year, soldiers of the National Liberation Front were predominantly South Vietnamese, not invading North Vietnamese.

Duncan also described the mass saturation bombing of a Vietnamese village:

I had seen the effect of the bombing at close range. Those bombs would land and go for about 15 yards and tear off a lot of foliage from the trees, but that was it. Unless you drop those things in somebody's hip pocket, they don't do any good. For 28 hours, they bombed that area. And it was rather amusing because, when I came out, it was estimated that they killed about 250 Viet Cong in the first day. They asked me how many Viet Cong did I think they had killed and I said maybe six, and I was giving them the benefit of the doubt at that. The bombing had no real military significance. It would only work if aimed at concentrated targets such as villages.

Duncan concluded that "communist or not, the vast majority of the people were pro-Viet Cong and anti-Saigon." American veterans just did not, in early 1966, go around saying the things Duncan did—at least not in print. *Ramparts* aggressively promoted the story, which blackened America's "good-guy" image for many readers.

Another writer who chose the pages of *Ramparts* to expose secret dirty work was Stanley Sheinbaum, the former coordinator of the Vietnam Project at Michigan State University. Sheinbaum left Michigan State to tell his story in *Ramparts* only two months after Duncan's confession hit the newsstands. Sheinbaum revealed that Michigan State professors had trained Diem's police, drawn up his budget, and written his constitution—with CIA money. Hinckle put Scheinbaum's story on the cover, where *Ramparts* depicted Diem's sister-in-law, the vitriolic Madame Nhu, as a Michigan State cheerleader waving a pennant. Inside, the magazine reprinted a Michigan State inventory that included itemized accountings for teargas projectiles, .50-calibre guns, grenades, and mortars. "The essential query, which must be asked before the discussion of Michigan State's behavior can be put into any rational perspective, is this: what the hell is a university doing buying guns anyway?", Scheinbaum wrote.

Once *Ramparts* had nailed down its stories, the magazine ballyhooed them in full-page ads in major newspapers. The frontal assault worked. *Ramparts'* circulation reached 250,000—by far the largest of any radical periodical—in the late sixties. Readers responded to *Ramparts* because it made the stories of the day seem as dramatic in print as they were in real life. The introduction to a heartbreaking photo-essay on the suffering children of North Vietnam in the January 1967 issue was written by Dr. Benjamin Spock, the famous baby doctor whose "permissiveness" was blamed for creating America's generation of peace activists and uppity journalists. Pictures of the torn and burnt flesh of the Vietnamese children were silent witness to the grisly effects of napalm and the bombing of civilians—horrors that radical underground publications were among the first to report.

As the war continued to expand, Wilfred Burchett bombarded readers of the *National Guardian* with increasingly anguished reports of civilian deaths from the U.S. bombing of the north. In the *Guardian*'s June 11,

1966, issue, Burchett quoted a North Vietnamese educator as saying, "We have absolutely abandoned multi-story buildings and every class-room has subterranean communication trenches starting right at the desks. . . . We cannot build complexes of buildings. Otherwise, the Americans will wipe them out."

Leading American newspapers sometimes alluded to communist re-ports of civilian casualties in the bombing, but they did not use their own reporters to confirm the accounts. The implication was that such reports were communist propaganda and therefore not to be trusted. The Penta-gon, for its part, continued to insist that American warplanes were hitting only military targets.

By mid-1966, however, noncommunist foreign media were joining their radical counterparts in reporting civilian deaths in North Vietnam. Both the *Sunday London Times* (which printed dispatches from Agence France-Presse) and *Le Monde* reported many civilian deaths in the raids. I. F. Stone summarized the foreign reports in the July 11, 1966, issue of his *Weekly*, commenting angrily:

> Washington officials quickly hailed the bombings [of oil refineries in Hanoi and Haiphong] as "superb" but assured us that they killed only "one or two civilians, if any," though admitting that heavy smoke hampered reconnaissance. . . . Their smug arithmetic of the bodycount is always being adjusted upward or downward as if with omniscient exactness, to prove our prowess or our rectitude.
>
> Hanoi is taking no chances on our highly advertised mercy. . . . Hanoi fears we may duplicate in North Vietnam the war crimes the Germans committed by bombing the dikes in Holland. This is the fear aroused as we tighten the screws in what Johnson blandly calls "a policy of measured response."

Toward the end of 1966, the international chorus of criticism of the U.S. bombing raids became so loud and so insistent that the *New York Times* sent a correspondent to Hanoi to take a look for himself. It was then nearly two years since the bombing had begun.

The *Times'* associate managing editor, Harrison Salisbury, filed his first dispatch on December 24, 1966. Appearing in print on Christmas Day, Salisbury's story confirmed what foreign media and the domestic radical press had long reported. "Contrary to the impression given by United States communiqués, on-the-spot inspection indicates that American bombing has been inflicting considerable civilian casualties in Hanoi and its environs," Salisbury wrote. He also seconded what Burchett and others had reported: the bombings had had little effect on purely military targets and seemed to stiffen the Vietnamese will to wage war.

Salisbury was compared to Tokyo Rose by William Randolph Hearst, Jr., and dubbed "Ho Chi Salisbury of the *Hanoi Times*" by the Pentagon; but his dispatches were verified in January 1967 by Associated Press reporters in North Vietnam. Americans were shocked by these reports of impersonal, casual cruelty, raising doubts where before most had been confident of the essential goodness of the American mission in Southeast Asia.

The *Times* backed up Salisbury's reporting by editorializing, on December 25, that "The tragedy of the bombing policy is that it extends rather than ends the war." *Times* editors had expressed misgivings in print about the administration's war policies before, but after Salibury's dispatches appeared their doubts seemed to deepen.

Salisbury's reporting had far more impact than did the many earlier reports in the radical underground media. By putting its imprimatur on the news, the *Times* legitimized it for less radical readers—"widened the pattern of acceptability," to use Salisbury's own words about his work. It was a pattern that would be repeated throughout the sixties and seventies.

Salisbury was nominated for a Pulitzer Prize in 1966, and again in 1967, but did not get the award either time. According to Turner Catledge, then executive editor of the *Times*, writing in his memoir, *My Life at the Time*, ". . . I was convinced that several of my colleagues made their decision on political rather than journalistic grounds—indeed, they made no bones about it. They supported the war, so they voted against Salisbury."

Wilfred Burchett, whose reporting on civilian deaths in North Vietnam had preceded Salisbury's by more than a year, was not nominated for a Pulitzer Prize. His partisanship, rather than the quality of his work, presumably disqualified him. While Salisbury's writing showed flashes of indignation and irony, Burchett wrote consistently with deep radical passion. In his report in the January 7, 1967, *National Guardian*, Burchett's lead sentence, referring to the bombing, read, "Truth will out—and it is murder, bloody murder."

Those were fighting words, meant to galvanize readers into action to stop the war. In the highly charged political atmosphere of the time, Burchett's words were not calculated to win prizes from juries of generally conservative journalists. He did, however, have the satisfaction of being solicited to write a series for the Associated Press in January 1967, in which he outlined North Vietnam's outlook toward the peace negotiations that always seemed to be pending. Burchett was chosen because of his excellent contacts with communist leaders. His pieces for the AP were widely read in official Washington, where they arrived on diplomats' desks in the pages of the *New York Times*, which had finally chosen to print his work.

As the year 1967 wore on, however, there was still no peace in Vietnam. That summer, a group of American radical journalists met in Czechoslovakia with representatives of the National Liberation Front of South Vietnam. Like the NLF, the Americans believed that U.S. intransigence, rather than communist aggression, was preventing a peace settlement. On the agenda were discussions of how the American radical underground media could help pressure the U.S. government to end the war.

One of the American journalists at the conference was Raymond Mungo, a recent graduate of Boston University and a past editor of the campus newspaper there. With his friend Marshall Bloom and several others, Mungo had been talking of starting a radical news service for underground and college media. Inspired by what he saw as the dedication of the NLF to the liberation of their homeland, Mungo proposed Liberation News Service (LNS) as the name for the new project. Bloom agreed, and LNS was born—two weeks before the mass exorcism of the Pentagon in October 1967 (the event described brilliantly by Norman Mailer in *Armies of the Night*).

LNS was the underground's United Press International to the Underground Press Syndicate's Associated Press. That is, it was a central news-gathering and dissemination agency, while UPS was a loose confederation of member papers that reprinted each other's material. With its worldwide contacts among Western radical groups and Third World guerrilla forces, LNS gave the underground press a global perspective it had lacked. First-person reports, news analysis, poetry, comics, photographs, and columns were sent out in thrice-weekly packets to media organizations throughout the United States and the world.

The news service was financed by hook and by crook. According to Mungo, some of LNS's equipment was "liberated," and many of LNS's bills went unpaid. Friends at the *Washington Post* helped develop LNS photographs on the sly, while typesetting equipment at the Institute for Policy Studies—Washington's leftist think tank—was commandeered for setting copy. In its early days, LNS shared a house with the underground *Washington Free Press* and Students for a Democratic Society. Staffers occasionally lunched with I. F. Stone, who took a paternal interest in the news service.

LNS published its first packets immediately after the march on the Pentagon. They included interviews with GIs assigned to defend the building, a report on the use of tear gas against the demonstrators, and an account by Mungo of conditions in a prison where arrested demonstrators were held. LNS's excellent, on-the-spot coverage of that major demonstration fleshed out many a local paper that would otherwise never have had firsthand radical views of the action for its readers. The following spring, LNS photographers inside the occupied buildings at Columbia spurned a big-money offer from *Life* and instead sent their exclusive photos of the rebellion to *Ramparts*.

Despite their initial successes together, the LNS staff was a fractious group, divided between emphasizing political or cultural revolution in their coverage and running the service collectively or continuing under the leadership of Marshall Bloom. The two groups split up in August 1968, with the Mungo/Bloom faction retiring to a Massachusetts farm, where the rigors of a New England winter soon put an end to their branch of LNS.

The split was a foreshadowing of the tension between anguish and whimsy that would later rend the movement as a whole. Reviewing the dispute in his engaging—if sometimes self-serving—memoir of LNS's early days, *Famous Long Ago* (published by Beacon Press in 1970), Mungo wrote:

> Their politics was communal socialism, ours was something like anarchism, and while we could cheerfully keep a few socialists around, they couldn't function as they planned with even one anarchist in the house, one Marshall Bloom, who would go out in the afternoon and buy a glorious collator, or take an unexpected trip. Their method of running the news service was the Meeting and the Vote, ours was Magic. We lived on Magic, and still do, and I have to say it beats anything *systematic*.

In October 1969, several months after the demise of the Massachusetts branch of LNS, Marshall Bloom took his own life, leaving notebooks filled with plans for a magazine called *Journal of the New Age*, that he would never see. The surviving branch of LNS in New York continued to thrive under the de facto leadership of Allen Young, a *Washington Post* dropout, who made it clear that LNS's job was to make the news as well as report it. "We select articles that best publicize and promote the movement," he said. By late 1969, LNS claimed four hundred subscribers, including several prestigious daily newspapers and major television networks. LNS also supervised a teletypewriter link among New York, Washington, Boston, and Berkeley.

The propagandistic nature of LNS was embedded in its coverage. Like any of the underground media, LNS often romanticized foreign revolutionaries, making them into larger-than-life superheroes with qualities that American radicals hoped they, themselves, would have someday. In one LNS piece, George Cavalletto described how NLF cadres published their own underground papers—literally underground, since some of them were printed in caves—in the midst of war. Cavalletto excitedly remarked that "in some ways, the papers remarkably resemble U.S. radical papers." "The typewriter and the gun," he wrote, "the propagandist and the soldier." In the *San Francisco Good Times*, Cavalletto's piece was headlined, "This Article Is Propaganda."

Activists throughout the underground media saw their work as political weapons for stopping the war. Even the less radical rock radio stations took propeace stands, giving airplay to antiwar anthems by the likes of Bob Dylan, Joan Baez, Pete Seeger, and Phil Ochs. By 1970, alienation from U.S. government policies was so great that San Francisco's KSAN radio, in search of reliable information about the U.S. invasion of Cambodia, called the head of the Provisional Revolutionary Government in Paris and broadcast the conversation in its newscasts. The station's reporters didn't trust their own government to tell the truth. As for the Vietnamese communists, they were regarded not as enemies, but as human beings whom it was possible to communicate with and even trust.

Radical filmmakers concentrated their efforts on producing fully human portraits of the Vietnamese by showing their constituents what radio and print could only describe. Radical cinema projects ranged from simple filmstrips to ambitious feature films. Like the Workers Film and Photo League's efforts of the thirties, they were intended to spur viewers into political action.

New York activist Kathie Amatniek produced a seventy-frame filmstrip in 1966 entitled *Our Enemy in Vietnam*. Designed to be shown to uncommitted audiences as a catalyst for discussion of the war, the strip sympathetically depicted NLF soldiers and peasants as simple people determined to defend their land against foreign invasion. (Renaming herself Kathie Sarachild, Amatniek, who had been writing critically about Vietnam since 1962, became one of the leaders of the pioneer feminist group Redstockings in the late sixties.)

Ironic juxtaposition was a prime characteristic of politically radical films on Vietnam. In Peter Gessner's *Time of the Locust*, a thirteen-minute, black-and-white film also released in 1966, scenes of peasants stooped in labor in their rice paddies are contrasted with shots of American GIs in Saigon brothels and a raucous rock soundtrack to dramatize the cultural dissonance that America brought to Vietnam. The film ends with a battle scene, while Lyndon Johnson's recorded voice unctuously tells us that "Every night before I turn out the light, I ask myself, have I done all I could to unite the people of the world, to bring peace?"

As the war escalated and was fought with more sophisticated weapons, radical films about the war—nearly all of them documentaries—also grew more sophisticated. *Inside North Vietnam*, a 1968 release by British filmmaker and author Felix Greene, depicted the war within the context of centuries of foreign invasion and successful resistance by the Vietnamese. The film boasted artful color camerawork and sensitive interviews with Vietnamese in all walks of life; it ran a feature-length eighty-five minutes.

By the early seventies, independent filmmakers in Hollywood's left-liberal community joined radicals in depicting Vietnamese revolutionaries sympathetically to Americans. Jane Fonda, Tom Hayden, and Academy Award-winning cinematographer Haskell Wexler collaborated on the 1974 feature *Introduction to the Enemy*. A well-realized political travelogue that pointed up the organic unity of Vietnamese culture, both north and south, and the Vietnamese will to win, *Introduction* was screened on campuses around the country—sometimes accompanied by Fonda and Hayden, who led discussions on issues raised in the film.

Also in 1974, Peter Davis and Bert Schneider committed to film the kind of historical overview of the U.S. presence in Vietnam that *Ramparts* had done a decade earlier in print. Their film, *Hearts and Minds*, dramatized the war by integrating battle footage and revealing interviews with architects of American Vietnam policy such as McGeorge Bundy and dovish former hawks such as Daniel Ellsberg. In 1975, *Hearts and Minds* won an Academy Award as best feature documentary—a development that would have been unthinkable in the early days of resistance to the war, before the underground media message softened up public opinion.

Underground periodicals were not able to dramatize the nature of the war in lager-than-life frames, the way filmmakers did, but the relative ease of producing and retrieving periodicals, pamphlets, and leaflets made print well-suited for conveying the nuts-and-bolts information that activists needed to oppose what was shaping up, in the late sixties, to be a protracted war.

The underground press augmented its dispatches on the war in Vietnam with reports on the war at home—the repression of peace demonstrators by authorities, maps and guides for major marches, notices of upcoming meetings and rallies. In 1967, folksinger Phil Ochs wrote an article for the *Los Angeles Free Press* announcing a "The-War-Is-Over" rally directly across the street from a $500-a-plate dinner for Lyndon Johnson in Century City. Ochs planned to charge a one-cent admission to his rally, at which radicals would celebrate the spirit of resistance and look to the day when the war was really over. When Los Angeles police, swinging nightsticks, broke up the demonstration, the event made national news. The following year, Ochs recorded his song "The War Is Over," which became one of his best-known efforts, pointing up the intimate connections among underground media, radical musicians, and the peace movement as a whole.

Pacifist publications such as *Win*—the magazine of the War Resisters League, founded in 1965—provided inspiration by publishing antiwar poetry and prose by Daniel Berrigan, David McReynolds, and Allen Ginsberg. The political posture of the pacifist publications, which included *Liberation* and the *Catholic Worker*, was one of the utopian anarchism and opposition to all wars by means of moral witnessing and nonviolent action. The combined circulation of the three leading pacifist periodicals at their peak was less than 150,000, but their influence on leaders of the antiwar movement, many of whom doubled as writers in their pages, was considerable. The pacifist magazines complemented their publication of poets and philosophers with down-to-earth information on resistance to war-tax surcharges and directories of sympathetic attorneys and draft counselors for readers facing conscription.

There was even a publication for and by the tens of thousands (their exact number is unknown) of young men who chose to avoid the draft by seeking sanctuary in Canada. *Amex-Canada* was started in Toronto in 1968 as a newsletter of the Union of American Exiles, an activist organization of American draft resisters and deserters living in Canada. The magazine (which continued publishing until President Jimmy Carter issued a conditional amnesty in 1977) combined leftist analysis of the Indochina war with hard information on how to survive in Canada: how to qualify for legal residency; where to stay; how to find a job; where and when meetings of war resisters were held; where to meet people. *Amex* also ran articles on Canadian history and society to help the new exiles ease into their new home. It published approximately every other month with the aid of liberal Canadian church groups. *Amex* served as a lifeline for transient war resisters, as a clearinghouse of information for mainstream reporters visiting Canada, and as a bulletin board for parents back home eager to contact their sons.

Amex was an irritant to American authorities, but it was hardly a threat. War resisters in Canada were, after all, a tiny minority, and they were out of the country to boot. Much more serious, from the U.S. government's point of view, were the dozens of antiwar papers that sprang up in the late sixties on and around military bases. Some of those publications—which bore names like *The Bond, The Ally, The Last Harass,* and *Up Against the Bulkhead*—were published by civilians who hoped to organize soldiers against the war. Others were issued by and for the GIs themselves.

The GI papers arose because official publications were unresponsive to the complaints of the draftees and enlisted men and women who did the dirty work and the bulk of the fighting in Vietnam. Most GI papers were awkwardly laid out and poorly written. But like other do-it-yourself projects that came into existence because they *had* to, the GI papers had a rough vitality and no-holds-barred honesty that went over well with their readers.

The soldiers of previous wars had laughed at the cartoons of artists like Bill Mauldin, who blasted the officer corps as pompous and removed from the troops, but supported the war he depicted—World War II—as a just war. Ted Richards, an Army sergeant who drew cartoons for Rip-Off Press after serving in Vietnam, attacked the very existence of the Vietnam war in his work. Richards' main character, a stoned, funloving young doughboy named "Dopin' Dan," lived to avoid fighting. In one Richards story, an eager young officer orders his troops to follow him to the attack, only to discover that their guns are aimed at him. The officer wisely calls down an air strike on the enemy instead: "Calling 'Tiger Balls,' this is 'Mad Gorilla,' we've run into *stiff resistance.*"

Material like that worried career officers, the "brass," who saw the GI underground papers as obstacles to running a finely tuned war machine and who tried to limit their circulation accordingly. Army regulations in the late sixties affirmed the right of soldiers to possess antiwar literature,

Former GI Ted Richards portrayed stoned,
peace-loving troops at war, their hearts and minds
more in tune with Jimi Hendrix than Lyndon
Johnson. (Courtesy of Last Gasp Comics.)

but not to distribute it. As a result, GIs were put in the stockade for passing out their underground papers, and their civilian allies were driven off base. Even so, the papers were read. Staffers for *The Bond* once drove alongside a military convoy and passed copies of the paper to soldiers in the trucks.

The Bond, started in Berkeley in 1967 and relocated to New York in 1968, was the first underground GI paper. It was distributed internationally on bases, on ships, even in Vietnam, and claimed a circulation of 100,000 in 1971. *The Bond* was arguably the most important GI underground paper. It was published by the American Servicemen's Union (ASU), an organization that claimed a peak membership of 11,000. The ASU argued that GIs had the right to bargain collectively, elect their officers, and "disobey illegal and immoral orders," among other things. *The Bond*'s editor, Andy Stapp, was an ex-private who joined the Army after being bounced from college for burning his draft card, specifically in order to organize a revolution in the ranks. Stapp received an undesirable discharge, as did editors of several other GI papers. He went on to write a book, *Up Against the Brass* (Simon and Schuster, 1970), and is now a reporter for the *Workers World* newspaper.

Despite official opposition, the antiwar GI papers were popular with soldiers who wanted a respite from the harsh indoctrination of military life and an alternative to fighting a war many of them felt they couldn't understand or support. Like other underground papers, which were also widely read among soldiers (the *Fifth Estate* gave GIs in Vietnam free subscriptions), the GI papers published listings of lawyers and antiwar groups, news of the war and resistance to it, and blunt criticism of the military. In his book *Deadline for the Media* (Bobbs-Merrill, 1972), James Aronson estimated that one hundred GI papers, many of them issued sporadically, were published in 1970.

The combined effects of antiwar organizing and publishing and the miseries of the war itself greatly strengthened antiwar feelings in the ranks. By the early 1970s, according to *The Nation*, desertions had soared to 250,000 annually. David Cortright—himself a GI activist—wrote, in a 1971 issue of *Liberation*, "American GIs were taken out of the war because the policy makers could no longer consider them politically and militarily reliable From the incidents of Hamberger Hill [when a number of GIs refused to continue fighting] to widespread reports of 'fragging' [GIs killing unpopular officers] to the recent stories of 53 GIs refusing to advance near Laos, the evidence is strong that large numbers of American servicemen will no longer risk their lives in a cause they do not support."

The American public, too, was growing disillusioned with the war. Their disenchantment was again given impetus by the independent media in 1969, when Dispatch News Service released Seymour Hersh's numbing story of the massacre of 109 unarmed South Vietnamese civilians at the village of My Lai. Unlike Wilfred Burchett, Hersh was not a radical, but, like Burchett, Hersh was forced to use alternative channels to circulate his most controversial work. A former Associated Press reporter, Hersh had tried to sell the My Lai story to *Look* and *Life* and gotten nowhere. Armed with a modest grant from the Fund for Investigative Journalism—a liberal funding organization based in Washington, D.C.—Hersh did the story for Dispatch News Service—also based in Washington—which had been founded only several months earlier by twenty-three-year-old David Obst.

Incredibly, the My Lai story had gone unreported for months, while rumors of the massacre, which took place on March 16, 1968, circulated informally. Ron Ridenhour, a former GI who had heard about the massacre, tried to place the story with a number of major news organizations without success. Ronald Haeberle, who had been an Army photographer at My Lai with Lt. William Calley and C Company, actually showed his photos of the carnage to an Ohio Rotary Club, but still the news didn't get out. Only when Hersh landed a crucial interview with Calley and went to Dispatch News Service, which pushed the story aggressively, did the biggest story of the Vietnam war surface.

It is no exaggeration to say that the news of the My Lai massacre sent shockwaves throughout the United States. Political activists who had been following the underground media were shocked, too, but they were not caught unaware. My Lai was the closing of a circle begun years earlier with Wilfred Burchett's reports from behind the lines in the *National Guardian* and Donald Duncan's tale of murder and mayhem in *Ramparts*.

By the end of the sixties, the combined effects of the antiwar media and movement had turned a significant minority of Americans against the war. News of My Lai, which broke on November 13, 1969, the same day that hundreds of thousands of Americans massed for a Stop-the-War Moratorium, made waging war all the more costly on the domestic political front for Richard Nixon, who had replaced Lyndon Johnson as Commander-in-Chief.

But still the war did not end. More convoluted negotiations, this time involving *Guardian* reporter Burchett directly, were in the offing. In the fall of 1971, Henry Kissinger waived the U.S. travel restrictions on Burchett's Cuban passport and invited the globetrotting writer to the White House for a breakfast of coffee and eggs and a blunt exchange of views. Kissinger (who does not mention the meeting in his 1,500-page memoir, *The White House Years*) assured Burchett that no one was more desirous of peace than he. According to Burchett's account in his own book on the Vietnam years, *Grasshoppers and Elephants* (published in 1977 by the leftist Urizen Books), Burchett promised to convey to Hanoi Kissinger's critical assessment of a Vietnamese peace proposal then before the U.S. Apparently the message got through, for those negotiations too collapsed.

The year 1971 was also the year that Daniel Ellsberg released the Pentagon Papers to the *New York Times*. Years of memoranda and reports showing that the Johnson administration planned to push a sweeping redefinition of the President's war-making powers months before the Gulf of Tonkin—and even planned to send bombers over North Vietnam as soon as the 1964 American elections were over—confirmed the case that antiwar activists had been making for years. By publishing the Pentagon Papers, the *Times* again put the seal of respectability on views that had once been considered paranoid, even traitorous.

To peace activists who had been informed by the radical underground and foreign media, the Pentagon Papers induced what-else-is-new shrugs. The June 23, 1971, issue of the *East Village Other* editorialized, "Now only a fool and a knave can look at those documents as secrets. There is nothing in them that we didn't know and rave about since this paper existed. They called us every name in the book—fools, hippies, trippies, and yippies—yet the fact remains we were right."

Coming after the news of My Lai and civilian deaths in North Vietnam, the revelations of the Pentagon Papers strengthened still further the antiwar constituency in America. Even the impact of the Pentagon Papers didn't halt the momentum of the war machine immediately, however; it had been building for more than a decade. The U.S. again attempted to drive the communists to the negotiating table with heavy bombing of Hanoi and Haiphong at Christmas 1972, and the response from the underground media was again strongly in favor of the revolutionaries. The New Orleans underground paper *Nola Express* graphically condemned the attacks, running a banner headline over a cover photo of American bombers that read "ENEMY BOMBS HANOI." To politically radical underground media, nothing short of victory for the revolutionaries was sufficient.

Underground media activists got their wish on April 30, 1975, when NLF and North Vietnamese troops entered Saigon after the shaky peace settlement signed in January 1973 had collapsed in mutual recrimination. The sharp demarcation between mainstream and underground media remained intact. America's major newspapers saw the collapse of the Saigon government as tragic but consoled themselves and their readers with the contention that America had done the best it could. The *New York Times* editorialized: "There are those Americans who believe that the war to preserve a non-Communist, independent South Vietnam could have been waged differently. There are other Americans who believe that a viable, non-Communist South Vietnam was always a myth. . . . A decade of fierce polemics has failed to resolve this ongoing quarrel."

Missing from the *Times'* assessment was mention of Americans who believed that the United States was not justified in waging war in Vietnam in the first place. It was the *Times'* position that reasonable persons disagreed only on tactics, not on the propriety of intervention. By implication, those who opposed the war on principle were unreasonable, and they were written out of the history of the conflict forthwith.

The response of the underground media could not have been more different. Radical newspapers like the *Guardian* highlighted the role of the American antiwar movement in restraining the U.S. war effort and celebrated the Vietnamese revolutionary victory as their own. The *Berkeley Barb*, founded to chronicle and encourage the antiwar movement with its first issue in 1965, hailed the end of the war in 1975 with a banner headline that read "LET SAIGONS BE BY-GONES." Inside, the *Barb* recorded the response of Berkeley radicals to the end of the war:

> People danced in the streets in small groups or in a large snake dance, victory joints and bottles of wine were passed around, and everyone agreed it had been a long time coming. . . .
>
> Nancy Kurshan, who was one of the organizers of the Vietnam Day Committee in 1965, said that the end of the war did not mean the end of the struggle. "Now we have to continue to change this country." Several people told me during the march that it was the greatest day of their lives.

The war without end was over, brought to a halt in part by the efforts of the American antiwar movement and its activist media. The underground media successfully challenged the formulae of objective newswriting with advocacy reporting that not only broke major stories, but humanized the statistics of the body courts, showing the Vietnamese as real people worthy of compassion and respect. The radical media helped provide a moral, intellectual, emotional, and political context in which consistent opposition to the war—the movement's finest hour—could flourish.

RAT
SUBTERRANEAN NEWS

june 15–28, 1968   n.y.c. 15¢   outside

five

The Media Guerrillas

THE COVER OF THE JUNE 15, 1968, issue of *Rat*, the New York underground paper, featured a drawing of Hubert Humphrey, dressed in riot control gear, with handcuffs and a canister of tear gas on his belt and a thin smile on his face. Behind him a guided missile lifted off, a huge dollar sign on its side, and a police armored car squatted ominously. The cover was *Rat*'s way of trumpeting the expected police repression of demonstrators at the Democratic Party's national convention in Chicago, scheduled for the last week in August. The war on the home front had been declared.

The bloody streetfighting took place outside the convention hall, as anticipated, and was televised nationwide—providing perhaps the most memorable media event of the sixties culture of protest. It was an event announced, planned, and debated in the underground media months before youthful protestors grabbed the attention, if not the approval, of American TV viewers. Together, the evolution and impact of the media strategy that produced the Chicago demonstrations compose a cautionary tale about the romantic media politics of the sixties.

Rat forecasted combat conditions in Chicago for the 1968 Democratic Convention. Abby Hoffman, on trial for conspiracy to riot, joined the battle with courtroom theatrics designed for media consumption. (Photo by Henrietta Haines.)

The Chicago demonstrations were called by three groups of youthful activists: "Clean-for-Gene" student volunteers who hoped to see their candidate, Eugene McCarthy, nominated for President; the National Mobilization Committee to End the War in Vietnam, which planned to protest frontrunner Humphrey's endorsement of Lyndon Johnson's war policies; and the hybrid group of hippies and New Left activists who called themselves the Youth International Party (YIP), who used satire and calculated outrage to assault the electoral system itself. Of the three groups, the Yippies left by far the clearest imprint on the tumultuous gathering.

The Yippies were media guerrillas, called into being in December 1967, when antiwar activist-writers Jerry Rubin and Abbie Hoffman, teacher-writer Keith Lampe, Paul Krassner, WBAI's Bob Fass, and several other underground media activists formed YIP in a stoned, marathon brainstorming session. At a climactic point in the proceedings, Krassner jumped out of his chair and shouted "Yippie! We're Yippies!" The others took up his cry, and the Yippies were off on their brief but colorful journey as media marauders.

The Youth International Party attempted to join the theories of the Che Guevara with those of Marshall McLuhan. The Yippies' battle plan was to emerge from their base in the underground media culture to stage media events—symbolic political dramas put on expressly to garner publicity—which the mass media would find so colorful, so compelling, that they would have to cover them. By portraying the Yippies shouting their slogans, staging their elaborate jokes, and flouting society's rules with their hirsute, studiously sloppy appearance, YIP theorized, the mainstream media would unavoidably transmit radical values to millions of Americans instantaneously. Instead of guns, the Yippies' revolutionary weapons would be the camera, the microphone, the tape recorder, the printing press, the put-on. It was an imaginative, often fascinating, ultimately self-defeating approach to social change. Chicago was both its *pièce de résistance* and its Waterloo.

The battle of Chicago was preceded by a number of skirmishes in which the media guerrillas honed the theory and practice of revolution-by-media. Rubin and Hoffman, in particular, had had success attracting mass-media coverage with audacious stunts before YIP was formed. In 1966, Rubin had mocked—with great attendant publicity—the once-feared House UnAmerican Activities Committee by appearing before the committee in the uniform of a Revolutionary War soldier—to show,

Rubin explained, that revolution was in the American tradition. The following year, Hoffman and a group of friends reaped similar mass-media coverage by tossing dollar bills onto the floor of the New York Stock Exchange, laughing as affluent stockholders scrambled after the greenbacks.

In the fall of 1967, the media guerrillas presented a dress rehearsal for Chicago. It was the exorcism of the Pentagon, an event stage-managed by Rubin, who abandoned plans to go around the world as a *Berkeley Barb* correspondent when *Liberation's* Dave Dellinger phoned and asked him to help organize the Pentagon demonstration.

This Rubin did, in the flamboyant style for which he became known. First, Rubin spread word of the demonstration in the underground media. Then he contacted the mainstream media with promises of the great, outrageous things to come—the exorcism of evil spirits from the Pentagon and the levitation of the building to a height of three hundred feet not least among them.

As promised, the happenings at the Pentagon made great copy. After Allen Ginsberg, the Fugs, and other poets and singers chanted "out, spirits, out" in front of the building, demonstrators charged lines of federal marshals, raised a National Liberation Front flag on the Pentagon flagpole, and succeeded in briefly entering the Pentagon itself. Perhaps equally important, from the demonstrators' point of view, the event was marked by a communal spirit that inspired much sharing of marijuana, blankets to ward off the evening chill, and food. The cooperation among New Left organizers, pacifist draft resisters, and dope-smoking hippies was unprecedented at a major peace demonstration. It was this exciting, and short-lived, coalition that gave impetus to the idea behind YIP and served as a model for future demonstrations.

No sooner had the Pentagon demonstration ended than the underground media were hashing things over, figuring out how to solidify and extend this potentially powerful coalition and garner more mass-media coverage in the process. Jerry Rubin, writing in the November 17, 1967, issue of the *Barb*, concluded:

> Our task is to create dramatic and creative confrontations which put people through tremendous radicalizing changes, releasing energy and exciting the imagination.
>
> The goal? A massive white revolutionary youth movement which, working in parallel cooperation with the rebellions in the black communities, could seriously disrupt this country, and then be an internal

catalyst for a breakdown of the American ability and will to fight guerrillas overseas. . . .

At the Pentagon we all smoked pot, we all realized the nature of imperialism, we all related to one another as living human beings, sharing food and living in collective fear in the face of armed soldiers. For two years, the so-called "hippy" rebellion demonstrated that a part cultural, and part religious, movement was needed to deepen the political consciousness of the New Left. The political movement is now becoming cultural and quasi-religious. We have our own press, our own music, our own communities, and our own myths.

In his *Barb* postmortem on the Pentagon, Rubin both articulated the philosophy of YIP and identified its hoped-for constituency: disaffected white youth. With YIP, Rubin, Hoffman, Krassner, and company attempted to fuse the politically radical "I Protest" of the New Left with the existential "I Am" of the counterculture. Such a fusion, they believed, would supply an inexhaustible source of energy for the revolution.

Like other New and Old Leftists, the Yippies were generically socialist. They believed in sharing the wealth in a post-industrial utopia of abundance, which they outlined in a leaflet circulated before the Chicago convention. The leaflet included a list of demands, including: an end to the Vietnam war; the abolition of money; the establishment of an ecologically sane society; free birth-control information and abortion on demand; "the open and free use of media. A program which actively supports and promotes cable television as a method of increasing the selection of channels available to the viewer." "It is for these reasons," the leaflet concluded, "that we come to Chicago."

The Yippies' grab bag of demands did not constitute a consistent, smoothly reasoned program. Indeed, the Yippies rejected the very idea of a program as hopelessly confining. Their chief doctrine, in Hoffman's words, was for people to "do whatever the fuck they want." By Hoffman's reckoning, ideology was "a brain disease." The only movement he claimed to believe in was "dancing."

The Yippies' unorthodox approach to revolution, which emphasized spontaneity over structure, and media blitz over community organizing, put them almost as much at odds with the rest of the left as with mainstream culture. Wrote Rubin in the *Barb*, "The worst thing you can say about a demonstration is that it is boring, and one of the reasons that the peace movement has not grown into a mass movement is that the peace movement—its literature and its events—is a bore. Good theatre is needed to communicate revolutionary content."

Many traditional leftists thought that YIP was *all* theatre—perhaps even a counterrevolutionary act. Marxist Irwin Silber, writing in *The Guardian*, called Rubin and Hoffman "the Katzenjammer Kids of the American Revolution," adding:

> The "freedom to do whatever the fuck you want," appealing and revolutionary as that concept may sound, is actually the underpinning of the capitalist system. Eliminate the expletive and the quote could as easily have been attributed to Ayn Rand as Abbie Hoffman. It was the rallying cry of the bourgeoisie which, in its struggle against moribund feudal society, was attempting to unleash the dynamic social forces inherent in a "free" labor market and the free enterprise system. . . . It is . . . not freedom but the absence of social restraint.

Despite a distinctly chilly reception in many leftist media, the Yippies pushed ahead with their plans for a massive demonstration in Chicago. At the heart of the Yippie scenario was a "Festival of Life" that would provide an alluring alternative to what they dubbed the Democrats' "convention of death." Exaggeration was the key to the Yippie style, so by the time news of the plan penetrated the mainstream media, the festival began to take on larger-than-life dimensions. The Yippies planned to summon a quarter million—no, a full million—young people to Chicago. Ten thousand—make that a hundred thousand—protesters would burn their draft cards. While the Democrats nominated their candidate under armed guard, the Yippies would nominate their candidate, a four-legged pig called Pigasus. All the top rock groups would play. The best poets would read. The holiest gurus would lead the people in life-giving chants. There would be free, healthy food for everyone, workshops on street demonstrations and first aid, and underground newspapers to keep everyone informed.

It was an ambitious plan for a group that had no political organization as such. The Yippies met and issued statements sporadically, hoping the media would do their organizing for them. The mass media did their part, publicizing the Yippie "invasion" of Chicago with wide-eyed credulity and not a little unease. To follow the mainstream media in the months before the August convention was to be convinced that a specter was haunting America: the specter of Yippie.

Privately, Yippie leaders knew nowhere near a million young people would show up. But they did expect a large crowd, and, by claiming it would be an event unprecedented in human history, they would challenge the thousands who did come to live up to the myth, and the Yippie dream would come true. That's how Yippie—how any media myth—was presumed to work.

While this unthinkably overblown scenario for revolution in Chicago was put out for mass consumption through the mass media, the nitty-gritty details of organizing such an event—and the wisdom of staging it at all—were debated in the underground media. Periodicals such as the *San Francisco Express Times* and the *Chicago Seed*, and other underground media outlets such as WBAI and Liberation News Service, crackled with news and analysis of the forthcoming extravaganza. Much of the news was alarming and the analysis often highly critical.

While Yippie leaders were proclaiming a Festival of Life to the mass media, they confided to their colleagues in the underground media that violence might attend the festival. In a prophetic interview in *Other Scenes*, a New York-based newspaper published by John Wilcock (for years a columnist with the *Village Voice* and later an editor of the *East Village Other*), Jerry Rubin allowed that "I think we have to worry about violence from the other side. . . . I mean, I think there'll be violence in Chicago and probably all of it will come from the law and order representatives in uniforms and licensed to carry guns and carry clubs." The issue was dated March 1968—five months before violence flared at the convention.

But even if violence did erupt, Rubin contended in the same interview, the drama of the fighting would work in the Yippies' favor. "What Chicago's going to do . . . you're going to dramatize that there are two sides and you can choose. It's not the Republicans and the Democrats, it's what America is doing and what it stands for and against. And when that becomes clear in every living room in the country, wow—our side's gonna win."

In the months preceding the convention, both Martin Luther King, Jr., and Robert Kennedy were murdered. The mood of the country was suddenly a lot grimmer and the stakes higher than they had been in the afterglow of the Summer of Love the previous year. Some underground media, attuned to the charged atmosphere of polarization, sharply criticized the Yippies for their plans to lead longhaired lambs to what looked like certain slaughter in Chicago and for their belief—basic to the Yippie media strategy—that intensified polarization of the nation would automatically benefit the radicals.

A passionate exchange of views took place in the May 1968 issues of the *San Francisco Express Times*, one of the more thoughtful of the underground papers. With its clean layout and partisan but literate writing, the *Express Times* was in some ways a precursor of the alternative papers of the seventies. Now the *Express Times* took aim at the Yippies' plans for Chicago. Michael Rossman, a leader of the Free Speech Movement and a personal friend of Jerry Rubin's, warned:

> . . . this style of organizing is dangerously irresponsible. For the formless publicity building the magical beckoning symbol of Music projects an image that is recklessly and inescapably slanted. It promises grooving and warmth, and does not warn that joy there must be won from within—not absorbed from others—in a landscape of total hostility whose ground conditions may well be the terror and death of one's brothers. . . . And once triggered, the energies there may not soon subside.

It was an accurate forecast of what eventually occurred, but the Yippies rejected Rossman's warning. Rubin fired off a letter to the paper affirming the appropriateness of the Yippie plan. "YIP will break people out of their psychological and geographical isolation . . . and give people the feeling: there are many, many of us; we can win! We are winning!" But before long, another personal friend, Eugene Schoenfeld ("Dr. Hip"), also decried the Yippie invasion of Chicago. In his influential syndicated column, published in the June 28 issue of the *Los Angeles Free Press*, Schoenfeld wrote: "German communists thought they would use Hitler and later take his power away from him. They would be among his first victims. Some of the Yippies feel that creating anarchy and chaos will indeed lead to a rightist reaction, but then a turn to the left. German communists believed the same until they were eliminated. . . ." "I'm not going to Chicago."

While criticisms of the Yippies in the underground press were occasionally hard, they were not harsh. The criticisms, after all, came from allies. The response from *Rolling Stone*, a fledgling rock-and-roll newspaper launched in San Francisco the previous year by Jann Wenner, a disgruntled ex-*Ramparts* staffer, was a different story. In a page 1 piece in the March 28, 1968, issue—headlined "Musicians Reject New Political Exploiters"—Wenner accused the Yippies ("a self-appointed coterie of 'radicals' without a legitimate constituency") of attempting to use the reputation of rock groups that would supposedly be performing in Chicago to lure young people to an ill-conceived political event.

Wenner didn't stop there. He assailed the very notion that politics could be a solution for young people, deferring to what he termed "the vague spirit of rock and roll" as youth's only hope to create something new and different. "The spirit of rock and roll, hippies, LSD-users, or the new youth, or whatever catch-all phrase may be used to denote this mood (which can't properly be called a 'movement'), wants no part of today's social structure, especially in its most manifestly corrupt form, politics, even 'new left' politics, which is, after all, still politics."

The critics of Yippie plans, each with a personal motive and degree of departure, had put their fingers on something basic: In the process of mustering the troops for the symbolic drama to be enacted for the mass media, the Yippies had given flesh-and-blood demonstrators an unrealistic idea of what to expect. The Festival of Life would be nothing of the sort. The Yippies were, to a considerable degree, manipulating the young people they sought to lead to Chicago. Instead of enlisting conscious, informed citizens empowered to make decisions and act in their own best interests, the Yippies viewed their supporters mainly as extras in their great media drama. Seeking to bring down what they saw as an impersonal political machine, the Yippies depersonalized their own supporters. By pointing this out, critics in the underground media both undercut the basis of the Yippie media strategy for Chicago and discharged their own responsibility to honestly inform their constituents.

The Yippies had their supporters, too, among such papers as *Rat*, the *Berkeley Barb*, *The Realist*, and the *Chicago Seed*. The *Seed* was, not surprisingly, more deeply involved than any other underground paper in helping to plan the events of August. The paper's office doubled as the Chicago nerve center of YIP. *Seed* staffers applied for the necessary permits from city authorities, and *Seed* editor Abe Peck took to signing his columns "Abraham Yippie." When convention week rolled around, the *Seed* published a special issue complete with a survival guide, cut-out press cards, maps, and other information suitable for an occupying army. "If you are attacked by several people," the *Seed* noted, "the best way you can protect yourself is by falling to the ground in a fetal position, covering vital organs with your knees. It is suggested that men wear heavy clothing below the waist."

The military language was appropriate. In the fear of the long, hot summer of 1968, initial hopes for a lovely, peaceful time in Chicago gave way to public battle plans. Chicago Mayor Richard J. Daley prepared for the acidheads and foulmouthed draft-card burners at *his* convention in *his* town by recruiting 23,000 police, National Guard, and regular Army troops to greet the demonstrators. Then he put out a message of his own: come to Chicago at your own risk.

Clearly, the convention was shaping up as a battle royal. The Yippies remained so convinced, however, that the inevitable bloodshed, telecast to America and much of the world, would show radicals in a favorable light, they would not—perhaps, at that late date, *could* not—call off their protests. In the final days before the convention, even the *Seed*, initially enthusiastic about rallying incoming demonstrators, expressed grave misgivings.

In an article entitled "The Great Media Backfire," Abe Peck, a member of the Free City Survival Committee, the Chicago group that hosted the counterconvention in association with the *Seed*, issued a statement warning incoming protestors of what they could really expect in Chicago:

> It's no go.
>
> Don't come to Chicago if you expect a five-day Festival of Life, music, and love. The word is out. Many people are into confrontation. The Man is into confrontation. . . . Cars and buildings may burn. Chicago may host a Festival of Blood. . . .
>
> We refuse to pose as front men for an alternative that no longer exists. . . .
>
> We refuse to lure you from your homes for an impossibility. . . .
> Don't come to Chicago.

But it was too late to stop everyone from coming, and the *Seed* staff wanted those who did come to have a reasonable chance to survive intact. So the *Seed* published its guide to the city, together with its grim warnings. *Rat* printed a similar issue and ran off 50,000 copies for the use of the demonstrators. *Ramparts* editors Warren Hinckle and Robert Scheer showed up too, with plans to issue a daily *Ramparts* wallposter consisting of news of past actions and previews of future ones. Ready or not, the confrontation was on, and Yippie media politics would get their trial by fire. "Hand John Wayne a flower," the *Seed* editorialized in a doomed voice. "He'll eat it and spit the petals at you."

The flowers left over from the Summer of Love—if, indeed, there were any—withered in the white heat of the Chicago convention. Demonstrators (numbering only an estimated 5,000 to 10,000), delegates, reporters, and bystanders alike were gassed and clubbed before the TV cameras in a melee that surpassed all but the most apocalyptic expectations. Six hundred sixty-eight persons were arrested during the five-day convention.

Among the hundreds beaten by Chicago police were many mainstream reporters caught up in the fighting. The September 9 issue of *Newsweek* published a photograph of six *Newsweek* reporters, detailing, in the caption below the photo, the injuries each had suffered at the hands of the Chicago police. The reporters posed for their group portrait in protective headgear. The floor of the convention arena itself was less physically dangerous than the streets, but nearly as acrimonious, as contending factions of the Democratic Party struggled for control of the proceedings and blamed each other for the chaos outside. In their zeal, convention security guards knocked down several floor reporters, prompting Walter Cronkite of CBS, on camera, to label the security forces as "thugs."

Outside the convention hall, underground journalists, who marched with protestors at any demonstration as a matter of course, were frequently battered. One of them was Robert Scheer. Scheer was enraged not only by the police tactics, but by his colleague Warren Hinckle's decision to remain ensconced in an expensive fifthteenth-floor hotel suite, watching the action on TV. Said Sheer, "It was like having two magazines. I went out on Michigan Avenue and got teargased and clubbed, and I never saw Warren for three days. His style there was offensive to me." Hinckle's lofty remove—and his huge hotel bill, reportedly almost $15,000—sparked a deep split between the two men that helped lead to Hinckle's resignation from *Ramparts* the following spring. Hinckle's response to his critics was succinct: "Fuck the New Left. I was supposed to go out in the streets and watch that shit?"

The *Ramparts* wallposters that Hinckle and Scheer were supposed to put out appeared infrequently but it hardly mattered. Since mainstream reporters were also caught in the police dragnet, they reported essentially the same facts as did underground journalists. The difference in coverage was largely one of tone. The mainstream media, while they condemned the actions of the police in unequivocal terms, seemed surprised by it; to conventional reporters, police violence was an aberration. *Rolling Stone* went further, condemning the violent overreaction of the Chicago police as typical of the establishment, while reaffirming its own stand against politics in general. In a post-convention analysis, the magazine described Richard Nixon as "ignorant" and Hubert Humphrey as "deluded and lost" and dismissed the New Left: "The left wing of politics is a completely frustrating and pointless exercise of campus politics in a grown-up world."

Underground reporters saw Chicago differently. They expected the onslaught of the police (the Walker Report to the President's Commission on the Causes and Prevention of Violence later termed it "a police riot") and, like their sisters and brothers on the street, considered police brutality routine. Underground journalists recognized that the presence of shaggy, shouting demonstrators had antagonized the police, but unlike the mainstream media, they did not criticize the demonstrators. The violence, some underground outlets maintained, served a useful purpose. *Rat* described Chicago as "a big hippie pogrom," but also found triumph in the fact that demonstrators were assaulted outside—and inside—the Conrad Hilton Hotel "because that is where the TV cameras are, and that is where the delegates are." Pro-Yippie underground media took the claim, chanted by the demonstrators during the battle, that "the whole world is watching" as *prima facie* evidence of success.

The *Seed*, which had to remain in Chicago after the demonstrators went home, was less enthusiastic. Its post-convention coverage featured a short item from LNS that claimed tests showed that one in five applicants for police jobs in Chicago was insane, plus several pages of angry, anguished letters from readers. Sighed one reader, "It's sad that things like this happen in our country, especially to people who are trying to help better it . . . As of tonight, I renounce my citizenship— because I do not wish to think of being in the same category as those pigs!" The *Seed* office also had a bullet shot through its front window, which staffers claimed was fired by marauding police.

Stew Albert, a Yippie journalist who "phoned in the news with tear gas in my lungs" to the *Berkeley Barb*, 2,000 miles away, remembered his hazardous legwork in Chicago as "true participant journalism, very partisan and agitational." Albert's reports were filled with news of a coalition between youth gangs and radical demonstrators, finding portents of a new, broader, tougher political base from which to challenge the establishment. Albert also sniped at the non-Yippie left, writing that "it all happened without a single leaflet being given to anyone and without a single white missionary getting a factory job."

Albert's writing shared with much of the New Left the romantic notion of an alliance between young, white, middle- and upper-class radicals and street-tough youth gangs and criminals. The news hit hard, then, when it revealed that one of Jerry Rubin's biker bodyguards was, in fact, an undercover Chicago police officer—not a revolutionary at all, although the Yippies remembered him as one of the most militant of their number. His testimony put Rubin on trial with seven other radical defendants the following year.

THE CHICAGO SEED

Chicago Tribune
THE WORLD'S WORSTEST PAPER

EXTRA: PIG WINS!

Washington, Nov. 5. (special to the Tripune). Thousands of people took to the streets this evening to commemorate the election of Swineburne P. Pig to the nation's highest office. Lining Pennsylvania Avenue, they cheered so fervently at the sight of Mr. Pig's bullet-proof sty that the seismograph at New York City's Fordham University had to be disconnected.

In an unrehearsed statement, Mr. Pig thanked the American people for their vote of confidence. He promised to continue in the American tradition of Garbage and..., stating that, from this day on, "no animal would be more equal than any other."

"This country has been for the Birds, and we're going to do our best to change that. During my barnstorming campaign, I learned merica is not

sick-- she's just a bit constipated."

After his spirited speech, Mr. Pig joined his Vice President for a victory dinner at the Feed Store.

Berkeley, Nov. 5.
Jerry Rubin, America's fair-haired boy wonder, led a torchlight parade through the streets of this city to express joy over the triumph of Mr. Pig. 55,000 people jammed Cody's bookstore to purchase The Collected Works of S. P. Pig, the President-elect's seminal work on American political theory. Rubin was heard to scream "Yippie" as he cashed his check from the First National Bank of Hanoi.

New York, November 5.
Abbie Hoffman and the Gypsy Digger Motorcycle club led the entire population of the Lower East side to the top of the Empire St. Building for a marathon electric yo-yo org 8,000 birds

were accidently killed when they flew into the T. V. tower.

Birmingham, Alabama, November 5.
George Corley Wallace expressed sorrow over "the choice of the American people." Wallace, speaking from the steps of the Veteran 's for a Third World War" lodge hall, announced that "after all, I'm a much bigger pig than that Swineburne fella. It must have been those Eastern monied interests."

New York, Nov. 5.
Richard Mildew Nixon tonight stated his hope that Mr. Pig would rejoin the two-party system. After reading an extremely brief press release, he was seen to turn and retreat into the shadows, muttering "Checkers, Checkers."

Minneapolis, Nov. 5.
Hubert Horatio Humphrey retu

The Chicago Conspiracy Trial took place in the tradition of Yippie media events, with Jerry Rubin and Abbie Hoffman dressing in judge's robes, holding spirited courtroom debates with the judge and prosecuting attorney, and jetting around the country to give attention-getting speeches on college campuses. The eight original defendants—Rubin, Hoffman, Dave Dellinger, Tom Hayden, Bobby Seale, Rennie Davis, John Froines, and Lee Weiner—were charged with conspiring to cross state lines to incite a riot and inciting to riot as individuals. The trial was held from September 26, 1969, to February 18, 1970, in federal district court in Chicago before Judge Julius Hoffman. (Seale's case was severed from those of the other seven in October.)

Attracted by Rubin and Hoffman's courtroom antics, the mass media gave extensive coverage to the trial, although the defendants got mixed reviews for their audacious performances. Coverage in the underground media, however, was exhaustive and uniformly friendly to the Chicago Seven, as they came to be called. Radicals and liberals agreed that the seven were being railroaded to jail by Judge Hoffman, an idiosyncratic, conservative jurist whom the defendants called "Mister Magoo" after the myopic cartoon character.

Underground reporters sat directly in back of the defendants' table, passing notes and exchanging winks. One of the radical journalists at the trial was Lionel (formerly Steve) Haines, an ex-reporter for the *Chicago Daily News*, whose voluntary downward mobility took him to the *Berkeley Tribe*. Haines, along with his wife, photographer Henrietta (née Marsha) Haines, was part of a rotating pool of radical journalists who covered the trial—and socialized with the defendants in their spare time. "We saw the trial as a gestalt," said Lionel Haines. "We saw the defendants at the Conspiracy office. We partied together. We ate together. We were part of the Conspiracy."

The underground media did everything they could to promote the idea that there *was* a conspiracy, and that everyone dissatisfied with the powers that be—millions of young people and a few sympathetic elders—were part of it. With the murder of Black Panther leader Fred Hampton by Chicago police on December 4, 1969, and the "Days of Rage" rampage through the streets of Chicago by the Weathermen immediately following the killing, promoting radical resistance to the establishment seemed more important than ever. Many underground papers carried large ads, free of charge, exhorting readers to "Join the Conspiracy!" and donate money to the Chicago Seven's defense.

After five long months, the verdicts came in: all seven defendants were

The Chicago Seed *helped organize the convention demonstrations and gave sardonic coverage to the election results that fall.*

acquitted of the conspiracy charges, and Weiner and Froines were acquitted in full. The remaining five were convicted on individual counts of crossing state lines to riot. Judge Hoffman also slapped all seven defendants, plus their lawyers, William Kunstler and Leonard Weinglass, with contempt sentences for their outspoken behavior in the courtroom. (The convictions were overturned on appeal in 1972. Kunstler, Hoffman, Rubin, and Dellinger were found guilty of contempt in a second trial, but did not serve prison sentences.)

Although the verdicts could have been much more severe, underground media activists, enraged that the defendants were convicted of anything, labeled the American justice system as the real criminal. Even *Rolling Stone* got into the act. The magazine's April 2, 1970, issue—which featured Abbie Hoffman on the cover—was a powerful indictment of Chicago justice. Freelancer Gene Marine, a veteran dissident journalist, recounted Judge Hoffman's courtroom biases in an article entitled "Chicago: The Trial of the New Culture." Wrote Marine, "Shouldn't we at least be asking ourselves, a little more often and a little more consistently, what kind of a country can do this thing, and what can we do about it, and isn't it time to get started? And can you—longhaired and freaky-clothed—can you handle, gently and without letting it turn you into just another kind of pig, the fact that it's you America is afraid of?"

Rolling Stone's political activism was shortlived. Sales of the issue bombed among the rock fans who read the magazine. A special "Pitiful Helpless Giant" issue published the following month, in the wake of the U.S. invasion of Cambodia and the shootings at Kent and Jackson State, fared no better. According to former managing editor John Burks, who supervised the two political issues, "Wenner hated them. He called a staff meeting and said from then on we wouldn't be doing political cover stories, because *Rolling Stone* was about rock and roll, not politics. I felt," Burks continued, "that we were certainly about rock and roll, but you couldn't look the other way, away from what was going on. However," he concluded, "*Rolling Stone* was Jann's magazine. He could do what he wanted with it. I thought things over for three or four days and resigned." With Burks' departure, *Rolling Stone* went back to its innocuous role as a bridge over troubled waters.

Amidst all the hoopla before, during, and after the Chicago demonstrations, the questions remained: Was it worth it? Did the demonstrations radicalize America as the media guerrillas said they would? Or was

Chicago just another media event, a brief taste of street theatre between the mouthwash commercials and the video nomination of Hubert Humphrey?

Hoffman and Rubin, along with their supporters in the Yippie school of media politics, continued to insist that Chicago was an unqualified success for their side. The demonstrations were dramatic, the broadcasts of the streetfighting showed people actually *doing* something, and they got on prime-time network TV to boot. Hoffman maintained that the government was forced to reveal the mailed fist inside its kid gloves and that the quick-cutting from the convention hall to the riots in the streets by the TV cameras amounted to "commercials for the revolution."

If so, American consumers weren't buying it. According to *Newsweek*, "one national survey found almost three out of four persons approving the police action. . . ." The media guerrillas made the mistake of thinking that getting into the mass media was the same thing as getting across their version of political reality. The confrontation in Chicago may indeed have strengthened the resolve of rebellious youth to resist the establishment, but, simultaneously, it appeared to strengthen the determination of Middle Americans to uphold the system. And they outnumbered by far the rebels and revolutionaries. Rather than rearranging the battle lines in the long-pending second American Revolution, the events in Chicago merely reaffirmed existing divisions and deepened the polarization of the nation.

Moreover, Jann Wenner was right in pointing out that the Yippies had no real constituency. The alliance with gang members and others in Chicago was strictly temporary, having little to do with the day-to-day lives of the people radicals were attempting to galvanize with media heroics. Michael Shamberg, writing in his book *Guerrilla Television* three years after the Chicago convention, made the point succinctly: "The now-legendary 1968 Democratic convention was energizing for people who were on the streets of Chicago because it was extraordinary in a superficial way that life is not: demonstrations and combat, staying up all night listening to music and smoking dope, a clear-cut enemy, and so on. That's exhilarating stuff, but totally unapplicable to an ongoing lifestyle. The streets may belong to the people, but they're a crummy place to live."

The hard lessons of media politics were demonstrated concretely in 1969, when Students for a Democratic Society organizers attempted to capitalize on what they thought were solid gains among white working-class youths after the battle of Chicago. Instead of being welcomed as liberators, however, SDS members were tossed off high-school campuses by the students they were trying to organize. According to Kirkpatrick Sale's definitive history, *SDS*, a group of teenagers in Columbus Ohio, threw punches at SDS organizers "and chased them from the neighborhood, where they were nevermore seen again."

The *kidpolitik* of the Yippies and Weathermen was an abject failure. American youths may have watched the same TV shows, seen the same movies, and grooved to the same records, but that did not, as some underground activists believed, make them a distinct class capable of rising and acting in concert to attain a political goal. Divisions of income, skin color, and gender were still there after the media flash faded, and they were stronger than the generational ties that bind. An eighteen-year-old scion of a wealthy white family, armed with a student draft deferment, had little in common with an inner-city black youth of the same age who was drafted and sent to Vietnam. The student could enjoy Yippie media events on his dormitory TV set; the soldier would hear about them at an almost surrealistic remove. Their lives after the war—assuming that the draftee survived the fighting—were likely to be equally dissimilar.

The Yippie commercials for the revolution failed, for all but confirmed partisans, because the Yippies didn't produce them; they were only the actors. It wasn't the radicals who called the shots, scheduled the programs, or—most importantly—defined the context for their messages. Writing about a Yippie "takeover" of the David Frost TV show in England, Shamberg noted that the Yippie action looked good on the jerky, rapid-fire videotape the Yippies themselves made of the event. But the same incident, broadcast over British television, seemed to favor Frost's smooth rationality and good manners because the format of the program—rational, restrained—was tailored to Frost's professionalism. "No alternative cultural vision is going to succeed . . . unless it has its own alternate [*sic*] information structures, not just alternate [*sic*] content pumped across the existing ones," Shamberg concluded.

America's media guerrillas had their own information structures—their own context—in the underground media, which were expanding rapidly in early 1968. When the Yippies tried to leapfrog the normal stages of development of their own media, they lost the ability to define the political situations into which they so eagerly thrust themselves. Abbie Hoffman may have made it onto the Merv Griffin show, but his attempt to shatter the bland talk-show format by wearing a shirt made of an American flag resulted in a blank spot on the half of the screen where

Abbie was supposed to be. As an example of network timidity, the exorcism of Hoffman's image was striking, but it's not likely that his disembodied voice convinced anyone to take to the barricades. "The revolution ended," Shamberg quoted his friend John Brockman as saying, "when Abbie Hoffman shut up for the first commercial."

Radical values were not able to survive transmission through mainstream media intact. Instead of a coherent radical vision, the mass media produced what was, in effect, a parody of radical politics. In trivializing the issues they were attempting to dramatize, the media guerrillas did unintentional damage to the movement for radical social change. Todd Gitlin, a past national president of SDS and the author, in 1980, of *The Whole World Is Watching*—a study of the mass media's coverage of the New Left between 1965 and 1970—observed, "When movements become too 'mediated,' it becomes hard to tell the difference between a movement and a fad, a movement and a trend, or just a press conference. The results are pernicious for movements. The lines between leadership and celebrity becomes very thin. It's easy for leaders to cross over and become wholly unaccountable to a movement base. The movement then becomes envious and bitter, forcing leaders even further into celebrity roles."

Hoffman and Rubin exacerbated this problem by maintaining the fiction that they were not leaders. Yet they gave the press conferences, conjured the images by which their brand of revolution would be known, wrote the books, and gave the campus talks that articulated Yippie media politics. It was always unclear whether Hoffman and Rubin were headed first to Havana or to Hollywood. In recent years, that question appears to have been answered. Hoffman's autobiography, published by Putnam/Perigee in 1980, is entitled *Soon to Be a Major Motion Picture*. True to the title, a movie version of Hoffman's book is reportedly being readied. (Hoffman delivered the manuscript of his book surreptitiously while he was a fugitive from charges of selling cocaine.)

Jerry Rubin also wrote a book of memoirs, *Growing (Up) at 37*, published in 1976, in which he described some of the pitfalls in his mass-media manipulation in the sixties and early seventies: "I purposefully manipulated the media but on a deeper level, I see that it was mutual manipulation. To interest the media I needed to express my politics frivolously. . . . Without being aware of it, I gave the media what it [*sic*] wanted. If I had given a sober lecture on the history of Vietnam, the media cameras would have turned off."

Rubin belatedly came to agree with the sentiments of Gil Scott-

Heron's popular poem, "The Revolution Will Not Be Televised." A mass-media TV show on revolution, Rubin realized, is just a TV show, after all.

The images of bloodletting in Chicago quickly sobered up radicals who had grown giddy with the expectation of easy victory. They responded to the establishment's show of force in two dramatically different ways: the acceleration of the back-to-the-land movement, with its attendant belief that the politics of confrontation are a deadend, and a bitter determination among the movement's street fighters to escalate their actions against the establishment and everyone believed to be part of it. According to Kirkpatrick Sale, Weatherwoman Bernardine Dohrn went so far as to praise, at a public meeting, the Manson family's commission of the Tate-LaBianca murders in Los Angeles in 1969, saying, "Dig it: first they killed those pigs. Then they ate dinner in the same room with them, then they even shoved a fork into the victim's stomach. Wild!" Dohrn later regretted those sentiments, but they showed how bitter, how desperate, some movement radicals became in the bleak days after the end-game in Chicago. Those two wildly divergent tendencies ended the alliance between cultural and political radicals that began with such high hopes at the Pentagon march, only ten months before the Chicago convention.

The underground media expressed both sentiments clearly and frequently. An LNS packet on the battle of Chicago also included an article entitled "What to Do Till the World Ends": "That a hard rain (of some kind) is agonna fall on America soon is a fact apparent to mystics and rationalists. . . . Whether it manifests itself in the form of a shifting of the earth's crust complete with sinking cities and tidal waves . . . or as a Good Revolution with the inevitable ironies and excesses . . . there are some of us, perhaps less dramatic by nature, who would first prefer to go on living." The LNS article advised readers to: (1) learn to eat weeds; (2) live like a gypsy; (3) learn a pre-industrial trade; (4) study preventive and emergency medicine; and (5) learn to build a solar water still.

The more radical New Left groups, most notably the Weathermen, condemned such tactics as bourgeois escapism. Better to have a gun handy and know how to use it, they argued. Just before they went underground to bomb symbolic targets in their attempt to become America's Viet Cong, the Weathermen changed the name of their newspaper, *New Left Notes*, to *Fire*.

The fire this time. The underground media both reflected and encouraged this apocalyptic outlook. By the end of the sixties, the mood of struggle-to-the-death gripped much of the underground. Wrote Rubin, in *Growing (Up) at 37*, "Reading the underground press at that time was hard to do because it seemed to spread the idea of preparing ourselves to die: Break up monogamy. Love is dead. Romance is over. Criticize yourself incessantly. Individuality is bourgeois. All nonviolence is bullshit. Bombs, guns, bombs." What Rubin had once described as "the beating heartbeat of the community"—the underground press—seemed about to burst.

That agony, more than anything, was the legacy of Chicago. Most radical activists didn't realize it at the time, but 1968–1969, which seemed to be only the beginning of greater things for the underground media culture, marked the beginning of its demise, as a conservative backlash against what was perceived as the excesses of the radical movements whipped through the United States. Widespread revulsion against the violence in Chicago helped Richard Nixon and Spiro Agnew to their narrow victory in 1968 and cast a pall over the efforts of political radicals to bring fundamental social change to America. Ahead lay the shootings at Kent and Jackson State, tougher antiriot and antidrug laws, stiffer jail sentences for protestors, secret surveillance of radical activists, and a highly effective attack on liberals in the mainstream media.

The underground media would feel the heat directly from this counter-offensive. Amidst the gathering gloom of radical disillusionment, the new administration stepped up a covert program of infiltration, surveillance, and disruption of underground media that can best be described as a secret war.

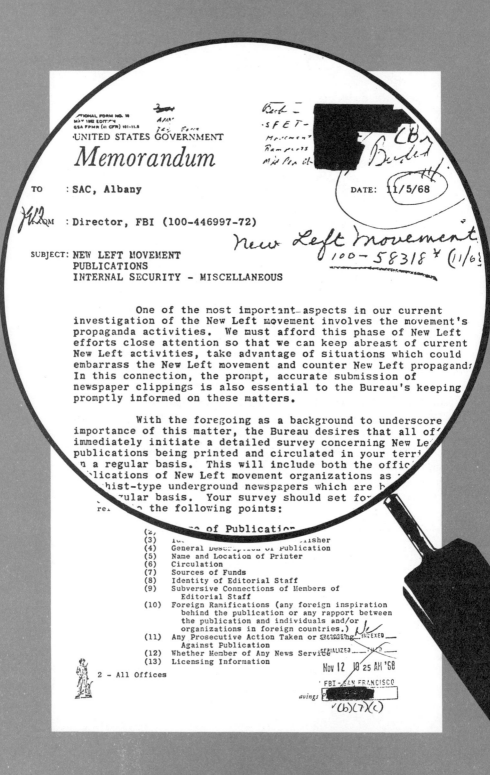

UNITED STATES GOVERNMENT

Memorandum

TO : SAC, Albany

DATE: 11/5/68

FROM : Director, FBI (100-446997-72)

new Left movement
100-58318 (11/6

SUBJECT: NEW LEFT MOVEMENT
PUBLICATIONS
INTERNAL SECURITY - MISCELLANEOUS

Bert -
SFET-
Movement
Rampurts
NW New Ch

CB
Bullet

One of the most important aspects in our current investigation of the New Left movement involves the movement's propaganda activities. We must afford this phase of New Left efforts close attention so that we can keep abreast of current New Left activities, take advantage of situations which could embarrass the New Left movement and counter New Left propaganda. In this connection, the prompt, accurate submission of newspaper clippings is also essential to the Bureau's keeping promptly informed on these matters.

With the foregoing as a background to underscore importance of this matter, the Bureau desires that all of immediately initiate a detailed survey concerning New Le publications being printed and circulated in your terri n a regular basis. This will include both the offic lications of New Left movement organizations as hist-type underground newspapers which are h ular basis. Your survey should set fo the following points:

(2) of Publication
(3) ...sher
(4) General Description of Publication
(5) Name and Location of Printer
(6) Circulation
(7) Sources of Funds
(8) Identity of Editorial Staff
(9) Subversive Connections of Members of
        Editorial Staff
(10) Foreign Ramifications (any foreign inspiration
        behind the publication or any rapport between
        the publication and individuals and/or
        organizations in foreign countries.)
(11) Any Prosecutive Action Taken or Pending
        Against Publication
(12) Whether Member of Any News Service
(13) Licensing Information

INDEXED
SERIALIZED

Nov 12 10 25 AM '68
FBI - SAN FRANCISCO

2 - All Offices

avings

(b)(7)(c)

six

The Secret War

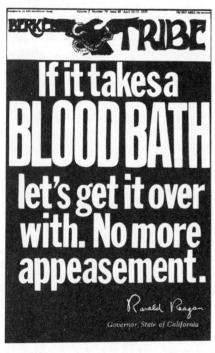

If it takes a BLOOD BATH let's get it over with. No more appeasement.

Ronald Reagan

Governor, State of California

ON NOVEMBER 5, 1968, Federal Bureau of Investigation Director J. Edgar Hoover sent a memorandum to local FBI offices. The subject was the underground media, in particular the periodicals of the New Left. Hoover ordered that "all offices immediately institute a detailed survey concerning New Left-type publications being printed and circulated in your territories on a regular basis." He instructed local offices to provide information on the identity of each paper's publisher; the name of its printer; "sources of funds"; "identity of editorial staff"; "subversive connections of members of editorial staff"; "foreign ramifications"; and "licensing information."

The FBI's covert surveillance of underground publications was the opening salvo of the secret war against the underground media. This offensive included a variety of repressive actions, including: the monitoring of personal finances of underground journalists; arrests and assaults on staff members; government-inspired distribution hurdles for radical

F.B.I. Director J. Edgar Hoover instructed agents to spy on underground papers in a memo written the day Richard Nixon was elected president. Future President Ronald Reagan, then Governor of California, issued a challenge of his own, which Berkeley Tribe *cover quotes.*

periodicals; loss of printing facilities; grand-jury subpoenas for editors and reporters; the release of "disinformation" falsely attributed to underground media; publication of "underground" papers secretly funded by the government; the bombing, burning, and ransacking of newspaper offices; and, possibly, the destruction of the transmitter of a listener-sponsored radio station.

Joining the FBI in its assault on the underground media was an alphabet soup of federal agencies, including the Central Intelligence Agency (CIA), Internal Revenue Service (IRS), Federal Communications Commission (FCC), numerous local police forces, and even the White House staff. Together, they effected systematic violations of First Amendment freedom of the press and Fourth Amendment freedom from unreasonable search and seizure. Thousands of underground journalists became unwilling victims of repression, and the growth of underground media was effectively halted.

Of the many eulogies to the death-of-radical-activism delivered since the early seventies, only a few barely noticed accounts have given full weight to the attack on the movement's means of communication as a leading reason for its collapse. Yet the story of the suppression of underground media is a crucial chapter in the recent history of radical activism in the United States.

Despite its longstanding reputation for freedom of the press, America has frequently seen fit to silence the press, particularly its radical and dissident branches. The first American newspaper, Benjamin Harris's *Publick Occurrences Both Forreign and Domestick*, published in Boston in 1690, lasted only one issue before colonial authorities shut down the paper. Much like dissident papers of later years, *Publick Occurrences* combined muckraking, gossip, and a nose-thumbing disregard for authority. Harris criticized Britain's Indian allies for alleged brutality toward French prisoners of war and published a rumor that the King of France was sleeping with his son's wife. One simply did not publish such items about a reigning sovereign in 1690, and, since Harris had neglected to apply to authorities for permission to publish his four-page sheet in the first place, there was never another issue.

Subsequent suppression of the press intensified in times of crisis, often erupting into violence such as that visited upon the abolitionist press in the nineteenth century and the socialist press in the post-World War I Palmer Raids (which the young J. Edgar Hoover helped lead). Later suppression of dissident media was often legalistic in form, such as the

impoundment (and subsequent release) of issues of *The Militant* for its
antiwar views in World War II, the 1955 deportation of *National Guardian*
cofounder Cecil Belfridge as an undesirable alien under the McCarran-
Walter Act, and the investigation—for alleged communist influence—of
Pacifica radio by the Senate Internal Security Subcommittee in the early
sixties (Pacifica was subsequently cleared).

The suppression of the modern underground media reached its zenith
in the Nixon-Agnew administration. It may not have been coincidental
that J. Edgar Hoover's go-ahead memo to FBI field offices was dated the
very day that Richard Nixon and Spiro Agnew were elected President
and Vice President, respectively. Both men were unremittingly hostile
to the media, under and above ground, which they viewed as infested
with radicals and liberals inimical to their interests.

Agnew's attacks in the fall of 1969 on "impudent intellectuals" and the
mass media were matched by his assaults on underground media, which
the Vice President pursued with relish. According to a confidential FBI
memo, when Agnew visited Pittsburgh in 1970, a member of the White
House staff asked for copies of that city's underground papers to provide
fuel for the fiery stump speech Agnew would deliver on the conspiracy
within.

Agnew was also vocal in his condemnation of drug-related lyrics in
rock songs, most of which were aired on underground FM radio stations.
Dean Burch, who chaired the FCC, let it be known that stations playing
drag songs—or songs the FCC believed to be drug songs—would not be
looked upon with favor by the commission. An FCC proposal to ban
broadcasting of drug-related lyrics was not adopted, but Agnew and
Burch's attentions had a chilling effect on underground radio stations,
subtly influencing not only their selection of records, but even the tone of
their public affairs programming.

According to Larry Bensky, news director at Metromedia's KSAN in
San Francisco in early 1970, there was "a war of memos" in the corporation's home office in New York about how to respond to the pressure
being put on broadcasters by the federal government. KSAN was
Metromedia's political problem child. Station manager Willis Duff was
strongly critical of KSAN's advocacy reporting, particularly Bensky's
partisan, on-the-scene accounts of the Chicago Seven conspiracy trial.
Coincidentally, the trial got underway just as Agnew's blasts at the
media were reaching their peak.

"I was in the courtroom the day Judge Hoffman bound and gagged
Bobby Seale," remembered Bensky, who, incensed, publicly compared

the trial to Nazi justice in his reporting. "That made management nervous," Bensky recalled. "That made 'em real nervous." Another thing that rattled Willis Duff and Metromedia was KSAN's ridicule of Nixon and Agnew in the station's collage newscasts. "We'd just play back what they said that day and put a song next to it. We didn't have to comment further."

While he did not receive direct orders about what to cover and what not to cover, Bensky remembered the tension generated in the station by the Agnew offensive as Duff grew more and more critical of Bensky's partisanship, his bordering-on-profane language, and his propensity for turning over the microphones to community people to air their complaints. In June 1970, after only three months as news director, Bensky was fired.

Meanwhile, back in Washington, government officials kept their eyes, as well as their ears, open for subversion in the media. According to documents released under the Freedom of Information Act (FOIA) in 1979, Richard Nixon himself demanded—in a memo dated September 1971—that all federal funding for the Public Broadcasting Service be cut off immediately because of the network's allegedly liberal bias. However, Nixon's staff advised the Chief Executive that this was politically infeasible.

According to former White House counsel John Dean in his book *Blind Ambition*, presidential aides also planned to leak to the mass media what they deemed to be damaging information from leftist filmmaker Emile de Antonio's FBI dossier should his anti-Nixon film, *Millhouse*, become a hit. When it didn't, the plan was dropped, but de Antonio was still named to the White House "enemies list"—the only filmmaker thus recognized.

While the executive branch of government was moving against the underground media on a wide front, the legislative branch was launching congressional inquiries and entertaining proposals for press sanctions. The Senate Internal Security Subcommittee again swung into action, investigating the finances of Liberation News Service in order to dig up the Moscow or Peking gold some Senators believed was buried in LNS's backyard. None was found. In 1970, Senator Thomas Dodd attempted to write press suppression into law, introducing what he termed the "Urban Terrorism Prevention Bill." Dodd's proposed law would have made it illegal to belong to an organization advocating the overthrow of the U.S. government or to publish a periodical that did. The bill, which would have outlawed newspapers such as *The Black Panther*, did not pass.

In a strictly legalistic sense, the suppression of the underground media did not compare with the outright bans and revocations of mailing permits experienced by earlier radical publications. Legislatures and courts upheld the right of underground media to exist. However, court rulings protecting antiestablishment media were sometimes ignored by law-enforcement agencies and private vigilantes. Ruth Marie Eshenaur, who published a doctoral dissertation at Southern Illinois University in 1975 on censorship of the underground press, observed, "Even though the majority of decisions upheld First Amendment rights, other types of . . . actions tended to deny them. . . . [The] post office, FBI, police, and prison officials suppressed [underground periodicals] in various ways. . . . Therefore, regardless of whether the final decision was favorable or unfavorable to the periodical, the fact that it had to expend considerable time, money, and effort in self-defense constituted a form of harassment. . . ."

Eshenaur also noted that of the underground journalists she surveyed, nearly twice as many believed that covert, illegal governmental actions posed bigger threats to them than did efforts at legal suppression. As we shall see, underground journalists had reason to be worried about official disregard for the law.

Of the federal agencies that sent agents into "deep cover," the CIA was traditionally the most secretive. Rumors in radical circles put CIA agents everywhere at once, infiltrating underground news staffs, sabotaging demonstrations, sowing paranoia.

The rumors proved to be more truth than paranoia when it was revealed in July 1979, in United Press International dispatches, that the CIA had kept tabs on domestic political demonstrations with spy satellites. Other reports uncovered both the CIA's extensive use of mass-media contacts to advance government policies and the agency's heretofore hidden manipulation of underground media.

Some of the CIA's policies toward the underground media were relatively innocuous. For example, according to FOIA documents, the CIA closely read and clipped underground and campus newspapers as part of a program called "Project Resistance" from December 7, 1967, through June 28, 1973. The agency used the clippings to predict the reception its recruiters would get on college campuses and to keep tabs on radical groups.

Most CIA operations went considerably beyond clipping newspapers. In 1966, the CIA—reportedly worried about a forthcoming *Ramparts* exposé of CIA funding of the National Student Association—collaborated with IRS officials to check the tax records of *Ramparts* owner Edward Keating for irregularities. None were found.

FOIA documents released in 1977 show that the CIA also secretly funded College Press Service (CPS), a Denver-based news service for campus papers. Seed money from the agency helped establish the news service in the early sixties. During the Vietnam war era, CPS struck an antiwar stance, sending correspondent Sal Ferrara to Paris, where he reported on peace negotiations between Vietnamese revolutionaries and the United States in the early seventies. In the process, Ferrara became close to officials of South Vietnam's Provisional Revolutionary Government (PRG) and to ex-CIA agent Philip Agee, who was then writing his exposé of the agency, *Inside the Company: CIA Diary*. Unknown to Agee and the PRG, Ferrara was a CIA agent. After planting a bugged typewriter on Agee (to give CIA officials advance warning of what Agee was writing), Ferrara funneled dispatches and background of his exclusive interviews of PRG representatives of the CIA. (Most CPS staffers did not know of the CIA involvement in the news service. CPS today is a popular and independent source of news for campus papers.)

Before going to Paris, Ferrara also worked with a Washington, D.C., debugging outfit, checking telephones of movement groups for hidden taps. Elsewhere in the nation's capital, the CIA planted an agent on the staff of the underground newspaper *Quicksilver Times*, giving the agency an inside look at a paper that often aided in planning and promoting peace demonstrations and hosted movement luminaries such as Abbie Hoffman and Jerry Rubin in the communal house where *Quicksilver Times* was produced. Spying on American political groups and American media directly violated the 1947 CIA charter, which forbade the agency from engaging in domestic intelligence operations against Americans.

As recently as 1976, the CIA was still involved with sabotage of radical periodicals such as the Washington, D.C.-based *CounterSpy*. Founded and initially funded by Norman Mailer to spy on the spy agencies on behalf of dissenting Americans, *CounterSpy* set off a furor when, in 1975, it published a list of CIA agents around the world. One of the agents named was Robert Welch, the CIA's station chief in Athens. Soon after the *CounterSpy* articles appeared, Welch was murdered.

The CIA publicly and bitterly blamed *CounterSpy* for Welch's death. Critical articles on the small (circulation 3,000) quarterly appeared in mass-circulation magazines such as *Newsweek*. The slain agent received a state funeral, and members of Congress—then investigating the CIA's covert operations—began asking if the CIA wasn't itself being sabotaged by too much public exposure.

Lost in the surge of emotion was the fact that, as Morton H. Halperin (a former National Security Council aide to Henry Kissinger) revealed, Welch had been warned by the CIA itself not to take up residence in a well-known CIA house in Athens, at the risk of assassination. The warning was given before the *CounterSpy* article appeared, but Welch ignored it. In January 1978, Halperin told the British news service, Reuters, "That the stories [appearing in the U.S. press] suggested that *CounterSpy* was responsible for Welch's death, was the result of a deliberate CIA manipulation of the press." The manipulation was successful. *CounterSpy* folded amid a barrage of criticism from Congress and the mass media.

If CIA agents dropped in on underground media circles from time to time, FBI agents practically took up residence there. Underground media activists had long suspected that the FBI monitored and attempted to disrupt their activities, but not until 1971, when antiwar activists broke into an FBI field office and made off with classified files, did they discover how much. The name of the Pennsylvania town where the files were taken was, appropriately, Media. Excerpts were published as "The Media Papers" in *Win* magazine in 1972. The documents revealed the existence of a top-secret FBI counterintelligence program (code name: "Cointelpro") to disrupt and discredit radical movements and media.

Additional details were added in the late seventies, after a joint lawsuit by freelance writer Chip Berlet, the Alternative Press Syndicate, and the National Lawyers Guild forced the Bureau to give up more documents, and FOIA suits and requests by other journalists and private citizens freed still more. While many documents were withheld from public circulation—and those that were released were usually censored, with much sensitive information blacked out—the outline of the FBI's battle plan against the underground media can be seen in the bureau's memoranda.

A reading of FOIA documents leads one to conclude that the FBI's primary role was to act as a political agency by opposing radical media and movements on principle, whether or not any laws had been broken. The 1968 memo from J. Edgar Hoover cited at the beginning of this chapter explained: "One of the most important aspects of our current investigation of the New Left movement involves the movement's propaganda activities. We must afford this phase of New Left efforts close attention so that we can keep abreast of current New Left activities, take advantage of situations which could embarrass the New Left movement and counter New Left propaganda." To this end, FOIA documents show, the FBI closely watched the Socialist Workers Party (SWP) and its newspaper *The Militant* for thirty years, even though the party was not accused of a single crime in all that time. As a consequence, the SWP has filed a massive, multimillion dollar lawsuit against the FBI (which has not been decided at this writing).

Another organization in which the FBI showed intense interest was Pacific News Service (PNS). Founded in 1970 by the Committee of Concerned Asian Scholars to provide in-depth reporting on Southeast Asia from an antiwar viewpoint, PNS was established as part of a radical think tank called the Bay Area Institute (BAI). Pacific News Service included scholars such as Franz Schurmann, a well-known author and lecturer, and Orville Schell, who has since gone on to success as an author of books on China and California Governor Jerry Brown.

The FBI saw PNS's antiwar roots as evidence that the news service offered—as a confidential memo put it—"an ideal outlet for 'New Left' and pro-Chinese Communist propaganda." The memo noted that results of the FBI's investigation of PNS would be "disseminated to USIS [United States Information Service], CIA and State Department, [and the] American Consulate General, Hong Kong." The FBI clipped PNS dispatches on domestic antiwar activity and national liberation movements abroad. The bureau was also interested in PNS's frequent articles on the U.S. military, based on what appeared to be excellent sources inside the military itself.

In addition, the bureau gave close readings to PNS's dispatches on the first stirrings of the environmental movement, which the FBI saw as dangerously subversive. Read a 1970 memo:

BAI has concentrated its efforts in the ecology area. The issue of ecology, for all practical purposes, has replaced the war as the major organizing tool for the left wing movement. Although the interjection of the Cambodian situation precluded a full swing to the ecology effort during the beginning of 1970, it is anticipated that in the near future ecology will become the most sophisticated anti-industrial effort by the left yet devised. It is not then by accident that leadership personalities in the ecology movement have long distinguished themselves in anti-establishment efforts and have been associated with movement activities that are antagonistic to our national security.

When the FBI could not find real underground publications to watch for signs of dangerous trends, the bureau made up its own—such as the *Denver Arrow*, an entirely imaginary newspaper in whose name the FBI rented a post office box so it could subscribe to the College Press Service without revealing its identity. The FBI also clandestinely sponsored two other "underground" papers, the *Rational Observer*, published at American University in Washington, D.C., and *Armageddon News*, issued at Indiana University. Hoover took a personal interest in *Armageddon News*, writing a memo to the field office that produced the paper urging them to toughen their antiwar viewpoint in order to better simulate a New Left paper.

Armageddon News criticized the war and the local campus administration but urged students to vote warmakers out of office rather than take to the streets in pursuit of their aims. The FBI felt it could live with—and even promote—mild antiwar sentiment; going outside accepted political channels was what the bureau felt compelled to combat.

In addition to publishing several newspapers anonymously, the FBI wrote anonymous letters seeking to promote splits within genuine New Left media efforts. In 1968, when Liberation News Service split into warring factions, the FBI clandestinely wrote and circulated to New Left groups a letter criticizing the Marshall Bloom/Ray Mungo group that had departed New York for a Massachusetts farm. According to Chip Berlet's research, the letter, entitled "And Who Got the Cookie Jar," labeled Bloom "a bit of a nut" and assailed the farm faction for turning LNS "from an efficient news service into a mess." The letter, taken as authentic by some of its readers, exacerbated already existing tensions surrounding the LNS split.

Even more than the CIA, the FBI placed agents and informers on the staffs of underground newspapers. The *Berkeley Tribe*, *Quicksilver Times*, and the *San Francisco Express Times* were among the papers the bureau infiltrated. FOIA documents show that the FBI paid an unidentified informer at the *Express Times* $380 to fly to Madison, Wisconsin, in late 1968 to report on an underground press convention there. The informer flew, he explained to his control officer, because he was afraid coworkers from the *Express Times* would smoke marijuana during the long drive to Madison and have an accident or get arrested.

Telephone conversations between *Express Times* staffers and members of the Black Panther Party were detailed by an informant placed in deep cover by the FBI at the Panther national headquarters in Berkeley. The FBI expressed keen interest in any signs of cooperation between under-

ground papers, especially if it involved the Black Panthers and their
newspaper. Bureau memos show accounts of phone conversations between Panthers and *Express Times* staffers about the possible loan of
production equipment to the Panthers for use on their own paper.

The *Black Panther*, a weekly tabloid with a peak circulation of 100,000
in the late sixties, was the object of FBI "destabilization" efforts as well as
routine surveillance. FOIA documents quoted by Berlet in an article for
Alternative Media magazine show that the New York City field office of
the FBI contacted "the shipper who transported bulk copies of *The Black
Panther* within the city." After talking to federal agents, the shipper
agreed to raise his rates to "the highest legal fee" for handling the Panther
paper. "This will amount to an increase of around $300 weekly in
shipments to New York City alone," Berlet quoted an FBI memo as
reading. "This counterintelligence endeavor . . . will definitely have an
adverse effect on the amount of incendiary propaganda published by the
BPP."

Numerous unexplained setbacks around the country struck the Panther paper during this period. In San Francisco in 1970, a warehouse
storing back issues of the paper burned down. *Black Panther* staffers
complained that their paper moved slowly, if at all, through the mails
and that persons vending the paper were frequently harassed by local
police who coordinated their activities with the FBI. Numerous
shootouts—sometimes with uniformed police, sometimes with unidentified parties—also claimed the lives of Panther members during the late
sixties and early seventies. Among them was Walter Pope, circulation
manager of the Panther paper in southern California, who was killed in
1969. Two years later, *The Black Panther*'s national circulation manager,
Sam Napier, was murdered in New York City.

With setbacks like those, it's not surprising that the paper declined in
circulation and influence. Originally a weekly, *The Black Panther* is now a
biweekly, and its circulation has dropped to 40,000—one-fifth of its peak
sales. Moreover, the paper still has frequent problems with the Postal
Service. The May 25, 1980, issue carried an item informing subscribers
that the Oakland Post Office had "forgotten," for two weeks, to ship bulk
copies of a previous issue. Like the Socialist Workers Party, the Black
Panthers are suing the FBI for a multimillion-dollar sum in a case that has
not yet been resolved.

Other antiestablishment papers suffered physical attacks in the politically polarized Nixon years. *Kudzu*, an irregularly published paper in
Jackson, Mississippi, was one such paper. *Kudzu* (named after a plant

that grows widely and rapidly in the South) editorialized against the Vietnam war and challenged Southern segregation while undergoing almost constant harassment by local police and FBI agents. One day in 1970, eight Jackson police officers entered the *Kudzu* office with drawn guns and ransacked the place, saying they were looking for Weatherman fugitive Mark Rudd. They left with three address books after roughing up a staff member, according to an account in the January 4, 1971, issue of *The Nation.*

Prior to the raid, *Kudzu* staff members' homes had been searched six times in two weeks by Jackson police and FBI agents, who entered without search warrants. According to *Kudzu* editor David Doggett, an FBI agent replied to protests by *Kudzu* staffers that their rights were being violated by snapping, "Punks like you don't have any rights."

Grimmer still were accounts of assaults on the underground *San Diego Street Journal* in the late sixties and early seventies by a paramilitary group calling itself the Secret Army Organization (SAO). The SAO, composed of ex-Minutemen (a rightwing vigilante group), wrecked the *Street Journal*'s office, destroying $5,000 worth of production equipment, in 1969.

When the *Street Journal* started digging into the San Diego power structure with reports on millionaire C. Arnholt Smith, a friend of Richard Nixon, the attacks intensified. The paper charged that Smith sold several enterprises—at inflated prices—to publicly owned corporations of which he was a director, making a tidy sum in the process. Shortly thereafter, shots were fired into the paper's office, with little subsequent police investigation.

The *San Diego* police, in fact, appeared to be extremely hostile to the *Street Journal.* One day in November 1969, five squad cars pulled up to the paper's office, and police stormed in without a warrant to search the premises. Later that year, police—again without a warrant—entered the "people's commune" where many staffers lived, arrested a guest on "suspicion of burglary," and then left without taking him to jail. In addition, "seventy-five of our street vendors were arrested," remembered *Street Journal* veteran Lowell Bergman, now a reporter for the American Broadcasting Corporation's "20/20" TV series.

The *Street Journal*'s staffers began to suspect that the SAO and the police were trying to tell them something. "We kept our house brightly lit and took turns standing guard with weapons," Bergman recalled.

The worst was yet to come. On January 6, 1972, the SAO shot into the home of antiwar professor Peter Bohmer, wounding Bohmer's companion—Paula Tharp, a former *Street Journal* staffer—in an apparent assassination attempt. Under the constant pressure of such events, the paper folded later that year.

Before long, however, reporters at the *San Diego Door*, an underground paper that outlasted the *Street Journal*, began investigating the SAO. Their research alleged that a leader of the paramilitary group, Howard B. Godfrey, was a paid FBI informer. Godfrey testified at the trial of a fellow SAO member in 1973 that he had, indeed, been an FBI informer over a period of five years. In 1975, an investigation by the American Civil Liberties Union concluded that Godfrey was telling the truth and documented that conclusion in a report for the Senate Select Committee on Intelligence. Committee sources, in turn, told the *New York Times* in 1976 that Godfrey's FBI control officer hid the weapon used to wound Paula Tharp "in his own home for half a year while the San Diego police searched for evidence. . . ."

These events were reported throughout the early seventies by the *Street Journal*, the *Door*, and other underground media, but San Diego's Copley-owned daily newspapers buried accounts of the action in their back pages. On January 11, 1976, the *San Diego Union* finally published a detailed account of the relationship between the SAO and the FBI and the deleterious effect it had on San Diego radicals and underground newspapers. The *Union* story substantiated in all important particulars the reports that had appeared earlier in the *Door*, but by then four years had passed and both the *Door* and the *Street Journal* were gone.

Harassment of underground journalists by vigilantes and local police—with or without FBI cooperation—was common in the late sixties and early seventies. The offices of underground papers were firebombed in Seattle (the *Helix*), Houston *(Space City)*, Los Angeles (the *Free Press*), and Milwaukee (both *Kaleidoscope* and the *Bugle American*). Moreover, the radio transmitter of Houston's listener-sponsored KPFT was bombed off the air—not once, but twice—in 1970. Station manager Larry Lee said that FBI involvement had long been suspected but never proven. A former Ku Klux Klan member admitted to the bombing, which attracted national attention and substantial donations to help repair the damage. The station went back on the air in 1971 after achieving the dubious distinction of being the first radio station in the history of American broadcasting to be blown off the air.

Local police agents, like their federal counterparts, wrought considerable havoc in the underground media. In 1970, an undercover narcotics agent on the staff of *View From the Bottom*—a New Haven, Connecticut, underground paper—arrested copy editor C. R. Lawn and several other key staffers on drug charges. The paper folded soon afterwards, and Lawn ended his probation by leaving New Haven and underground journalism. A graduate of Yale law school, Lawn now tends an organic farm in Maine and pursues a lawsuit against New Haven police for what he said was illegal wiretapping leading to his arrest. It would be simplistic to ascribe the surge of the back-to-the-land movement entirely to the repression of political radicalism, but, as Lawn's story shows, that was certainly a contributing factor in its growth.

Many other underground papers were subjected to a variety of abuses from local authorities, and, like *View From the Bottom*, many collapsed under the pressure. Some papers experienced mass arrests of their street vendors or discovered that peddler's licenses costing up to $100 a day were needed to sell their papers—and only *their* papers—on the streets. Still others found themselves involved in a flurry of drug arrests. One paper, the *Philadelphia Free Press*, was harassed in a variety of ways all at once. In its August 2, 1970, issue, the paper told readers that local police had:

> 1) beaten one *Freep* staff member; 2) on several occasions taken staff members into "preventive detention" and released them without even the pretense of a charge; 3) arrested three staffers on charges which were thrown out of court without trial; 4) threatened staffers with physical assault; 5) threatened, before witnesses, to drive the paper out of town; 6) on four occasions broken into the homes of staffers without warrants; . . . 11) engaged in intimidating surveillance by as many as six cars at a time, and by gun-flourishing stakeout men.

The mass media might have been able to rally public opinion to the side of their counterparts in the underground media if they had cared to do so. But generally, they ignored, downplayed—and, in a few cases, encouraged—the pressure on the underground. This hurt antiestablishment media even more, and it largely restricted the news of their suppression to their own still limited circles, ensuring that the secret war remained secret from most Americans.

Ruth Marie Eshenaur reported that the *Philadelphia Bulletin* published articles on the *Free Press* based on confidential files made available to the daily by the Philadelphia police, the U.S. Department of Justice, and the Selective Service System. One of the articles was headlined "100 Hardcore Revolutionaries." After the *Bulletin* articles—which were generally critical of the *Free Press*—appeared, the paper lost many advertisers, a staff member lost his "straight" job, and the paper's printer refused to continue printing the *Free Press*.

Many printers, repulsed by the controversial content of radical papers, simply refused to handle them. The Milwaukee underground paper *Kaleidoscope* was forced to journey out of town to Port Washington, Wisconsin, to find a sympathetic printer. There, Bill Schanen, a commercial printer who owned three small papers of his own, fought a boycott by local advertisers who tried to pressure him into dropping *Kaleidoscope*. Rather than give in to the boycott, Schanen sold two of his three papers for operating capital. (In February 1971, Bill Schanen died of a heart attack. He was fifty-seven.)

Most radical publications did not find printers with as much character and courage as Schanen, as the experience of *Scanlan's Monthly* shows. Founded in 1970 by former *New York Times* reporter Sidney Zion and Warren Hinckle (who had left *Ramparts* the previous year), *Scanlan's* put together a special "Guerrilla War in the USA" issue. The issue featured maps of bombings by radical groups and speculations about how, when, where, and why urban guerrillas would strike next. Although *Scanlan's* did not advocate bomb-throwing, the magazine's printer refused to touch the issue. "The guys in the shop wouldn't print it," Hinckle recalled. "They said it was unpatriotic." Every other American printer that Hinckle contacted—about fifty in all—thought the same thing. The issue was finally printed in a small Quebec town, but Canada was then under martial law (Prime Minister Pierre Elliott Trudeau had invoked the War Measures Act to combat Quebecois separatists) and the Royal Canadian Mounted Police seized most of the copies. "I've got a bunch in my basement," Hinckle said.

(*Scanlan's* also ran afoul of the Nixon administration when the magazine published a memo, supposedly written by Spiro Agnew, linking the Vice President with a top-secret plan to cancel the 1972 elections and repeal the Bill of Rights. The satirical memo, which *Scanlan's* invented, deeply angered Richard Nixon. According to John Dean's *Blind Ambition*, Nixon ordered an IRS investigation into the magazine's finances, but was frustrated because the six-month-old magazine had not yet filed any tax returns.)

Scanlan's folded in 1971 after only a year of publication—in part, co-editor Zion told the *New York Times* in 1976, because "third parties" had approached major national distributors and advised them not to carry *Scanlan's*. Zion believed that the mysterious third parties were government agents.

And still the war against the underground media escalated. In Syracuse, New York, a conservative local publisher led a devastating attack on the alternative *Nickel Review*. The cause of the commotion was a special supplement, edited by the poet Walter Lowenfels, commemorating the hundredth birthday of Lenin in 1970. The supplement was more literary than inflammatory—it contained a Langston Hughes poem and numerous intellectual essays—but just mentioning Lenin in a positive light was dangerous in conservative Syracuse.

The *Fayetteville Eagle Bulletin*, a staunchly Republican weekly paper, editorialized: "The unmistakable connection between international Communism and the leftwing radical underground . . . publications . . . has been well established. The Federal Bureau of Investigation and its director, John Edgar Hoover, have produced evidence of the chain of Marxist-Communist influence through national organizations to state and local levels and into local schools. . . ."

The *Eagle Bulletin* was joined in its attack on the *Nickel Review* by the daily *Syracuse Herald Journal*, which urged local merchants to withdraw their advertising from the *Review*. This they did, many of them switching to a free, largely apolitical student shopper called the *Orange Pennysaver*, a weekly published by Ken Simon, a young Syracuse University journalism graduate.

"No local printer would touch us," recalled *Nickel Review* editor-publisher Walt Shepperd. "We had to drive two hundred and fifty miles round trip to Gouveneur [New York] to be printed. A few of the advertisers stuck with us, but most of them left, quickly." The double punch was too much for the *Review*, which folded in the summer of 1970.

The human cost of the offensive against the underground media can be heard in Shepperd's voice when he remembers what the conservatives' prosecution of the *Nickel Review* meant to him. "It took me a couple of years to get over it. It drove me back to tobacco. And I'm still in debt." Shepperd tried to resurrect the *Nickel Review* as a literary magazine in 1979, but it failed when Syracuse's only periodical distributor—mindful of the controversy in 1970—refused to handle it.

The demise of the original *Nickel Review* cleared the way for the commercial success of the *Orange Pennysaver* (renamed the *Syracuse New Times* in the fall of 1970) and watered down alternative journalism in that city. The *Review* had been frankly partisan, championing the New Left and the counterculture, publishing original work by talented writers such as Ishmael Reed, Julius Lester, John A. Williams, and David Henderson and serving as a relatively early supporter of women's rights. The *New Times* was not a conservative paper, but it was far from radical,

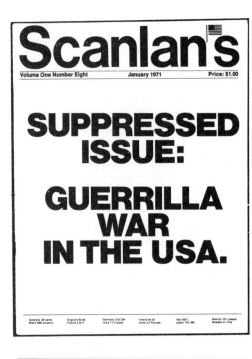

Scanlan's

Volume One Number Eight   January 1971   Price: $1.00

SUPPRESSED ISSUE:

GUERRILLA WAR IN THE USA.

Australia 30 cents   England 6s 6d   Germany 3.65 DM   Ireland 6s 5d   Italy 835 L   Mexico 12½ pesos
Brazil 5000 cruzeiros   France 5.35 F   India 7.5 rupees   Israel 3.5 Pounds   Japan Yen 360   Sweden 6.1 Krs

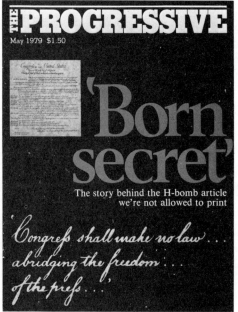

*Political repression of radical periodicals
spans the sixties and seventies. Scanlan's
special issue on guerrilla war reached few
readers. The Black Panther reported police raids to all who would listen. In 1969
the Barb summed it up in one word. In
1979 The Progressive suffered the first
use of judicial prior restraint in history.
(Covers courtesy of respective periodicals.)*

Berkeley Barb

Vol. 9, No 8, Issue 210, August 22-28, 1969
2042 University Ave., Berkeley, Ca. 94704   849-1040

PUBLISHED WEEKLY   204

15¢ BAY AREA

25¢ ELSEWHERE

PARANOIA

and it lacked the *Review*'s depth. The *New Times*—largely a consumer guide—published extensive entertainment listings and reviews and lighter-than-air profiles of local personalities, anchored by occasional antiwar articles and think pieces. This editorial mix proved to be more acceptable to Syracuse conservatives than the *Review*'s challenging journalism.

This pattern was to be repeated throughout the country. By the late seventies, most major American cities and many college towns had consumer-oriented alternative newspapers aimed at the market of 18-to-37-year-olds. Indeed, the growth of alternative consumer papers was a journalistic phenomenon of the late seventies, much as the mushrooming growth of back-to-the-land periodicals like the *Whole Earth Catalog* and *Mother Earth News* was a journalistic phenomenon of the late sixties and early seventies. Although those two trends were dissimilar in many ways—one being primarily urban and geared toward the accumulation and enjoyment of consumer goods, the other essentially rural and dedicated to mysticism and self-sufficiency—they have at least two important features in common: Both trends took hold among the young, white, college-educated middle class, and both were triggered, in part, by the suppression of radical underground publications in the Nixon era.

As a rule of thumb, politically radical media efforts suffered the sharpest restrictions of First Amendment rights. The courts in the sixties were not as enthusiastic about violating press freedom as their predecessors had been, but, as the sixties faded into the seventies and the Nixon administration became more deeply entrenched, legal decisions began running against underground and mainstream journalists. This was particularly true for underground media that aimed their efforts at captive audiences such as high school students, whose limited autonomy was written into law.

Underground high school newspapers, which numbered an estimated five hundred in 1969, issued aggressive challenges to dress codes, pushed for curriculum changes, and inveighed against the Vietnam war. Often such publications were banned from schoolgrounds by principals and school boards, setting up courtroom showdowns. The thrust of court decisions upheld restrictions on the sale of underground papers on school campuses, but permitted students to publish without prior administration review. This limited triumph was limited still further, however, when many schools simply ignored court rulings they didn't like, expelling student journalists on a variety of charges and sinking their papers.

According to Ruth Marie Eshenaur, student staffers at *When the Levee Breaks*, in North Chelmford, Massachusetts, had copies of their paper taken from them and thrown in trash baskets by school authorities. A student told Eshenaur that staffers were also suspended for "miniscule and unrelated violations of school rules, such as truancy, smoking . . . [and] 'rebellious attitude' . . ." Eshenaur recorded that statement in 1973, after most of the favorable court rulings had been handed down.

Journalists in other branches of the underground media entered the legal arena with almost equally dismal results. In 1970, *Kaleidoscope* editor Mark Knops was subpoenaed by federal and state authorities after his paper received a "communiqué" from a small radical group that bombed the Army Math Research Center at the University of Wisconsin, inadvertently killing a civilian researcher. Knops, who felt his paper's duty was to report news without serving as a conduit to police, served four months in jail rather than breach the confidentiality of his sources.

In 1974, a similar situation arose when the Symbionese Liberation Army (SLA)—the group that brutally murdered Oakland school superintendent Marcus Foster and kidnaped Patricia Hearst—sent a tape recording defending their activities to KPFK radio in Los Angeles. The Weather Underground (who changed their name from the Weathermen) had sent the station a letter explaining one of their own bombings earlier that same week. The FBI, given copies of the communications, demanded to see the originals, but KPFK general manager Will Lewis refused to produce them. Lewis, like Mark Knops, served time in prison (sixteen days, in Lewis' case) rather than compromise the confidentiality of his station's sources.

While Lewis awaited a decision on his appeal of a contempt-of-court ruling, the station got yet another communiqué—this one from the New World Liberation Front, another underground group. Asked by the Los Angeles Police Department for the original, Lewis again refused. On October 10, 1974, city police arrived with a search warrant. They stayed for eight hours (without finding the original). KPFK broadcast the entire search live.

On February 14, 1975, the U.S. Supreme Court refused to reverse Lewis' conviction for contempt of court, so Lewis turned over the documents in all three cases to a federal grand jury. Clearly crestfallen, Lewis remarked, "Any time the general manager of a radio station has to go before a grand jury in circumstances like these, it is an intrusion in our newsroom."

With the penalties for holding onto original communications stiffening and the novelty of radical groups such as the SLA and the Weather Underground gradually fading, most media outlets routinely turned over underground messages to authorities. And few of the media bothered to reproduce or broadcast the turgid, military-style communiqués in full, as the originating groups demanded.

Faced with the increasing difficulty of transmitting their messages through the media, the fugitives of the Weather Underground came up with a logical solution: start media of their own. Thus began a strange episode in the history of American media in which the media ventures themselves were perfectly legal, but the people producing them were not. The Weather Underground clandestinely published and distributed a quarterly magazine, *Osawatomie,* and joined with filmmakers Emile de Antonio, Mary Lampson, and Haskell Wexler to make a documentary entitled *Underground.*

When, in the summer of 1975, the FBI attempted to coerce de Antonio, Lampson, and Wexler into revealing the circumstances of the filming, the Hollywood film community—mindful of its collapse before McCarthy's pressure tactics in the fifties—circulated a statement of support for the filmmakers and helped assemble a high-powered legal team. The FBI backed off. However, few people saw the poorly distributed film, and splits in the Weather Underground finished off *Osawatomie* in 1976 after little more than a year of publication. Thus ended one of the more unusual, if shortlived, experiments in the American underground media.

The history of media suppression did not end with the end of the sixties, or with the eventual collapse of the Nixon administration. Legal challenges to press freedom still occur, as do physical attacks on journalists in alternative and mainstream media. Political activists point to a passage in an FBI memorandum, dated April 27, 1971, which supposedly announces the end of Cointelpro. The passage reads: "In exceptional instances where counter-intelligence action is warranted, it will be considered on a highly selective individual basis with tight procedures to insure absolute secrecy." Some activists interpret that to mean that covert FBI actions against radicals and dissenters, far from having been stopped, have simply gone deeper undercover.

Unexplained attacks on alternative media enterprises in recent years suggest that such could be the case. In 1975, the offices of the Denver-based feminist newspaper *Big Mama Rag* were ransacked, with ink and glue poured over telephones, files, and other production equipment. A similar attack took place that same year on the New York offices of *Majority Report*, a now-defunct national women's newspaper. In 1977, night raiders systematically destroyed the Oakland, California, printing facilities of Diana Press, the nation's largest feminist publishing house, leading directly to Diana's demise.

Other frightening assaults on alternative journalists have taken place even more recently. The most deadly of these occurred in 1979, when Michael Eiken—a former editor of the alternative *Austin Sun*, and a prominent Texas antinuclear activist—was mysteriously murdered while working on a story about safety violations at a nuclear power plant.

Legal battles continue to dog the alternative media as well. In 1979, *The Progressive*, a left-leaning national magazine, was slapped with the first judicial prior restraint order in American history. The cause of the commotion was an article by freelance writer Howard Morland, who collated publicly available information about the manufacture of hydrogen bombs. The point of Morland's piece, according to *Progressive* editor Erwin Knoll, was to demonstrate that many regulations classifying information about America's nuclear weapons program are inefficient and contradictory. Often evoked in the name of "national security," they keep essential information on the arms race from reaching ordinary citizens, who have a right to know. The Supreme Court disagreed, invoking the historic prior restraint order and delaying publication of Morland's article for several months until *The Progressive*'s December 1979 issue.

The Progressive attracted the attention and support of, among others, the Reporter's Committee for Freedom of the Press and the American Civil Liberties Union. Belatedly, some mainstream journalists have recognized that the suppression of antiestablishment media is not likely to remain divorced for long from suppression of the mass media. Recent exposures of domestic intelligence schemes targeting the media have lent credence to this belief.

A *New York Times* investigative series in December 1977 revealed that the CIA had extensively manipulated the mass media even as it moved to penetrate the underground media. Freedom of Information Act documents forced from CIA hands by lawsuits exposed agency funding for well-known foreign journals such as *Paris Match* and American propaganda outlets such as Radio Liberty and Radio Free Europe. The CIA also received information from dozens of friendly mainstream journalists, viewed outtakes (until the early sixties) of Columbia Broadcasting System TV news feeds, and sponsored publication of over a thousand books. Research published in 1976 by the *Columbia Journalism Review* revealed that a CIA operative even reviewed a book by another CIA operative in the *New York Times*. (The book, author, and reviewer were not named.)

Such in-depth exposures have, in essence, confirmed reports of covert operations—for years dismissed as paranoia and propaganda—in the underground media. In a speech in Berkeley in January 1974, *Washington Post* reporter Bob Woodward told an audience, that "The underground press was largely right about governmental sabotage, but the country didn't get upset because it was the left that was being sabotaged. The country got upset," Woodward said, "when the broad political center, with its established political institutions, came under attack."

"The *Washington Post* is a centrist paper and I'm a centrist person," Woodward offered. "That's the trouble with the *Post* and people like myself. When we first heard of dirty tricks being used against the left, we didn't care, because they weren't directed against us. We figured, 'Well, that's a fringe element.' It's something that calls for some introspection on my part."

Woodward's turnabout—and the more recent support by some mass-media organizations for *The Progressive*—is in marked contrast to the hostility of daily newspapers in Philadelphia and Syracuse toward underground media and the studied indifference of the dailies in San Diego a few years earlier. Today, however, the radical papers in those cities, and in many others, no longer exist. Reviewing the government strategy to bury the underground media, Tom Forcade, head of the Underground Press Syndicate, said: "With obscenity busts, they get your money; with drug busts, they get your people; with intimidation, they get your printer; and if you still manage somehow to get out a sheet, their distribution monopolies and rousts keep it from ever getting to the people."

Forcade's rueful comment underlined an essential truth about governmental suppression of underground media: The prosecution didn't have to prove its case to win. Most of the underground journalists formally accused of crimes were acquitted. But the effort involved in self-defense drained small, financially insolvent media, contributing to the demise of some and making it difficult for others to carry on. By weakening the means by which the movement for social change communicated with itself and with society as a whole, the government scored a valuable victory in its effort to preserve the status quo.

The big stick of repression effectively crippled the underground media. They would falter for other reasons, as well—reasons directly linked to the underground's own contradictory character—as erstwhile activists chased the carrot of commerce.

seven

The Selling of the Counterculture

A PHOTOGRAPH of several scruffy, solemn-looking young men gathered in an unfurnished apartment appeared in a number of underground publications in late 1968. From looking at the photograph, one would assume that they were conspiring to storm the Winter Palace, or at least attending a meeting of the Weathermen. But no. It was an advertisement placed by Columbia Records. The tagline below the photo read: "The Man Can't Bust Our Music."

The executives at Columbia had not gone over the wall. Rather, in the composition and placement of the ad, Columbia Records—a profitable subsidiary of CBS, Inc., which also owned CBS-TV and radio, the Discount Records chain stores, and other mainstream media enterprises—acknowledged the public impact of the radical movement and began to use the symbols of the youth revolution—long hair, hip argot, secret cell meetings—to sell Columbia products. By

The Barb, *like many underground papers, sold sex to make a buck. With the birth of* Rolling Stone, *"radical rock" was packaged and sold much more effectively. (Premier issue courtesy of* Rolling Stone.*)*

keying its ad to underground publications, the company acknowledged the crucial role of the underground press in reaching young consumers. By accepting the ads, underground periodicals in turn acknowledged their need to compromise in order to survive in the market economy; in effect, they accepted the megacorporations of the entertainment industry as the Medicis of the revolution. This symbiosis was to benefit the corporations far more than the underground media in the long run. Indeed, it was a key element in the selling of the counterculture.

The penetration and ultimate assimilation of much of the underground media culture was part of a familiar pattern of commercialization: Typically, an idea is developed by a creative community of artists and political rebels. It is given form in increasingly successful experiments by the alternative media. When the experiments show a positive response from the public, indicating the presence of a sizable potential market, mass media—often with the aid of alternative media workers who wish to "go commercial"—merchandise the concept in a no-sharp-edges package. Removed from its original context, the idea becomes a commodity. Its former constituency either becomes part of the market or goes packing in search of another idea, which, if successful, attracts merchandisers, beginning the process again.

The result of this process for mainstream culture is a replenishment of ideas and styles. Countercultural language ("do your own thing," "uptight," "ego trip"), dress (unisex clothing), food (organic), sexuality (ostensibly free and easy, without "hangups"), and sophisticated rock music were introduced by the underground media of the sixties. In the seventies, these innovations were stripped of their countercultural context—which presupposed a new way of living, rather than piecemeal modifications of earlier lifestyles—and disseminated on a wide scale throughout society by the mass media.

For the alternative media culture, the consequences of commercialization are distinctly mixed. On the one hand, alternative ideas and values travel widely in American culture through the commercialization process, and, since America is in many ways a social laboratory for the world, they eventually travel in many cultures. On the other hand, those ideas and values, once removed from the seedbed of alternative media culture, are altered in ways their creators usually did not intend and are, therefore, no longer radical. That is the essential paradox confronting alternative media culture, presenting both opportunities and traps and testing that culture's ability to retain both its identity and its integrity.

Many underground media ventures could not escape the snares of commercialism, for built into their concepts and structures were many of the values that underlie any business enterprise. Underground periodicals, for example, were quick to condemn the rise of rival publications such as *Rolling Stone*, accusing competitors of packaging the youth culture for pecuniary gain. Yet, as Greil Marcus, a writer for both *Rolling Stone* and the underground press, pointed out, "Papers like the *Los Angeles Free Press* and the *East Village Other* packaged it too. They took all the ads they could get. And a lot of underground writers wanted to move up. They didn't need to be seduced."

There is much truth in that. With the exceptions of radical left and grassroots community media, underground media aggressively pursued advertising dollars. For many, this took the form of inviting record company subsidies; for others, the selling point was sex.

With prostitutes and pornographers buying increasing amounts of space in underground periodicals, profits replaced free speech as the main rationale for running sex ads, and the openness and sharing of the first personal classifieds gave way to a new type of grotesquerie: "I dig dogs," read an ad that ran for years in the *Berkeley Barb*, "the bigger the better. That's why I got the world's biggest breed to satisfy me. For pictures of 'Wolfy' and me, send $3 to . . ."

The underground's approach to sexuality, at first innocently libertarian, had turned cynical and greedy by the late sixties, as underground papers sold titillating caricatures of hippie "free love," mostly to older consumers. In the long run, however, several important underground papers that prospered with "adult" ads ended by strangling on them. Among the victims were the *Berkeley Barb*, the *Los Angeles Free Press*, and the *East Village Other*.

The *Barb*'s sex ads, which made up most of the paper's advertising by 1969, led directly to the rejection of the paper by the women's movement and indirectly to a rejection of one-man rule and the profit-making corporate structure by the paper's staff. *Barb* workers cast a cold eye on employer Max Scherr in the summer of 1969, after a local satirical sheet called the *Berkeley Fascist* added up the ads in the *Barb* and estimated that Scherr was clearing $5,000 a week from the paper.

Shocked staffers, who hadn't thought to compute advertising column-inches themselves, demanded that Scherr do something revolutionary with all that money—like give it away to free clinics, emergency soup kitchens, bail funds, and other projects the hip community needed.

The staff also wanted to be paid more than the $5 to $10 per article they were getting. They wanted press passes, and they wanted Scherr to pay the bail of reporters arrested covering demonstrations. In addition, writers wanted a say in how their stories were edited and headlined. Scherr refused to make those concessions, but he did offer to sell the paper to the staff for $140,000, a price they conceded was more than fair, since the *Barb*, in its four years of existence, had grown from a thin, virtually worthless radical sheet to a business estimated—by the staff itself—to be worth one million dollars.

Negotiations between Scherr and the staff fell through, however, when Scherr presented terms of sale that former *Barb* writer and editor Jim Schreiber described as "fragmented, complex, involuted, and slippery." The terms called for remaindered payments of $140,000 and personal as well as collective liability on the part of the staff; should the *Barb* not come out one week, or should the money in its account fall below a certain sum, the paper would revert to Scherr, along with personal property of the buyers—a setup Scherr maintained was required by law.

Instead of buying the *Barb*, the staff walked out, publishing a special "*Barb* on Strike" issue. The following week, on July 16, 1969, Scherr sold the *Barb* to anthropologist Allan Coult, and the strikers—calling themselves the Red Mountain Tribe, after a cheap red wine favored by Berkeley radicals—launched a paper of their own, the *Berkeley Tribe*. The founders of the new paper hoped that by instituting a cooperative communal structure—a tribe—they could successfully challenge the profiteering, one-man rule to which the *Barb* had supposedly lost its soul.

The *Barb* did poorly under Coult, boycotted by most politically radical readers, who saw the *Tribe* as the *Barb*'s legitimate heir. The *Tribe* flourished for a time with a semicollective structure. The paper was staff-owned, and, while not legally incorporated as nonprofit, the *Tribe* donated money to community causes, as its staff had urged Max Scherr to do. The paper's editor and other key workers were selected by a vote of the staff. All staff members earned the same $30-a-week salary, regardless of their jobs. The *Tribe* was, in its first six months of existence, an exciting paper—publishing first-person reports of the Chicago Seven Conspiracy Trial, introducing one of the first environmental columns in any newspaper (Keith Lampe's "Earth Read-Out"), even printing a radical astrology column by Antonia Lamb ("August 22—a good day for fleeing the country; fly or drive . . . some paranoia around midday, but try to slough it off.")

There were tensions within the *Tribe*, however, between political radicals—who wanted to follow the streetfighting example of the Weathermen—and cultural radicals—who felt more affinity for the nonviolence of the hippie movement, with its freeform music and art. There was also resentment of leaders in key positions by some staffers with more workaday jobs, such as selling the paper on the street or pasting up the copy. Before long, those divisions would tear the brave new paper apart. At a staff Christmas party in 1969, the tension flared into violence, when a Tribe member who felt himself excluded from the inner circle pulled a knife. Other staffers (most of them high on LSD at the time) talked him into dropping it, but, for the *Tribe*, the party was over. Fourteen staff members from the cultural wing—about half the staff—left the *Tribe*, which eventually deteriorated into a rhetorical sheet, complete with the sayings of Kim I Sung and diagrams of how to make guns. The utopian experiment had self-destructed.

Moreover, the *Tribe* never solved the question of how to support itself without giving in to the demands of the market economy. The paper sought and printed numerous record-company ads and, despite the *Tribe*'s criticism of Scherr, a few sex ads, as well—although most of them were printed after the split, and even then the *Tribe* printed far fewer than its crosstown rival, the *Barb*. Perhaps pornographers simply preferred the *Barb*, which actively solicited sex ads until 1978.

In Los Angeles, a series of events centering on sex advertising, nearly as tempestuous and complex as those in Berkeley, took place. Like the *Barb*, the *Los Angeles Free Press* was heavily dependent on money from pornographers who, *Free Press* founder-editor Art Kunkin recalled, "felt themselves to be social rebels and identified with me. They became close personal friends in some cases." Eventually, Kunkin got to know several pornographers better than he wanted to know them and in a way he hadn't anticipated.

In 1971, after Kunkin lost a lawsuit filed against him two years earlier for printing the names and home addresses of California narcotics agents, his printer dropped the *Free Press*. Kunkin tried to protect the paper by arranging to buy a printing press of his own, but the huge, quarter-million-dollar press turned out to be a financial drain, and Kunkin was unable to make the payments. His creditors then sold the *Free Press*—which Kunkin had put up as security—to pornographers from San Diego, who incorporated under the misnomer New Way Enterprises. The new owners gave Kunkin a two-year contract to edit the *Free Press*. The week the contract expired, Kunkin was fired from the paper he had started. "It came kind of suddenly," Kunkin recalled. "I wasn't aware it was the last week."

That was in 1973. The *Free Press* survived for five more years as little more than a wraparound for pornographic ads. In 1977, *Hustler* magazine owner Larry Flynt acquired the *"Freep,"* promising to rejuvinate the paper. Instead, the *Free Press* was permanently silenced after unknown assailants shot and wounded Flynt outside a Georgia courtroom in February 1978, and the Flynt organization, seeking to cut costs in that moment of crisis, lopped off the *Freep*.

If the fate of the *Los Angeles Free Press* seems similar to that of many other business-as-usual propositions, that's because it was. Always operated for profit, with a hierarchy like that of conventional corporations, and financed mostly by the sale of sexual services and stereotypical images of women, the *Freep* replicated some of the most exploitive aspects of the culture it was created to counter. In the end, the *Free Press* floundered on its own inconsistencies.

Despite their serious shortcomings, the *Free Press* and the *Barb* at least attempted to present editorially a view of sexuality consistent with visions of a new world. By the end of the sixties, some underground publishers dispensed with even the *Barb*'s and the *Freep*'s sharply compromised views and sold sexuality, simply and purely, for profit. Publications such as *Screw*, *Suck*, *Pleasure*, *Kiss*, the *New York Review of Sex*, the *San Francisco Ball*, and the *L. A. Star*—"pornzines" as they are called in the trade—arose from the underground in the late sixties, offspring of older radical publications that soon outgrew their parent papers.

The underground credentials of many pornzine publishers were impeccable. Feminist Germaine Greer, author of *The Female Eunuch*, was on the staff of *Suck*, a European sex paper. *Pleasure* was founded by the business manager of *Rat*. The *East Village Other* published *Kiss*, after pornzines had stolen much of *EVO*'s circulation, and the *New York Free Press* weighed in with the *New York Review of Sex*.

The first and most successful pornzine was *Screw*, a joint venture of Al Goldstein, a writer for several lurid tabloids, and Kevin Buckley, an editor and typesetter at the *New York Free Press*. *Screw* grew to become the *Consumer Reports* of the sex business, rating vibrators and condoms for commercial appeal, reviewing sex books and movies, and offering assorted scatological tales and hot photos. From its first twelve-page issue in November 1968, *Screw* was a success, in part, because it dispensed with the challenging radical politics of *EVO* and other undergrounds and got down to the business of selling pounds of flesh. "We've learned that the left is just as fucked up as the right when it comes to sex," the paper editorialized.

The underground sex papers stripped sexuality of the political context in which other underground media had been careful to put it. While many underground publishers sold sex to move their papers, and most unabashedly celebrated sex, the pornzines posited sex as the end-all of liberated lifestyles, not simply an important ingredient in them. From attempting to liberate Americans' sexuality from Puritanical repression, the underground raised it to the status of an obsession. This, of course, dovetailed neatly with the conventional usage of sex to sell products and with the promotion of sex by slick, mass-circulation magazines such as *Playboy* as the most desirable product of all. Far from challenging conventional notions of sexuality, the porno sheets served as the sleazy underside of sex publishing. Their self-conscious raunchiness was also a boon to slick mainstream publishers, for, by challenging restrictive obscenity laws, the pornzines helped clear the way for the four-color raunch of *Penthouse* and *Hustler*, magazines even further removed from radical visions of sexuality.

The effect of *Screw* and other sex papers on politically radical underground papers was disastrous. The pornzines siphoned off income and circulation from other underground papers, prompting at least one, the *East Village Other*, to enter the pornzine publishing field itself. Thus the birth of *Kiss*—an eleventh-hour attempt to drum up revenue for its parent publication. But the attempt came too late. *Screw* and other pornzines were already well established. *EVO* folded in 1972. *Screw*, by way of contrast, remains prosperous, in spite of numerous courtroom battles over its alleged obscenity. The weekly paper now publishes East and West Coast editions and claims a paid circulation of 100,000.

Equaling even sex as a come-on in the selling of the underground media culture, rock music served as the commercial basis of numerous periodicals and radio stations. Since one could actually *hear* the music on the airwaves—not just read about it—rock radio proved to be a particularly kinetic, and eventually profitable, medium.

Underground rock radio stations shrewdly fused music and drug references in commercials aimed at youthful listeners. The irony was apparent: drugs, hailed by counterculture gurus as tools to attain mystical states, were evoked on rock radio to sell all manner of products on the material plane. Repetitions, distortions, or reverberations of key words were matched with snatches of popular songs in "psychedelic" ads, and underground bands cut commercials for such notable aboveground advertisers as Coca-Cola and Levi Strauss.

Attracted by the growing response to underground radio, mass-media advertisers flocked to rock radio, enlarging the audience for their version of the underground, increasing the frequency of commercials, pressuring broadcasters to tone down controversial public-affairs programming, and driving up ad rates. That, in turn, drove off the small community merchants who helped finance FM rock in the first place. To longhaired disc jockeys dismayed by the influx of corporate sponsors, KSAN station manager Tom Donahue offered these words of advice: "If you get in bed with the devil, you'd better be prepared to fuck."

Before long, business realities began shortcircuiting the radical public-affairs programming that accompanied rock songs on some of the stations. KSAN management fired controversial news director Larry Bensky in 1970, thirty minutes after he interviewed employees of Jeans West—a big KSAN advertiser—who told listeners that Jeans West forced workers to take lie-detector tests about marijuana smoking, in apparent contradiction of the company's hip image. Bensky's firing dramatized the conflicts between radical staffers' desire to apply their values to their work and management's desire to get and keep commercial accounts.

In 1980, looking back at the clash between profit-minded executives and staffers dedicated to social change, Bensky said:

> It makes them [executives and advertisers] nervous to think that there is social ferment, because there is a reluctance to participate in the consumer economy by people who think that they're going to be drafted or bludgeoned or beat over the head in their beds. . . . They forget to go out and buy TVs. When times like that are going on, you'll find that the sales people at a radio station will be saying that "Life isn't like that." Because, for them, life isn't like that. They live in, usually, isolated communities, with very little contact with the realities of inner city life, or protest life, or anything like that. So you have a class difference, a difference of outlook . . . and all that contributes to tension at a [commercial] radio station.

This conflict between management and staff was played out, in revealing detail, at KSAN. Tom Donahue, the broadcaster who popularized freeform rock radio, left KSAN to launch his own syndicated programming in early 1969. His successor was Willis Duff, whom Bensky described as "a real straight Texan, professional radio person, relatively young, [but] with no exposure to radical politics," who was "being pushed out of his tree" by the rebellious staff.

Duff pushed back, firing Bensky after the Jeans West episode, and, before that, firing news collagist Scoop Nisker. With several leading radical staffers gone from the station, Duff went on to play an important role in the selling of the counterculture. He devised a galvanic skin-response test that measured listeners' involuntary responses—sweaty palms, warming or cooling skin—to underground radio personalities and newly released rock songs, with specially designed electronic equipment similar to that used in biofeedback. But whereas biofeedback teaches people to use their minds to control supposedly involuntary body responses, Duff's testing helped commercial broadcasters devise programming to manipulate people subliminally, repeating and refining subtle features that drew positive involuntary responses in Duff's testing.

Larry Bensky, squeezed out of commercial radio, took a very different path. Bensky went to work for listener-sponsored KPFA in Berkeley as an unpaid volunteer, doing a six-hour program on Saturday nights that blended jazz, poetry, interviews, and politics in an unpredictable, freeform style. His mentor at KPFA was Roland Young, a gifted black disc jockey who was fired from KSAN for reading—on the air—a listener's letter in support of Black Panther David Hilliard, then under arrest for allegedly threatening the life of Richard Nixon at an antiwar rally.

KPFA and other listener-sponsored stations provided alternatives to commercial underground rock radio. They were able to do that for several reasons. First, Pacifica stations are determinedly noncommercial, operated by a foundation set up to provide educational, not profitable, programming. Second, unlike rock stations, Pacifica outlets didn't cater to young, white listeners; rather, they provided programming for and by a broad spectrum of people, admitting a greater range of interests and a greater tolerance for a variety of opinions. Finally, Pacifica didn't play mainly rock and roll, but featured opera, classical music, blues, bluegrass, jazz, electronic avant-garde music, poetry, theatre, and many other forms of art and entertainment—not as novelties, but as integral parts of its programming. Rock radio stations, while they were unpredictable compared to tightly formatted Top Forty AM stations, were relatively simple and predictable compared to Pacifica outlets. Taking in the broad range of Pacifica programming almost demanded that one stretch one's mind to comprehend it. That kind of diversity, because it is difficult to contain in a commercial package, is not aired by commercial radio stations anywhere in America.

Bensky, Nisker, and Young's enforced departure from commercial underground radio was duplicated at other rock FM stations around the country, illustrating the limits of commercial rock radio as an alternative medium. Like other merchandisers of hip culture, rock radio executives and advertisers felt more comfortable with flower-child programming than with the edges-and-elbows politics of iconoclasts like Bensky. In fact, they originated some flower-child programming themselves.

In the spring of 1970, the American Broadcasting Corporation's FM rock stations were converted to "Love Radio." Love Radio was a tightly coordinated concept that featured soft rock; quiet, mushy poetry à la Rod McKuen; and a minimum of challenging social commentary. Selling the listenership of Love Radio to prospective advertisers was part of the package too. As ABC's ad copy informed would-be advertisers, "Like any successful business, we invest in new products too. One of our latest ones is called LOVE . . . it communicates to a new kind of audience . . . the audience that thinks, feels, and buys in the same way. A group with whom the buying power of the country rests. And LOVE is the only concept on radio that's effectively reaching them."

Stations like KSAN retained progressively watered-down versions of freeform programming until the late seventies, when the novelty and popularity of the form was exhausted. The exciting but shortlived experiment of freeform rock enriched commercial radio, enabling broadcasters to attract young listeners who had begun to drift away from less sophisticated AM outlets. By the end of the seventies, however, freeform radio survived only where it had originated, in the noncommercial stations that gave homes to innovators such as Bob Fass and the radical refugees from KSAN.

The assimilation of rock radio was paced by the absorption into mainstream culture of rock journalism—the chronicling, analysis, and celebration of rock music. The form began in the middle sixties with mimeographed sheets passed hand-to-hand and proceeded apace until the middle seventies, when even conservative daily newspapers felt compelled to hire rock writers and snare young readers with syndicated material from *Rolling Stone*.

Although *Rolling Stone* quickly became the most commercially successful rock publication after its founding in late 1967, it was not the first of its genre. Rock criticism, as such, began in early 1966, when Paul Williams, a Swarthmore College student, issued a mimeographed newsletter (later a printed magazine) called *Crawdaddy*. In June of that same year, Richard Goldstein, fresh from Columbia University, inaugurated a weekly column in the *Village Voice* called "Pop Eye," in which he reported and analyzed developments in the new music. Williams, Goldstein, and their young colleagues wrote about rock in ways no one had ever dared or cared to do before, bringing passion and developing intellectual standards to music that had been considered inconsequential. In the process, they helped validate the music and enlarged the audience for it. "Back then," remembered Williams, "we were interested in writing about our lives when we wrote about records. Everyone listened to the same ones, so there was a common reference point. We could touch on anything through them. . . ."

The underground media gave rock a new legitimacy. Established media had long ignored it, except as a curious youth phenomenon. When they covered rock at all, they did so with anthropological detachment. The trade papers saw rock only in dollar-and-cents terms, entirely missing its cultural significance. The fan magazines were, well, fan magazines, worshipful adjuncts to the industry, more concerned with publishing color pinups of pop stars than with probing the depths of their music.

It didn't take long for the music industry to realize that underground media spoke intimately to the audience for rock. Record companies hired "house freaks" from the hip community to cue them in on how that community lived: its unwritten rules, its true language, its unexamined assumptions. By 1967, the music industry was cultivating the underground press. Musicians freely gave interviews to rock writers, and their parent companies took out ads. The businesses' more astute promoters leaked exciting music news to the underground.

The Monterey Pop Festival, held in California in June 1967, was the first major international music festival to feature rock. Monterey was promoted largely through the underground press. In an article published in the *Los Angeles Free Press*, Derek Taylor, the Beatles' press officer, invited the young and hip to Monterey: "The Festival plans to attract tens of thousands of pop followers—the young and those who remember, the free and those who would like to be—to watch and hear and absorb and enjoy some of the world's best young entertainers in the hippest surroundings, piling music upon music, hour upon hour, into a sapphire evening."

The cultural/spiritual wing of the underground press, epitomized by psychedelic papers such as the *San Francisco Oracle*, happily went along for the ride on the peace-and-love trip of the Beatles and lesser flower-power bands. Other branches of the underground—critical of corporate control of rock, and believing that rock was, by definition, revolutionary—tried to call forth the legions of a rock-and-roll army to do battle with the establishment.

The most effusive and ambitious of those papers was Detroit's *Fifth Estate*, which published the writing of John Sinclair, head of the White Panther Party, a radical white youth group inspired by the Black Panthers. Sinclair wrote page after page of kick-out-the-jambs prose, declaring that the program of the White Panthers was "dope, rock-and-roll, and fucking in the streets." Sinclair believed that rock was revolutionary because the music forced kids "into" their bodies, causing a break with Puritanical repression, and because it was usually played in a group rather than by an individual. Leni Sinclair, John's wife, was at least equally enthusiastic, proclaiming, "The turning point in the history of Western civilization was reached with the invention of the electric guitar."

The White Panthers attempted to practice what the Sinclairs preached in the *Fifth Estate*, sponsoring "people's ballrooms," where young people in Detroit and nearby Ann Arbor got high and danced. The *Fifth Estate* devoted voluminous coverage to the MC 5, a rock band managed by Sinclair, and generally promoted the idea of "free music for the people." The paper's equation of "high-energy" rock with radicalism was simplistic, however, as individualism and machismo—not very promising qualities for a revolution—were deeply embedded in the music.

The flirtation between rock and revolution was a quarrelsome one, ending when rock stars jilted their would-be radical allies. In a statement written for the British underground paper *Black Dwarf*, John Lennon, believed to be the most radical of the Beatles, summed up his philosophy in a "Very Open Letter": "Until you/we change your/our heads— there's no chance. Tell me of one successful revolution. Who fucked up communism—christianity—capitalism—buddhism, etc? Sick heads, and nothing else. . . . You destroy [the system], and I'll build around it."

Rock, as Lennon's comments implied, gave voice to an essentially cultural, gradual, personal kind of change—one which, while rebellious, was not revolutionary. The most influential portrayals of rock lifestyles—movies such as *Monterey Pop* (1969), *Easy Rider* (1969), and *Woodstock* (1970) and the play and cast recording of *Hair* (1968)—steered clear of politics, unless one defines politics in the most reductive (the paranoia of *Easy Rider*) or amorphous (the communal euphoria of the others) sense.

While they helped seed lifestyles based on rock, underground media did not share in the commercial harvest. Entertainment industry executives generally—like the Metromedia managers who toned down rock radio—were uneasy about the political content of underground media, and, as the size of the youth market became apparent, launched media enterprises of their own. Slick magazines such as *Cheetah* and *Eye* were started to steal the underground's thunder. *Cheetah* enlisted Richard Goldstein, Robert Christgau, and Ellen Willis (one of a very few female critics in the man's world of rock-and-roll), but the magazine was shortlived. A similar fate awaited *Eye*, the Hearst entry in the rock sweepstakes. *Cheetah* and *Eye* were just too slick for the countercultural audience, too transparent in their attempts at co-optation, to succeed.

Bounded by the hip slicks on one side and by the funky underground papers on the other, a publishing vacuum developed. On November 7, 1967, the first, 24-page issue of a new biweekly published in San Francisco arrived to fill that vacuum. It was called *Rolling Stone*.

Rolling Stone was the brainchild of Jann Wenner, a 21-year-old former *Ramparts* staffer piqued by *Ramparts'* refusal to cover rock-and-roll in the style he believed it deserved. *Rolling Stone* was neither newspaper nor magazine, but a hybrid of both, published on newsprint with a magazine's long-range perspective on events. Wenner started *Stone* with $7,500 he borrowed, in part, from his mother and from Ralph J. Gleason, the *San Francisco Chronicle*'s respected jazz and pop critic.

Gleason already covered rock and the counterculture with a more than sympathetic eye in his *Chronicle* column and in *Ramparts*, where he once contributed an effusive cover story on Bob Dylan. But Gleason left *Ramparts* after editor Warren Hinckle did a scathing story on Haight-Ashbury, scoring the community's hip businessmen as "merchant princes," deriding Tim Leary as a charlatan, even divining traces of fascism in some of the occult theories of the hip world. Gleason needed some other periodical in which to invest his time and considerable energy—one that would permit him to wander farther afield than he could do in the *Chronicle*. He was delighted to help fund *Rolling Stone*.

From the start, Wenner distanced himself and his publication from the underground press. *Rolling Stone* was professional: nice-looking in an almost traditional way, neatly laid out with conservative column rules, carefully quarter-folded. The stories were accurate and the magazine was generally free of typographical errors and other youth-culture blemishes. Moreover, it had an instantly recognizable style. Rock music became "rock & roll," with an ampersand. The many photographs of rock stars by the magazine's first staff photographer, Baron Wolman, were well composed and clearly reproduced. When Annie Leibovitz replaced Wolman as *Stone*'s star photographer in 1970, she brought a portfolio of airy, romantic shots to the magazine, giving *Rolling Stone* a touch of *Vogue* or the old *Esquire*.

And *Rolling Stone* was careful about politics. Most of its stories were about music—not about corporate control of rock, or the music's revolutionary potential in political terms, but music itself and the high-rolling, free-flowing, dope-smoking, get-it-on lifestyle that went with it. Enjoyment of the music was equated with freedom, and consumption of the music was identified with rebellion, even revolution. Organized political activity was simply suicidal and probably morally wrong besides, in editor Wenner's reckoning.

"His [Wenner's] basic attitude is that violence is abhorrent," Greil Marcus told Lawrence Leamer, author of *The Paper Revolutionaries*, "but that any kind of resistance—not only violent resistance, but resistance even in print—is ridiculous, because we're going to win. We're younger and we're going to take over. You know, the establishment has committed a hideous atrocity, but the Black Panthers, or whoever, were acting stupidly or foolishly. The message of the article is that it's too bad, but they got what they deserved."

Rolling Stone occupied the middle ground in the ideological wars of the late sixties, asserting that rock and the rock life were, alternately, "beyond politics" or else the better part of politics. Wenner's occasional editorials criticizing both the establishment and its young opponents were buttressed by columns in which Ralph Gleason—very much the avuncular, older hipster—advised young radicals they were irrelevant. Gleason often began paragraphs with a blunt "Look." Or "Listen." Even more than Wenner, he was convinced that revolution was something records did when they spun on a turntable.

As a writer for both *Rolling Stone* and the San Francisco *Express Times*, Greil Marcus had a foot in each world. He contrasted the two periodicals by commenting, "Marvin Garson [editor of the *Express Times*] didn't edit the paper, he inspired it. You were always free to come up with something deeply felt. There was a format at *Rolling Stone*, and a certain tendency to censor yourself. It was always a product of editing."

Rolling Stone was edited skillfully and purposefully. The pages of *Rolling Stone*, like the pages of the early *Time* and *Playboy*, defined a world. It was a world in which benevolent superstars did miraculous things with sound, in which barriers to developing consciousness were overcome with good vibrations, a world whose residents believed in the redemptive powers of rock-and-roll music and were blessed in their faith.

Wenner recruited many of the best rock writers to articulate the growing myth of rock-and-roll as the music that could set you free: Jon Landau, Langdon Winner, Michael Lydon, Ed Ward, Michael Goodwin, Marcus. Not infrequently, their writing on rock was more vivid and dramatic than the music they raised to mythic status. In a piece on an album called *Born to Run*, by Bruce Springsteen, Marcus wrote, "Springsteen's singing, his words, and the band's music have turned the dreams and failures two generations have dropped along the road into an epic—an epic that began when that car went over the cliff in *Rebel Without a Cause*." Although Marcus' Springsteen review was written in 1975, it was not unrepresentative of the writing in the early *Rolling Stone*.

Rolling Stone made money, although modestly at first. As *Rolling Stone* gathered momentum, its circumspect youth-culture slant drew advertising away from the underground press. According to Lionel Haines, business manager of the *Berkeley Tribe*, major record companies suddenly pulled most of their ads shortly after the start of the Chicago Seven Conspiracy Trial and the Weathermen's "Days of Rage." "We lost $17,000 a month in revenue," Haines recalled. At the same time, the *Tribe* lost most of its classified advertising to a new, free-circulation, apolitical shopper called the *Classified Gazette*. The double punch staggered the *Tribe*, suddenly unable to pay its printer and its street vendors. "Our circulation dropped from 60,000 in November 1969 to 29,000 at the end of November," Haines said. Similarly, "within months, most of the viable underground papers around the country were crippled. With the big national ads going to *Rolling Stone* and the local classifieds going to free shoppers, there was no economic base." Underground journalists accused *Rolling Stone* of using its sales pitch to urge record companies to pull their ads from underground papers. Whether or not *Rolling Stone* did that, record companies did switch their advertising to *Rolling Stone*, helping to ensure the survival of the underground press' chief competitor.

Rolling Stone also got a badly needed injection of business expertise in 1970, when Max Palevsky, who had parlayed Scientific Data Systems into a multimillion-dollar company, bought stock in the magazine and revamped its business procedures. Wenner was also briefly in business partnership with Mick Jagger in a British edition of *Rolling Stone*; the prospect of the magazine's reviewing its part-owner's music apparently didn't concern either Jagger or Wenner.

According to a lengthy, two-part feature in *New Times* magazine in 1976, Wenner and *Rolling Stone* were also chummy with several of the biggest record companies in the business. Robert Sam Anson, the *New Times* writer, reported:

> In the early years, *Rolling Stone* . . . was distributed by Independent News Service, wholly owned subsidiary of the Warner Communications. . . . The relationship . . . was terminated several years ago, but while it lasted, Independent played a crucial role in keeping *Rolling Stone* together, especially in 1970, when, virtually bankrupt, Wenner obtained a $100,000 advance from Independent against future sales—in effect, an unsecured, interest-free loan. During the same period, Wenner also obtained advances against future advertising of more than $25,000 each from Atlantic and Columbia records.
>
> Columbia agreed to have its salesmen distribute *Rolling Stone* through record stores, a mutually lucrative arrangement that accounted for more than 15 percent of *Rolling Stone*'s single-copy sales. Next it was advice: [Columbia's then-president Clive] Davis steered Wenner to a management consultant. Meanwhile, he had Columbia's art department design a direct mail campaign for the magazine. At one point, *Rolling Stone*'s advertising salesmen were working directly out of Columbia's offices.

The recording industry had taken a special interest in *Rolling Stone* almost as soon as it began publication. In 1968, after the magazine did a fulsome piece on an unknown Texas blues-rock guitarist named Johnny Winter, the musician was signed to a lucrative $600,000 recording contract. His label? Columbia Records.

As *Rolling Stone* grew it became a model for newer publications that aspired to its expanding influence and professionalism. Alternative publications in the early seventies were strongly influenced by *Stone*, adopting its bemused tone, its mix of personality profiles and reviews, its bright layout, even sharing several of its writers. Jon Landau, a longtime *Stone* contributor, took up residence as the star critic at Boston's *Real*

Paper in the early seventies. The exchange of writers went in the other direction, too, as reporters like Joe Klein and Timothy Crouse (Crouse wrote the engaging book *The Boys on the Bus*, about the presidential press corps, in 1973) went from Boston alternative papers to the staff of *Rolling Stone*.

As early as 1969, *Rolling Stone* was beginning to make its impact felt beyond the world of rock and counterculture politics. Wenner was the subject of profiles, published in the same week, by *Time* and *Newsweek*. He assured *Time* that, while "Rock-and-roll is now the energy core of change in American life . . . capitalism is what gives us the incredible indulgence of this music."

Respect gradually came to *Rolling Stone* from mainstream journalists whose approval Wenner and his magazine seemed to court. *Rolling Stone* scored a breakthrough in early 1970, when it published a lengthy report on the disastrous rock festival at Altamont, California, where Hell's Angels murdered a young black man while the Rolling Stones cavorted on stage. In a special report headlined "Let It Bleed," *Rolling Stone* laced into the band, their management, their lawyer Melvin Belli, and the Hell's Angels for ruining the festival with violence and greed. The piece opened with a gripping eyewitness account of the murder and closed with images of scavengers sifting the mountains of trash left behind for things they could sell. *Rolling Stone* also quietly donated money to the family of the victim, something the Stones were asked to do, but did not.

It was a superb report that earned *Rolling Stone* a National Magazine Award for Special Journalism in 1971 and a measure of legitimacy from the mainstream media. The award citation honored *Rolling Stone* for publishing "material that challenged the shared attitudes of many of its readers." Yet *Rolling Stone*'s report, well-executed though it was, challenged mainly the conduct of the rock business at Altamont, not the nature of the business or the values on which it drew.

In an analysis distributed by Liberation News Service, Todd Gitlin described Altamont and the social forces that produced the horror there:

"We're all here to have a party," Stones manager Sam Cutler announced over and over. . . . It wasn't so. From the start, most of us were there as spectators. The event was outside us, out there on the stage. No wonder hundreds, thousands, had to crawl over each other to Get to the Stage. The rhetoric has it that the action is in each of us. . . . Brave words, but they haven't ever been the whole truth . . . the action is still centralized, whether on the flickering tube or on the poorly built stage. Freedom, in the aggregate, turned out to be a spectator sport. . . .

Dots on the periphery of a large circle, with the music at the center. Dots on the periphery don't establish relations with each other. They relate to the center. A crowd of dots. Dots will not take responsibility for each other. Dots will crawl over each other to get a better piece of the real action—the "really heavy music."

Dots with long hair and dots stoned on who knows what—still dots. Dots invented by the elite of mass communications. Dots turned on not to each other, not to the communal possibilities, but to the big prize, the easy ticket, the "good trip."

"The youth culture is still thin," concluded Gitlin, "more *managed* than self-directing. . . . The question is whether the youth culture will leave anything behind but a market. . . ."

Gitlin's angry, incisive writing, published by a small radical news service, did not win any awards. But his work, more than any other, uncovered the essential flaw in the commercialized versions of the youth culture: its passivity. In its pursuit of profit—and its promotion of the star system, competition, hedonism, and, above all, a kind of sated passivity—*Rolling Stone* became the antithesis of what cultural and political radicals intended when they launched the underground media.

The rejection by radicals hardly hurt *Rolling Stone*'s quest for respectability. Nor did the splashy, manic coverage of the 1972 Presidential race by Hunter Thompson, a former *National Observer* writer who broke the sedate rules of campaign journalism and got away with it. In the middle seventies, *New York Times* managing editor Abe Rosenthal sheepishly confessed that his writers regularly combed *Rolling Stone* in search of story ideas. So did many other mainstream journalists, attracted by the magazine's audacious New Journalism and convinced that *Rolling Stone*, and only *Rolling Stone*, had the key to the mysterious lifestyles of the young. As rock grew to dominate the music industry, *Rolling Stone* grew apace. In the early seventies, Wenner and his wife owned a Victorian home in San Francisco staffed with Chinese servants and drove his and her Mercedes-Benzes. In 1977, the magazine relocated from San Francisco, the psychic capital of the counterculture, to New York, where, Wenner told a reporter, "the people with ambition live." At the dawn of the eighties, *Rolling Stone* had a paid circulation of 600,000, roughly four times the circulation with which it began the seventies. Its parent corporation, Straight Arrow Publishing, was a $20-million company with 135 employees, managed by a Harvard Business School graduate.

The music *Rolling Stone* was founded to celebrate is now the heart of a $4-billion-a-year industry. Openly consumerist and conservative by sixties countercultural standards, *Rolling Stone* supported Jimmy Carter for president in 1976 and published a 176-page tenth-anniversary issue in 1977, stuffed with ads for cars, cameras, clothes, and liquor. Accomplished work still appears in the magazine—Robert Palmer's writing on jazz and blues and Howard Kohn's antinuclear muckraking, among others, come readily to mind—but it seems almost out of context in a magazine that is safely assimilated, like rock and the youth culture, into the mainstream of American life.

The stylized freedom of rock radio, the commercial empire-building of *Rolling Stone*, the tawdry trafficking of the pornzines, the compromises of underground periodicals that used rock and sex to sell papers—all contributed, in varying degrees, to the co-optation of whole segments of underground media culture. The commercialization that proceeded apace in the late sixties was the complementary opposite of the political suppression of the same era—the profitable pull to the push of the repression of radical media.

The results of this dynamic could be seen throughout American society, in bland movie portrayals of the youth culture such as *Woodstock*, and in the bellbottomed jeans and marijuana roach clips in suburban shopping malls. The corporate captains of the leisure-time industry shrewdly posed consumption as an alternative to protest—even, as in the case of "revolutionary" records, as a form of protest—and, by absorbing the radical changes propounded in the underground media, managed to contain them. Underground media activists complained bitterly of colleagues who "sold out," but paradise wasn't lost in a day; had there been no internal contradictions in underground media culture, there would have been nothing to co-opt.

Underground media activists had underestimated the adaptability of mainstream culture. Like architects who design highrise buildings to withstand gale-force winds by swaying to avoid crashing to earth, American social engineers had constructed an edifice that figured to last for a while. The message of media activists changed accordingly as the underground media gave way, at the turn of the decade, to the new activism of alternatives.

TIMES UP

joe llego

I first came to the Good Times a couple of years ago. I had known one of the staff members a year before in New York, where we both worked on a radical paper together, Like all radical/revolutionary/underground papers, the hours were long, the pace rough. Our work was made even more difficult, however, by taking place within what we felt to be a confining hierarchical structure that compartmentalized one's work to the same degree that it is boxed in in the capitalist society around us. We often felt ourselves to be little more than "employees."

Well, it ended for both of us, and we went our separate ways, me to Los Angeles, him to San Francisco. On a vacation trip to San Francisco I looked him up on an impulse, and found him at work here at the Good Times.

What a difference! Where he had been the office hippie back in New York, with his talk of "creative anarchy" and "fuck hiearchy," touting the wonders of "living the revolution," here in San Francisco at the Good Times everybody talked that way. Oh, I felt there was some overdone surface faddism, such as regards hair and dope, but I was easily captivated by the warm, quiet spirit that permeated the place. I first got here in Thanksgiving, 1970, and every time I fell by afterwards it felt like Thanksgiving, in that quiet hour after a full meal, when one contemplates one's stomach and soul, life . . .

I would come here to get away from L.A., to enjoy the adventure of the drive up here, to see San Francisco--and always would end up passing the whole weekend in the house, curled up in a beanbag, stoned, digging the wonderful slow spiral of the collective organic consciousness here. people were constantly coming and going, and there was not too terribly sharp a division between the Good Times and its "constituency," as SDS would have said, centuries ago.

First off, its constituency was, after all is said and done, white. But these "whites" were determined to stretch the meaning of that term--mostly they just ignored it. So in some ways they remained white. They could

p.6

guy

Good Times is not "dead!" It's deep frozen, or into spining a cocoon so as to be able to metamorphose into something else. Unless we disperse,(not now having the binding force of a production schedule) we will continue to generate some kind of mind and spirit nourishment We aren't apathetic and not yet scattered, but confronted with the dual reality that 1. "underground papers" as a media form have outlived their time; the form is dead. And 2. a group of eight or ten people is physically incapable of organizing writing, producing and distributing a twice-weekly, getting-into-mass-media-consciousness-newspaper for very long. A twice-weekly is a great idea and with a little more help a little sooner we might have been able to pull it off and remake the underground press into a more immediate and valuable instrument of alternative communication.. We tried very hard, but finally reached an innate limit and had to stop.

But a little history of the recent drains upon the Good Times. I have only lived here for about six months. When I first arrived I participated as the paper tried to increase its human resources by adding a new house and more living space to the commune. Another basically good idea; yet two houses turned out to be a communal and financial disaster. It pointed up one basic problem of a self-sufficient communal news enterprise, made up of basically good hearted freaks. We found we allowed ourselves to support far too many non-contributing people --- members of the commune, yes; members of the collective, no. It was always the energy put into the newspaper collective that ultimately supported the commune. Non-collective members of the house became an unbearable economic, and, if we couldn't relate personally to our boarders, an energy drain as well. Thus, interestingly, our houses eventually became two seperate worlds, one mainly full of newspaper people, the other mainly full of non-newspaper people being mainly supported by the efforts of the newspaper staff. It became totally unfeasible to maintain two houses and still

p.3

benhari

Revolution. What do you think when you hear that word? What did you think when you heard it a few years ago? If its meaning hasn't changed for you, you were either an incredible visionary or you're now hopelessly out of date.

It used to be said proudly, "I'm a revolutionary like Che or like Malcolm or like Uncle Ho." Brilliant, loving dedicate, men. But it turned out that most of the people who took on the label were not like Che or Malcolm or Ho, they were slender intellectual idealists, slobbering Meth heads, egomaniacs, bum artists, con men, faddists, opportunists, romantic or fucked up middle class kids who knew what's happening in America just ain't right.

Some people, like Bernardine Dohrn, or Karl Armstrong, Bobby Seale, or Cesar Chavez, many others WERE (and ARE) actually together enough to take actions they felt necessary to initiate this revolutionary process, to do the hard, hour by hour struggling that is necessary to overcome this inhuman system which allows 2% to live in undreamed luxury while millions scramble for the simplest necessities.

And it took most of us some time to learn that revolution is a PROCESS, not a product. We can't just go to a 4-day festival and think the revolution is won. We're not going to slip acid into the water system s of all the major cities and wake up the next morning and find all our dreams realized. We're not going to all drop out and toke hash and see the American colossus suddenly stop in its tracks.

It's going to take all these things to keep the revolutionary process flowing. It's also going to take yoga & guerrilla actions & food conspiracies & organizing workers & orgies & prayer & street demonstrations & alternative schools and dropping acid & voting and : . .well, Malcolm said a few years back "--Revolution by any means necessary." Revolution by EVERY means necessary. Revolution by any means POSSIBLE.

The revolution is happening. Too bad about all those drugged out people with long hair panhandling spare change on every downtown street corner, outside every rock show. Too bad about

p.8

marcia

This will be the last issue of Good Times for a while. We're taking a breather--a time to mellow out and absorb what we've learned. Maybe we'll try something new--we have hundreds of ideas. But first we'll probably take it easy.

It will mean a startling change in my life. I've lived the Good Times for the past two years. In that time I've always been Marcia from the Good Times. Our identities have been merged, both in my head and to the world. Now i'm kind of striking out on my own, leaving my security blanket behind. It's a heavy thing to do-- especially for a female person-- to regain my identity again.

I think we've carried the idea of Good Times as far as it will go. When I first met GT, I learned about this exciting experiment that was happening. No more commuting to work. Not even from up the street. The main people on the paper lived and worked together. A blending of life and work. After a few months contact benhari and I (we're married) moved in, knowing that we were about to get into something that was going to completely take over our lives and change our heads. No more schizophrenia. Everybody I associated with had to come to GT to see me. All my secrets were out. Cause in a working commune, there's no place to hide, not even in yourself. The daily contact is so close, and at GT the desire for positive change and willingness to struggle together so ever present, that you've either got to let it all hang out or move. I chose to stay.

So did many others. And for a while we were a stable group that had finally learned to accept and work with each other. We pretty well trusted each other's political motives. Trusted each other with our lives. And so together we put out what we all envisioned, and what many people have told us, was the best underground paper in the country.

At that time we had really managed to combine, each one of us, the culture and the politics of the revolution. We were a bunch of people who dug dope, expanded our heads with it, changed our lives, opened them up, learned to live together and build a family, learned that ecology meant

things like leaving the car at home. We maintained that imperialism, oppression and capitalism must end and sought to live our lives as far outside that system as we could. We also learned that we've got a lot to learn, but that it's okay because once you've started changing your life, and see it doesn't hurt, it's not so hard to go on.

When I talk about us, I also have to include our little compound. Our house is in the middle of two other identical Victorians. We share a backyard. But we've shared lots more than that.

The Breidings on one end were a family of country farming oriented freaks. They lived for four years getting together the money to buy a farm. In March they finally split to live that dream. We didn't always agree. They were much quieter than us, they held communal readings at night, some of them had straight jobs. But we got to know each other. We learned to live together. I think we even learned we could feel the other was righteous and love each other. Also count on each other. We were part of the same family.

The Gibbs on the other side were a whole other story. Eight brothers and Ma and Pa. Plus assorted lovers and renters. Each brother radically different (from an intellectual seaman to a doping drag queen) yet somehow living together and with us too.

We were always in and out of each other's houses. When we ran out of cups we just went next door and rounded some back up. Same with almost everything. We were almost forced to be more sharing than just with our own family, and it worked out okay. At least I never heard any really bitter or lasting complaints. Few of the Gibbs still live next door.

We got it from all ends and in our own house as well. Cause we never let each other off easy. Though we complained constantly of never "confronting the 'real' problem" some way or another it always came out.

(For those of you who lived in communes I hope you know what I'm talking about. If others, it's a good idea to find out if you don't know.)

Our kitchen table was probably the heaviest in town. Our regular Sunday night meet-

p.

The San Francisco Good Times *told readers "good-bye" and explained why in its last issue.*

eight

A Time of Transition

IN THE WANING WEEKS OF 1968, copies of a remarkable new periodical began appearing in hippie communes and a few bookstores. The publication was oversized and a bit awkward to hold, but on the cover was a stunning color photograph of the Earth, all blue and green and circled with white clouds, floating in the blackness of space. Inside were trenchant reviews, diagrams, and advice on how to make and do things—information essential for argonauts of the New Age to chart their course in and around mainstream society. The publication was called the *Whole Earth Catalog*.

The *Whole Earth Catalog* heralded a new kind of media activism. Like the underground media, the *Catalog* aimed to transform society, and, like them, it addressed readers informally, almost conspiratorially. Unlike the underground, however, the *Catalog* utterly rejected the confrontational mode of politics. "We were apolitical," the *Catalog*'s founder,

The back-to-the-land proselytizing of environmental media, symbolized by this picture of the earth taken from space, largely replaced the New Left's confrontational politics.

editor, and publisher, Stewart Brand, acknowledged. "The New Left wanted in the centers of power. And I worked in the centers of power [the U.S. Army and International Business Machines] and didn't want to go back there."

Rather than seizing power, the *Catalog* and its readers attempted to create an embryonic alternative culture in the margins of the old, a culture capable of sustaining them in what, it was now clear, was a lifetime task: transforming the United States of America. Frustrated and frightened by the co-optation of underground attitudes toward rock, sex, and drugs, the repression of radical media, and the shooting of students at Kent State (four dead) and Jackson State (two dead) in May 1970, media activists began the slow, patient construction of alternative institutions. In doing so, they also transformed their own media.

The change from underground to alternative media did not occur overnight, of course. Publications like the *Whole Earth Catalog* and *Mother Earth News* coexisted with fiery underground papers in a tense and often ambiguous time of transition. As the seventies unfolded, however, the nuts-and-bolts practicality and live-and-let-live philosophy of alternative media attracted more support than did the heated language and to-the-barricades agendas of the underground. The process accelerated after January 1973, when the Paris Peace Accords and the end of the military draft removed the leading *raison d'etre* of the underground media: the Vietnam war.

The differences between underground and alternative media were sometimes striking. The underground media were staffed, in their prime, by inspired amateurs; the alternative media began similarly, but, as time went on, they developed a core of experienced professionals. The underground's unabashed and often simplistic celebration of sex was replaced (especially in feminist media) by criticisms of the depersonalization of women as sex objects and, in most alternative media, by examinations of the Baby Boom generation's encounters with adult sexuality and sex roles: living together, living alone, open marriage, divorce, parenthood, and so on.

Rock music and drugs were also handled differently by the alternative media. While the underground viewed rock as revolutionary, the alternative media—if they covered rock at all (the environmental media didn't; most other alternative media did, in varying degrees)—saw rock as entertainment and saw stereo systems and records not as ammunition in a generational war but as accoutrements of the good life. Similarly, drugs, hailed as radical consciousness-expansion agents by the underground, were portrayed in the alternative media as hedonistic accessories or as vaguely embarrassing reminders of youthful excesses.

The origin of the word *alternative* to describe grassroots media is unclear, but in the early seventies a number of media outlets began calling themselves alternatives. In 1973, the Underground Press Syndicate, convening in Boulder, Colorado, formally changed its name to the Alternative Press Syndicate (APS). The name change came about in part, according to APS chief Tom Forcade, because member-papers, reeling from government harassment, believed that calling themselves alternative was less provocative—and so, less dangerous—than presenting themselves as radical underground papers.

As it turned out, the early seventies were the last hurrah for many of the papers represented, regardless of what they chose to call themselves. *San Francisco Good Times* (the renamed *Express Times*), short of money and staff, called it quits in the fall of 1972. So did *Kaleidoscope* in Milwaukee and *Quicksilver Times* in Washington, D.C. Boston's radical *Old Mole* (". . . our old mole, who knows so well how to work underground, suddenly to appear: the Revolution"—Marx) folded even before the conference. Chicago's *Seed* was soon to follow.

Fear of repression was a grim reason for adopting a new name, but there were positive reasons for adopting "alternative" to describe grassroots media as well. Underground had always seemed a dramatic but somehow restrictive term, as though the media it designated were fated to remain forever out of public view, agitating *against* things. "Alternative" augured something better. It was positive, constructive, with an implicit message that working models of reality substantially different from mainstream culture already existed. Many alternative media, while forgoing the "off-the-pig" rhetoric of the underground, were fully as activist as their predecessors. Theirs was activism predicated on persuasion rather than polarization as a means of effecting social and personal change. The tone of alternative media reflected this change of emphasis. They were inviting where underground media were abrasive.

Despite the new name, and the very real differences between underground and alternative media, there were important points of continuity between them too. The cooperative workstyles at the radical *Berkeley Tribe* were paralleled by the fluid staff structure of *New Age*, a leading exemplar of the spiritual movement media of the seventies. The distain for militarism that marked pacifist magazines such as *Liberation* was echoed in the *Whole Earth Catalog*, where enlightened invention was designed to replace warfare for problem-solving. The determination shared by all underground media—that their constituents be free to define themselves through their own life-improvisations rather than received definitions—was held equally sancrosanct by the alternative media.

Moreover, the deep concern for the environment that marked the emergence of alternative media had roots in the underground, which not only recorded but helped launch the ecology movement. This commitment to defending the natural world from encroachment, and developing skills that would allow human beings to live lightly on the earth, provided a natural bridge between underground and alternative media.

Several weeks before the violence in Chicago in August 1968—which inspired the New York branch of Liberation News Service to issue its article advising readers to "learn a pre-industrial trade"—the cultural radicals in LNS made their celebrated hegira to a Massachusetts farm. There, the emigre journalists grew less interested and able to keep up with movement news and furnish dispatches on the war. At first the farm branch of LNS published twice a week, then once a week, then every two weeks. Finally their delapidated press, which the farmer-journalists kept in a cow barn, fell silent altogether. Explained Steve Diamond, one of the prime movers of LNS-Massachusetts, "We simply didn't have anything more to say, other than perhaps get some land, get your people together, and see what happens." For the back-to-the-land renegades of LNS, the message had consumed the medium.

Almost. Although the cultural branch of LNS ceased publication in February 1969, its young veterans turned out several books in which they proselytized for their return to the land. Wrote Raymond Mungo in *Famous Long Ago*, "Here's the beginning of the 'peace movement' of the 1970s, here's a clumsy attempt at self-sufficiency, here's a bigger underground press than ever, for each one hath one and is one. The word is spreading faster than the wind can carry it."

The LNS veterans didn't leave the word to the wind, however. In the decade ahead, they founded the Marshall Bloom Institute of Media Studies (after the late cofounder of LNS), a countercultural enterprise that sponsored several books and films, an occasional magazine (*The Green Mountain Post*), and dozens of articles in alternative periodicals. One of Mungo's cohorts, Harvey Wasserman, emerged in the middle seventies as a leading writer and spokesperson for the Clamshall Alliance, a pacifistic antinuclear organization in New England, cementing the link between sixties revolutionaries, the back-to-the-landers, and a new, holistically inclined, back-to-the-world movement in the late seventies.

The concern for holistic health alternatives and personal growth in the back-to-the-land movement dovetailed with the humanistic psychologies then being developed by the Esalen Institute and similar therapeutic groups. Combined, the two strains of thought emerged in the middle seventies as a significant force in American life, known variously as the "human potential movement," the "consciousness movement," and the "New Age" and hailed—depending on who was doing the evaluation—as humanity's last, best hope or America's final descent into solipsism.

The underground media covered and encouraged this groundswell as it began to stir in the late sixties. Even in city-based media, the cultural wing of the underground placed great store on self-sufficiency and getting back to nature. Jeannie Darlington's column on gardening ("Grow Your Own") for the *San Francisco Good Times* was widely reprinted in the underground press. Ron Cobb, the editorial cartoonist for the *Los Angeles Free Press*, designed the symbol of the ecology movement—an ellipse made by putting a lowercase "e" inside the letter "O". The symbol, which Cobb bequeathed to the public domain, became internationally known. With the bold eclecticism characteristic of the underground, Cobb explained that the "e" stood for "Eden," "evolution," and "ecstasy," as well as "earth," and the "O" stood for "om," "orgasm," "orgy," and "oneness."

Eclecticism, of course, was common coin in the underground press and was both a strength (it gave readers a number of topics to choose from and constituted a wide-ranging vision) and a weakness (there was frequently a lack of cohesion in the pages of the papers and among their staffs). These strengths and weaknesses were concentrated with special intensity in the *Berkeley Tribe* immediately after that paper split off from the *Barb* in late 1969. With a diverse staff of cultural and political radicals, the *Tribe*, more than most underground papers, showed potential for evolving into a particularly vital alternative paper—providing its unstable elements could be synthesized.

The most prominent alternative-style feature in the *Tribe* was "Earth Read-Out," a weekly column on the environment by Keith Lampe, a former Queens College teacher and cofounder of the Yippies. Lampe intended "Earth Read-Out" to inspire a radical change of consciousness about the earth. He introduced readers to Paul Erlich, author of *The Population Bomb*, and promoted the whole-earth theories of Buckminster

Ray Mungo (on jeep) and Marshall Bloom cofounded Liberation News Service and led the return to the land. (Photos by Peter Simon.)

Fuller. In a particularly prescient column in the July 10, 1969, issue of the *Tribe*, Lampe accurately anticipated a softening of the us/them dichotomy that characterized both sixties politics and the underground media themselves: "Note well: present U.S. policies are killing half a million annually in Vietnam and at home—but *our* present policies will kill half a billion on this earth in the next fifteen years. Within this cataclysmic context, there's no polarization yet, no good guy/bad guy, no we/they, because neither side of the political spectrum has been paying adequate attention to it."

In that same week's column, Lampe spelled out the implications of that insight for radicals: "Almost certainly within six or eight months there will occur among most young activists a shift of consciousness emphatically away from campus-and-Vietnam issues and energetically into issues pertaining to the ecological emergency. As this shift occurs, we activists will have to deal with such complex forms of information that we'll probably grow nostalgic for the relative simplicity of the earlier issues."

Lampe's prophecy stands as an epitaph for the New Left, the underground media, and his own newspaper, for the complexity he anticipated helped shatter the bedrock of belief on which the New Left and media like the *Tribe* rested. The final schism in the *Tribe* (mentioned in the previous chapter) between cultural and political radicals was closely tied to the shift in consciousness Lampe predicted, dooming the *Tribe's* chance to make the transition from sixties radicalism to seventies alternative activism.

One of the fourteen cultural radicals who left the *Tribe* at Christmastime 1969 was photographer Henrietta Haines. A decade after the event, Haines remembered the impact of the violence of the late sixties on the cultural staffers of the *Tribe*. "We wanted to kill pigs," she said, "but we didn't want to kill some person. And we didn't want to get hurt." Like the paper, "the movement was never monolithic," and after the violence against young whites escalated, both the movement and its media started coming apart. "All of a sudden, there were defections to the country, and to gurus."

After the split, Henrietta Haines and her husband, reporter Lionel Haines moved to the woods of Marin County, near San Francisco. The *Tribe's* circulation manager, Gentle Waters (Marlon Ayott), meandered to a rural commune. Like the Haineses, Waters left not only the city but also underground journalism in the process. Another *Tribe* staffer who left the paper was Keith Lampe. Lampe shed his old identity and his old name. Indian-style, he adopted the totem-name Ponderosa Pine and took to playing an unidentifiable stringed instrument and singing at public events in a wordless, droning voice. His life—from teacher to revolutionist to protector of trees and singer of chants—was a microcosm of changes in the underground media culture itself.

With the exodus of the cultural radicals, the *Tribe* lost the unique chemistry that made it an exciting paper. Instead, the paper became increasingly taken with the rhetoric of armed struggle. By the time the *Tribe* folded in the fall of 1972, former staff photographer Alan Copeland remembered, "the paper read like the *Pyongyang* [North Korea] *Times*."

The identity crisis faced by many radical activists after the dissolution of the New Left was anticipated in several remarkable films by independent filmmaker Robert Kramer. A cofounder of Newsreel, Kramer made uncommonly introspective films on his own even as he worked with the radical documentary group. So stark was his vision—and so ambiguous were his conclusions—that Newsreel declined to distribute Kramer's films, feeling that his work projected "negative energy." Nonplussed, Kramer used his network of contacts to distribute the films himself.

Kramer's first feature, a 60-minute, black-and-white film entitled *In the Country*, released in 1966, portrayed a young radical's life underground and his anguish at not being able to stop the Vietnam war. The following year, Kramer weighed in with a similar film called *The Edge*, about a group of fugitives, one of whom attempts to assassinate the President but fails, implicating his comrades in the process. In 1969, in a third feature, entitled *Ice*, Kramer portrayed a group of isolated guerrillas in a future fascistic America who, despite their determination to smash the state, are killed one by one by authorities.

After having, in effect, predicted the dead end of armed struggle in America in his films of the sixties, Kramer described the complexity of post-New Left culture in his major effort of the seventies, *Milestones*. This three-hour, color docudrama, released in 1975, depicted political and once-political figures who disappeared into the woodwork of American society as acupuncturists, potters, organic farmers, draft resisters, and, in one case, a factory organizer in Detroit. Beginning with an elderly woman recounting her memories of growing up in the immigrant ghetto of New York, *Milestones* ends by recording the birth of a child in a California commune established by former radicals.

Called "something of a masterpiece" by critic Richard Eder in the *New York Times*, *Milestones* reflects the fragmented nature of post-New Left culture. Unlike the agitprop Newsreel films he helped make between 1967 and 1970, Kramer's ambitious personal work resists posting political direction-finders for the viewer. "You're sort of required to deal with the films the way you deal with your daily life," said Kramer. "Instead of being didactic, the films are this invitation to enter into a relationship, the kind you have to your own experience. There's a lot of space for people to thrash around in."

Kramer's eagerness to explore the interior of radical life in America, and his openness to experience, were unusual in leftist underground cinema but were also very much in tune with alternative film-and-videomakers of the seventies, whose work generally avoided heavy-handed didactism while reflecting their creators' values in editing and choice of subject matter. Michael Shamberg's Raindance Corporation, renamed Top Value Television (TVTV) in 1972, was one leading video-documentary group to take this approach.

TVTV turned out tightly edited pieces that rank with the best alternative documentary work. In "Four More Years," a tape of the 1972 Republican convention in Miami, TVTV developed its point of view not through exhortations to smash the Grand Old Party, but by juxtaposing shots of Henry Kissinger stepping out of his limousine with footage of Vietnam war veterans in wheelchairs. The tape also shows an interview with a young Nixon delegate who refers to the demonstrators by saying "We could have a Kent State-type incident here," allowing as how that might not be so bad.

In "Chic to Chic," made for the Public Broadcasting Service, the group taped a lavish party at the Iranian embassy in Washington D.C. TVTV staffer Megan Williams interviews the furred and bejeweled guests in footage that reveals their indifference to the brutality of the regime that footed the bill for the bash. "If all the Americans could eat at the Iranian embassy, they wouldn't have to spend anything on food," exclaims one elderly guest.

"Savior of the World" is a tongue-in-cheek documentary of a religious extravaganza—billed as the greatest event in human history—held in the Houston Astrodome. The event featured the Guru Maharaj Ji, (a pudgy Indian teenager with a host of American disciples), a speech filled with platitudes about world peace, an orchestra to hail his arrivals and exits, and an extravagant car to transport his corporal presence around the material plane. Again, TVTV made adroit use of interviews, allowing the guru's followers to express their worshipful enthusiasm. One of the Mahara Ji's followers was former Chicago Seven defendent Rennie

Davis, depicted with his wife humbly following several paces behind, who avers that the young guru is God incarnate.

Pointed without being ponderous, the TVTV tapes were shown on public and cable television systems around the nation to enthusiastic audiences far larger than the cult following that viewed most earlier alternative video. No longer were TVTV's tapes (or those of other videomakers following their lead) aimed primarily at audiences of cultural and political radicals. The TVTV group, however, remained true to Raindance Corporation's original premise of making use of the latest portapak technology to record for television the kind of video that commercial broadcasters couldn't or wouldn't do.

Such work included unstructured spiritual programs considered too difficult for average viewers to grasp by commercial producers and politically irrelevant by leftists. However, the seventies proved to be prime time for a fusion of videotechnology and spiritual visions of the type presented by artists such as Stephen Beck. Beck is a San Francisco artist who creates subtly shifting images with a videosynthesizer of his own invention that allows him to take apart and recombine images.

Beck describes his work as "kinetic sculpture—forms in motion, usually set to music, which shift and change colors in a calming, meditative way. In a tape called "Anima," we see a moving figure of light that gradually becomes clearer, evoking, by the end of the tape, the suggestion of a human form. In "Union," a body coursed through with light illustrates the meridians of energy that are said to be activated by tantric yoga. This was technology with a human touch, if not a human face. Said Beck: "In the sixties, technology had a certain negative quality. One associated it with napalm and so on. So I thought, what can you do with technology other than blow things up? I was interested in images I could see with my eyes closed, things I saw as a kid and with psychedelic drugs. I found a more definite approach through meditation. With technology, I found I could recreate those images."

Many alternative media activists shared Beck's feeling that technology could be harnessed and used as a tool by people to free themselves and chart their own directions in life. The most popular of all alternative media rooted in that premise—and in many ways the one whose influence has lasted the longest—was the *Whole Earth Catalog*.

The *Whole Earth Catalog* was subtitled "Access to Tools." "We are as Gods," proclaimed the first issue of the *Catalog*, "and might as well get good at it." If there was a single quality that characterized the *Catalog*, it was an attitude of cosmic practicality: roughly, the belief that the universal principles of science—including the laws of interdependence and natural balance revealed in the study of ecology—can be applied to human affairs to make a better world.

This can-do attitude was, in part, attributable to the influence of Buckminster Fuller on the *Whole Earth Catalog's* founder, Stewart Brand. Fuller was the inventor of the geodesic dome, an ingenious use of light metallic materials to construct airy structures that were easy to build and take apart. Many a hippie commune threw up geodesic domes among its tipis and log cabins; the U.S. exhibit at Montreal's Expo '67 was housed in a Fuller dome. Fuller also employed computers in his "World Game" to identify the earth's resources and track their patterns of use as a preliminary means of reallocating them equally in a just, rational world. His most popular concept was the idea of the planet earth as a spaceship on which we all ride, utterly interdependent, irrespective of national boundaries and other divisions. The photograph of the earth on the cover of the *Whole Earth Catalog* was an illustration of Fuller's Spaceship Earth metaphor.

Like Fuller, Brand had little use for politics, feeling that it only pitted people against one another. And, like Fuller, Brand was a "pragmatist" in the American vein—a problem-solver with a basic faith that people would put aside their quest for power and riches if they could only be made to see that there is room enough on the planet for us all. The *Whole Earth Catalog*, from its inception, was a testament to this whole-hearted, innocent belief in rationality and selflessness.

Brand and several helpmates printed a thousand copies of the first 64-page *Catalog* at the tail end of 1968. It was oversized (11″ × 14½″) and cost five dollars, a hefty sum in those days, especially for an unknown item. Some of the goods the *Catalog* touted were available from the While Earth Truck Store, a retail operation run by the magazine's staff. A few copies of the first issue were mailed directly to buyers, but mostly Brand and staff trucked them around by themselves.

That was easier said than done, because Brand's friends and potential readers were scattered to the winds—human seedlings in the back-to-the-land movement that the underground press had already helped to start. When they reached their new home, the young migrants found they needed to know how to do things: how to plant, how to build, how to make clothes, even how to make music. How-tos. That's where the *Whole Earth Catalog* came in. It was the counterculture's first how-to publication.

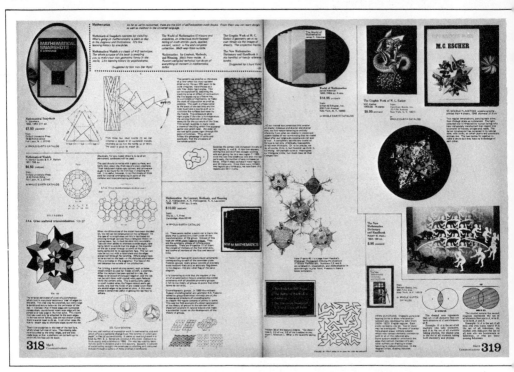

The Whole Earth Catalog *was a crazy quilt of technical data, hippy aphorisms, and uncategorizable odds and ends. (Catalog pages courtesy of the Point Foundation.)*

Stewart Brand, who founded and edited the Catalog, *for a few friends "and any one else who was interested," soon had a phenomenon on his hands that sold two million copies and replaced the family bible for latter-day pioneers. (Photo by Janet Fries.)*

Issue Number 2, stuffed with the concise reviews, diagrams, mail order offers, and odd bits of humor and insight that became the *Catalog's* trademark, came out in January 1969. It was twice as thick—128 pages—and a dollar cheaper than the first issue. This time the press run was larger, and copies of the book-sized periodical were quickly snapped up. Word had spread.

The *Catalog's* functional model was the *L.L. Bean* Catalog of outdoor gear. Brand dreamed of an "access service—a catalog of goods that owed nothing to the suppliers and everything to the users." He never accepted advertising and never needed to. Readers loved the *Catalog*. It was useful, fun to look at, and read in spots like a hip allegorical novel. In its last regular issue (Summer 1971), the *Catalog* published a novel (Gurney Norman's *Devine Right's Trip*), positioned in the lower right-hand corners of right-hand pages like a serial. By that time, the magazine was 144 pages thick and cost only three dollars.

The *Whole Earth Catalog's* size and declining cost alone would have made it unique, but what was most engaging about the publication was its attitude and its built-in notion of access. The *Catalog* was positively nostalgic for the future and, in its writers' speculations and fantasies, displayed an almost tangible hunger for another, newer, better world, one its contributors had as yet only glimpsed. What kept this yearning from inducing only fantasy and passivity was Brand's regard for his readership as a constituency, not a market.

The *Catalog* was an example of what Michael Shambert termed "process journalism." It engaged readers, got them to participate in the process that is an alternative medium. The *Catalog* did this not only by offering mail order goods—lots of magazines do that—but also by soliciting reviews and other articles from readers who had themselves tested the items and taken the journeys they described. Such readers Brand recognized as next-of-kin. As a result, the *Catalog* became, to a considerable degree, a reader-written magazine, not a publication composed by professional journalists. Shamberg also pointed out that the random factoring of the *Catalog* format and readers' tendency to absorb it in skips and jumps made the *Catalog* similar to electronic media. In this, too, it was distinctly different from the linear, top-down packaging of conventional magazines.

The *Catalog* was distinctive in yet another way: It folded at the peak of its success, on purpose. After three years of publishing, Brand and his staff were drained. Nothing unusual there: many staffers on other magazines feel the same way. In addition to being tired, though, Brand was curious. What would happen if he just shut down this roaring success? Would anything spring up to replace it, improve upon it?

To find out, Brand folded the magazine in 1971. Then he threw a *"Whole Earth* Demise" party and gave away $20,000. People in attendance debated whether it was wise to accept the money and, once accepted, what they should do with it. In addition, Brand founded the nonprofit Point Foundation, gave away a. million dollars to ecology groups and political organizations like *COYOTE*, the San Francisco-based prostitutes' union, and financed the start of the *CoEvolution Quarterly*, his current magazine, in 1974. So the money that came from the *Whole Earth Catalog's* community returned to that community in an imaginative act of journalistic recycling.

The *Whole Earth Catalog* was published regularly for just three years. It brought forth sixteen issues through the end of 1971, plus an *Updated Whole Earth Catalog*, a *Last Whole Earth Catalog*, and an *Epilog* in 1974. Another issue, the *Next Whole Earth Catalog*, which Brand described as a compendium of "all the 'best' tools seen in thirteen years of watching, . . . 1500 items of pure cream," was published in October 1980. The mammoth (608 pages), relatively cheap ($12.95) volume was compiled by the staff of the *CoEvolution Quarterly* and distributed by Random House.

Although the early *Catalog* spawned a host of imitators (some of them tongue-in-cheek, such as the *Whole Cat Catalog)*, the originals still sell. Sales totalled two million at last count. More importantly, for the future of alternative media, it set an example of success achieved on its own terms and helped speed the maturation of alternative media by establishing a standard of excellence. The *Catalog* directly inspired a number of New Age periodicals, as well as *the* alternative publishing success of the seventies, *Mother Earth News.*

Mother Earth News was born in the first month of the new decade, the product of round-the-clock effort—and a $1500 grubstake—by John and Jane Shuttleworth. The January 1970 issued was pasted up on the kitchen table of the Shuttleworths' Ohio farmhouse, and it looked it. Its typography was a mish-mash of styles and sizes, layout was rudimentary, the paper was cheap newsprint. The publication looked and read homemade in every way.

But just as those characteristics marked *Mother* (as the magazine styles itself) as hopelessly amateurish to media professionals, they added to its authenticity for the readers at whom the magazine was aimed. Like the magazine itself, they were poor; like the magazine, most of them were young; like the magazine, they were struggling but hopeful, possessed by a dream they were just beginning to articulate. So *Mother's* crudeness did not deter this readership; rather, they were attracted by its vitality and the chance to grow along with the magazine.

Like Stewart Brand at the *Whole Earth Catalog*, Jann Wenner at *Rolling Stone*, and Warren Hinckle at *Ramparts*, *Mother Earth News* was largely the product of one person's vision—in this case, John Shuttleworth, a former advertising executive on Madison Avenue, public relations savant for Boeing Aircraft, and road manager of a folk-rock group. Like his predecessors, Shuttleworth was driven. Hundred-hour work weeks were common in the early days as the magazine struggled to stay afloat.

From the beginning, *Mother Earth News* was an unusual publication, influenced in equal parts by the *Catalog*, the underground press, and nineteenth-century farm magazines that offered everything from wood burning stoves to crackling good yarns to warm up isolated farmers on winter nights. Many of *Mother's* first readers were isolated too. Theirs was psychic rather than a physical isolation, and they wanted to ground themselves in communities of like-minded people, preferably in the country, to end that isolation. Shuttleworth designed *Mother Earth News* to help them do that. He recalled, "We wanted to publish . . . a magazine that would interest *us*. Not advertisers, not distributors, not the 'average' reader, not the pseudo-intellectuals. Us. We wanted a periodical that would: (1) help other little people just like us live richer, fuller, freer, more self-directed lives, and (2) ease us all into more actively putting the interests of the planet above any personal interests."

Eschewing theory, Shuttleworth emphasized nuts-and-bolts information for the here-and-now. "All you got to do to lose my interest— immediately!—is to start dropping words like 'proletariat' into your magazine. . . . The only people in the world who talk that way on purpose are college sophomores . . . and they only impress each other." *Mother Earth News'* premiere issue featured a simple cover drawing of the sun rising over the earth with the words ". . . a new beginning" emblazoned alongside. Inside, the new publication had the earmarks of a standard countercultural publication of the time: an egalitarian masthead from which no one's rank or role was discernible; a generous supply of plugs for underground publications; membership in the then-Underground Press Syndicate. Several articles, including the leadoff essay by poet Gary Snyder, were reprinted from the *Whole Earth Catalog*. Others were taken from mainstream publications, such as a "Living High on $6500 a Year" reprint from the *Saturday Evening Post*.

Snyder's article best exemplified the applied philosophy of *Mother Earth News* and the groundswell of which it was a part:

> Since it doesn't seem practical or even desirable to think that direct bloody force will achieve anything, it would be best to consider this a continuing "revolution of consciousness" which will be won not by guns but by seizing the key images, symbols, archetypes, eschatologies, and ecstasies so that life won't seem worth living unless one's on the transforming energy's side.
>
> Our community: Without falling into a facile McLuhanism, we can hope to use the media. New schools, new classes—walking in the woods and cleaning up the streets. . . . Let some groups establish themselves in the urban centers, and let them work together, a two-way flow of experience, people, money, and home-grown vegetables. Investigating new lifestyles is our work. . . . .
>
> Our own heads is where it starts.

Shuttleworth grounded Snyder's vision by telling readers how to integrate their lofty goals into daily life. *Mother Earth News* celebrated the mundane: composting, natural childbirth, clothes-mending, chicken-farming, home doctoring, sprout-growing. After the first few issues, *Mother* came to rely mostly on readers for its tips. Like the *Whole Earth Catalog*, it became a largely reader-written publication. And after the *Catalog*'s demise it became the journalistic heir to the hip how-to tradition.

Except that "hip" became less and less of a consideration. Through the first few issues, *Mother's* masthead dedicated the magazine to "today's influential 'hip' young adults, the creative people, the doers, the ones who make it all happen." By the end of the first year of publication, the "'hip young adults" were replaced on the masthead by "turned-on people of all ages" who wanted to live in harmony with the earth.

This was a striking break with the underground tradition, which had been dedicated almost exclusively to the Baby Boom generation. *Mother Earth News* broke out of that generational ghetto, carrying countercultural values of natural living to society at large. It shattered the implicit premise that the counterculture was only for the young and enlarged the operating premise of alternative media as well.

Shuttleworth proved to be a maverick in other ways too. He championed the old-fashioned American virtues of thrift, self-reliance, and hard work—learned, he said, in his parents' home as an Indiana farmboy. Shuttleworth also broke with the counterculture belief that money was evil by telling his readers, over and over, that they could profit from survival: "How to Work For Yourself!" "Make A Living Along Shore . . . Digging Clams!" Make "a full $10,000 *profit . . . per acre!*" by learning the ins and outs of "the secret art of frog farming!" Shuttleworth took his own advice, applying the profit motive to his magazine's operations. After its first few shaky years, *Mother Earth News* grew into the only commercial success to emerge from the environmental media.

Mother Earth News was thus a unique combination of old-fashioned virtues, bootstrap capitalism, and forward-looking thought—a periodical that searched for the best of all possible worlds and found it in Jeffersonian America. The combination clicked. By the end of 1972, *Mother* had a paid circulation of 60,000 and a pass-along readership of perhaps a dozen times that. In 1973, the magazine moved to Hendersonville, a small town in the mountains of western North Carolina, where Shuttleworth realized another dream: building a research center.

Like all alternative media visionaries, Shuttleworth didn't just want to publish a successful magazine. He wanted to use his publishing success to make things happen. In *Mother Earth News's* research center, Shuttleworth's tinkers and inventors came up with an automobile that runs partly on electricity and partly on conventional fuel. Cars powered by methane gas and houses heated by solar, wind, and biomass energy are other projects championed in the pages of the magazine—and attempted concretely in the research center by the latter-day Edisons on Shuttleworth's payroll.

By the dawn of the eighties, *Mother Earth News* had grown tremendously. The magazine is now published in bimonthly issues of 196 pages, stuffed with classifieds, mail-order offers, and expensive, four-color display ads. Many of the mail-order goods are sold by *Mother Earth News* itself. *Mother* also syndicates a how-to column three times a week to over 100 newspapers, with a combined circulation of 10 million, and produces three-minute radio tapes mailed free of charge to 900 AM and FM stations. The paid circulation of *Mother Earth News* reached 600,000 in 1980, making it a real-life Horatio Alger success story—one of the 100 largest magazines of any type in the United States. Among the periodicals broadly classified as alternative, only *Rolling Stone* is larger.

There is nothing alternative about the way the magazine is run. *Mother*

Earth News is owned (and until 1980 was also published and edited) by John Shuttleworth, who turned it from a small, struggling child of the counterculture into an efficient midwife of mom-and-pop capitalism. With success, the old egalitarian masthead has been jettisoned, as has UPS (now APS) membership. The informality that was once an organic part of *Mother Earth News is* now stylized; people are "folks," going is written "going'," and there are more three-dot sentence breaks in *Mother's* tightly edited copy than anywhere since the passing of Walter Winchell. *Mother* has also given columns to several "name" writers. Paul and Anne Erlich write a bimonthly column on the state of the world environment, and Scott and Helen Nearing, pioneers in the back-to-the land movement (and now in their nineties and seventies, respectively), regularly contribute how-to tips. *Mother Earth News'* increasing professionalism is probably of interest mainly to magazine critics, however, since the publication's formula for success has changed not a whit.

Like the *Whole Earth Catalog, Mother Earth News* succeeded because it helps people *do* things. Many were the ecology journals launched with high hopes in the early seventies—*Clear Creek, Earth, Earth Times,* and *Not Man Apart* among them. Most are now defunct, and none has had the impact of *Mother Earth News* or the *Whole Earth Catalog.* In the final analysis, reportage and ruminations by name writers and environmental movement stars has not proven as meaningful to readers as concrete information they can use in their own lives.

The long-range influence of *Mother Earth News* and the *Whole Earth Catalog* has extended far beyond their original counterculture readerships. Their success presaged the popularity of how-to books and natural lifestyles that surfaced—usually in more commercialized, diluted forms—in the middle seventies with the popular passions for running, backpacking, alternative sources of energy, appropriate technology, hot tubs, home childbirth, holistic health, and health food. In their way, they have helped heal American's Vietnam-war wounds by showing—again, in concrete terms—that all are subject to pollution. There has been little "us versus them" in their pages. There is, finally, only us.

Within the alternative media culture itself, the *Whole Earth Catalog* and *Mother Earth News* signaled major changes. The underground media also provided concrete information—*Rat's* survival guides to New York and Chicago, among others, come to mind. But the underground's guides to action were often for exceptional events (big demonstrations and confrontations with authorities) or for subsisting on the throwaway goods of the mainstream economy. The alternative media, exemplified by the *Catalog* and *Mother*, have refined and extended this approach, helping their readers to integrate the extraordinary experiences and insights of the underground into their daily lives and to become self-reliant producers of their own goods—in short, to evolve as people.

The self-reliance forged in the alternative media presuppose an adult sense of responsibility and long-term commitment which the underground media culture, with its on-the-road restlessness and desire to change the world—didn't have. In the early seventies, the alternative media culture left the road for the pleasures of place and the responsibilities of community.

R. Crumb dramatized the battle over "red-tagging" between hippie home-builders and state authorities for the Mendocino Grapevine. *(Cartoon courtesy of Crumb.*

nine

The New Provincials

IN JANUARY 1973, a young Midwesterner named Stu Chapman started a newspaper he called the *Grapevine* in his adopted home, California's Mendocino County. Chapman published the monthly paper to serve counterculturists and ex-radicals who, like himself, had moved to rural Mendocino intent upon bringing the pages of the *Whole Earth Catalog* to life by living simply, independently, and quietly on the land.

Barely a year later, however, the *Mendocino Grapevine* and many of its readers found themselves embroiled in a heated political controversy. The homes that young migrants had built by hand—cabins fashioned from used lumber, using solar and wind generators instead of electricity from the local utility, and with compost privies in place of flush toilets—violated the State Uniform Building Code. Homeowners who ignored the code to build what they believed to be ecologically sound homes were hauled before trial juries on criminal misdemeanor charges by local authorities who thought the houses unsanitary and unsafe.

The Grapevine gave form to the resistance with hard-hitting editorials and by throwing its pages open to the home owners. Cover courtesy of the Grapevine.*)*

The young homesteaders decided to fight back, using the *Grapevine* as an organizing tool. Stu Chapman fired editorial salvos criticizing the housing code as an infringement of personal liberty, and unecological to boot. But Chapman did more than write in favor of the settlers and their association. United Stand (US). He invited the migrants to write about themselves, donating space in the *Grapevine* for US to reproduce its newsletter. This provided an essential communications link for US, as many of its backwoods members didn't have telephones. By reading the *Grapevine*, they found out the times and places of meetings and kept posted on what state and local officials were doing. After a two-year impasse, the state of California relented, revising the housing code to accommodate many of the homesteaders' innovations and dropping the misdemeanor charges. The migrants had won an important legal victory, thanks in large part to the *Mendocino Grapevine*.

The lesson of the housing struggle was not lost on Chapman. The *Grapevine* and its constituents would have to participate in local politics, like it or not, or see their interests ignored. The *Grapevine* revamped its format accordingly. The paper published biweekly, then weekly, re-cording county supervisors' meetings, printing paid legal notices, cover-ing elections, and distributing issues of the paper countywide (the only newspaper in Mendocino to do so). In the process of changing itself, the *Grapevine* also changed its community. Longtime residents began read-ing the paper and tolerating, if not accepting, the countercultural values which the *Grapevine* now trumpeted in a more muted fashion.

The *Mendocino Grapevine* determinedly local, reform-minded, freshly planted—was broadly representative of the trend to regionalism in the alternative media in the seventies. The phenomenon embraced city as well as county and included all branches of the alternative media. There were new urban alternative papers in Boston and San Francisco, com-munity radio stations in Minnesota's Iron Range, regional filmmakers at work in the Deep South, independent book and magazine publishers articulating regional sensibilities in all parts of the country.

Like the *Grapevine*, these new local media sometimes got involved in community issues because they had to. Richard Parker, a cofounder of the *Santa Barbara News & Review* (and later a cofounder of *Mother Jones* magazine), attributed the rise of localism in part to the slow expiration of the Vietnam war. "When we started planning the paper in the fall of 1971, interest in the war was peaking," Parker recalled. "Even people in the GI movement were burning out. There was a real sense that we had to get to work on local community stuff, to ground ourselves in the community."

Parker's comment illustrates both the negative and positive reasons for the growth of local and regional media. Frustration, a sense of not getting anywhere on the war, was the negative reason, and there a lowering of expectations was evident. In the desire to put down new roots, however, there was also a willingness to accept responsibilities, to make commitments in concrete, sustained ways. This implied a form of activism that Gurney Norman, a Kentucky writer who contributed to the *Whole Earth Catalog*, dubbed "the new provincialism."

It was *new* provincialism because, as Stu Chapman's move to Mendocino showed, many community media were started by newcomers to the places celebrated in their coverage. Unlike most established media, which invited industrial development as a means of modernizing their home territories, the new provincials were unanimous in their commitment to preserve the natural environment. New provincial media were also highly critical of the cultural corollaries of industrialization: standardized fast food, network TV news reporters whose regional accents were carefully expunged . . .and standardized conceptions of how to build a home. The new provincials found value in diversity—not a separatism rooted in ignorance of the outside world, but a worldly respect for one-of-a-kind places, plants, and people.

Their political stance, which seemed radically new, was, in fact, traceable to something very old in American life: the ideals of Thomas Jefferson, who located virtue in a self-reliant society of small towns, family farms, and balance between local and national authority. Jefferson's vision, although it was overridden in Alexander Hamilton's successful promotion of strong central government and urbanization as a prelude to industrialization, survived in the counterculture's dream of self-reliant, ecologically balanced communities, rooted in regional identity and linked by networks of alternative media. In the *Grapevine*'s clash with state authorities could be heard echoes of Jefferson's lifelong debate with Hamilton, a conflict taken up anew by the new provincials in all forms of media.

The first urban alternative newspaper to articulate a revitalized regional sensibility was the *San Francisco Bay Guardian*. Founded in 1966 by Bruce Brugmann, an ex-daily-newspaper reporter, the *Bay Guardian* was partially funded by local environmentalists. The paper's name reflected one of their prime goals: halting the filling of San Francisco Bay for housing subdivisions and industrial parks.

The *Bay Guardian* (no relation to the *National Guardian*) began modestly. It published sporatically at first, hard-pressed to match the razzle-dazzle of the underground press and carefully distanced from the underground's radical politics. "I've always been a reformer," Brugman said, "I'm not interested in destroying the system." Although the *Bay Guardian* consistently opposed the Vietnam war, Brugmann believed that the underground media drew too much of their identity from their antiwar stand, "'Sooner or later,' I told the underground people, 'the war will be over, and you'll have to go back to being ordinary citizens'."

Brugmann was determined to avoid the underground's mistake. He positioned the *Guardian* as a muckraking reform paper, specializing in local issues. This gave the *Guardian* an identity all its own, and a reputation that grew rapidly when the paper began breaking major local exposés.

In 1967, the *Guardian* revealed that most members of San Francisco's draft boards did not reside in the districts they represented, as required by law. The paper also documented abuses of federal law by Pacific Gas & Electric, the local monopoly utility; uncovered real-estate speculation accompanying the construction of the Bay Area Rapid Transit system; and took aim at the prolific construction of highrise buildings in downtown San Francisco. *Bay Guardian* writer Burton Wolfe coined the term "Manhattanization" to dramatize the changing city skyline and to point out the transformation of San Francisco from a blue-collar port and home of light industry into a corporate headquarters city cluttered with highrises, like New York. The word effectively played on the provincial pride of San Franciscans, aghast at the thought of their soft, Mediterranean-style city becoming like slick, hard, fast Manhattan. More importantly, the *Guardian* showed—in extensive cost/ benefit analyses—that the highrises were costing the city more in municipal services than they were bringing in in taxes.

"We should have gotten two or three Pulitzers for our highrise stuff," asserted Brugmann. "We changed the complexion of the debate on highrises in San Francisco and all over the country, by moving it from an esthetic, emotional argument to an economic one." In 1971, the *Guardian* published a collection of its highrise stories in a book called *The Ultimate Highrise;* the volume was used as a reference and action guide by environmental groups in cities across the United States. In San Francisco, citizens' groups, spurred by the *Guardian*'s is muckraking, put on the ballot an initiative to limit the height of highrises. However, the measure failed at the polls.

Despite the defeat of the highrise initiative, the *Bay Guardian* became a force to be reckoned within local politics. The paper compiled exhaustive election guides, which featured the voting records of local and state officeholders. Moreover, the *Guardian* tendered highly promoted election endorsements. This had the effect of endorsing not only individual candidates, but electoral politics itself as a preferred form of political activity—something that radical media scorned as cosmetic and the countercultural media ignored as mundane.

The *Bay Guardian's* election guides became one of the paper's trademarks, as did its guides to entertainment: wine and cheese, local restaurants, used-book stores, and "best buys." In this, the *Guardian* anticipated a major trend of seventies journalism: the consumer-oriented "city magazines" (of which Clay Felker's *New York* was the prototype) and detailed guides to local nightlife that came to dominate many urban alternative newspapers.

In 1966, the same year the *Bay Guardian* was founded, a new paper composed entirely of guides and reviews got underway in Boston. That publication, called *Boston After Dark (B.A.D.)*, began as a supplement to the Harvard Business School newspaper. By 1969, the weekly paper was solely owned and published by Stephen Mindich, a young Boston University communications graduate. *B.A.D.* built up circulation by giving away the paper on Boston's numerous college campuses and selling it elsewhere in town. For three years, *B.A.D.* had the lucrative college market to itself.

In 1969, Mindich's paper was challenged by a new weekly that attempted to fuse the entertainment listings and reviews of *B.A.D* with the cityside muckraking of the *Bay Guardian*. The *Cambridge Phoenix* published its first issue in September 1969 under the aegis of Jeffrey Tartar, a Vietnam veteran who wanted to publish a "writer's paper" like the *Village Voice*. Tartar assembled a talented staff from Boston's deep pool of writers and artists, but by the spring of 1970, with a paid circulation of only 800, the paper was sinking fast.

Tartar sold out to Richard Missner, a wealthy young Harvard Business School graduate, and Ray Reipen, a local lawyer who also owned pieces of WBCN radio and a local ballroom called the Boston Tea Party. Missner and Reipen promptly hired Harper Barnes, a young *St. Louis Post-Dispatch* reporter, to beef up the paper's editorial side. With Reipen's contacts, Missner's money, and Barnes' editorial flair, the *Phoenix* began to prosper. The new paper followed Stephen Mindich's lead by giving copies away on campuses and added a twist of its own by recruiting a highly visible army of vendors to hawk the *Phoenix* downtown and draw attention to the paper. Before long, the *Phoenix* surpassed *B.A.D.* in journalistic quality.

During Barnes' tenure, the *Phoenix* ran tough pieces on the segregationist policies of the Boston School Committee, the easy access to customers' financial records given local authorities by Boston banks, and the role of Harvard and the Massachusetts Institute of Technology in development schemes in Cambridge. The paper leavened the heavy going with numerous reviews and tips on "coping" with city life. In its September 5, 1970, issue, a column called "The Pennypincher" advised readers on how to make smart buys at auctions. That issue was 40 pages, a hefty size for a newspaper barely a year old. The *Phoenix's* success forced Stephen Mindich to make changes in *Boston After Dark*, using street vendors to sell the paper, closely copying his brash competitor's layout and design, and, most importantly, initiating local reporting and news analysis.

Both the *Phoenix* and *Boston After Dark* were very much Boston papers. Like the *Bay Guardian*, they emphasized local news and features. When national or international stories made the papers, the editors usually gave them a local twist. Both papers were also stuffed with free readers' classifieds and comprehensive guides that told young readers what was going on in Boston. That, too, gave the papers a strong local slant and helped strengthen a sense of community among the 500,000 persons between 18 and 30 in metropolitan Boston who formerly had to rely on posters, leaflets, word of mouth, and the inconsistent efforts of the local underground media to find out what was happening. This dense concentration of young people, unmatched in any other city in the country, put the Boston weeklies on firm financial footing.

Like the *Bay Guardian*, the Boston papers differed markedly from the underground sheets they replaced. While both opposed the Vietnam war, neither the *Phoenix* nor *B.A.D.* openly and consistently identified with militant international movements. Politically, the new papers were reform-oriented rather than radical. Ted Gross, an editor at *B.A.D.* and the *Boston Phoenix* in the early seventies, told Andrew Kopkind, writing in the theoretical journal *Working Papers*, "We weren't political activists, really. . . . Our paper was supposed to be 'radical,' of course. But it was going to reach out to the community. . . . deal with local problems, deconceptualize the rhetoric that was killing the *Old Mole*. So we were

Boston Phoenix *owner/publisher Stephen Mindich turned a small, local enter-tainment sheet called* Boston After Dark *into the nation's largest alternative weekly with eclectic cultural coverage, a liberal slant on city and state politics, and a sharp, expansion-minded business sense. (Photo by Peter Simon.)*

allowed to flatter ourselves and believe that we were doing something radical and at the same time feel superior to it."

But while the political stance of the Boston papers may have induced a kind of journalistic schizophrenia in some staffers, their increased mainstream orientation gave them commercial viability. Rhetoric didn't bring in advertising, but record and restaurant reviews did. As a consequence, both the *Phoenix* and *B.A.D.* did well financially. But they were splitting the market.

This worried both *B.A.D's* Mindich and the *Phoenix's* Missner, who, after buying out Reipen, became the paper's sole owner. In the summer of 1972, Missner shocked the *Phoenix* staff by selling the paper to his archrival, Mindich. Reading from a typewritten announcement, Missner coldly informed his staff they were fired. Chuck Fager, the president of the in-house Phoenix Employees Union, remembered, "Missner threw us out of the offices on four hours notice. We were just plain—bam! It was really something to lose a job at noon and be on the street at four. No compensation, no severance pay, absolutely nothing."

Missner and Mindich expected that to settle the matter, but it didn't. The ex-*Cambridge Phoenix* staff, regrouping from the surprise firing, launched a paper of their own, which they dubbed *The Real Paper* to distinguish it from Mindich's "phony *Phoenix*," now the consolidated *Boston Phoenix. The Real Paper* was slightly to the left of the new *Phoenix*—not so much in its coverage as in the internal operation of the paper. *The Real Paper* was a staff-owned business that hired and fired by consensus and gave every worker, regardless of position, one vote in making major decisions.

Like their predecessors, both papers thrived in the unique Boston youth community, the *Boston Phoenix* more so because of Mindich's established reputation as an entrepreneur. By the middle seventies, the two papers published fat issues, in several sections, and both claimed circulations of just over 100,000, of which nearly half were paid.

The success of the Boston papers inspired dozens of similar efforts around the country, the most notable of which was a newspaper based in Amherst, Massachusetts called the *Valley Advocate*. Debuting as an unprepossessing 24-page biweekly in September 1973, the *Valley Advocate*, by the early eighties, was the flagship of a regional newspaper chain in the Northeast with a combined circulation of 350,000. (For an analysis of chain ownership in alternative media, see Chapter Fifteen.)

Like the Boston papers and the *Mendocino Grapevine*, the *Valley Advocate* drew upon and helped define the social mileu of a geographic community—in the *Advocate's* case, the Pioneer Valley of western Massachusetts. The *Advocate* covered a three-county area which, like Boston, boasted a large number of college students and, like Mendocino, hosted numerous young adults engaged in countercultural pursuits: organic farming, cooperative businesses, assorted arts and crafts. Many of the *Advocate's* readers were originally from somewhere else, drawn to their new home by its beauty, its relaxed pace, and its tolerance of unorthodox lifestyles.

The *Valley Advocate* was founded by Geoff Robinson and Ed Matys, two young copy editors at the daily *Hartford Courant*, and Linda Matys, Ed Matys' wife, who was a former moderator for public television. All three had roots in New England: Ed Matys grew up on a Massachusetts farm; Linda Matys attended college in the Pioneer Valley; and Geoff Robinson lived in neighboring New Hampshire. Following the lead of the Boston weeklies, the *Valley Advocate* was given away on college campuses, both to introduce the new paper to its intended readers and to guarantee a large circulation to advertisers. The premier issue of the *Valley Advocate*, dated September 19, 1973, articulated a consciously regional editorial policy:

> A growing awareness of regional identity in the Pioneer Valley has produced a need to examine issues and events which affect the three counties [Hampden, Hampshire, and Franklin]. But shortsightedness and self-imposed limitations of the press have limited our access to information which would benefit individuals, communities, and the Valley.
>
> The *Advocate* seeks to correct this myopic lack of regional perception. . . .
>
> The *Advocate* seeks to correct this myopic lack of regional percep-for those whose lack of establishment status denies them full access to the public arena of ideas.
>
> Institutions which bear directly upon our lives should be laid open to intense scrutiny and criticism. At the same time, the legitimacy of alternatives to these institutions should be fully recognized and accepted, to provide a forum for new thinking.

The *Valley Advocate's* first issue featured stories on local women's services, a community men's center, a survey of nearby banks and an evaluation of their loan policies, a spate of reviews of books and movies, a calendar of local music ("Beer and Boogie"), and a lengthy, well-researched article critical of Northeast Utilities' plans to build a nuclear power plant near the Pioneer Valley town of Montague. The writer, Dorothea Katzenstein, was a former *Bay Guardian* reporter who served as press coordinator of the Western Massachusetts Public Interest Group, a Ralph Nader organization.

Reporting that local officials had been wined and dined by the utility company prior to official approval of the plant, Katzenstein quoted scientists critical of nuclear power, concluding with a question that her article, by inference, had already answered: "Is contemporary society . . . to be trusted with the handling of such power—and risk?" Accompanying the story was a list of regional and national antinuclear organizations and a large photo of a weather observation tower erected by Northeast Utilities on the site of the proposed plant.

Six months after the *Valley Advocate* article appeared—on Washington's Birthday, 1974, to be exact—a young activist named Sam Lovejoy knocked down the observation tower in an act of civil disobedience and turned himself in to Montague police. Lovejoy was an organic farmer and friend of the alternative media activists who ran the nearby Bloom Institute of Media Studies. Nuclear power, to Lovejoy, was not a far-off, abstract issue, but a concrete threat to his home. His action, the generally favorable response by local residents, and Lovejoy's subsequent acquittal on criminal charges were the subject of Green Mountain Post Films' *Lovejoy's Nuclear War*, a 60-minute film that became a popular organizing tool for the antinuclear movement.

The *Valley Advocate* covered Lovejoy's trial closely, confirming the paper as an antinuclear stalwart. The writer of many of the *Advocate's* articles on nuclear power was Harvey Wasserman of the Clamshell Alliance. Seven of the articles in his book *Energy War: Reports From The Front*, published in 1980, originally appeared in the *Valley Advocate*. When Northeast Utilities tried to counter the *Advocate's* antinuclear reporting by buying an ad in the *Advocate*, the paper refused to sell the space. "We're not an ideological paper," said Ed Matys, "but we are antinuclear and they [the utility] have plenty of money to tell their story. They tell it every day."

The *Valley Advocate's* energy policies meshed with its announced intention to bolster alternative institutions in the Pioneer Valley when the paper cosponsored the Toward Tomorrow Fair at the University of Massachusetts in the mid-seventies. The fair featured local arts and crafts, displays of appropriate technology, and visits by leading alternative energy advocates such as Buckminster Fuller and Amory Lovins. In this way, the paper was both local and global in focus, as well as providing the alternative advocate its name promised.

The growth of local and regional papers like the *Valley Advocate* was the leading development in the alternative press in the seventies. By the end of the decade, statewide weeklies were published in Maine, New Hampshire, and Illinois (all called the *Times*, all independent), A weekly paper in Chicago (the *Reader*) racked up a free circulation of 97,000 doing only local stories. Much smaller papers in college towns such as Chico, California (the *News & Review*), and Ithaca, New York (the *Times*), outgrew their original campus audience to become citywide papers. Alternative papers took as their beats the vastness of Alaska (the now-defunct *Alaska Advocate*) and the Byzantine compactness of Washington, D.C. (the *D.C. Gazette*).

The papers vary in style and tone. The *Chicago Reader's* soft features bear little resemblance to the *Bay Guardian's* crusading news reporting. Their commonality is the strong local slant of nearly all their editorial content, a policy that encourages readers to see the world in microcosm in their communities, as philosophers search for the secrets of the universe in grains of sand.

This determination to ground activism in local and regional communities was exemplified in magazine and book publishing as well as in newspapers. A prime example was the Cascadian Regional Library (CAREL), founded in 1977 at a conference of community activists from all over the Pacific Northwest. Held during the spring equinox, and appropriately called the Equinox Gathering, the conference was called to discuss the Columbia River system as a unique bioregion—a place defined by natural features held in common, such as plants, animals, sources of water, and climate. Discussion centered on how living in the Northwast helped shape the lifestyles of ecologically minded people, and it went on to considerations of how local problems and projects could be approached on a regional basis. The conference ended with a resolution to make the Equinox Gathering an annual event. CAREL was set up to coordinate future meetings, open local offices to serve as information centers, and begin publication of a regional magazine.

The magazine, called *Cascade*, began bimonthly publication later that year. *Cascade* printed overviews of subjects of wide regional interest, such as appropriate technology, New Age spirituality, farming and gardening in the rainy Northwestern climate, and earning a livelihood ("Rainbow Flute thought I should write you because . . . you might be of some help to me; I am looking for a job in a wood shop—Carol.") Every article included a resource directory so readers could follow up the subject of the piece. Dense with data and published unceremoniously on newsprint, *Cascade* is not an artistically rendered publication, but its utility in informing, and sometimes inspiring, Northwesterners is evident. Wrote one reader, "Out here in Wheeler County (one square person per mile), we sometimes feel terminally isolated from most forms of wit and wisdom. . . . Magazine such as [*Cascade*] give us hope and the knowledge that we're not alone."

Other regions host alternative magazines whose styles vary as much as do the areas they represent. *Southern Exposure*, a book-length quarterly published in North Carolina, is as artistic as *Cascade* is utilitarian. With large, handsomely bordered photographs, interviews with traditional craftworkers (one issue featured a conversation with a ninth-generation Southern potter), and first-person essays on the region's tumultuous politics—factory organizing, say, or the civil rights movement—*Southern Exposure* is an evocative blend of work and play, the personal and the political. The magazine frequently prints bibliographies of books and articles on the South and resource guides to political action. Like *Cascade*, *Southern Exposure* invites readers to *do* something, to get involved in the life of the region, not just admire it.

A similar activist ethic informs *New Roots*, a bimonthly magazine published in the *Valley Advocate's* home turf of western Massachusetts. *New Roots*, as the magazine's masthead puts it, "celebrates the Northeast as a unique cultural and geographic region," enlisting, among others, writers from the *Advocate* newspapers and *Maine Times* to do it. The magazine combines regional reportage ("Who Owns New England's Farms?)" with advocacy of solar and other alternative forms of power for an energy-starved region largely dependent on outside sources of fuel. The message of *New Roots* is that appropriate technology and cooperative enterprise can revitalize the historic but hurting Northeast.

Across the continent, in northern California, an occasional publication called *Raise the Stakes* takes regional identity to its logical political conclusion: separatism. Publisher Peter Berg assails what he terms the "global monoculture . . . that methodically reproduces itself in fast food chains, advertising images, freeways, and industrial-designed environments." In addition to publishing *Raise the Stakes*, Berg employs an imaginative form of communication he calls "bundles." Issued under the auspices of the Planet Drum Foundation, Berg's bundles focus attention on a given bioregion—the Rocky Mountains, for example—by furnishing a map of the area, plus transcribed conversations with environmental activists, wall posters listing animal species native to the region, poems and broadsides—all printed on separate pieces of paper in different sizes, shapes, and colors. By making use of this flexible, unpredictable form, Berg's media work begins to approximate the *aliveness* of the ecological processes it is intended to describe.

Berg believes the uniqueness of each bioregion can best be protected from outside government and business depredations by declaring them independent. As such, his publications support nearly every political separatist group in the world. "Separatist groups differ like species of plants and animals, or the natural regions where they occur," Berg writes. "They are the closest political manifestations to the unrepentant diversity of the biosphere itself and they persist like any native thing." Planet Drum has published books by Berg (*Reinhabiting a Separate Country*) and former *Village Voice* writer Michael Zwerin (*Devolutionary Notes*) that seriously propose separatism as a political alternative to the highly centralized nation-state.

This approach could be read as narrow and sectarian—the *old* provincialism, in short—if Berg didn't have a unifying ecological vision. "I think we can have roots in particular places, although our heads are everywhere," Berg offered. What his polemics ultimately point to is a type of world federalism, with each region retaining its identity while cooperating on large-scale issues—pollution of the oceans, say. This makes Berg something of a latter-day Jeffersonian, an identity he shares with several other writer-publishers.

A rough equivalent of Berg's thinking appeared in fiction in 1975, when *Film Quarterly* editor Ernest Callenbach self-published his futuristic novel, *Ecotopia*. *Ecotopia* (the title is a combination of the words ecology and utopia) was rejected by twenty mainstream publishers who told Callenbach, "the ecology fad is over." He proved them wrong. Callenbach sold 37,000 copies of the book through publicity in the alternative media and by word of mouth. In 1977, Bantam Books issued a mass-market paperback edition of *Ecotopia*, a fiction rooted in the real-life social experimentation of the Pacific Northwest.

Ecotopia traces the adventures of a New York City reporter who visits the new nation of Ecotopia—northern California, Oregon, and Washington—after it secedes from the United States in the 1980s to form an ecologically attuned society. As the cynical reporter explores the new nation's nonpolluting public transportation, war games for channeling aggression, cooperative business, its citizens' high regard for nature, and their decentralized, noncoercive form of government, he is won over. In the end, the reporter abandons his job, trading his assignment for a new life.

Ecotopia is at times awkwardly written fiction, but Callenbach's ideas excited readers interested in their real-life applications. Eugene, Oregon, proclaimed an "Ecotopia Day," as civic leaders extolled bicycles, trees, and renewable sources of energy. In Eureka, California, local craftworkers built an Ecotopian school where Callenbach's humanistic vision of education could be put into practice. Ecotopia's influence was, finally, felt as far away from its Northwest setting as New York, where WBAI radio broadcast readings of the entire 167-page book on two occasions.

A more literary approach to a new provincial sensibility can be found in Ishmael Reed and his partner Al Young, proprietors of Y'Bird Press in Berkeley. Reed's connection with alternative media goes back to 1965, when he helped plan publication of the *East Village Other*. Reed left *EVO* early on to write novels, experiencing immediate success with books such as *The Freelance Pallbearers* and *Yellowback Radio Broke Down*, for major publishers.

But Reed wasn't satisfied. Feeling he was a token black writer in the white world of letters, and convinced that New York's domination of publishing was forestalling the development of a diverse, democratic American literature, Reed moved to the West Coast. He teamed with Young in 1971 to start Yardbird Press. (The name was changed to Y'Bird after a falling out with business partners in 1977.) Reed and Young published several book-length anthologies, consisting mainly of minority writers, most of them from the West Coast and other points far from the true north of mainstream publishing in Manhattan. The anthologies were well received, eliciting praise from the *New York Times* and winning two Pushcart Press Awards for small-press publishing.

In 1979, Y'Bird published a book consisting entirely of work by California writers dating from the eighteenth century to the present. The book, *Calafia*, was named after the mythic black queen of California. *Calafia* blended Reed's interest in regional writing with his concern with invoking a multicultural mosaic to succeed the old American ideal of the Melting Pot. Operating Y'Bird, Reed figured, would serve the dual purpose of promoting multicultural art and decentralizing publishing:

> I travel all around, and I see a lot of manuscripts that some editors never see. And the thing you find out is that talent is common. A lot of New Yorkers put down other writing, because there's fierce competition in this industry, you know. So you can't go around telling everybody that there's this guy in Lawrence, Kansas, who can write too. I mean, the Southwest is very different from the Northeast, the

Southeast is very different from the Northwest. There's all kinds of cultures going on.

While Reed didn't second Peter Berg's proposal of political separatism as a solution for cultural centrism, his comment underscores the belief characteristic of all new provincial media: the conviction that there is value in diversity and worth in local and regional identities. Far from being esoteric, this belief is deeply embedded in the American grain and shared by residents of all parts of the country. It makes strange bedfellows of people who would otherwise barely speak to one another.

In 1976, amid an atmosphere which people on the scene later likened to an old-fashioned barn-raising, a broad spectrum of community people in Grand Rapids, Minnesota, pitched in to raise the transmission tower of a listener-sponsored radio station. KAXE-FM promised to be a left-of-center station, yet it was partially funded by the local Rotary Club. The Kiwanis Club donated money too, as did the Chippewa Indian nation. These diverse donors were united on perhaps only one thing: they wanted a local, open-access radio station, and they were willing to help make that station a reality.

KAXE was founded by Suzi McClear, a native Minnesotan, and her husband, Rich McClear, who hailed from New Jersey. The McClears were able to attract such a broad base of support because they believed that access to the station by a cross-section of local people was both necessary and desirable. "If we didn't put some conservatives on the board [of directors]," Rich McClear said, "then we really weren't a community radio station. Senior citizens, Native Americans, and far-right conservatives are as disenfranchised from the national media as anyone."

Broadcasting with a powerful 100,000 watts, KAXE's signal comes in loud and clear up to sixty miles from Grand Rapids, near the Canadian border. "Northern Community Radio," as the station bills itself, has become a strong cultural force in the area. KAXE sponsors live peformances of local musicians and airs programming on the diverse ethnic enclaves in the state, such as the Russian Orthodox community. Announcers are local people who often speak with strong Iron Range accents which the station management makes no effort to change. Rich McClear, who has experience in commercial radio in New York, said, "I don't like people to sound like radio announcers. Ours don't, and they're good." McClear defined the purpose of the station as ". . . rebuilding community. There's a strong feeling of self-reliance here in northern Minnesota. We are part of that. People are discovering that they have talent, that they can do it, and that we can share our very worthwhile heritage."

Few community FM stations can equal KAXE's 100,000 watts, but all of them match KAXE in their dedication to local community. KOTO, in Telluride, Colorado, operates on all of 10 watts. Small though it is, KOTO has proven its importance to the community, which awarded the station municipal funds to go on the air in 1974. In return, the station carries all City Council meetings live.

KOTO and KAXE are among the nearly sixty members of the National Federation of Community Broadcasters (NFCB), an organization formed at an alternative radio conference in Madison, Wisconsin, in 1975. The NFCB, which admits only noncommercial stations with clear commitments to access by community people, exists to share information and otherwise further the interests of community radio. To this end, the organization maintains a national office and lobbying arm in Washington, D.C.

NFCB stations (which include the established Pacifica outlets) view themselves as alternatives not only to commercial radio, but to the federally funded National Public Radio (NPR) network as well. George Stoney, codirector of the Alternative Media Center at New York University, has said that the ease of public access to community stations is the main thing that distinguishes them from both commercial and public radio stations. "NPR says, 'We know what's good for you.' Community radio says, 'We want to determine ourselves what's good for us.' "

The growth of community radio stations, most of them at least partially funded by listeners' donations, accelerated rapidly during the seventies. Numbering, at most, a dozen at the beginning of the decade, community stations totaled about thirty by 1975 and nearly twice that number by 1980. Since most broadcast frequencies in or near major cities have long been taken, the growth of community radio has been chiefly in small towns and rural areas, where sophisticated programming of the type that Pacifica stations have done for years is only now beginning to be heard. Most of the new stations, while they belong to the NFCB, guard their independence zealously. Attempts by the NFCB's Washington office to coordinate national and regional planning are watched closely by members stations for signs of incipient centralization and bureaucracy. That may signal an overraction by some members, but it is indicative of their first priority: service to their own communities, in their own way.

Independent filmmakers released several important films with regional themes in the late sixties and seventies. Most of them were documentaries, but one key film was feature-length fiction. The filmmakers' purposes, like their styles and choice of subjects, varied greatly. Some were content to make melancholy records of disappearing regional cultures, while others actively sought to rekindle regional pride and identity, and, with it, a still-simmering sense of social justice.

Les Blank is a documentarian who began his career making industrial films for corporate clients. In the late sixties, he gave it up in order to film evocative documentaries about regional cultures that have somehow survived in the margins of the industrial world. Since the late sixties, Blank has made films about the backwoods culture of black Louisiana Cajuns, the Texas-Mexican musicians of south Texas, the rhythm-and-blues subculture of New Orleans, and blues musicians Lightnin' Hopkins and Mance Lipscomb. Blank's profiles of individual musicians focus as much on the cultures of which the musicians are a part as on the musicians themselves; it's Blank's way of showing that the human being and his or her culture are indivisible.

Blank has a passion to record these cultures before they are absorbed into the monoculture—a process, he reported, that is well underway: "One of the hardest parts of making these films is asking people to turn off the TV and talk about their own cultures. It's really sad." Blank's work maps the inroads that modern society has made into regional cultures even as it celebrates the vibrancy of what remains: communal feasts, work, parties, humor, and earthy wisdom. Much of the quiet philosophizing in Blank's films comes from the people his camera catches in the act of exchanging—often reluctantly—one way of life for another. A black Cajun woman in his film *Dry Wood* tells the camera:

When I was younger, I thought it was a great thing to be on earth and be alive, because you knew the meaning of every day. . . . When it was a holiday, we used to get together at my grandmother's house. She'd cook in a big washpot outside under the trees. We'd hang some meat in front of the fireplace and we'd just sit down and talk, talk about life. But now we don't have time to do that no more. Now life is too fast. . . . As the children grow up, there's no jobs, nothing for them to do. They're leaving, one by one.

The subtle sociology in Blank's films—made with foundation grants when he can get them, loans, investors' money, and his pay from filming TV commercials—have been well received by film reviewers and by

Novelist Ishmael Reed left New York for California and became a publisher himself to counter the centralization of power in American publishing. (Photo by Dave Patrick.)

Independent filmmaker Les Blank lives and works with the people whose lives he documents, such as these Chicano musicians in Texas. (Photo courtesy of Flower Films.)

much tougher critics as well: the people the films are about. Blank routinely screens his work in union halls, churches, social clubs, and bars, incorporating many viewers' suggestions during and after filming into the finished films. Blank does not live permanently among the people whose lives he documents, nor are his films overtly political. But Blank's work, powerfully democratic and decentralist, identifies him as a new provincial.

Other alternative media activists turned out explicitly political films during the seventies which shared Blank's respect for the dignity of the films' subjects, but rejected the resignation implicit in his work—the feeling that, despite their great music, great food, and great talk, nothing can be done to save these beautiful losers. Radical filmmakers such as Ciné Manifest used the film medium to convey a very different message. In 1976, the San Francisco-based Ciné Manifest group journeyed to North Dakota to film *Prairie Fire*, a documentary on a turn-of-the-century populist organization called the Nonpartisan League. Despite their acknowledged leftist politics, Ciné Manifest was funded, in part, by the state of North Dakota, which was eager to reclaim a nearly forgotten part of its history. When Ciné Manifest showed *Prairie Fire* around the state, the film sparked memories of the Nonpartisan League among descendants of the original organizers.

Ciné Manifest worked simultaneously on a fictionalized dramatization of the Nonpartisan League, called *Northern Lights*. Director Rob Nilsson was a young Californian whose grandfather had been active in the league back in North Dakota. Casting only three professional actors, Nilsson and his colleagues teamed them with nonprofessionals from the farms and small towns in the area. Many of the amateur actors were also descendants of league members. The result was an elegiac black-and-white film that effectively evokes the Scandinavian immigrant culture and stark beauty of the Northern Great Plains. In 1979, *Northern Lights*, made on a budget of just over $300,000, won a coveted Golden Camera award at the Cannes film festival and earned limited theatrical distribution.

Although the era depicted in *Northern Lights* (and in *Prairie Fire*) is distant, the lack of control over their markets which spurred farmers to join the Nonpartisan League remains, and the type of collective political action they took could happen again. Rob Nilsson was candid about hoping that *Northern Lights* would have precisely that effect. "I hope the film moves people to be resistant, rebellious," Nilsson said, "not to put up with business as usual, but to stand up and create new forms of cooperation rather than competition. I don't want it to be sentimental. I want it to be a film for people to promote political and social change."

Bringing about social change on a regional scale is the express purpose of a multimedia collective in Whiteburg, Kentucky, called Appalshop (short for Appalachian Film Workshop). Cofounder William Richardson described Appalshop as "the only show in town for 13 to 15 million people in Appalachia who are totally unrepresented in the media." Appalshop was one of eight regional film projects set up by the federal Office of Economic Opportunity in 1969. When federal officials saw the challenging films Appalshop was making, the organization's funding was cut off, but Appalshop persevered without federal money.

The project has made some two dozen films, many of them highly partisan. Appalshop's most powerful work, an hour-long film called *Buffalo Creek Mining Disaster*, released in 1975, documents a dam break in West Virginia in 1972 which wiped out fifteen towns and 5,000 homes, injured some 3,000 people, and killed 125 more. Appalshop's documentary charged Pittston Oil, the company that maintained the dam, with negligence in the disaster. *Buffalo Creek*, which took three years to finish and was made on a budget of only $7,000, was shown to the West Virginia State Legislature during an official investigation of the dam break. Selections of the film were also aired nationally on PBS-TV.

"Our political films are our bestsellers," Richardson said. "People love'em, they want to see good, solid economic, social, and political films about the region."

Appalachia was the scene of a major development in American media during the 1950s, when cable television was developed to bring TV reception to remote parts of the mountaineous region, where over-the-air broadcasting proved impossible. Since then, cable systems have been established in all parts of the United States (20 percent of American homes had cable service in 1980), often offering programming too specialized or too challenging for network TV.

Alternative media activists saw the sheer number of channels in cable systems—up to forty channels each, all in need of programming—as providing their best chance to gain access to the country's most pervasive and influencial medium. Minimizing the ownership of many cable systems by media giants such as Time, Inc., Some activists believed that alternative programming transmitted over local cable systems would spark a revolution in American television.

So far, however, cable TV has been considerably less than revolutionary. Under FCC regulations formulated in 1972, cable systems with more than 3,500 subscribers had to provide unused channels and production equipment, at their own expense, to community groups. However, those regulations were declared invalid by the Supreme Court in 1979. Even publicly owned cable systems have pulled back somewhat from their commitments to public access in the wake of the Supreme Cout ruling.

The few public-access channels that have been developed and maintained have created openings for social-change groups to put their work before the public from time to time. One such organization is Marin Community Video (MVC), founded in 1973 to bring grassroots television to Marin County, just across the Golden Gate Bridge from San Francisco.

According to former MVC director Ray Rodney, the project was started . . . "to make TV responsible to people and usable by people in a community context. TV, in its commercial form, is a waste of a tremendous resource." The nonprofit MVC teaches production skills to community residents and provides production assistance to local schools. In Rodney's opinion, failure to teach children weaned on commercial TV how to make their own TV programs "is like teaching kids how to read but not how to write."

Young people wth access to MVC's equipment have produced a number of videotapes: for example, a program on unemployed youths produced by unemployed teenagers themselves and funded by a CETA grant. The MVC staff has also made tapes on social problems in Marin, a beautiful, generally affluent county which, incongruously, includes San Quentin Prison. "Inside San Quentin," a 90-minute color tape by MVC, was a video veritélook at the bureaucracy and barely supressed violence of the prison. Shown locally on cable TV and on public television, the tape was an effective counterweight to the "mellow" image of Marin usually transmitted by other media.

Appalshop is also active in cable TV. In addition to making films and tapes *about* the people of Appalachia, Appalshop teaches local people how to make films and videotapes themselves. "A bread and butter task of ours is to record and preserve parts of the region that we feel are real," said William Richardson, "and teaching local people to do media work is a good way to do that." Appalshop staffers hope their efforts will help correct damaging "hillbilly" images in the mass media and serve as antidotes to the homogenization of regional culture by conventional media, especially network TV.

Appalshop also swaps videotapes with Broadside TV of Johnson City, Tennessee. Between those two alternative media projects, local people are able to view—and in some cases participate in—shows depicting traditional mountain culture, such as healing with herbs and the telling of tall tales. Frequently the old stories, such as the Br'er Rabbit tales, are told by elderly people, a group usually ignored by national commercial media. By using the latest communications technology in a democratic way, Appalshop and Broadside TV preserve the oldest of all "media," the oral tradition, in hopes that that cultural circle will be unbroken.

For some alternative media activists, however, petitioning for access to local cable systems just isn't enough. In Los Angeles in 1974, video activists established a viewer-sponsored TV station. Their purpose was to broadcast to the entire city, airing programming which they, themselves, selected, and which they would show without commercial interruption for as long as they chose. KVST (Viewer-Sponsored Television), Channel 68, also hoped to teach technical skills to local people, encouraging the community to produce its own programming. Kim Weir, who worked at the station, explained: "[Commercial] TV controls the way people are represented. It takes them out of their element and into traditional programming structure. People have a very good instinct that commercial media are not out to help them. They're thrust into high pressure situations . . . where they don't feel comfortable."

Unfortunately for the activists who hoped to change that state of affairs, KVST was plagued by poor transmission and other technical difficulties and was perceived by the city's large Mexican-American community as an essentially "Anglo" project—and thus off limits to Chicanos. Moreover, as veterans of the experience reported, KVST staffers never focused clearly on whom they wanted to address and what they wanted the station to say. KVST went off the air in December 1975, after only a year and a half of programming.

KVST, Appalshop's videotapes and films, *Northern Lights, Ecotopia,* the *Valley Advocate,* the *Mendocino Grapevine*'s work with United Stand—the media that succeeded, and the media that didn't—shared a determination to empower geographical communities of which they were integral parts. This was was their common ground—not leftist, liberal, or rightist politics, mutually exclusive categories into which the new provincial media did not fit comfortably. When the *Grapevine* stood against restrictive housing codes, it was both radical and conservative—conservative because the paper championed individual rights, self-reliance, and resistance to centralized authority; radical because it also challenged the basis of industrial society: enforced standardization.

It is tempting to label new provincial media as nostalgic. Peter Berg's advocacy of separatism sounds backward—a pining for the good old days when every tribe had its verdant summer meadow. But just when that temptation presents itself. Berg or other new provincials remind us that their vision is futuristic and planetary as well as ancient and local: "We can be rooted in particular places, although our heads are everywhere." The new provincial media are, then, both forward-and backward-looking, radical and conservative, and, above all, American. They speak from and to a basic part of the national heritage when they talk of local control and regional identity.

At about the same time that the new provincial media were putting down new roots, the era of another kind of alternative media—also promoting empowerment—was beginning. These media were rooted in communities of interest rather than in particular locations. Feminist and gay media, based on gender rather than geography, took as their territory the lightly explored regions of sexuality.

ten

Sexual Politics

ONE OF THE FIRST and most significant feminist newspapers, a monthly called *off our backs*, began publication in Washington, D.C., in early 1970. The paper's name had a double meaning: It signified the end of sexual passivity by women and announced a determination to end unjust social systems everywhere by getting the oppressors off the backs of the oppressed. "We seek," read the paper's founding statement, "through the liberation of women, the liberation of all peoples." *Off our backs* exemplified radical feminist media. It was militant, internationalist, nonprofit, collectively operated, and written almost entirely by nonprofessionals—women from all walks of life with something to say.

The second wave of American feminist media of which *off our backs* was a part followed by nearly a century the historic efforts of Susan B. Anthony and Elizabeth Cady Stanton's *The Revolution* and suffragist publications like the *Woman's Journal*. Founded to subvert the sugar-and-spice images of women in popular magazines such as *Godey's Lady's*

Casey Czarnik rolls the presses at Diana Press, one of dozens of feminist publishing houses that sprang up in the late sixties. Off our backs was one of the first and most respected women's newspapers. (Photo by Kay Radditz. Cover courtesy of off our backs.)

Book (coedited, for 41 years, by the author of "Mary Had a Little Lamb") and to jolt the abolitionist and labor movements into taking women's rights seriously, such publications sowed the seeds of media which blossomed in remarkable number and variety in this century.

Like their predecessors, alternative media activists found demeaning sterotypes of women in general and lesbians in particular in the mass media. Homosexual men fared no better. Even supposedly radical underground media seemed unresponsive to the demands of newly awakening women's and gay liberationists. The solution, for activists schooled in the antiwar and civil rights movements, seemed obvious: start media of their own.

In the ensuing decade, the history of feminist media and the media of lesbian feminists and gay men inspired by the women's movement closely paralleled that of other alternative media: There developed a creative core of radical outlets, limited in resources but significant in influence, from which have come the fundamental values of sexual liberation; "bridge" media, such as *Ms.* magazine, which transmit diluted feminist ideas to a broader public; and purely commercial attempts at co-optation by periodicals such as *Savvy* ("The Magazine for Executive Women") and *Self*.

The most authentically alternative media efforts are those that attempt to reassess basic ideas about human beings, asking: What is a woman? What is a man? What are the varieties of sexual experience, and how do they interrelate with social values? How can sex roles be revamped to make them fluid and equitable?

Attempts to answer such complex questions necessarily take many forms, but common to all feminist, lesbian-feminist, and gay media are the quest for authentic identity and the overriding goal of empowerment. As do other alternative media, they provide not only information but also confirmation, enabling sexual radicals to shape their future and reclaim their past.

Modern feminist media began symbolically in 1965, when two white women activists, Mary King and Casey Hayden, wrote what they called "a kind of memo" and mailed it off to other women "in the peace and freedom movements." The subject of King and Hayden's memo was the status—or, rather, lack of it—of women in movement politics. In their memo, King and Hayden observed uncomfortably that women, like blacks, seem to be caught in a common-law caste system that operates, some-times subtly, forcing them to work around or outside hierarchial structures of power which may exclude them. Women seem to be placed in the same position of assumed subordination in personal situations too. It is a caste system which, at its worst, uses and exploits women.

. . . Having learned from the movement to think radically about the personal work and abilities of people whose role in society has gone unchallenged before, a lot of women in the movement have begun to apply those lessons to their own relationships with men. Each of us probably has her own story of the various results.

King and Hayden's paper received wide circulation among female activists, many of whom agreed with its insights. A month after the two activists mailed their memo, a group of women walked out of the national convention of Students for a Democratic Society. The following spring, the paper was reprinted in *Liberation*, where it attracted more attention and served as a radical complement to Betty Friedan's influential book *The Feminine Mystique*, published in 1963.

Throughout the middle sixties, emerging feminists worked within the radical leftist media, advocating what they saw as a revolution within the revolution—the liberation of women. A few underground outlets were sympathetic, providing space and airtime for feminist views. In 1970, *Win* devoted an issue to the women's movement, while women at Liber-ation News Service at about the same time sponsored a "radical women's conference" to address problems of sexism—inequitable treatment on the basis of gender within the movement media. Even *Ramparts,* preoc-cupied with romantic guerrilla actions in the late sixties, opened its pages in 1971 to an influential essay by Susan Griffin—previously a *Ramparts* staffer—on rape. Griffin's article provided the first analysis of a rape as a crime of violence, not of passion, created and sanctioned by a sexist society as a crime against all women. Griffin's piece laid the theoretical groundwork for Susan Brownmiller's landmark book on the subject, *Against Our Will*.

Feminists also established toeholds in other underground media. At New York's WBAI radio, Nanette Rainone, a volunteer programmer who later became the station's program director, started a program called "CR" (for consciousness-raising). Although most male staffers were critical of the program, "CR" was warmly received by female listeners, who were surprised and pleased to find a program on the radio that spoke directly to their lives. A typical "CR" show featured a discussion of popular topics such as marriage and divorce, culled from edited tapes of consciousness-raising group sessions and followed by telephoned comments from listeners which were broadcast live, turning WBAI into a medium for conducting citywide electronic teach-ins on sexism.

The underground media—despite the occasional cooperation of WBAI, *Ramparts*, and a few others—were not much more receptive to feminism than were the mass media. At the New York underground paper *Rat*, women staffers, incensed by the paper's reliance on pornographic ads and sensationalist covers, ejected editor Jeff Shero and took over the paper. The first women's issue of *Rat*, published in January of 1970, included a scathing essay by poet and journalist Robin Morgan which immediately became a classic of feminist polemics. Entitled "Goodbye to All That," Morgan's furious declamation ran down a lengthy list of complaints against men in the New Left and the counterculture that took on aspects of a magical chant of exorcism:

> Goodbye to the inaccurate use of the phrase "male chauvinism." Male chauvinism in an ATTITUDE—male supremecy is the OBJECTIVE REALITY. . . . Goodbye to the Conspiracy who, when lunching with fellow sexist bastards Norman Mailer and Terry Southern in a bunny-type club in Chicago, find Judge Hoffman at the neighboring table—no surprise: IN THE LIGHT, THEY ARE ALL THE SAME.
>
> Goodbye to Hip Culture, and the so-called Sexual Revolution, which has functioned toward women's freedom as did the Reconstruction toward former slaves—reinstituted oppression by another name . . .
>
> Let it all hang out. Let it seem bitchy, dykey, catty, frustrated, crazy, . . . nutty, frigid, ridiculous, bitter, embarrassing, man-hating, libelous, pure, unfair, envious, intuitive, low-down, stupid, petty, liberating. We are the women that men have warned us about.

Morgan went on to fame as the editor of *Sisterhood Is Powerful*, an influential anthology of feminist writings—most of them drawn from the underground and women's press—published by Random House later that year. *Rat* published for another three years in an attempt to meld a leftist and feminist approach to sexual politics—but without Morgan and other staffers who felt that women's media should focus fully on women's issues, not on a leftist vision propounded by women. Rooted in that conviction, radical feminists, in the underground media tradition, set off to establish media of their own.

The second wave of American feminism proved to be a highly literate and prolific movement. Between March 1968 and August 1973, according to Ann Mather in the scholarly magazine *Journalism History*, "more than 560 feminist publications appeared in the United States alone. . . . The majority of the American feminist publications were newsletters, although there were also 60 newspapers, nine newspaper/magazines, and 72 magazines and journals. They appeared in all but seven states."

The new women's periodicals bore names that reflected flair and determination: *It Ain't Me Babe; The Furies; Tooth and Nail; Battle Acts; Amazon Quarterly; No More Fun and Games; Women: A Journal of Liberation; Up From Under.* Most of these quickly published and perished, unable to survive changes in the movement and its media, but early feminist publications served the purpose of providing the emerging women's movement with reliable sources of information and put women in different parts of the country in touch with each other. This was particularly true of women's newspapers, which raced to cover and promote the expanding movement—often in an angry, confrontational style reminiscent of early underground papers.

The first feminist newspaper was the Berkeley-based *It Ain't Me Babe.* Staffed by female veterans of the New Left, *It Ain't Me Babe* was a broadly political paper which identified and supported women all over the world, especially those in national liberation movements (such as that in Vietnam) and socialist countries (Cuba and China). *It Ain't Me Babe* fused the anger of early feminism with the energy and hope of international revolution, associating aggression and war with "male culture." The front page of the paper's first issue, dated January 15, 1970, was devoted to a discussion of karate for self-defense. Several months later, when the U.S. invaded Cambodia, *It Ain't Me Babe* ran a cover illustration depicting Richard Nixon, with a missile for a phallus, raping Cambodian women and children. Although it was published for less than a year, *It Ain't Me Babe* exemplified the spirit of feminist broadsides.

Off our backs, which started only six weeks after its West Coast counterpart, shared the latter's anger, energy, and internationalism. Founded by New Left veterans such as Coletta Reid, Marlene Wicks, and Marilyn Webb, a former writer for The *Guardian, off our backs (oob)* published a centerspread on the history of International Working

Women's Day in its first issue. The new paper's global coverage was balanced by excellent local and national reporting. News stories about Betty Friedan's testimony against Harold Carswell—a Nixon Supreme Court nominee—and the beginning drive to pass the Equal Rights Amendment (ERA) fleshed out *oob's* first twelve-page issue.

The *off our backs* staff collective considered humanistic politics some-things to apply in the operation of the paper, not just material for the editorial pages. In its second number, the staff explained the lateness of the issue by confiding that Marilyn Webb and Coletta Reid had both given birth to daughters the preceding week "Unlike most male-dominated enterprises, we are happy and willing to meet the human needs of our staff."

Functioning harmoniously and collectively was easier said than done, however. The original *oob* staff split along lines of experience versus amateurism and residual leftist politics versus the nascent lesbianism of some staffers. Toward the end of 1970, Webb was asked to leave the paper. "Partly this was because I had been a key founder of the paper, I was told, and thus had tremendous power," she remembered. *Off our backs* also lost five of its twelve members shortly after Webb's explusion, when lesbian staffers decided to set up independent media enterprises to explore the lesbian experience. (Lesbian-feminist media are explored later in this chapter.) *oob* was shaken by the split, but the paper survived.

Off our backs has gone on to become the most widely respected newspaper of the women's movement. Subtitled *A Women's News Journal*, *oob* is generally accurate, well researched, and fair, despite its obvious parti-sanship. The paper's quality and national circulation prompted Kirsten Grimstad and Susan Rennie, coeditors of *The New Women's Survival Catalog*—a commercially published resource guide to feminist alternatives—to describe *off our backs* in 1973 as "The *New York Times* of the Women's Movement. *Oob* was the first feminist paper (and one of the first papers of any kind) to report the torture of women prisoners of war in South Vietnam. It was also the first to publish Jane Alpert's mani-festo, "Mother Right," in which Alpert, a former *Rat* staffer and radical leftist who had gone underground to escape bombing charges, aston-ished her former comrades by denouncing the chauvinism of the "male left" and committing herself to feminism.

Following *off our backs* and *It Ain't Me Babe*, feminist newspapers were born throughout the country in the early and middle seventies. There was *Ain't I a Woman*, a lesbian-feminist paper published in the heartland of Middle America: Iowa City, Iowa; New York City had *Majority*

Report; in Los Angeles, there were *Sister* and *The Lesbian Tide;* Denver had *Big Mama Rag;* feminists in Rochester, New York, started *New Women's Times;* in the San Francisco area a $1500 grant from the *Whole Earth Catalog* helped a group of radical women begin publication of *Plexus.* There were many others.

Such papers were essential links in feminist and lesbian-feminist communities starved for information that seldom passed through the mass media unaltered by a nonfeminist (even an antifeminist) vision. The commitment of feminist newspapers to women's issues sometimes re-sulted in early reports of news of critical importance to women. Ann Arbor, Michigan's *Herself,* for example, reported on the cancer-causing properties of DES—the hormone used in "morning-after" pills—before such dangers were widely publicized in the mass media. In 1973, *Herself* also unearthed news of fetal damage from X-rays and reported on new techniques in breast biopsy, stories picked up later that same year and passed on to larger audiences by *Ms.*

Feminist newspapers were nearly all collectively edited and produced, bringing their internal structures into line with their democratic vision. Feminists, then and now, associated hierarchies and competition with what they termed "patriarchal culture" and determined to avoid them in their own work. At today's *off our backs,* each member of the collective is responsible for editing and laying out one page of the paper. *Plexus* assigns small "task forces" to each phase of production (typesetting, layout, editing, and so on), with the overall direction of the paper determined by the staff as a whole. At *Big Mama Rag,* all copy is read and evaluated by the staff collective prior to publication. Some feminist periodicals also print financial statements, sharing with constitutents information that is usually off limits to readers.

By sharing power among staff members and information among readers, feminists infuse their media with the alternative message of empowerment. Having left the New Left because they felt that a socialist revolution, if successful, would only exchange one group of male rulers for another, feminists determined to operate their own media in an essentially anarchistic fashion. As an outgrowth of that policy, there were supposed to be no stars in feminist media—only low-profile leaders validated by and responsible to their colleagues. Building community, rather than reinforcing individuality, was and is the purpose of feminist media.

By the middle and late seventies, feminists had established communi-ties in which women determined their own values, sometimes in concert with men, often without them. Such "woman-identified" communities boasted their own coffeehouses, restaurants, bars, galleries, crisis centers, and bookstores—more than a hundred of them, according to Polly Joan and Andrea Chessman's *Guide to Women's Publishing*. Together, they comprised an embryonic but distinctive women's culture, a feminist body politic in which feminist media served as synapses, relaying essential information to their public.

Feminist media activists in radio, video and film, while they have yet to achieve the pervasiveness of women's print media, have made important contributions to the alternative women's culture.

The now-defunct Feminist Radio Network (FSN), for example, was founded in the early seventies to do on a national scale what Nanette Rainone had done for women in New York: give exposure to feminist ideas that were otherwise missing from the airwaves. The FSN set up a tape exchange program, enabling locally produced programs on subjects such as antirape actions and interviews with feminist leaders to find larger nationwide audiences.

In 1977, Marlene Edmunds, a worker at Zodiac News Service—a source of short items for radio stations and newspapers—started a women's news service she dubbed Her Say, to disseminate news from a feminist perspective to alternative and mainstream outlets alike. By 1980, Her Say, owned and staffed entirely by women, had one hundred radio subscribers, in addition to magazines such as *Ms.* and *Mother Jones*.

The surge of interest in video that marked the late sixties and early seventies moved feminist media activists to become involved in the new medium. Video Women, a collective of New York feminists, was started to record feminist conferences and produce interviews with individual women on topics such as sex and marriage. Video Women's documentaries were complemented in the late seventies by the work of woman videomakers such as Kim Ecclesine, whose tapes dramatize fictitious but true-to-life situations. In a series of tapes called "Work Vignettes," Ecclesine focuses on the demeaning character of women's work. In one scenario, the camera steadily records an "interview" in which a woman seated behind a desk rattles off her impressive credentials (an advanced university degree, years of work-related experience) only to pull away at the last moment to show the woman—a secretary, not, as the viewer has supposed, an executive—literally chained to her male boss' coffeepot.

Feminist video retains its exciting educational potential, but it has not been fully developed artistically and put before large audiences. Independent women filmmakers have done somewhat better, screening their films widely on campuses, at feminist conferences, and in community centers, sometimes joining forces to distribute their work. One cooperative feminist effort (and one of the few that occasionally works with men) is the Columbus, Ohio-based New Day Films.

Like many alternative media ventures, New Day Films was born of necessity. The roots of the project go back to 1971, when filmmakers Julia Reichert and Jim Klein completed a film called *Growing Up Female*. *Growing Up Female* viewed the socialization of women through the lives of six females, ages 6 to 34, who talked about their lives and allowed the camera to follow them in their encounters with parents, teachers, guidance counselors, boyfriends, and husbands. The result was a revealing but slow-paced film with little of the visual pyrotechnics that commercial distributors and exhibitors look for. No established distributor throught highly of *Growing Up Female* as a drawing card, nor would any distributor grant rental discounts to women's and community groups, as Reichert and Klein wanted. So the filmmakers decided to distribute the film themselves. They even printed their own promotional posters on what Klein described as "a terrible old movement press."

Their efforts did not go unrewarded. "In 1971–1972," Reichert recalled, "we were getting thirty to forty bookings a month, but that was Harvard, Brandeis, Vassar, and women's centers. The next year, we started noticing Y's and churches, nursing schools, technical schools." Encouraged by this response, and convinced that filmmakers benefited by controlling the business end of filmmaking themselves, Reichert and Klein teamed wih feminist filmmakers Amalie Rothschild and Liane Brandon in 1972 to form New Day Films as a distribution co-op. The four filmmakers put together packages of films for audience discussion, eventually including *Men's Lives* (examined later in this chapter)—a film made by and for men—which they considered a profeminist film.

Whenever possible, the New Day filmmakers would accompany their films to screenings. Reichert described the experience as "exciting," adding, "I'd show a series of films and afterwards we'd talk about the films and the local situation. You'd see people groping and excited— women who hadn't met before talking for hours and then deciding to meet again. Consciousness-raising groups, women's centers, and all kinds of activities around the country started with film being a catalyzing force."

It was this involvement with the constituency for their films, fully as much as the content of the films, that set feminist filmmakers apart from commercial producers. Viewers of feminist films didn't expect to be entertained for an evening and then go home. They saw films as tools with which to take control of their lives.

Childhood conditioning is a frequent subject for dissection in women's films, particularly lesbian-feminist films. In Jan Oxenberg's *Home Movies*, footage of Oxenberg as a child, grimacing and clutching her doll, is interspliced with work by Oxenberg as an adult which explicitly rejects the inherited sex role the child disliked. The film closes with a scene showing a group of women playing an unladylike game of football, then falling into a cozy heap, cuddling one another while (presumably heterosexual) spectators look on in stupefaction.

Although radical women, particularly lesbian feminists, angrily reject training for traditional sex roles, they express great interest in reclaiming what they regard as their authentic "herstory." Often this search takes the form of making films about women of distinction, some of them historical figures such as Gertrude Stein, others elderly but still living, such as the conductor Antonio Brico.

The women's movement's search for accomplished women of the past extends to other movements in which women have played crucial, if barely acknowledged, roles. In 1976, Julia Reichert and Jim Klein teamed with Miles Mogulesque to produce *Union Maids*, a documentary which juxtaposes historic footage of union organizing drives of the thirties with contemporary interviews with three women veterans of those days—two white, one black—who analyze their victories and defeats. *Union Maids* emphasizes that women did not constitute a mere auxiliary in labor struggles, but sometimes assumed leadership.

Lorraine Gray's *With Babies and Banners* (1978), a documentary on the 1937 sit-in at the General Motors plant in Flint, Michigan, which forced the company to recognize the fledgling United Auto Workers Union, is structured similarly and explores an identical theme. Presentive vintage footage of the Women's Emergency Brigade (WEB) marching, smashing windows to let tear gas escape from the occupied plant, and being hauled off in paddy wagons juxtaposed, with discussions of the sit-in forty years later, the film gives a stirring composite view of women's role in winning the strike. *With Babies and Banner* ends by recording a fortieth-anniversary dinner commemorating the sit-in. Noting that women are entirely absent from the speakers' rostrum, WEB veterans in attendance send up a clamor from the floor until one of their number is permitted to speak. A moving scene which comments effectively on sexism in the labor movement today, it makes *With Babies and Banners* much more than a nostalgic document.

The role of women in waging a contemporary strike is one of the prime themes of Barbar Kopple's *Harlan County USA* (1976). The Academy Award-winning documentary shows wives of striking Kentucky coal miners planning strategy and bolstering union militancy during the often-violent 1973 strike, which claimed the life of a male miner when gun-carrying vigilantes attacked a picket line.

Harlan County USA, With Babies and Banners, and *Union Maids* are not feminist films per se, but their direction and scope demonstrate the influence of the women's movement and media on other social movements. With the notable exceptions of films such as *Salt of the Earth*, traditional leftist filmmakers did not emphasize the centrality of women in the labor movement. Even the New Left filmmakers of the middle sixties seemed largely unaware of women's contributions. By fusing a femnist consciouness with labor militancy, contemporary filmmakers have taken beginning steps toward healing the breach between these two movements.

Healing, in one form or another, was the major theme of independent women's book publishing in the seventies: healing (and preventing) disease; healing psychological and emotional trauma; curing society of its poisonous attitudes toward the female majority. This healing took place on practical and mythical levels, both of which were explored in depth in feminist publishing.

The most eminently practical book to emerge from the women's movement was *Our Bodies, Ourselves*, a comprehensive self-help volume written by the Boston Women's Health Collective and originally published by the leftist New England Free Press. Since—collective members reasoned—most women knew little about the workings of their bodies, and since medical science, dominated by male physicans, "mystified" health care for power and profit, the group would demystify women's health. Collective members wrote a series of practical papers on topics such as anatomy, physiology, sexuality, birth control, pregnancy, childbirth, and the health-care establishment. The authors consulted with sympathetic health-care professionals and incorporated comments and criticisms from women who followed the advice in early drafts of the articles. Then the papers were revised, collected, and stapled into a newsprint book, 136 pages long, which sold for 75¢. The first edition was published in December 1970.

Our Bodies, Ourselves, was an immediate success, going into a number of subsequent printings, some of which sold for as little as 35¢. Readers valued the book for its wealth of practical information and its we're-all-in-this-together philosophizing. The chapter in anatomy and physiology reads; in part,

> Our society adds insult to injury by demanding that the truly "womanly" woman be soft, somewhat weak and awkward—in short, physically unfit. We contribute to this by, for example, wearing high healed shoes that keep us in our place (we can't run). Our physical limitations are more apparent than real, however, and exist today because we don't have the opportunity to defend ourselves, and men and the pressure exerted by our male-dominated society tell us what is good, what is bad (a strong woman is considered "masculine" and undesirable as a woman). We want to become physically healthy and strong and enduring, through exercise, proper eating, and training (like karate), and proud of our bodies. Proud because we feel good ourselves, not because we look good for others.

Our Bodies, Ourselves, sold 250,000 copies in its first year in print—solely on the strength of publicity in feminist and other alternative media. In 1975 the publication rights were sold to Simon and Schuster, which issued a revised and expanded edition. "Going to a capitalist publisher was one of our biggest struggles," recalled collective member Judy Norsigian, "but it was the only way to reach a mass audience."

The move was successful. By 1980, *Our Bodies, Ourselves,* had sold two million copies and been translated into thirteen foreign languages. The original collective worked with foreign feminists in the preparation of the foreign editions, earmarking the profits for feminist health projects in those countries. The group also arranged 70-percent discounts on the book for nonprofit women's health centers in the United States.

Our Bodies, Ourselves, played a crucial role in catalyzing a nationwide, grassroots women's health movement that now counts over a thousand women's clinics and health groups in the United States. Belita Cowan, executive director of the National Women's Health Network, told *New Roots,* "I truly believe *Our Bodies, Ourselves* has touched the life of every woman in the country, whether she realizes it or not. . . . It allowed a national network of groups to develop. . . . It gives women that sense of entitlement, that they have a right to know." Its voluminous sales—and, particularly, its concrete effects on women inside and outside the women's movement, on an international scale—make *Our Bodies, Ourselves,* the single most successful effort of any any kind to emerge from the alternative media.

Self-expression and self-assertion, along with the sharing of practical information, have dominated feminist book publishing. Some feminist authors have self-published their work without embarrassment, happy to have editorial and artistic control of work which male-dominated mainstream publishers—and most male-dominated small presses as well—deemed unpublishable. The San Francisco area feminist Alta printed her poetry herself on a used press in her garage, trimmed and bound her books, and sold them herself. Alta called her imprint Shameless Hussy "because that's what my mother called women she didn't approve of." Gradually, Shameless Hussy Press began publishing other women writers (and even a few men), including early work by Susan Griffin and Mary Mackay, who went on to score commercial success for Doubleday with her satirical novel *McCarthy's List* in the late seventies.

Shameless Hussy won national attention in the middle seventies by publishing Ntozake Shange's biting collection of poems, *For Colored Girls Who Have Considered Suicide When the Rainbow Is Enuf.* Reworked as a play, *For Colored Girls* was performed in New York, where it was lavishly praised. A pioneering work that put the sexual politics between black women and men under a microscope, *For Colored Girls* sparked bitter controversy in the black community over its unflattering portrayal of black men. Shange's work was one of the first fusions of black and feminist consciousness, anticipating Michele Wallace's highly publicized book, *Black Macho & the Myth of the Superwoman,* by five years.

Other feminist imprints issued books designed to be both inspiring, like *For Colored Girls,* and practical, like *Our Bodies, Ourselves.* The Feminist Press produced nonsexist children's books with titles like *Firegirl* and *My Mother the Mail Carrier*—well-received books intended to instill positive self-images in girls and show children of both sexes that inherited sex roles don't have to be passively accepted. The Feminist Press matched its concern for the future with its dedication to clarifying the past. The nonprofit company published biographies of "lost women"—accomplished women whom history has unjustly ignored— and reprinted forgotten feminist writing such as Charlotte Perkins Gilman's *The Yellow Wallpaper.* Originally published in 1892, Gilman's novel details the fate of a woman who is sent to a sanitarium to cure her melancholia when she fails to properly appreciate life as a wife and mother. By exhuming the book, The Feminist Press submitted a history lesson its editors believed had relevance for women today. Many of the Feminist Press' books are popular in college women's studies programs, where they are used as texts.

Up Press, a small, independent imprint in Palo Alto, California, carried out a similar reclamation project in 1976, when it published *The People's Bicentennial Quilt: a Patchwork History*. The book consists of a series of photographs of squares sewn by a large group of women for a cooperatively made quilt. Each square, accompanied in the book by explanatory text, represents a scene from America's radical history: the trial of Sacco and Vanzetti, the life of Sojourner Truth. Wrote Connie Young Yu in the preface, "Bea Keesey, the great-granddaughter of John Brown, stunned us all by passing around an old worn Bible the famous abolitionist carried with him on the fateful raid on Harper's Ferry. She recalled how her grandmother would look at what the school texts said about her father and write 'Not True!' on the margins." By combining historical research and the traditional women's craft of quiltmaking with publishing, the women who initiated this imaginative project gave readers a challenging, unconventional view of the American past.

Lesbian-feminist writers offered equally aggressive challenges to contemporary views of women and sexuality. The most popular fiction to emerge from the women's press was Rita Mae Brown's funny, sexy novel of a lesbian life, *Rubyfruit Jungle*. Unlike most conventional fiction, *Rubyfruit Jungle* presented lesbianism as a fact of life, not a freakish subject for exploitation. Published by Daughters, Inc., a leading feminist publishing house, and produced by women printers, *Rubyfruit* sold 70,000 copies before Bantam brought the book in 1977.

Brown's work helped undermine one of the most damaging stereotypes of the women's movement: that it had no sense of humor. So, too, did women's media enterprises such as *Wimmen's Comix*, a series of comic books drawn by female cartoonists. Although much of the humor was bleak—filled with fantasies of revenge and it-only-hurts-when-I-laugh stories about birth-control snafus and demoralizing jobs—*Wimmen's Comix* allowed women cartoonists to turn the tables on men with pointed satire and candid treatments of sex from a woman's viewpoint.

Feminist books, films, video, and radio join with women's magazines to form an information environment within which many female activists choose to live their lives. While most feminist media concentrate on getting out information about where women are and where they have been, several key periodicals—journals of politics and art—play an equally important role: that of exploring possible alternative futures from feminist points of view.

The leading feminist journals are deeply involved in the alternative women's culture—one might call it a female counterculture—into which some feminist activists have found it necessary to withdraw, to live and work with other women as a means of defining themselves and developing ideas that would later be offered to mainstream culture through the feminist media. This process has created the apparent paradox of a separatist culture that has proven influential in the culture from which it has attempted to remove itself.

Although most women activists of the seventies remained in heterosexual relationships, a significant and unspecified number of leading writers and artists agree with *Village Voice* writer Jill Johnston's dictum that "Feminism is the theory, lesbianism is the practice." Homosexuality is nothing new, of course, but telling the world about it in forthright, sophisticated terms was a daring innovation in American media. This was the province of feminist magazines of theory and experience, many of which were of specifically lesbian-feminist character.

The few lesbian publications that existed before the seventies generally published in isolation. *The Ladder*, a lesbian magazine founded in 1956, argued first for the protection of homosexual women under the law and later—as the magazine grew more sophisticated—for the rights of all women as first-class citizens not only in a legalistic sense, but as economic equals of men. *The Ladder*, featuring fiction and poetry as well as expository writing, published until 1972, when financial shortfalls finished the magazine. Although it was an important pioneering publication, most issues of *The Ladder* read like quaint tracts from another century compared to the no-holds-barred polemics of later lesbian publications such as *The Furies*.

The Furies was a lesbian-feminist offshoot of *off our backs*, founded at about the same time that other *oob* staffers left the paper to start Diana Press, a leading feminist publishing company. The Washington, D.C.-based magazine (named after the snake-haired female spirits of Greek mythology who avenged victims of unpunished crimes) began publication in January 1972. The staff included Rita Mae Brown and Charlotte Bunch, a leading writer and organizer. "To be a lesbian," Bunch wrote, "is to love oneself, woman, in a culture that denigrates and despises women, LESBIANISM THREATENS MALE SUPREMACY AT ITS CORE. When politically conscious and organized, it is central to destroying our sexist, racist, capitalist, imperialist system."

The Furies ceased publication in June 1973, but excerpts from the magazine were reprinted by Diana Press and circulated throughout the nation, where, according to *The New Women's Survival Catalog*, they "have had a profound impact on radical feminism." After leaving *The*

Furies, Charlotte Bunch helped found *Quest* Magazine and contributed articles to *Ms*. Other ex-*Furies* staffers started Olivia Records, an all-woman recording company, Diana Press, and Women in Distribution (WIND), an all-woman distributing company that carried feminist small-press titles. (WIND went bankrupt in 1979.)

The Furies set a militant, ambitious example for other lesbian periodicals, which numbered about fifteen in 1978 according to Polly Joan and Andrea Chessman. Gay women's publications stand critically apart from a society their staffs and readers feel oppresses them doubly as women and as lesbians. Some espouse a separatist society, harkening back to a prehistory, real or imagined, in which matriarchies in tune with the moon and stars ruled the earth. In their search for female archetypes, lesbian-feminist periodicals come perilously close to embracing the stereotypes of the intuitive, nurturing Earth Mother promoted by the hip counterculture and long enshrined by mystics. Lesbian media activists, in an attempt to further separate themselves from patriarchal culture, often refer to themselves in print as "wimmin" or "womyn."

Picking up the torch from *The Furies*, a magazine called *Amazon Quarterly* published well-written theoretical pieces in the middle seventies on subjects such as the nonlinear functions of the right brain (which, the magazine contended, are more prominent in women than in men), nature-based religion, and the healing arts traditionally practiced by witches, midwives, and other laywomen. *Amazon Quarterly* folded in the mid-seventies, but, like *The Furies*, it set standards of militance and quality for later feminist politics and arts journals—of which some, like *Sinister Wisdom* and *Conditions*, were lesbian-feminist periodicals, and some, like *Heresies* and *Chrysalis*, were more broadly based in the alternative women's culture.

Conditions is a quarterly journal in whose pages may be found experimental poetry, fiction, and essays, as well as thoughtful book reviews, many of them analyses of feminist-press books passed over by established periodicals. The magazine has also focused on feminist politics in articles and special issues such as a late-seventies number on black feminists, guest-edited by Barbara Smith, a black professor of psychology at Harvard. *Conditions* also published an intriguing article by Julia P. Stanley and Susan J. Wolfe on "naming—finding one's own words with which to described one's experience. In sympathetic magic, to name a thing is to know it, to enter into it. By naming their experience, feminists claim language and culture as their own.

This theme has also been explored in *Sinister Wisdom*, a quarterly journal coedited by the r·spected feminist authors Michelle Cliff and Adrienne Rich, who wrote *Of Woman Born*, a feminist study of motherhood. *Sinister Wisdom* has published science-fiction writer Joanna Russ' futuristic visions of a peaceful, democratic world run by women. The magazine has also featured feminist scholarship such as Mary Daly's investigation into the history of English words commonly used to dismiss or degrade women—the word "haggard," for example. Wrote Daly:

> Although haggard is commonly used to describe one who has a worn or emaciated appearance, this was not its original or primary meaning. Applied to a hawk, it means "untamed." So-called obsolete meanings given in Merriam-Webster include "intractable," "willful," "wanton," and "unchaste." The second meaning is "wild in appearance, as a) of the eyes; wild and staring b) of a person: WILD-EYED." Only after these meanings do we find the idea of "a worn or emaciated appearance." As a noun, haggard has an "obsolete" meaning: "an intractable person, especially: a woman reluctant to yield to wooing."

Daly's article showed how, over time, the meaning of haggard—which could originally have signified strength of character, e.g., the refusal to be wooed and "won"—has been changed into a word describing physical appearance, specifically, an ugly woman—a "hag." By digging to the root of this and other words, Daly argued, women could reclaim prejoratives as words of female identity, pride, and beauty.

Radical challenges to received reality were implicit in the name of the feminist magazine *Heresies*, while the evolution of the mundane into beauty was evoked in the name of another: *Chrysalis*. Describing itself as "a magazine of women's culture." *Chrysalis* was founded in Los Angeles in 1977 to provide a national forum for radical reassessments of art and politics. The magazine fueled the interchange between theory and practice by including in each issue a resource catalogue on such topics as holistic health, women's theater, grantsmanship, and feminist publishing. Like other magazines whose function was to examine and encourage the female counterculture, *Chrysalis* was operated on the assumption that the bodily experience of women differs markedly from that of men, and in that difference lies the germ of a uniquely female sensibility.

Chrysalis attracted 13,000 paying readers (one of the highest circulations among radical feminist periodicals) with articles on subjects such as the importance of female support networks to activists like Lillian Wald, Crystal Eastman, and Emma Goldman. *Chrysalis* helped inspire a women's support network of its own with its resource directories and evocative articles such as Kathleen Barry's analysis of Patricia Hearst's kidnaping and trial. In contrast to most media portrayals of Hearst as a "spoiled rich kid," Barry portrayed Hearst's treatment by her captors, the media, and much of the public as that of a victim—raped both physically and metaphorically—who did what she had to do to save her life. After Hearst's trial and brief incarceration, the public view of Hearst shifted much closer to Barry's *Chrysalis* analysis.

Radical feminists and their media reach the American public directly only occasionally, but, when they do, those encounters are often memorable. Long lines and extensive mass-media attention greeted feminist artist Judy Chicago's exhibit, *The Dinner Party*, when it was shown at selected museums in the late seventies, for example. An ambitious setting of ceramic plates with painted vaginal and psychological imagery meant to suggest the personal qualities of famous women of history, *The Dinner Party* drew a generally admiring response from the public even as it bitterly divided critics over whether it was art or propaganda. The challenging imagery could have been lifted intact from the pages of *Amazon Quarterly*. But it was not that late magazine that introduced uncompromising feminist art to the public; it was the mass media, attracted by the novelty and audacity of *The Dinner Party*.

This points up a deep dilemma of the feminist media culture: Despite the impressive outpouring of feminist art and thought, it is the mass media—and the "bridge" media that connect them to feminist alternative media—which decide, in effect, how much of the emerging female sensibility most Americans will encounter—and how they will encounter it. The role of these connecting media is very important, for they both introduce feminist values to mainstream culture and, by their very nature, ensure that those values are diluted. The most important bridge-media outlet is the monthly magazine *Ms.*

At its founding in 1972, *Ms.* was something new in feminist media. It was a magazine that owed more to the world of commercial publishing than to grassroots political activism. *Ms.* was bankrolled with over a million startup dollars, an enormous sum compared to the shoestring budgets of radical feminist periodicals. It was openly commercial and considered advertising both as necessary for survival and as a vehicle for transforming stereotypes of passive female consumers. The magazine was printed on slick paper with four-color covers, forgoing the homemade look of most other feminist periodicals.

There were other differences as well. *Ms.* coeditor Gloria Steinem and copublisher Pat Carbine were experienced media professionals whose contacts were invaluable in getting *Ms.* off the ground. *Ms.* debuted as a 44-page insert in *New York* magazine in December 1971. *New York* was then owned by Clay Felker, an editor at *Esquire* when Steinem published her first freelance pieces there. *New York* solicited the ads for *Ms.*'s introductory issue and paid all publishing costs—an unusual arrangement for a publication that was not a subsidiary of its benefactor. *Ms.* also snared a million-dollar investment from the Warner Communications conglomerate and a much smaller sum from Katherine Graham, publisher of the *Washington Post*. The magazine published a spring preview issue and commenced monthly publication with its July 1972 issue.

The premiere issue of *Ms.* featured a cover illustration of Wonder Woman towering many stories in the air and dashing to the rescue of a worried world. The inside front cover was given over to a Coppertone ad—the traditional bikinied blonde woman on the beach beside the trademarked terrier tugging at the briefs of an embarrassed little girl, also blonde. Several pages on, however, readers encountered a very nontraditional image of a woman worker installing new equipment, the centerpiece of a Bell Telephone ad. With that ad, *Ms.* introduced one of its recurring concerns: placing women in jobs traditionally reserved for men.

Editorially, the new magazine presented a wide range of topics: an interview with Simone de Beauvoir, articles on "getting angry," the ERA, "lesbian love and sexuality," a story by Germaine Greer on female apparel. (From the latter: "Ideally, women should not be judged by their clothes any more than men. As long as women are judged easy or provocative because of their chosen mode of dress, they are being judged as beings with significance only through their relationships with others.") The first issue of *Ms.* also amplified themes pioneered by The Feminist Press, initiating a regular feature on "Lost Women" and nonsexist "Stories for Free Children."

There were no articles on snagging and keeping a man, but there was an optimistic statement by the founders of *Ms.* about the magazine's goal of serving as an organizing and outreach resource for the women's movement. It was a long way from *Ladies' Home Journal* and like-minded women's magazines, in which women were seen as wives and mothers primarily and independent persons and political beings not at all.

The early *Ms.* came close to meeting its goal of being the connective tissue in the feminist body politic. There were numerous reports from grassroots women's organizations, articles on abortion and the effects of

LORIA STEINEM
N HOW
OMEN VOTE

ONEY FOR
OUSEWORK

Ms.

NEW FEMINIS
SIMONE
DE BEAUVOIR

BODY HAIR: T
LAST FRONTI

VONDER WOMAN FOR PRESIDEN

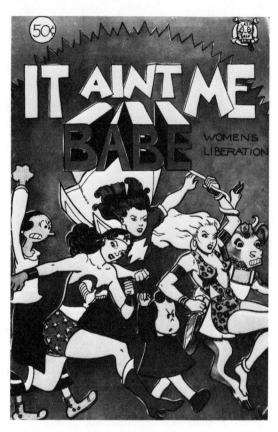

A sampler of women's periodicals (clockwise from top): the militant reportage of It Ain't Me Babe; *the explorations of art and politics of* Sinister Wisdom *and* Chrysalis; *the mainstream feminism of* Ms. *(Covers courtesy of respective periodicals.)*

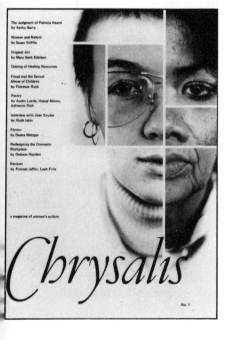

The Judgment of Patricia Hearst
by Kathy Barry

Women and Nature
by Susan Griffin

Original Art
by Mary Beth Edelson

Catalog of Healing Resources

Freud and the Sexual
Abuse of Children
by Florence Rush

Poetry
by Audre Lorde, Honor Moore,
Adrienne Rich

Interview with Joan Snyder
by Ruth Iskin

Fiction
by Deena Metzger

Redesigning the Domestic
Workplace
by Dolores Hayden

Reviews
by Frances Jaffer, Leah Fritz

a magazine of women's culture

Chrysalis

No. 1

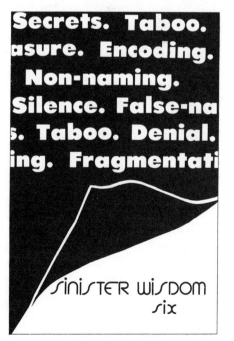

poverty on women, accounts of international women's conferences. "Name" feminist authors—Andrea Dworkin, Robin Morgan, Ellen Willis, Steinem herself—shared the pages of *Ms.* with unknowns. The magazine was edited and operated cooperatively, with staff members' names listed alphabetically on the masthead. *Ms.* also established the legally separate, nonprofit Ms. Foundation for Women, which, according to Steinem, provided "early grants for women's projects in . . . health, employment, reproductive rights, the prevention of violence against women and children, and nonsexist multiracial education."

But while *Ms.* was far from a traditional "ladies' magazine," it was not a radical publication either. There was a tension between women-as-constituency and women-as-market in its pages. Although *Ms.* pledged to eliminate demeaning images of women from its advertising, this pledge was not consistently kept—the Coppertone ad in its first regular issue is one example. In other cases, the pledge was trivialized. A photograph of an expensively gowned young woman in a Drambuie liquor ad in 1980, for instance, carried a headline that read, "Isn't It Time You Knew an Exciting Drink to Order—Instead of Taking a Man's Suggestion?" Ads like that implied that the proper channel for feminist assertiveness was the purchase of commodities, equating the right to make one's own decisions with the right to become a conspicuous consumer.

Ms. also departed from the radical feminist aversion to stars, with cover photographs and inside stories that focused on successful women as role models for women who hadn't "made it" yet in a man's world. Sometimes they were movement figures; Bella Abzug was frequently featured. At other times female celebrities from the worlds of entertainment and business were chosen. *Ms.'s* celebrity-watching was of a piece with other not-so-liberated features of the magazine.

In "The Conservatism of *Ms.*"—written in 1975, after she left the magazine's staff—Ellen Willis enumerated what she saw as the hidden conservative biases of *Ms.*: "an obsession with electoral politics, as if women's liberation will be achieved by integrating the ruling class"; an emphasis on personal, rather than collective, liberation; a tendency to gloss over real political differences between women in deference to "a mushy, sentimental idea of sisterhood"; an emphasis on changing sex roles rather than structural change; a "pervasive class bias" in favor of upper-middle-class women. Concluded Willis, "The common theme is a denial of the need for militant resistance to an oppressive system. We don't need to fight men, only our own conditioning. We don't need to attack the economic system; we too can make it. At best, *Ms.*'s self-improvement, individual-liberation philosphy is relevant only to an elite; basically it is an updated women's magazine fantasy."

Willis' insider's criticisms became more telling toward the end of the seventies, when every other *Ms.* cover featured photos of female celebrities to go with articles that extolled famous women—such as a more-than-sympathetic profile of Jacqueline Kennedy Onassis by Steinem in 1979—and tips on corporate gameswomanship. Warned *Ms.*'s June 1977 issue: "Above all, don't show emotion and *never* cry in front of a male co-worker. Men have spent their lives learning how to repress tears. Women have a lot of catching up to do."

The getting-yours theme is echoed in the magazine's advertising columns. Fairly representative is a full-page ad for a car rental agency in which a young businesswoman stands, car keys and briefcase in hand, while a trio of uniformed working-class men service the vehicle. "Don't get mad," these articles and ads advise, "get ahead." The same message appeals, unadorned, in magazines such as *Savvy* and *Working Woman*—slick monthlies that dispense with *Ms.*'s qualified feminism to get down to the essence of life: a career of one's own.

To radical feminists, *Ms.*'s emphasis on forging personal solutions within the system is evidence that the magazine has it all wrong. While women mustn't be confined to hearth and home, they argue, neither should they adopt the John Wayne model of personhood. "Feminism is for women en masse or it isn't feminism," editorialized *off our backs* in 1980. "Superwomen aren't feminists."

Ms., then, is neither a conservative ladies' magazine nor a hotbed of radicalism. In both its editorial and its advertising policies it follows a program of liberal reform akin to that of the National Organization for Women. Left-wing viewpoints and expositions on the women's culture celebrated by lesbian feminists do not often appear in its pages. *Ms.* is very active in its own version of politics, however.

The Ms. Foundation for Women (which began publishing the magazine as a nonprofit venture through a subsidiary, the Ms. Foundation for Education and Communication, in 1979) gave away some $220,000 in grants in 1978. Moreover, with a nationwide circulation of 500,000, *Ms.* has the contacts, money, and expertise to promote its political vision widely. *Off our backs*, by way of comparison, has a circulation of about 10,000. While *Ms.* has failed to impress most radical feminists, to many mainstream Americans it is *the* feminist publication.

Ms.'s influence extends to traditional women's magazines such as

Redbook, Cosmopolitan, and *McCall's.* No longer do women's magazines assume that their readers are wives in traditional nuclear families or that they are ingenues eager to take their places as champions of apple pie and motherhood. Today's women's magazines, following *Ms.*'s lead, address readers in recognition that they may work outside the home (*McCall's* publishes the slick monthly, *Working Mother*), that they may live alone, and that they face choices of greater significance than which household cleanser to use on waxy yellow buildup on the kitchen floor.

Women's magazines are also now more candid about sex. Birth control and abortion are discussed, if not promoted, and recognition that sex occurs outside of marriage informs their pages. Mainstream women's magazines have also decided that it's OK for women to regard men as sex objects in much the same way that men have long regarded women— thus the nude male centerfolds in *Cosmopolitan* and *Playgirl*, the swinging bachlorette's guide to the good life.

Ms. occupies the center of the political and journalistic spectrum, flanked by feminist alternative publications like *off our backs* on one side and gloves-off career guides like *Savvy* on the other. *Ms.* serves chiefly as a bridge between these opposites, over which radical ideas pass on their way to being accepted or rejected by mainstream society. The radical feminist media, for their part, supply *Ms.* with many of its grassroots-oriented story ideas and a few of its writers. In relying on *Ms.* to popularize their ideas, radical feminists live in uneasy coexistence with the magazine, since, by popularizing feminist values the way it does, *Ms.* also inevitably dilutes and sometimes neutralizes them.

While feminists were busy launching women's media enterprises, men committed to revamping traditional sex roles created media of their own. The early seventies saw the advent of a shortlived phenomenon called the men's liberation movement. Periodicals such as *Brother, Double F,* and *The Effeminist* (which sold for 10¢ to "women, children, older men, Third World, and gay men" and 25¢ to "known white, straight males") were published by this movement. They sought to do for men what feminist periodicals had done for women: provide useful information and a trans-formed sense of identity, arrived at by working with feminists toward shared political goals. The May 1971 issue of *The Effeminist,* for example, carried articles by men condemning the Vietnam war as an outgrowth of heterosexual male aggression, and a story by a woman—headlined "Smash Phallic Imperialism"—which compared sex with men to "doing alienated labor so that on with power could make good profit of [sic] my surplus labor." Early men's liberation periodicals were comparable to underground papers in their militant, confrontational styles. Paralleling the development of other alternative media, this militance soon gave way to low-key attempts at persuasion.

The most successful of the alternative men's liberation media efforts was *Men's Lives*, a film made in 1975 by Will Roberts and Josh Haning. *Men's Lives* featured interviews with people—most of them male—from all walks of life, showing how men are socialized into rigidly aggressive roles: a barber, a basketball coach, a factory worker, a female schoolteacher who allows that she forces her boy students to be more competitive than girls because they will have more responsibilities as adults. A quiet but evocative film, *Men's Lives* reveals the depth of emotional repression that underlies our culture's ideals of masculinity. *Men's Lives* won an Academy Award in 1976.

The Oscar helped bring *Men's Lives* to a wide audience. Some 900 prints of the film were sold to schools, libraries, and museums—far more than average for an independent film. The 43-minute color documentary was also used as an educational tool by men's consciousness-raising groups, fulfilling what Roberts described as a "springboard" function.

Despite the far-reaching implications of men's liberation, the movement and its media didn't get very far. Most men, believing the men's movement to be rooted in guilt, rejected the helpmate role proposed by men's liberationists, most of whom were gay or bisexual. Gay men were more successful in developing media for men only. Gay media espoused male homosexuals' desire to relate exclusively to other men, while not necessarily working in concert with feminists or criticizing the machismo for which some gay men are known.

The first militant media effort for gay men was a program called "The New Symposium," first aired on WBAI by Baird Searles in April 1969. Searles forthrightly declared his love for men and proceeded to tackle a variety of controversial subjects: gay sex, gay relations with police, what gays saw as their oppression in straight society. Listeners lit up the station's call-in lines to talk with Searles on the air about being gay. "The New Symposium" was the first public rallying point for New York's gay men. The second one was the rebellion at the Stonewall Inn, a popular bar on New York's Christopher Street, where several hundred homosexual men fought police who attempted to arrest patrons. The Stonewall rebellion erupted in June 1969, two months after Searles went on the air.

After Stonewall, gay liberationists started periodicals in several cities to spread the word about their new movement. There were *Come Out!* in New York, *Gay Liberator* in Detroit, *Fag Rag* in Boston, *Gay Sunshine* in Berkeley. *Fag Rag* was a fairly representative gay publication. Started in 1971, it embraced a plethora of then-current causes, opposing the Vietnam war and all forms of aggression, which the paper linked with heterosexual male machismo. *Fag Rag* posed an alternative by frankly celebrating gay sex with homoerotic photographs and poetry in the deliberately provocative manner of the early underground papers.

However, of the early gay militant periodicals, only *Fag Rag* made it through the seventies in anything like its original form. *Come Out!* and *Gay Liberator* folded by the halfway point of the decade, as alternative publications replaced militant papers. *Gay Sunshine* epitomized that change. Originally published by the Berkeley Gay Liberation Front, the magazine ceased publication when the staff collective foundered on the shoals of gay politics. In 1971, *Gay Sunshine* was revived by a former Catholic priest named Winston Leyland. Leyland moved the publication to San Francisco and turned it into a literary magazine, blending excerpts from works-in-progress, suppressed gay writings of the past, and interviews with luminaries such as Allen Ginsberg. Gay Sunshine Press, an offshoot of the magazine, published generally high-quality books by homosexual writers such as Frank O'Hara and Harold Norse which served to remind us of the considerable contributions that gay men have made to American letters.

In the middle seventies, gay periodicals—paralleling developments elsewhere in the alternative media—became slicker and more narrowly focused on entertainment and local news. Out went the crude layout and revolutionary zeal of *Come Out!* and *The Effeminist*; in came comprehensive entertainment listings, more restrained writing, clearly composed pages, and relatively artful cover designs. The political focus of gay male media changed correspondingly, going from agitation for broad-based liberation to the measured though persistent advocacy of legal reform and the celebration of hedonism.

Indeed, hedonism became the central focus of several gay publications. Beefcake magazines like *Mandate* and *Blueboy* and the slick arts and entertainment magazine *After Dark* dropped nearly all references to gay liberation, viewing the movement as, well, a little tacky, and preferring to depict the gay experience as essentially pleasurable. These gay slicks targeted the well-paid gay professional with articles on food, wine, and travel and attempted to lure lucrative national advertising by ballyhooing their upscale demographics. *Blueboy* claims its average reader had an income of $24,000 in 1979; in keeping with this relative affluence, the magazine is listed on the New York Stock Exchange.

In 1976, the evolution of gay media took another turn when a monthly magazine called *Christopher Street* arrived on the newsstands. A fusion of the hedonism of the other gay slicks and the literacy of *Gay Sunshine*, *Christopher Street* printed professionally written reviews of books, theatre, and music, along with witty cartoons that earned the magazine a budding reputation as a gay *New Yorker*. That reputation was enhanced in 1979, when *Christopher Street* published a series of articles by journalist Edmund White, who crisscrossed America visiting gay baths and bars and exploring the varieties of homosexual experience. White's reports were published in book form by Dutton in 1980. The book, *States of Desire*, won critical praise from a number of mainstream reviewers.

Gay newspapers shared in the trend toward arts and news and away from polemics. This was best exemplified by *The Advocate*, a national biweekly published in a suburb of San Francisco by David Goodstein. A former Wall Street executive, Goodstein saw *The Advocate* as a responsible news medium—concentrating on reports of legislative and legal battles for gay rights—rather than as an incendiary sheet.

The February 21, 1980, issue of *The Advocate* is fairly representative. That 80-page issue devoted several pages to news briefs, led by an account of a meeting between White House staffers and gay activists; included interviews with lesbian writer Sally Gearhart and gay filmmaker Guy Hocquerghem; carried 20 pages of reviews of movies, music, theatre, and books; and featured an editorial in which Goodstein gently chided gay men for being obsessed with sex. A look at the rest of the paper proves Goodstein's rather disingenuous point: 32 pages were devoted exclusively to sex ads as explicit as any in the underground press: "Hot buns can't say no to extra long & thick studs that won't quit."

Like many publications for gay men, *The Advocate* draws much of its revenue from ads for gay pornography and assorted sexual services. And, like other periodicals for gay men, *The Advocate* has tried—with some success—to sell national advertisers on its 110,000 Audit Bureau of Circulation certified readers, who had average household incomes of $23,600 in 1977—or 50 percent above the national average. This sharply distinguishes gay periodicals from publications for lesbians—who, as women, are usually paid less than men and sometimes have children from previous marriages to support as well. *The Advocate* and most other gay periodicals also differ from lesbian publications by their warm embrace of hierarchical decision-making and the profit motive.

Although the streetfighting polemics of gay liberation are mostly a thing of the past, gay media still crusade for the legal rights of homosexuals, and, in cities with large gay populations, gay media swing some political clout. The *San Francisco Sentinel,* a biweekly paper with a circulation of 17,000, publishes political columns and endorses candidates for public office right next to photo spreads on Halloween drag balls and reports on the sado-masochism scene. In 1980, presidential candidate John Anderson—seeking to snare the gay vote—wrote an article for the *Sentinel,* becoming the first major presidential candidate to openly court the gay press.

Such a turn signifies a measure of acceptance of homosexuals and gay media by mainstream society, but it also indicates that gays and their media can be absorbed without changing society fundamentally. This is made possible by the relatively modest (except to the organized right) political agenda of gay media, which begins and ends with the advocacy of civil rights. While that is a necessary first step to full citizenship, it is a far cry from the calls to liberation by early gay media—or the challenging radical visions of contemporary lesbian-feminist media. Instead of changing the world, gay media seem content to work diligently for a comfortable place in it. Unlike feminist media, whose attempts to dig to the root of things are radical in the original sense of that word, gay papers—with their pages of ads for restaurants, baths, and pornographic movies, their hierarchies and profit-making operations, their advocacy of political gradualism, and their celebration of hedonism-cum-narcissism—present a slightly distorted mirror-image of the status quo.

Mainstream society has shown that it can absorb a number of once-threatening ideas from sexual radicals and turn them into throwaway consumer items. Thus, the freedom from confining clothing advocated by Germaine Greer and other feminists becomes, in the commercial context of network TV, the come-on of "jiggle" shows, where bra-less lady detectives solve crimes of passion in exotic locales. The sexual self-determination of feminist fiction becomes the obsessive, egocentric search for "the zipless fuck" in Erica Jong's *Fear of Flying.* The purposeful internationalism of *It Ain't Me Babe* becomes the celebration of the perfect paté in *Self.*

Yet it would be a mistake to assume that the innovations of feminist media have been altogether trivialized. Articles on birth control, living alone, single parenting, day care for working mothers, and related stories now common in the feature pages of daily newspapers are there by courtesy of the feminist media and movement. Syndicated columnists such as *Ms.* contributing editor Lindsy Van Gelder and *Boston Globe* writer Ellen Goodman—who writes wry, mildly feminist stories on the family and modern life—bring a reform version of feminism to those same pages. The mainstream media, while they are a long way from being strong supporters of feminism, have modified their formats in an apparent attempt to keep up with the changing lifestyles of their readers.

Feminists and gay media have also strongly influenced other alternative media. In addition to bridge periodicals like *Ms.*, urban weeklies such as the *Boston Phoenix* and *The Real Paper* give space to articles by and about feminists, as do left-leaning magazines such as *Mother Jones*. Feminists and gays have figured prominently in the *Village Voice* since the late sixties, when the paper published Jill Johnston's lesbian odysseys. Alternative media regard sexual politics as a beat, covering issues such as equal pay for women, the civil rights of homosexuals, and the right to abortion frequently and empathetically, if not with the passion those subjects evoke in feminist and gay media.

Thanks to the creative core of feminist media, the topics of abortion rights, access to birth control, the ERA, pornography, the heretofore hidden epidemic of battered women, and the crusade to stop rape and end the once nearly universal tendency among police and courts to blame the rape victim for her assault—all have been placed on the national political agenda, amplified by *Ms.* and other alternative media, and partially ratified by the mass media. The fact that many of these innovations are now under attack as part of a coordinated right-wing offensive is another topic of much concern in the alternative media (see Chapter Fifteen).

Little of this variety and depth of activity seemed in the offing in 1965, when Mary King and Casey Hayden sat down to communicate with other women by writing "a kind of memo." Taken together, the alternative media have deepened the authentic expressions of feminism and gay liberation that stir beneath the patina of commercialism.

eleven

The High Society

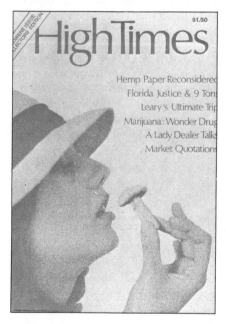

IN THE YEARS SINCE the underground media heralded the delights of drugs, dope in America has gone middle-class. The substances that were once the preserve of hirsute radicals and street hippies are now taken at high-school graduation parties, in plush lawyers' offices, reportedly even in government circles. America has become the High Society, and underground and alternative media deserve the lion's share of the credit—or blame—for that development.

In the process of transition from radical fringe benefit to national pastime, the nature of drug-taking has changed fundamentally. Drugs—seen by the underground media as consciousness-expanding and radicalizing agents—have become mere commodities. Instead of being used to see God or smash the State, popular drugs such as marijuana and cocaine have become accoutrements in the modern American lifestyle, hedonistic props for making life more comfortable rather than for changing life's direction.

The selling of the drug culture began as soon as dope left the small circle of Beat acolytes, who guarded the flame of drug-inspired wisdom

Tom Forcade, Underground Press Syndicate coordinator and High Times *founder, dressed in black and averted his face in photographs. Forcade's eccentricities won him a reputation as the Howard Hughes of the underground. (Photo by John Burks. Cover courtesy of* High Times.*)*

in the forties and fifties, for wider popularity in the hippie underground. In a 1976 interview in *New Age,* one of the leading alternative spiritual magazines, Pierre Delattre—a Protestant minister and former editor of the underground poetry magazine *Beatitude*—recalled seeing incipient signs of commercialization back in the sixties and being startled by them:

> The thing that really amazed me the first time I came back from Mexico, after I'd really gotten into psychedelics, was the way the hippies were . . . walking through supermarkets, buying things. I thought everybody would be on a very spiritual trip. I used to go to the Northpoint in North Beach . . . and there were all these hippies, stoned out of their minds, walking around the hot fudge counters and going wow—picking up one thing after another. That's when I realized that dope is the perfect stimulant to the economy, because once you're stoned, you don't worry about the price; you've got to have it.

The mass-media merchandisers of pop culture had the same realization, but, unlike Delattre, they were not dismayed. By the end of the sixties, only half a decade after the drug culture was introduced to large numbers of people by the underground media (and several prescient record companies), drug lingo and adaptations of the drug sensibility were well on their way to being absorbed by mainstream culture. Hollywood movies affected psychedelic colors and swirls, and several releases—*Blow-Up, Head, The Trip, Yellow Submarine, Easy Rider*—were developed specifically to appeal to young drug users—"heads" and "freaks," as they called themselves. Graphics in the print media took on the shimmering, flowing qualities of psychedelic experience. Language, too, reflected the influence of the drug culture as Middle Americans accepted "turn on" and "ego trip" into their daily speech. Dope also helped relax sexual inhibitions; many were the heads whose long hair was let down under the influence of drugs.

The results of all that apparent success, however, were not what underground media proselytizers had expected. Instead of being transformed by psychedelic drugs, mainstream culture absorbed them as psychological and commercial tributaries while maintaining its essentially competitive, materialistic qualities. (A small but significant exception was the drug-related birth of the New Age movement and media, which forked off from the drug culture, largely leaving the commercial path. These phenomena are examined in Chapter Thirteen.) An important byproduct of the curious commercial success of psychedelics—for the drug culture and its media—was a dilution of visions and values that had once seemed truly radical.

This cultural and journalistic cul-de-sac was a far cry from what drug visionaries in the underground media, and even before, had forseen. Drug hedonism, while not foreign to the early Beat and hippie scenes, did not dominate them either. The psychedelic elders of the forties and fifties bequeathed to the early hippies their conviction that drugs were a means to liberation. Mind-expansion, it was called, and, if one did it properly, negative conditioning from the "straight" society into which one was born could fall away like the cocoon from a butterfly.

Although they believed in the power of drugs to change society for the better, underground media activists did not believe that all drugs were beneficent. Underground figures such as Robert Crumb, the cartoonist, issued warnings in their work against dangerous drugs like "speed" (amphetamines), much as celebrities of their parents' generation had warned against taking that last martini for the road. Drugs, to the underground media, were not ends in themselves, but means to transpersonal goals. Underground media heralded the psychedelics—peyote, mescaline, psilocybin, and chiefly LSD—as ways of confronting oneself in cosmic dramas and, hopefully, learning from the experience. Marijuana, too, was favored as a means of relaxing in a supercharged, competitive society and throwing off the inhibitions of the Puritanical past. In short, instead of using drugs to escape from reality, the underground media culture advocated the use of drugs—some of them, anyway—to escape *to* reality.

Early underground media were quite definite about what drug use meant in a social context. Specifically, it meant one was *for* peace, long hair, cooperation, open expressions of sexuality, and a spiritual approach to life and *against* anything that threatened those values. Selling drugs was an honorable occupation so long as unseemly profits did not accrue to the seller. Lots of dope was given away.

In the early seventies, all that changed. Unlike the underground, the alternative media did not proselytize for drugs. The alternative media's tone was cooler, less certain. Sure, our constituents use dope, they seemed to say, but they use it to have a good time or just to get through the day, not to meet God and get His address. The economy was tighter, so it was OK to sell drugs, and at higher prices. The spiritual path was not for everyone, so it was OK to use drugs strictly for pleasure— particularly the expensive white powder called cocaine, a kind of super- speed that largely replaced LSD as the drug of choice. The preoccupa- tion with self that critics would later call narcissism interfaced with changing drug habits to give the seventies a self-contained tone that contrasted sharply with the self-scrutiny of the sixties.

The receding tide of confrontational politics and flamboyant hippie lifestyles also gave way to a more scholarly, legalistic approach in the continuing efforts to legalize—or at least decriminalize—drugs. The alternative media were very much involved in this change of strategy and, indeed, helped make it happen. *High Times* magazine, the largest and most influential alternative publication devoted to drugs, helped bankroll the National Organization for the Reform of Marijuana Laws (NORML), an organization founded in 1970 by a young lawyer named Keith Stroup. NORML's main function, as distinguished from radical agitation for broad-based change, was professional lobbying at the state and federal level for a single-issue goal: the reform of antimarijuana laws. Whereas sixties radicals had gone out of their way to assert how different they were from Middle Americans, NORML members emphasized how similar they were to everyone else—respectable, hard-working people who sought to peacefully persuade other respectable, hard-working people that the antimarijuana laws were unfair.

The alternative media culture produced scholars and intellectuals to buttress arguments for decriminalization, hoping to convince lawmakers that most drugs, when properly used, were harmless and had long histories of use in cultures all over the world besides. One such drug scholar, Michael Aldrich, established a library in San Francisco devoted exclusively to drug studies. Called the Fitz Hugh Ludlow Memorial Library, after a nineteenth-century drug scholar and author, the Ludlow Library gathered rare manuscripts, letters, and scientific reports on drug experiences and collected drug-inspired artwork such as the psychedelic posters of the sixties. Thanks largely to Aldrich's efforts, the newly emerging area of drug scholarship became an almost respectable field of research.

Alternative book publishing also zeroed in on the drug culture. In 1973, Ron Turner—owner of Last Gasp Eco-Funnies—and Sebastian Orafali—a student of the mystical Gurdjieff tradition and a member of a psychotherapeutic group that used the reputed "love drug," MDA— started an independent publishing house called And/Or Press. And/Or produced nothing but drug books in its first several years—lavish, colorful books that caught much of the "feel" of the drug experience. And/Or's books did not generally associate drug use with a radical movement, but celebrated drugs as exotic items to be savored by connoisseurs of mind-expansion—well-traveled, tasteful persons of the world who knew good hashish, or a good book about hashish, when they saw it. "It's virtually impossible to build a culture from scratch," explained And/Or's executive editor, Peter Beren. "However, it is possible to build a publishing company. We don't really concentrate on the political ramifications."

And/Or built its business rapidly. The company's first book, published in 1973, was entitled *Laughing Gas* and covered the history and uses of nitrous oxide. One of the book's coauthors was David Wallechinsky, who went on to fame as coauthor of *The People's Almanac* and *The Book of Lists* for mainstream publishers. *Laughing Gas* was followed by the republication of *History of Coca*, W. Golden Mortimer's long-out-of-print classic on the South American coca leaf and its popular derivative, cocaine. The book included fascinating ethnographic and botanical material and featured fine line drawings which had graced the original 1901 text. *History of Coca* introduced twin themes that were to recur in many alternative drug ventures: an intense nostalgia for earlier eras, when forbidden drugs were legal and easily available, and a romantic view of the faraway cultures that produce the raw materials for American noses, lungs, and veins.

In 1976, And/Or published a *Marijuana Grower's Guide*, a complete how-to book on the cultivation and appreciation of *cannabis sativa*. The *Grower's Guide* put And/Or on the alternative publishing map, with 100,000 copies sold in a deluxe edition and another 400,000 in a cheaper paperback version. The *Marijuana Grower's Guide* confirmed that the constituency for drugs and drug-related items had become an eager, growing market. The lesson was not lost on other entrepreneurs.

At about the same time that And/Or's presses were beginning to roll, an alternative media activist on the other side of the continent was considering the publishing possibilities of the drug culture. He was Tom Forcade, a Yippie media activist who had been the national coordinator of the Underground Press Syndicate and publisher of an underground magazine called *Orpheus*, which he and a peripatetic staff produced from a 1946 Chevrolet bus while they drove around the country.

Forcade was an unlikely activist. The son of a Goldwater Republican, he liked to shroud his past in mystery. Born Gary Kenneth Goodson in 1945, he grew up in Arizona, graduated from the University of Utah with a degree in business administration, and went into the Air Force. After only a few months, Goodson was discharged from the service, where he had become increasingly critical of the Vietnam war. At about age twenty, for reasons known only to himself, Gary Goodson changed his name to Tom Forcade (pronounced like *fasçade*). Shortly thereafter, he began publishing *Orpheus*, a drug-and-revolution magazine that advo-

cated the establishment of "liberated zones" occupied by hippies and
other dropouts on remote North American land, the legal ownership of
which was in doubt. *Orpheus* also carried the cryptic logo "This magazine
has been shot with a Colt .45 automatic" on the cover.

With *High Times*, Forcade's interests in business, politics, publishing,
and drugs congealed. Forcade claimed he got the idea for *High Times*
when he and a few cohorts from the underground press were inhaling
copious quantities of nitrous oxide in a Greenwich Village apartment one
night. Wouldn't it be great, someone said, if there were a magazine that
did for drugs what *Playboy* did for sex: popularize new, liberating attitudes, fuse the culture and business of dope, and do it in an accomplished
manner, enlisting the highest heads among underground artists and
writers as contributors. Such a magazine could blow things wide open
and be a success atistically, commercially, and politically, bringing
"far-out" lifestyles to millions.

Forcade decided it *would* be great and he would do it. Together with a
few friends, Forcade began working on the new magazine in a Greenwich Village basement apartment. The first issues of *High Times* were
reputed to be bankrolled by big drug dealers—friends of Forcade's—or
through a big drug deal by Forcade himself. When asked about that,
Forcade shrugged and replied, "Who *hasn't* dealt?"

In the summer of 1974, *High Times* emerged from the underground to
tell the world about dope. The first issue featured a cover photograph of a
young woman about to eat a psychedelic mushroom. The magazine was
48 pages long, published on slick paper, and cleanly laid out, with
conservative column-rules and a fair amount of white space. Editorially,
it was a mixed bag; alongside news of drug arrests and draconian government politics appeared features such as an "interview with a lady
dealer" and a history of cigarette papers used for rolling joints of marijuana. The magazine also published straight-faced market reports on the
type, price, availablity, and quality of drugs all over the world: "Mexican
as high or higher than NYC . . . Colombian and Jamaican rare and
high. . . . heroin on Coast, and potent. . . . Hash oil very available in
Eugene and Springfield . . . some domestic, but quality ragged."

The new magazine also delivered a strong dose of dopers' paranoia.
High Times assured charter and future subscribers that its mailing list was
known only to the publisher and the publisher's lawyer and would not be
divulged to anyone else "under any circumstances, period." Forcade's
name did not appear on the masthead or anywhere else in the magazine,
and it would not until after he died.

In a three-dot, Walter Winchell-style section called "Flashes," *High Times* indirectly described the situation that led to its own birth:". . . lots of new books on dope and a few on daily use of those things, but few worth reading. . . . Anyway, some of the best highs are not from drugs, but from far-out . . . records, music, and various mental disciplines, from yoga to biofeedback."

High Times made occasional reference to nondrug highs, but it seldom explored them with the relish and detail it devoted to drugs. Instead, *High Times* embraced what Christopher Lasch called "the propaganda of commodities"—selling drugs and drug-related products as substitutes for inner resources. This was contrapuntal to evolving Aquarian spirituality, which also claimed roots in the drug culture. In this way, drugs paradoxically sparked a spiritual renaissance in American life and contributed to is debasement. *High Times* played a leading role in this cultural passion play.

From the beginning, *High Times* seemed marked for success. The first issue sold out its conservative press run of 25,000 copies in head shops and hip bookstores. The second issue, published in the fall of 1974, did equally well. It was more artistically produced, and had the splashes of color that became the magazine's trademark, and boasted a feature story right out of the underground press tradition of "true fiction" and calculated outrage. It was called "I was JFK's Dealer" and purported to be an interview with an anonymous Ivy Leaguer who supplied John Kennedy with marijuana to ease his chronic back pain. The "dealer" also confided that the reason Ted Kennedy lost his head at Chappaquiddick was that he had filled it with LSD before driving off with Mary Jo Kepechne. There was no way for a reader to verify this story, but it intrigued and entertained with its "revelations" that the Kennedys, their teenage children, and many high government officials were heads, secretly working to do away with antidrug laws and hasten the triumph of Good.

High Times' second issue introduced another item that was to become a recurring feature of the magazine: the dope centerfold. The dope centerfold was a full-color photo of the object of *High Times'* affections—dope—taken in extreme closeup and printed on glossy stock in pornographic detail, so the reader could pick out every bud, blossom, and blemish of the exotic brand of drug on display.

The parallels with *Playboy* didn't end there. Early issues of *High Times* incorporated columns on sex and drugs based on readers' queries about those tender topics, with generally well-thought-out, reliable advice. While *High Times* took a clearly prodrug stance, the magazine showed

As this High Times *centerfold shows, marijuana now moves in bulk, earning big bucks for savvy adventurers. More often than not, drugs also lubricate the lifestyle*

of those who seek the enjoy the world as it is, rather than envision the world as it might be. *(Photo courtesy of* High Times.*)*

responsibility by, for example, advising readers that there was such a thing as too much cocaine and warning pregnant smokers to abstain from marijuana during the first trimester of pregnancy. Still other similarities to *Playboy* were highlighted in later issues when *High Times* initiated "the *High Times* [celebrity] interview" and published a "Dope in the Cinema" series, complementing *Playboy's* well-known "Sex in the Cinema" feature.

High Times proved to be the ideal vehicle for the increasingly commercialized drug culture of the middle seventies. It lent a touch of class to what had heretofore been a tattered underground phenomenon, provided dopers and their dealers with a means of expression, and articulated the growing importance and self-consciousness of the drug culture. After one year of publication and only four quarterly issues, *High Times* had a paid circulation of 250,000—ten times that of its first issue.

Forcade developed an editorial mix for *High Times* that soon settled into a predictable, but successful, formula. Nearly every issue had stories of drug busts and raids ("Pot Plane Shot Down in Dogfight"); potshots at Washington drug officials ("Study Shows Grass Laws Promote Selective Enforcement"); first-person reports from the exotic locales where dope is produced; swashbuckling tales of drug smuggling; interviews with pioneering dopers and other culture heroes; prominently displayed color comics; book and record reviews; columns on law, health, and sex; and letters from readers.

Reader input at *High Times*, while it never approached the levels in the *Whole Earth Catalog*, was substantial. The market quotations often came from readers, and debates on matters of concern to drug users frequently surfaced in *High Times'* pages. Once a flood of complaints about the dishonesty of drug dealers in Tucson, Arizona, prompted a defensive letter to the dope community from a Tucson dealer (unnamed, of course) who insisted that Tucson dealers were *too* honest. Many were the readers who sent in photos of their "stash"—their supplies of marijuana, cocaine, or whatever they had on hand—with all the pride that other people reserve for pictures of children and pets. Some *High Times* readers mailed the magazine snapshots of their pets *with* their stash, a popular feature that is, fortunately, limited to the pages of *High Times*. *High Times* published their shots long with elaborate work by professional photographers whom the magazine described as "dedicated lenspersons who can make a simple brick of dope or line of coke into a visual high fit to frame beside the noblest works of Rembrandt, Picasso, and Dali."

The skyrocketing success of *High Times* did not go unnoticed in the publishing world. Attempts by other dopezines—magazines devoted mostly to covering the glories of drugs—to cash in on this lucrative trend were made, and periodicals with names such as *Rush, Head, Flash*, and *Marijuana Monthly* briefly peaked, then crashed to earth. Only *High Times* persevered. In part, this was due to Forcade's editorial touch—his ability to stay a step ahead and to fuse the best graphics in the field with punchy writing that was both a parody of the pulp magazines of the thirties and a tribute to them.

Under Forcade's direction, *High Times* also indulged readers' desires for vicarious adventure by publishing photos and hair-raising accounts of drug cultivation, harvesting, trading, and smuggling in such faraway places as Marrakesh and Afghanistan. Despite Forcade's New Left background and the avowed radicalism of many *High Times* contributors, *High Times* did not explore the often-oppressive living conditions of the peasants who produce America's not-so-cheap thrills, except when—as was the case when the local gendarmes got angry—those conditions affected the dope business.

Thanks, in part, to the efforts of *High Times*, the dope trade was one of the leading growth industries of the seventies. In 1978, *High Times* estimated that yearly sales of marijuana and cocaine were between $4 and $6 billion. Some government sources put the figure even higher. In the late seventies the dope industry generated more revenue than network television, movies, or music. The trade and cultivation of marijuana alone accounted for more revenue than tourism in Hawaii, more than lumber in heavily forested northern California, and more than coffee in Colombia.

Such was the business that *High Times* helped expand, and from which it drew its identity. Like *Rolling Stone*, *High Times* glamorized the source of its income and identity, writing about the dope trade in the first person and setting up a we/they dichotomy in which youth, style, and freedom were identified with using drugs, much as the same qualities were associated in *Rolling Stone* with buying records and going to concerts. The two magazines, like the products they promoted, were complementary. One read *Rolling Stone* to decide which concert to go to and *High Times* to discover which drug would enhance the music most. Together, the two publications defined a world that was consumerist, hedonistic, insular, seamless.

But not all the world was enamored of *High Times*. Greece burned copies of the magazine and Canada banned it—actions which added to the mystique of *High Times*, as "the most dangerous magazine in

America," according to *High Times'* own ad copy. "No magazine or newspaper covers this beat. It's where dope, sex, and politics melt, mingle, and fuse into ideas too hot for the official culture to handle. Ideas too mad, bad, and dangerous to know."

Like any enterprise that conjured a heaven, *High Times* had to have evil spirits. It found them in agents of the federal Drug Enforcement Agency—archfiends who stood between *High Times* readers and their achievement of perpetual chemical bliss. Forcade himself, fearing a raid on the magazine's office, went into hiding and ran *High Times* from a pay phone booth for a time. On another occasion, believing that *High Times* was infiltrated by agents, Forcade fired the entire staff. He rehired most of them, though he still believed several were agents out to ground *High Times*. Forcade's personal life reflected his political paranoia. He lived in hotels, hopping from one to another, for a seven-year stretch. Together with his business acumen, Forcade's obsession with secrecy earned him a reputation as the Howard Hughes of the underground.

Forcade used his new wealth and power to launch a frontal attack on federal and state drug laws. In addition to donating money on a periodic basis to NORML, he gave the organization free ad space in *High Times*. The remnants of the Yippies were also beneficiaries of Forcade's largesse. He gave money and advice to the Yippies' irregularly published newspaper, *Yipster Times* (now called *Overthrow*), and donated free ad space for their political street theatre, especially the Yippies' annual Fourth of July Smoke-In across the street from the White House.

Forcade also bankrolled a number of related alternative media projects. He kept the nearly moribund Alternative Press Syndicate alive and published *Alternative Media*, the organization's more-or-less quarterly magazine. He opened a bookstore, backed several aborted films, and published High Times books. All of the latter were insiders' looks at drugs, bearing titles such as *The Pleasures of Cocaine*, *Sex Drugs and Aphrodisiacs*, and the *High Times Encyclopedia of Recreational Drugs*, a 512-page volume. All were attempts to move society in his and *High Times'* direction, and all were consistent with Forcade's description of himself as "a social architect."

His radical past and plans notwithstanding, Forcade was a sharp businessperson. By 1977, he had built *High Times* into a 400,000-circulation monthly with a pass-along readership of nearly four million. The magazine's parent Trans-High Corporation, through which Forcade operated his various enterprises, was a $6-million-a-year business; most of its income came from *High Times*.

High Times' success was due not only to Forcade's keen appreciation of the drug scene as a culture, but also to his knowledge of the complex and fascinating business that flourished behind the scenes. *High Times* parted the curtain on this hidden industry, running tantalizing features on dope lawyers, bush pilots, growers, tasters, and other key figures, and speculated about the industry's potential value to the American economy. "What's good for America's dope dealers is good for America," read one *High Times* article, and the statement was made only half in jest.

Forcade described the drug paraphernalia industry in 1978 as a $30-million-a-year business "at least," and *High Times* reflected his determination to control that market. Before *High Times*, head-shop operators and paraphernalia manufacturers were relatively isolated; with the advent of *High Times*, they secured a tribune that defended their interests and a vehicle in which to display their wares.

A single issue of *High Times* in 1979 carried ads for: T-shirts proclaiming the wearer's favorite brand of pot (choice of "Maui Wowie," "Thai," or "Sinsimilla"); an elongated pipe disguised as a walking stick scales for weighing one's stash; a hydroponic system for growing one's stash; a device that purported to extract the active ingredient in marijuana to make stronger dope; alternative comic books; and rolling papers.

High Times ads are like ads in any commercial magazine: long on promises, short on guarantees, frequently for nonessential items, often relying on sex to make the sale. Drugs—especially marijuana, cocaine, and tranquilizers sold under the trademarked name Quaalude—are valued as relaxants and sexual stimulants, and ads for drug paraphernalia make full use of that fact. A single issue of *High Times* had a display ad for a penis-shaped pipe with woman climbing the stem; a pitch for rolling papers with a female model about to lick their gummed edges; and an ad for a bong (an elongated water pipe) which a woman mouthed suggestively.

High Times' ads are a long way in content from the ads in *Ms.* —another magazine that teeters on the banks of the mainstream. In *Ms.*'s case, the products advertised beckon the reader to move up the social and economic ladder; in *High Times*, they invite the reader to lay back. There's not much difference, however, beween the underlying message of Ms.'s "assertive woman" Drambuie ad and that of *High Times'* thumb-your-nose-at-authority "Maui Wowie" T-shirts. Both suggest that you can become the person you want to be by buying a new product. This, of course, is the message of all advertising, showing how little marginally alternative magazines like *Ms.* and *High Times* differ from the periodicals to which they supposedly offer alternatives.

Forcade closely linked the fate of *High Times* with the paraphernalia industry—the makers and sellers of pipes, strainers, bongs, and other drug-related devices. In 1976 he launched a trade publication, aimed at the paraphernalia industry, called *Dealer.* That this was serious business was made clear by an editorial in the first issue of *Dealer:*

> A remarkable new marketplace is emerging in America because the marijuana subculture of the 1960s has established itself as the center of the major new leisure market of the 1970s.
>
> Grass and related highs have become commonplace in American life. Decriminalization of marijuana will continue with growing speed. A revolution in retailing on all fronts . . . will continue as paraphernalia retailers try to capture the imagination of the doper consumer.

High Times' ties to the industry that foots its bills become more apparent when industry interests are threatened. In 1978, when reports in *High Times* and other alternative media suggested that the spraying of the toxic herbicide paraquat on Mexican marijuana fields might be harmful to American pot smokers, *High Times* published a toll-free number which customers could call for paraquat information and an address where they could send anonymous, numbered samples of their pot to be lab-tested. But, while NORML emphasized the possible dangers of paraquat and advised consumers to stop smoking Mexican weed (which then comprised the bulk of the U.S. market), *High Times* pooh-poohed the warnings, declaring that it was all a government plot to scare smokers into giving up grass. Very few authenticated cases of paraquat poisoning were reported, but its long-term effects on smokers are unknown.

In the late seventies, conservative politicians on local, state, and federal levels gave the dope business another scare by attempting to ban the sale of drug paraphernalia to minors and, in some cases, to anyone. Most such laws face stiff courtroom challenges, but the time and expense of fighting the regulations have given the legal tip of the drug industry headaches. Again, *High Times* jumped to the defense of the industry, this time defending buyers' and sellers' rights to buy paraphernalia as part of every American's inalienable right of freedom of choice. Given *High Times'* obvious self-interest in matters affecting the dope trade, one may ask whether it was primarily principle or profit that lit the fires under *High Times'* writers and editors.

High Times also aggressively editorializes against the arrest and surveillance of drug magnates and consumers, hailing the dope industry as a cornerstone of "pure capitalism" and an exemplar of "free enterprise."

High Times' accolades are partly in fun, written as parodies of chesty Chamber of Commerce press releases, but they aren't far from *High Times'* true position. As a founding coeditor of the magazine told William Novak, the author of *High Culture*, "There's a very important need in this country for a bad-boy press. But a bad-boy press is not necessarily a left-wing press."

High Times admires the dope trade and is, indeed, part of it. As media reports of the late seventies made clear, the dope industry is not an admirable business, filled as it is with murder, fraud, and the apparently increasing participation of organized crime. This is particularly true in drug-drenched Colombia, where drug fortunes are made overnight and judges, merchants, and law-enforcement officers alike are subject to quick and violent deaths.

One violent death in Colombia may have profoundly affected the life of *High Times* itself. In mid-1978, a close friend of Forcade's—reportedly in Colombia on a dope-smuggling run—died in a mysterious plane crash. His friend's death depressed and frightened Forcade, who suspected foul play. Forcade began taking Quaaludes in large quantitites, becoming less and less communicative. On November 16, 1978, the publisher shot himself in the SoHo loft he shared with his wife, Gabrielle Schang. He died the following day in the hospital. A Colt .45, the weapon that "shot" *Orpheus* magazine, was the gun that Tom Forcade, the transplanted Westerner, used to kill himself.

After several months of corporate infighting, Schang—a former *Berkeley Barb* associate editor and layout artist and a cable TV personality in New York—became president of Trans-High and publisher of *High Times*. Schang immediately announced big changes, citing her determination to turn *High Times* into "the cultural magazine of the eighties." "We just have to expand the concept of high," she went on, "to include running, camping out, falling in love, dreaming." In line with that pronouncement, Schang subtitled *High Times* "the magazine of feeling good."

Feeling good did not meaning living an ascetic life, however, as the magazine's staff continued to live and work in ways far removed from those advocated by the psychedelic shamans of the sixties. Leslie Bacon—who was, like Schang, a former *Barb* staffer who emigrated to New York to work on the "new" *High Times*—described as routine "hundred-dollar dinners at the Plaza Hotel with Madison Avenue types," generous allowances of drugs and cab fare, and a promotional party that set the magazine back $5,000. "I suppose it was sort of decadent," Bacon said, "but the people there [at *High Times*] before us spent even more money on stuff. Compared to them, we were wholesome reformers."

The reformation was shortlived. Less than a year after taking the helm of *High Times*, Schang was ousted in another palace revolt by staffers who felt that her plans for the magazine jeopardized its survival. Schang was replaced as publisher in the summer of 1980 by Andy Kowl, who was then publisher of *Accessories Digest* (formerly *Paraphernalia Digest*). Kowl, who is well connected in the paraphernalia industry, is expected to return *High Times* to the narrow focus on drugs that characterized the magazine's headiest days.

While there is no doubt that there is plenty of money in drugs, it is questionable whether *High Times* will continue to prosper. The magazine's circulation fell to 350,000 in 1979 from its peak of 400,000; the industry from which *High Times* draws most of its ad revenue is under legal attack and likely to remain so in the foreseeable future; its young (average age 23), male (70 percent) readers are not the kind of upscale consumers that financially solvent magazines like to have; its founder and guiding spirit is gone.

There is no question that Tom Forcade had a flair for the dramatic. Just starting *High Times* and bringing a magazine dedicated to the care and feeding of illegal substances out in the open, was daring. And billing *High Times* as "the most dangerous magazine in America" was a nervy attention-getting device.

One might ask, however, to whom *High Times* was more dangerous: the scorned establishment or the avowed radicals on the magazine's own staff. *High Times* shook up one part of the establishment, certainly. Conservative church leaders, politicians, and law-enforcement officers were shocked and dismayed by the appearance of a periodical devoted to the promotion of illegal drugs, as their legislative curbs on the paraphernalia industry have shown. But other parts of "the system" were easily able to absorb dope and dope media. To hedonistic young moderns in the mainstream, drugs were simply instruments of pleasure—aids to better sex, better music, better eating—and a matter of personal choice besides. This was consistent with the American tradition of individuality, and conservative groups such as the Young Americans for Freedom and the Libertarian Party have acknowledged this by coming out for the legalization of marijuana. It can be argued, therefore, that drugs, to borrow from the drug lexicon, have mellowed out the system without really changing it.

To a considerable extent, *High Times* mirrored and helped bring about the changed role of drugs in American life in the seventies. For many drug consumers, self-discovery turned into decadence as LSD was replaced by cocaine—a drug which *High Times* and other dopezines did much to glamorize as the drug of the beautiful people. While LSD, inexpensive yet extremely powerful, was used by Aquarian argonauts to shed their egos, costly cocaine was used to reinforce them.

A new feature, instituted in *High Times* in 1978, further exemplifies the growth of hip materialism. This was a column by "R," a self-described "dope connoisseur," who announced that the time was at hand for someone—"R." in fact—to write about the taste, bouquet, color, and overall esthetics of dope the way other writers have long written about wine. The addition of "R's" writing to *High Times* was a political statement by the magazine, but it was not a dissenting one. Instead, it confirmed that drugs were no longer a means of throwing off mainstream conditioning, or of clearing the way for an alternative society, but had become accoutrements in the rarified world of connoisseurs, a world in which the best of everything mattered: the best car, the best running shoes, the best wines, the best marijuana.

Other media ventures inspired by the dope culture took similar turns. Said And/Or Press' Peter Beren, "We are not innovators, we're middlemen. We work with sixties political ideas and put them in a commercial context. For example, we took the political slogan 'seize the time' and put it on a calendar. For those who remember, it's a joke; for those who don't, it works anyway." Like *High Times* in its shortlived reformation, And/Or Press is diversifying, publishing books on holistic health, UFOs, and travel. Asked what criteria he uses to decide whether or not to publish a book, cofounder Sebastian Orafali laughed and said, "whether it'll make money."

The mechandising of the drug culture began in the sixties with head shops, personality posters, and water pipes. It continued apace, with greater sophistication, in the seventies. *High Times* and its less successful imitators were central to that process. They provided the nationwide communications vehicles and standards of professional excellence the industry needed to come at least partly up from underground. In the process of using *High Times* to radicalize dope smokers, however, Tom Forcade succeeded mainly in selling consumption in the guise of rebellion.

According to Christopher Lasch, writing in *The Culture of Narcissism*, "the propaganda of commodities serves a double function. First, it upholds consumption as an alternative to protest or rebellion." Instead of attempting to change the fundamental political and economic structure, the consumer—hip or otherwise—buys something to make life a little easier: a bong for the den, perhaps.

Second, writes Lasch, "the propaganda of commodities turns alienation itself into a commodity." That's where *High Times* and its penis-shaped pipes and romantic tales of beating the law to the cache of the right stuff come in. *High Times* does not propose a sustained alternative to life as it is; rather, it offers the means to make life more comfortable. It seeks not to replace the system, but to redeem it, all the while offering readers a feeling of camaraderie based on shared symbols and language which suggest that they are beating the system.

In short, *High Times* defines freedom as the freedom to consume. It is not alone in that regard. *Rolling Stone* and *Ms.* do the same, as do a dynamic group of alternative newspapers that grew to prosperity in the seventies—the free, controlled-circulation urban weeklies.

*Style pushes news and
analysis off page one in
many urban weeklies, as
this sampler shows. (Covers
courtesy of respective periodicals.)*

twelve

Ten Great Places to Find Croissants After Midnight

IN THE SPRING OF 1978, readers of the weekly *Boston Phoenix* discovered a new magazine called *Savor* tucked among the pages of their paper. Published on slick paper, with plenty of color and attractively designed ads, *Savor* told *Phoenix* readers how to mix good-tasting drinks, the secrets of rating imported beers and preparing Indian cuisine, and where to go in Boston for low-cost, quality meals. And the magazine's editors did not neglect to instruct their readers on the art of appreciating fine wine.

Savor was hailed by *Phoenix* publisher Stephen Mindich as a great leap forward in newspaper marketing. "To our knowledge," Mindich wrote, "the creation of *Savor* as a standard-size, four-color, glossy magazine presented as part of a weekly (or daily) publication is a unique concept in newspaper publish-

Survival is a daily challenge for many of the world's people, but merely a chic diversion for conspicuous consumers. (Courtesy of Eva Yarmo.)

ing. . . . *Savor* is intended to become a monthly addition to the *Phoenix* as a guide to the delights of dining, drinking, and anything else that may appeal to the well-savored life." Concluded Mindich, "*Savor* is another step in the *Phoenix*'s constant effort to respond to the needs of our market."

Savor was an outgrowth of a major development in periodical publishing in the seventies: the rise of marginally alternative newspapers and magazines—usually distributed free—as.how-to guides for coping with and enjoying city life. The new urban periodicals, most of them weekly newspapers, both reflected and helped stimulate the "gentrification" of America's metropolitan areas by well-educated young adults, most of them white, often without children and with disposable incomes, in search of sophistication that suburbs and small towns didn't offer. They were the Woodstock Generation a decade later, looking for a condominium rather than a tab of LSD, the 18-to-37-year-olds coveted by advertisers.

The urban papers played a major role in packaging young consumers for advertisers and helping to entice them away from the challenging world of radical politics, with a plethora of listings, service features, and ads keyed to the leisure-time market. To a considerable extent, the urban periodicals benefited from the work of their radical predecessors. Challenges to matrimony first articulated in feminist and leftist media helped create a phenomenal increase in single-member households and single-parent families. Women had children later or not at all. And those single people, both female and male, took advantage of their mobility to flock to the cities looking for jobs, apartments, independence. Once they got there, devoid of traditional community, they plugged into elaborate networks of service industries devised to meet their needs. The urban weeklies composed a communications network through which those services were advertised and made available. In the process, they helped define a community of interests that replaced the geographic communities of the past.

By defining this community of interests in an intensely commercial context—the music, bars, nightclubs, self-improvement centers, and physical therapy courses to which the upwardly mobile young moderns flocked were not free—the urban weeklies also helped displace the corresponding community of interests provided by radical politics, which had generally existed in a less commercial context (generally, but not always; the books and posters popular among radicals were not free either). In this way, periodicals of the seventies that were only marginally alternative joined with broader social forces—the tightening of the economy, the end of the Vietnam war as a unifying issue—to undermine radical culture and radical media. Much of the counterculture, as Chapter Seven showed, was co-opted as early as the late sixties.

How alternative are the urban weeklies? Many are cleanly designed, carefully edited periodicals that differ from conservative daily newspapers in several important ways: their relative ease of access for unknown or offbeat contributors; their use of the personal voice in writing; their willingness to do in-depth, magazine-style features about issues generally skimmed by daily newspapers and electronic media; their willingness to jab at the local power structure. They are alternatives in the broadest sense.

Not radical papers themselves, the urban weeklies give occasional access to radical writers. One such writer is David Moberg, a staff reporter for the socialist newspaper *In These Times,* who also contributes to the weekly *Chicago Reader.* Says Moberg of the *Reader*: "The *Reader* is an alternative in that it is relatively open to a wide range of contributors. The editors, in general, disagree with the things I write, but as long as I write them well, make a convincing case, and they seem to be well researched, they they'll use them. They are less staid than a lot of publications, more open to things that are unusual."

The urban weeklies that came of age in the seventies are hybrids incorporating features of several older publications and types of publications. The *Village Voice,* for one, is a marked influence. The *Voice* was the first American weekly newspaper to successfully "target" the young, mobile, educated, urban reader with both advertising and editorial content. The *Voice* covered what that group wanted to read about: theatre, film, books, art, city politics, and the politics of race, gender, and class. And it told readers where to find their hip oases in the concrete jungle. In the process, the *Voice* greatly aided the growth of off-Broadway theatre and the prosperity of small merchants who catered to the market of young urban professionals. Equally importantly, the *Voice* did all that with literacy and wit which the alternative periodicals of the seventies respect and to which they aspire.

The second influence on the urban weeklies was the humble "shopper"—a paper issued strictly to direct buyers to bargains in their localities. The urban weeklies adapted the free circulation of the shopper, its distribution to selected readers, and its profusion of service-oriented classified and display ads to their own purposes.

The third influence was Clay Felker's *New York* magazine. Founded in

1968 as a spinoff of the deceased *New York World Journal Tribune*, *New York* soared in popularity in the early seventies with breezy, provocative formula writing and ads geared to affluent "upscale" readers. Published weekly on glossy paper, *New York* expertly combined shopping tips (a guide to ten great places to find croissants after midnight) and consumer muckraking (mouse droppings on the premises of the croissant manufacturers).

New York was not a magazine to be read at leisure, but skimmed in haste, and the design by graphic artist Milton Glazer reflected that fact. "The magazine is not designed to look beautiful," Glazer told the *Columbia Journalism Review* in 1974, "but to convey a sense of energy, compression, density, information. We want it to be fast-paced, like the city, easily accessible, undemanding. We want people to get in and out of it very easily." Many of these qualities were imparted to *New York*'s own spinoff, *Ms.*, itself a kind of consumer's guide to feminism.

The urban alternative weeklies have borrowed freely from all three sources, but they are not carbon copies of any one influence. While most urban weeklies stress good writing, only the most accomplished of them—the Boston papers, Seattle's *Weekly*, Portland, Oregon's *Willamette Week*, Baltimore's *City Paper*, New England's *Advocates*—approach the quality of writing in the *Voice*, and only a few replicate the *Voice*'s passionate involvement in local and national politics. Most have gone to the targeted free circulation of the shoppers, but their editorial content makes them much more serious as newspapers than the shoppers. Though all have aimed for the flashy graphics and copied the "best-bet" listings of *New York* and other slick city magazines, they are not city magazines. The urban alternative weeklies aim at a younger market than do the city magazines, and their readers are more likely to actually live in the city, rather than the suburbs, in which city slicks find a large part of their audience. And while alternative weeklies are usually more cautious about political advocacy than the *Voice*, they are much more likely to take sides on matters of civic concern than are the city magazines.

The political slant of the urban alternatives is liberal and left-liberal. They are a far cry from the radical underground papers of the sixties, few of which made the transition from the explosive, outer-directed activism of the sixties to the quieter, localized politics of the seventies. Latter-day pundits such as *Pacific Sun* editor-publisher Steve McNamara hold that the only link between radical underground and city weeklies is technological—i.e., both were made possible by the advent of cheap, simple offset printing—but that is an oversimplification.

The underground press, in effect, did the marketing research for its successors, identifying a large constituency of young readers—mostly the white children of the Baby Boom—and helped make them a self-conscious social and political entity through its first-person, rally-round-the-flag advocacy journalism. The urban weeklies of the seventies have further developed the marketability of that generation—now older, less politically radical, more affluent—with more refined reporting and soft lifestyle features. The urban weeklies offer a very different agenda than did their radical predecessors: pleasure rather than struggle; status rather than the erasure of privilege; enjoyment of the world as it is rather than visions of the world as it might be.

The earliest and most spectacular successes of urban alternative newspapers came in Boston, where the *Phoenix* and *The Real Paper* each racked up circulations of around 100,000 (half paid, half distributed free on campuses), and threw a scare into the mighty *Globe*, the city's leading daily newspaper. Both papers are nationally known among mass-media and alternative mediaphiles alike, and their editorial mix and advertising base are widely imitated.

Editorially, both papers feature heavy doses of local and state politics, which they leaven with profiles of Boston's colorful ethnic "pols." Much of the weeklies' political coverage is on the order of high-level gossip— who is doing what to whom in the back rooms and what it will mean for the winner's career—although the voting records of the principals are not forgotten.

The January 15, 1980, issue of the *Phoenix* carried the following cover lines, ballyhooing an inside story on Massachusetts Governor Edward J. King: "The governor's government is of, by, and for his own kind. Renée Loth looks at his pawn game, and Richard Gaines analyzes the firing of Ron Brinn, the press secretary who couldn't sell King's own self-image."

The other stories promoted on the cover of that issue included a feature story on the lifestyles of people who work in the Massachusetts woods, a theatre review and a feature on the conversion of Boston movie houses into mini-theatres, and a profile of a local rock band. The inside pages also contained a serious and well-written feature on elections in Zimbabwe Rhodesia, a column on the fortunes of the Boston Celtics pro basketball team, and reviews of film, art, and music. Editorial copy shared the paper with twelve pages of classified ads, extensive calendars and listings, and a voluminous amount of display advertising for stereo systems, car rentals, clubs, records, liquor, cigarettes, and restaurants. The issue was exactly 100 pages long, thin for the *Phoenix* (blame it on the post-holiday slump) and a little thicker than the average issue of *The Real Paper*.

The editorial mix of that issue was broadly representative of both papers, with its emphasis on culture and entertainment, its lengthy news features on state and local politics, and its dollop of international news. The tone of the writing was consistent with the tone of most *Phoenix* and *Real Paper* articles: informed, interested but not passionate, a bit bemused.

This approach has netted both papers, especially the *Phoenix*, the trust of local advertisers who would probably feel threatened by a consistent advocacy of radical politics. That they don't feel threatened by the *Phoenix* and *The Real Paper* is indicated by the frequent appearance in both papers of special supplements—up to 48 pages in length—on food, drink, sound equipment, cars, and fashion. The supplements include bows to bargain-hunting, but often also make outright appeals to snobbery. Read an article on footwear in a *Phoenix* fashion supplement: ". . . a heady sort of status comes from possessing, let's say, a set of Galubier Superguides (mountaineering boots for approximately $100) or a pair of Justin country boots made of genuine alligator." The operative assumption of such appeals seems to be "You are what you buy."

The *Phoenix* has always maintained a lead over *The Real Paper* in snaring upscale advertisers, partly because the *Phoenix* is the older (by six years), more established newspaper. From the beginning, the *Phoenix* has also been under the direction of one person, founder-publisher Stephen Mindich, a brassy, self-described "supersalesman" who never made a secret of his desire for material gain.

The Real Paper, by way of contrast, was collectively owned from its founding in 1972 (see Chapter Nine) until the staff, exhausted by the demands of having to obtain everyone's approval for major decisions and still produce a weekly paper, sold to outside interests in 1975. Even when *The Real Paper* was collectively owned, it installed a hierarchy for day-to-day operations and attempted to match Mindich's success at the *Phoenix* with advertising supplements, cultural coverage, and listings. The paper was just getting by—hampered by a reputation in the business community as a radical organ—when the staff sold the paper.

The new owners were Martin Linsky, a former Republican state legislator, who became editor; well-connected Boston lawyer Ralph Fine, who took over as publisher; and David Rockefeller, Jr., son of the head of Chase Manhattan Bank, who moved in as executive vice president. The new triumvirate intensified the frankly commercial orientation of *The Real Paper*, publishing more supplements and pushing for more ads, and taking out a full-page ad of their own in a trade publication, announcing, "*The Real Paper* is run by a bunch of young freaks like Marty Linsky, Ralph Fine, and David Rockefeller, Jr." The ad also listed some of *The Real Paper*'s "freaky, way-out advertisers": Trans-World Airlines, American Motors, Heublein.

Even with its aggressive new campaign, *The Real Paper* was left playing catch-up with Mindich's *Phoenix*, though not as desperately as before. By the late seventies, both papers produced issues in several sections. The *Phoenix* published issues as long as 308 pages, and Mindich drove to the paper's modern offices in a Rolls Royce, a diamond ring sparkling on his little finger.

"I guess for some people I'm supposed to be a hippie, but that's not for me," Mindich told novelist Dan Wakefield, writing on the Boston weeklies in the *New York Times* magazine. "I wear a suit and a shirt with cuff links. If I have to see a banker, I don't want to show up wearing a leather headband and dungarees and play a role."

The tension between money and ideals at the Boston weeklies was the theme of a feature-length movie, released in 1977. Joan Micklin Silver's *Between the Lines* portrayed staff members at the mythical *Back Bay Mainline* as ambitious, frightened, and lost in the machinations of an aggressive publisher and outside business interests. The movie, based loosely on the sale of the old *Cambridge Phoenix* to Mindich, and written for the screen by a former film reviewer for the two papers, showed ideals running a distant second.

As successful as Mindich has been in Boston in real life, however, he may be nearing the limits of growth there. Boston is not especially large (population 560,000), and he has to share it with a competitor which many readers confuse with his paper. As a consequence, Mindich is thinking of finding other properties in which to sink his profits—estimated to be $500,000 a year against revenues of nearly $6 million in 1979. In the early seventies, Mindich tried unsuccessfully to establish papers in Cleveland, Philadelphia, and Miami. They failed for a variety of reasons, none of which seems to have discouraged Mindich more than temporarily. He has other plans.

Mindich has said, "I've always had the ambition to own a radio station, so I'm in the market for one of those. And there may be an opportunity for us to expand by helping out other, foundering weeklies, thereby acquiring either majority or substantial ownership in them."

Such help, of course, would not be altruistic. The *Phoenix*, like any business, is subject to the first commandment of capitalist enterprise: Expand or die. For all its often-sympathetic coverage of alternative social movements, the *Phoenix* is a conventional enterprise whose internal operations are strictly business.

The *Phoenix* and *The Real Paper* inspired weeklies in other cities, one of which rivaled their success by the late seventies. The *Chicago Reader*, distributed in Chicago's business district and its North Shore lakefront neighborhoods, was modeled directly on *Boston After Dark*, which *Reader* cofounder Bob Roth read during a summer stay in Boston. The *Reader* publishes issues that approach 100 pages in length and distributes 97,000 copies of each issue. Going the Boston weeklies one better, all copies of the *Reader* are free, as are most of its popular classified ads.

The *Reader* was launched in the fall of 1971 by four young graduates of Minnesota's Carlton College and was published out of what the paper's first managing editor, Nancy Banks, remembered as "a slum apartment." Roth, who became the paper's editor and publisher and is still the guiding force at the *Reader*, explained that, "I could see Chicago was in need of a good youth market publication." The *Reader* grew slowly but steadily, targeting students and young professionals, outdistancing several competing periodicals, including the *Chicago Seed*.

The *Seed* played a pivotal role in the Yippie invasion of Chicago in 1968, but by the early seventies the fires of insurrection were burning low. The *Seed* published its flamboyant calls to arms more and more irregularly until, in 1972, the paper folded. David Moberg recalled, "The *Reader* had a lot of impact because it was financially successful, and it had a lot of financial success because it departed from a lot of the more socially and politically conscious formulae published earlier."

Like most other alternative city weeklies, the *Reader* downplayed radical politics. Although the *Reader* published an occasional political article, the consumer guides and cultural coverage that Roth built into the paper brought in more advertising revenue. The ads, in turn, were aimed at the newly prospering, youthful community emerging in the early seventies in Chicago. "Not until the Baby Boom generation got out of college did that community really exist," said Nancy Banks. "The *Reader* helped those people recognize each other."

At about the same time, opposition to Mayor Richard Daley's political machine was growing in Chicago. This feeling was strong among young people in the lakefront neighborhoods, where the *Reader* circulated, carrying occasional features on reform politics by writers such as Moberg and freelancer Don Rose, an antimachine activist. In 1978, the antimachine sentiment that gathered momentum throughout the seventies resulted in the surprise election of Jane Byrne as the recently deceased Daley's successor. Byrne's campaign manager was Don Rose.

But while the *Reader* opened its pages to reformers from time to time, the paper did not crusade or even take clear positions on political issues as a paper. In large part, this was attributable to Roth, who, although he studied political science in the University of Chicago's graduate school, was steadfastly apolitical as an editor. Instead of hardnosed reporting or polemics, Roth filled the paper with lengthy, magazine-style features on "soft" cultural subjects and reviews of local theatre, music, and art. While the *Reader*'s political influence was almost inadvertent, its cultural impact was deliberate and considerable. Remembered Moberg: "A relationship existed between the *Reader* and a loose kind of community. Because of the *Reader*, art got covered, music got covered. Much later, local theatre got covered." Compared to the desultory coverage in the dailies, the *Reader*'s cultural writers were empathetic and informed about local arts.

Much of the *Reader*'s editorial content was well written, but editorial content was never the main attraction of the *Reader*; its ads and listings were—e.g., classified ads to find an apartment, listings to find cheap movies or good wine. By the end of the seventies, the *Reader* was 65 percent advertising, about the same percentage as a successful daily newspaper. And the *Reader* charged twice as much per thousand readers (the standard measurement) for ads than the Chicago dailies, because response to *Reader* ads was so strong. Not only did they pull lots of customers, they pulled the "right kind" of customer. Said one *Reader* advertiser in a *Wall Street Journal* feature on the *Reader* in 1979, "It reaches the kind of person we want, the kind who doesn't care about saving a nickel or a dime."

As for editorial, "If they read the articles, fine," Roth told the *Journal*, "if they don't, fine."

The secret of the *Reader*'s success, according to Roth, is strict adherence to what he terms "*Reader* theory." "*Reader* theory tells you to devise a publication that will be interesting to nonreaders," Roth told Michael VerMeulin in an article for an in-flight airline magazine. One section of the *Reader* is a compilation of entertainment listings, publicity photographs, and capsule reviews of music, film, theatre, and art. Another is composed entirely of advertising, both classified and display. The leadoff section features a long cover story and a number of short, snappy features on Chicago people and places.

"Another thing that *Reader* theory tells you to do is to infuse your paper with a kind of hipness," Roth continued. "The paper has to be witty, sophisticated, and with it." That goes, he said, for display ads and headlines as well as writing. "The most important thing about your editorial is that it have a reputation for high quality—but other than that, anything goes."

A look at what VerMuelin called the *Reader*'s "quirky, laissez-faire" editorial content shows that Roth wasn't kidding when he said that anything goes. If Roth likes an article, it runs, and never mind what it's about. In one issue of the *Reader*, for example, one finds a well-written, well-researched article on the transformation of Chicago's Pilsen district from a community of white, working-class ethnics into a multicultural artists' colony. In another issue, one finds a 19,000-word cover story on beekeeping which doesn't seem designed to be read by anyone in particular; perhaps it wasn't.

As Roth's casual approach to editorial policies indicates, making money is the main reason for publishing the *Reader*. In line with that, Roth—like the *Phoenix*'s Mindich—is expansion-minded. The *Reader* collects royalties for the use of the name *Reader*, its logo, and several other features that are leased to the *San Diego Reader*—another free-circulation weekly, published by a former *Chicago Reader* ad director. In addition, Roth and company publish a much thinner, 30,000-circulation free weekly, launched in 1978, in Los Angeles. There it competes with several other free papers, chief among them the *L.A. Weekly*—like the *Reader*, a nicely designed tabloid feature paper.

Reader theory is being tested in other locales as well. A third *Reader*-type paper—the independent *Twin Cities Reader*—is published in Minneapolis, and a fourth was started in Berkeley/Oakland by Chicago alumna Nancy Banks in 1978. Banks' free weekly, the *East Bay Express*, is her paper, but it is partially financed by investors in Chicago, including Roth. True to her *Reader* background, Banks steers the *Express* down a generally apolitical, service-feature-and-listings track. "People start newspapers for one of two reasons," she said, "because they have an ax to grind, or because they like good writing. I'm in the good writing camp. I don't think politics provides many answers. I have more questions than answers." The *Express* has, accordingly, published first-rate writers such as music critic Lee Hildebrand and social historian John Krich, who writes about Oakland's history and culture with insight and wit.

The commonalities among the various *Readers* and *Reader*-type papers is their lack of a consistently articulated point of view, their determined localism, and their emphasis on arts and entertainment coverage. For most of them, that approach has paid off handsomely. The *Chicago Reader* grossed nearly $2 million in 1978, with revenues running 38 percent higher than that as of late 1979. That's up sixty-five-fold from 1972, the *Reader*'s first full year of operation.

The most clear-cut triumph of seventies merchandising over sixties radicalism was in the San Francisco Bay Area, where the *Berkeley Monthly* and the *San Francisco Bay Guardian* blunted and finally buried the *Berkeley Barb*. Ironically, the biggest success of all, the *Berkeley Monthly*, was started by two former *Barb* staffers.

Tom and Karen Klaber worked on the *Barb* in 1969 during a strange interlude in the paper's history, when Allen Coult—an anthropologist, teacher, and author of a cult classic entitled *Psychedelic Anthropology*— bought the *Barb* from its founder, Max Scherr. According to Tom Klaber, Coult's purchase of the *Barb* was designed to purge the paper of New Left politics and transform it into a spiritual herald.

"Berkeley was very polarized in those days," Klaber remembered. "There were a lot of riots, and Allen saw a lot of the hate emanating from the *Barb*." To start the community on the right path, Coult and the young people who lived and studied with him, including Karen and Tom Klaber, published several issues of a newspaper of their own in 1969. "It was called the *Berkeley People's Paper*," Tom Klaber said, "and when you turned it over, it said *Berkeley Fascist*." That was to show the unity of opposites and suggest that radical and reactionary politics were just two sides of the same coin. The paper criticized the very notion of politics with detached amusement, using parody to make its point.

Coult and his staff of eager devotees didn't have the *Barb* for long. A lawsuit by Scherr—having second thoughts about letting the *Barb* go— wrestled the paper from Coult's hands, after only six months, in December 1969. Coult died several months after losing the *Barb*, but before he did, he advised the Klabers to publish a shopper and attain financial security—advice that perhaps only an American guru could give.

In 1970, the Klabers produced the first issue of a newsprint magazine called the *Berkeley Monthly*. It had no editorial content at first, only ads. But the ads were elegantly designed, with clever borders and lots of white space. The magazine was given away in retail outlets, some of which had been "trashed"—their windows broken, political slogans spray-painted on the doors—only months before in one of Berkeley's many street actions. Many of the *Monthly*'s first advertisers were, like the Klabers, young and hip and just beginning their small businesses. After several well-received issues, the *Monthly* added editorial material—

photo-essays and columns on astrology and natural foods. There were no
political articles. Explained Klaber:

> Karen and I were never political. We came from a spiritual back-
> ground. I never believed in politics as a solution. We believed the thing
> to do was to be an example, to make yourself whole.
>
> We didn't want to put anything negative in the *Monthly*. There was
> no other periodical in Berkeley where people could get away from
> politics. So we produced a periodical consisting of pleasing, inviting
> ads. Regardless of their background, people like to save money, they
> like to go out to eat, wear nice clothes. So the ads became a universal
> feature.

The *Monthly* provided a medium for hip young businesspeople to
announce their presence and affirm their collective identity. They were
lawyers who dropped out of the legal profession to start bakeries,
teachers who decided they really wanted to be chefs, typesetters who
opened pleasant, airy shops to sell macramé and ceramics. Usually their
work was of high quality—and expensive. To entice consumers into the
new shops, the *Monthly* printed coupons which were presented to re-
tailers for discounts. Inside the stores were more copies of the *Monthly*.

The magazine was distributed in Berkeley and Oakland neighborhoods where people whom the *Monthly's* advertisers wanted to reach
lived, people with taste and money. By proclaiming and encouraging the
growth of elegant specialty shops and other personalized services, the
Monthly helped change the popular perception of Berkeley as a hotbed of
radical politics to that of a pleasant place to shop. Following this percep-
tual shift, more businesses located in Berkeley, and the cycle intensified.

Radicals were critical of the *Monthly*, labeling it reactionary, but the
Klabers saw the conservatism of their publication as a natural progres-
sion. Reasoned Tom Klaber, "Young people are idealistic. When you
have nothing, you want to change everything. But you grow up, and
when you do, you start acting instead of reacting. It's inevitable, you get
more conservative. I don't think that's bad."

The *Monthly's* advertisers didn't think so either. The magazine drew a
strong response from shoppers that far outstripped the area's daily
papers, the University of California student paper, and radical alternatives such as the *Barb*. By 1980, the *Monthly* had a controlled circulation
of 70,000 in Berkeley and Oakland and a spinoff edition in Boston, where
Karen Klaber is publisher. The *Boston Monthly* follows the Berkeley

formula of artistically designed ads and light features in its attempt to compete with the *Phoenix* and *The Real Paper*.

The larger weeklies appear well equipped to meet the *Monthly*'s challenge, but smaller community papers are not so well fixed. Not long after the *Berkeley Monthly* expanded to Boston in 1979, the *Newton Times*—a small community paper that sold for 25¢—went out of business. The *Times*' managing editor, Barbara Kravitz, termed the intrusion of free papers supported by advertisers "a very dangerous phenomenon." Kravitz added that "a small independent newspaper simply doesn't have the tools to compete with that. There is a very real danger that alternative voices will be snuffed out."

Apparently unconcerned about their impact on other periodicals, the Klabers push on with plans for expansion and improvement. The *Berkeley Monthly* is now a smoothly edited professional product. Herbert Gold has published fiction in its pages, and Theodore Roszak has contributed essays. According to Tom Klaber, the *Monthly* will begin to cover politics in an evenhanded way, "with no ax to grind, no rigid point of view." The Klabers hope to turn their monthlies into classic American magazines, with local editions in cities around the country and production centralized in Berkeley. To pick up tips from publishing professionals, they have lunched with Clay Felker and Rupert Murdoch, Felker's successor as owner of *New York*, *New West*, and the *Village Voice*.

If all this sounds terribly traditional, Tom Klaber is unworried. "The *Monthly* looks so conservative," he smiled, eyes shining, "but what has a front has a back. Who would think that something that appears so conservative would be run by two old acidheads?"

While the *Berkeley Monthly* was making its steady climb to success, other Bay Area periodicals used the free, controlled circulation format to ride to prosperity or at least to revitalize sagging fortunes. Even the *Bay Guardian*, the liberal San Francisco weekly that had long prided itself on hard-nosed reporting, in 1979 began giving away an entertaiment section—with twice as many pages as its news section—which sold for 50¢. The following year, the *Bay Guardian* began giving away the entire paper, save for a home-delivery edition for which a few subscribers still paid. Wrote *Guardian* editor-publisher Bruce Brugmann, in a burst of hyperbole in the paper's May 29, 1980, issue:

Now, when times are tough and the price of just about everything is going up, you can get *free* each week, the consumer advice and information the *Guardian* has become famous for. . . . We recognize that in recent years the world has become a tougher place to get by in. . . . As times have gotten harder, it seems, good and reliable sources of information have grown fewer. . . . We've now decided to go against that trend. . . . We'll be as good and timely as ever . . . but we'll be free.

As the success of liberal giveaway papers in Boston and Chicago show, however, the *Guardian* was not going against the trend among city weeklies, but with it, often with unhappy consequences for readers. The free distribution of a *Bay Guardian* laced with entertainment listings was the culmination of a trend that began in the paper's pages in the early seventies, when guides and lists of "best-ofs" started appearing. Excellent consumer reporting was also published in the paper then—much of it by Jennifer Cross, author of *The Supermarket Trap*—on price "ripoffs," labeling loopholes, and the like. But by the middle seventies, stories by other reporters took a fluffier turn, and hard news was pushed aside to make room for listings and reviews keyed to advertising supplements. The paper's other publishing activities reflected the change. In 1971, the *Bay Guardian* staff compiled a book that critically examined high-rise development; in 1975, the paper produced a guidebook to San Francisco (issued in a revised edition in 1980).

Brugmann explained the change in emphasis by citing readership surveys in which "everyone says they love our PG&E stuff [exposés of the local utility]. But if they love it as much as they say, we'd have sold more papers. So we had to broaden the base of the paper with more consumer and entertainment stuff, and more lists, while retaining the core of our politics."

There is still some good reporting in the *Bay Guardian*, to be sure. In 1978, staff reporter David Johnston's lengthy exposure of a San Francisco politician's wheeling and dealing scotched a Presidential appointment for the politician, and the series was nominated for a Pulitzer Prize. But that kind of story is more the exception than the rule in the *Bay Guardian* long a favorite of media critics looking for a feisty little community paper to praise. More characteristic of the paper today is a special ski issue—published at about the same time as Johnston's stories—which advised readers on "how to cope with the biggest ski season in ten years," or the *Bay Guardian*'s annual summer guides to California wines and nude beaches.

The prosperity of radical alternative periodicals in the Bay Area, as elsewhere, declined in almost direct relationship to the rise of consumer guides among the affluent young liberals they helped develop into big spenders. Many radical periodicals expired. One of them was the *Berkeley Barb*, started in 1965, at its end the oldest survivor of the sixties underground press. Reaching a peak circulation of 93,000 paid weekly copies in 1969, just before the exodus of staffers from Max Scherr's regime, the *Barb* sold only 1,500 biweekly copies before it folded with the July 3, 1980, issue—just over one percent of its peak circulation.

Writing in 1977, Morris Dickstein singled out the *Barb* by observing, in his book *Gates of Eden*, "The history of the sixties was written as much in the *Berkeley Barb* as in the *New York Times*." The history of the *Barb* in the seventies, however, is the story of a paper that failed to redefine itself when redefinition was crucial to maintaining the *Barb*'s impact. Scherr's shocktroop journalism was out of place in a community that was defecting to the commercial elegance of the *Berkeley Monthly*, and he was unable to stem the tide. In 1973, Scherr left the helm of the *Barb*, although he remained as a paid consultant. In its seven remaining years of existence, the *Barb* had eight editors-in-chief and went through several format changes in a vain effort to recover its vitality. Although good work often appeared in the *Barb*, the paper, crippled by its well-deserved reputation for sexism and by an ever-shrinking editorial budget, was unable to break through to a wider readership.

In 1978, in desperation, the *Barb* adopted the free-circulation format that proved so successful for other papers, spinning off its notorious sex ads into paid weekly appropriately called *The Spectator*. The "new" *Barb* scored occasionally with hard-hitting local reporting; one story, which showed that developers of a Berkeley industrial park had mob links, helped to defeat the reelection bid of the town mayor, who backed development of the park. The paper also gave more frequent coverage to radical and minority issues than did the *Bay Guardian* and other qualified alternative papers.

But while the *Barb* didn't wholly renounce the radical editorial slant of its past, the paper's editors did make concessions to the ten-great-places-to-find-croissants-after-midnight syndrome. Staffers wrote up their favorite restaurants, and advertising and editorial content was closely coordinated in guides to local shopping districts. The gamble didn't pay off. The *Barb*'s lingering reputation as a radical paper hampered efforts to attract new advertisers, while its editorial compromises failed to attract and hold a radical readership.

To make matters worse, International News Keyus (INK), the corpo-

ration of tax lawyers and accountants that took control of the *Barb* from
Scherr in 1973, made only sporadic efforts to promote the brave new
Barb. In early 1980, claiming losses of nearly $200,000 since the switch to
free circulation, INK fired several key staffers, cut the *Barb*'s press run
from 40,000 to 5,000, and put the cover price back at a quarter. The
paper continued to lose money. Six months later, INK called it quits and
folded the *Barb*. (The profitable *Spectator* survives.)

Shannon Bryony, the *Barb*'s last editor, attributed the paper's long
goodbye to the rise of the right and the supposed apathy of former
radicals "who have lost their vigor, the belief that their convictions can
actually be practiced." Bryony was also highly critical of the *Barb*'s
publishers, whose successful law firm reportedly draws considerable
income from other projects and properties. "I feel," she said, "that the
owners should be morally obligated to maintain the life of the paper,
because in several years [after a spell of conservative government] people
are going to need it again."

The rightward drift of the late seventies undoubtedly hurt the *Barb*.
So, too, did its erratic management. Equally important, however, was
the competition from watered-down, free-circulation periodicals with
generally unchallenging content that pleased advertisers, attracted revenue, and permitted those periodicals to outflank and finally kill the *Barb*.

Free urban weeklies compete with conventional media and radical alternatives alike in nearly every large American city and in some college
towns. Compared to the often-dreary daily papers, grown complacent
from years of monopoly, they are lively and irreverent. But the urban
weeklies, having found the road to prosperity straight and true, are also
awash in commercialism. As time passes, they become more and more
alike, and their once-fresh approach runs the risk of becoming formulaic.

Thus it is that as spring and fall fashion supplements appear in the
Advocate newspapers in New England, similar sections stuffed with ads
and editorial copy tailored to the needs of advertisers appear at about the
same time in New Orleans' *Figaro*. As the *Santa Barbara News &
Review*—a generally fine community weekly—circulates a compendium
of listings geared to young consumers and given out free, so *The Aquarian
Weekly*—a highly successful paper in New Jersey and eastern
Pennsylvania—gives away guides to rock music and other entertainment
at retail outlets. A reader driving from one place to another sampling the
alternative weeklies finds some local and regional differences, but the
day when there is a Howard Johnson's-like sameness to the papers may

not be far off. Publishers, who regularly read one another's papers, are quick to transplant features that succeed elsewhere to local soil.

Most of the urban weeklies belong to the National Association of Alternative Newsweeklies (NAAN), a loose trade association formed in 1978 (as simply the National Association of Newsweeklies) to facilitate socializing and the exchange of information between members. NAAN has largely supplanted the once-thriving Underground Press Syndicate and its successor, the Alternative Press Syndicate (APS). That was not hard to do. When *Enlisted Times*—an alternative news-monthly for soldiers—joined APS in 1979, publisher Steve Rees called APS head-quarters in New York, curious to learn why the organization hadn't cashed a check he sent to cover *Enlisted Times'* membership fee. When he finally reached the APS office at mid-day, a stoned/sleepy voice asked Rees what time it was. Too late for APS, apparently.

NAN's founding conference attracted the amused attention of *New Yorker* columnist Calvin Trillin, who contrasted the businesslike atmos-phere with the anarchic journalists who attended an underground press convention in Boulder, Colorado, five years earlier:

> One of the prominent participants in the Boulder conference—the proprietor of an underground press service [Tom Forcade]—showed up with a friend at the Seattle conference for an appearance that was considered significantly brief. Looking more or less like a retired punk rock star and his manager, they made their entrance into a room where forty or fifty respectable-looking people, some of them in tweed sport coats, were discussing such things as circulation acquisition. The news service proprietor and his companion sat down for a few minutes and then quietly took their leave—like a couple of massage parlor operators who had rushed over to work the largest convention in town without first having bothered to find out that it was a conference of Lutheran liturgists. For the remainder of the conference, they were referred to as "the two gentlemen in costume."

The atmosphere at the association's 1980 conference in San Francisco was equally clubby. The representatives of member papers, most of them well-groomed white males in their thirties and forties, arrived punctually for meetings about promotional campaigns and employee relations, where they discussed marketing concepts such as psycho-graphics (defining groups of consumers by their interests, such as boat-ing or skiing), positioning (how a paper is defined vis-à-vis the competi-tion), and penetration (how deeply a paper is rooted in its market). Not all the papers represented were doing well, but the collective prosperity of the association's forty-odd members, with a combined circulation of 1.5 million, was evident from the well-appointed hotel in which the conference was held. The meeting closed with cocktails atop the high-rise world headquarters of the Bank of America.

At the convention's only lively discussion of editorial content, Pacific News Service managing editor Sandy Close exhorted the papers to cover international news, minorities, youth, and the poor. "These people are on the cutting edge of change in America today," Close said. "There's a massive illegal underground economy in American cities—drugs, street hustling—stories on how people survive. For the first time in American history [because of our faltering economy] children will make less money, as adults, than their parents." Close's pep talk was well received by some of the assembled journalists but rejected by many others, to whom coverage of local politicians and entertainment was more appealing. Mark Hopp, publisher of the *Twin Cities Reader* (circulation 100,000), dismissed extensive national and international coverage with the remark that such material "has a narrow readership band."

At the final business meeting of the convention, the ailing *Berkeley Barb*, only two months away from folding, threw the association a curve by applying for membership. After several members criticized the *Barb*'s association with *The Spectator* as "dirty money," *Barb* editor Rob Howe—his voice trembling with anger, sixties-style long hair cascading down his back—denounced the assembled journalists as hypocrites. The association's bank account in the Bank of America, an investor in racist South Africa, was dirty money too, Howe said, as was the Rockefeller money in *The Real Paper*. After reading his statement, Howe withdrew the *Barb*'s application and stalked out of the room. "Oh, we probably could have weathered the debate," Howe recalled, "but I really felt that someone needed to knock those people in the teeth." It was the only moment of the convention in which sparks flew over matters of principle and member papers tried to come to grips with what "alternative" means, or could mean.

As the dizzying heights of the Bank of America tower indicated, NAAN isn't the underground press, nor is it a radical press. The urban weeklies shun any association with the underground press—*The Weekly*'s publisher, David Brewster, sniffed in an article in his paper about "the odd eruptions of the 1960s underground"—fearing it will blur their image among advertisers. The papers were almost equally reluctant to describe themselves as alternative publications until I. F. Stone and

Village Voice media critic Alexander Cockburn, speaking at the association's 1979 conference in Boston, lectured the assembled publishers and editors on their social responsibilities. Properly chastened, the newspaper officials added the word "alternative" to the association's name.

The change, however, was more cosmetic than substantive. Most urban weeklies are the property of venture capitalists. Most operate with conventional hierarchies. Most are frankly commercial enterprises which have both capitalized on and encouraged the enfranchisement of a hip, young consumer class in the nation's affluent city neighborhoods. In all those respects, they reinforce the status quo—hardly an "alternative" course of action. Other conservative qualities are traceable to the reliance of many urban weeklies on free circulation, their fascination with celebrity, their solipsistic regard for media.

The success of free-circulation papers makes one wonder whether readers really like and read the papers or just pick them up because they're free. *Creative Loafing*—a free Atlanta weekly that describes itself as "America's most unique newspaper"—consists almost entirely of ads, listings, and short reviews. In 1978, *Creative Loafing* published a news section which sold for 25¢. The paper bombed. Within months, *Creative Loafing* was a free-circulation entertainment guide again. When the *San Diego Reader* tried to charge for its paper, it experienced similarly dismal results and soon returned to free circulation.

Free circulation has undoubted advantages for publishers. It reduces the amount of returns (unsold papers, or papers not picked up by readers); eliminates the handling of small change by merchants, distributors, and readers; and allows publishers to expose their papers to more readers (the *Bay Guardian's* circulation nearly doubled to 40,000 after the paper went free) without requiring a commitment on the part of the reader to purchase the paper. Some two-thirds of the NAAN members give away their papers. The business advantages to free circulation are, however, more than offset by disadvantages on the editorial side.

It is difficult for editors of a free-circulation paper to gauge reader response to editorial content. Letters to the editor and readers' remarks are helpful, but seldom representative, since only people who care deeply about something bother to write or call a periodical. Issue sales are a more reliable indicator, but for free-circulation papers there are no issue sales. That makes advertising the main measure of reader response: did the paper's audience clip and return so-and-so's discount coupon, or patronize such-and-such a store that was featured in the supplement on outdoor gear? Free circulation fundamentally changes the relationship between a periodical and its readers. In place of constituents who pay to support a paper they like are consumers whom the paper delivers as a market to advertisers who, in turn, bankroll the paper.

As its extreme, such a setup can produce papers like *The Aquarian Weekly*. In its August 6, 1980, issue, *The Aquarian* published a 160-page issue devoted mainly to its free, semiannual directory of local bands and clubs. That issue had eight pages of news and news features—about 6 percent of the paper—and even that miniscule figure was padded with celebrity-oriented shorts from Zodiac News Service (costing about 25¢ per published story) and substantial but inexpensive features from Pacific News Service (about $3.00 per published story). Two-and-a-half pages were written by the two *Aquarian* news staffers, who share the paper with a home furnishings editor, a fashion editor, thirteen ad sales representatives, and twenty-five regular music reviewers. Consumers, not readers interested in serious issues, are what *The Aquarian* appears to want most.

Of course, only consumers with money to spend are of interest to advertisers. The *Berkeley Monthly* has its issues delivered door-to-door in middle-class and affluent neighborhoods. Poor people in its circulation area are, in effect, too poor to receive this free periodical. When banks refuse to make loans to residents of poor neighborhoods, the practice is called redlining. Many free-circulation papers, including some that criticize banks for discriminating against the poor, engage in a form of journalistic redlining.

With advertisers footing all the bills, the temptation to devote space to airy promotional features that will please them—and water down items that might offend them—is enormous. Ed Matys, co-owner of the *Advocate* newspapers, defended free circulation, arguing that, with a large number of diversified advertisers, "no one has a dominant voice." Matys added, "We've stood up to major advertisers," but allowed, without elaboration, that "we're not stupid about it."

Such comments conjure images of cigar-chomping advertisers threatening editors with the loss of crucial ad revenue if that exposé of the new performing arts center isn't killed, but crude threats are fairly rare, and in any case they are usually unnecessary. Self-censorship is more common, and more effective, in chastening periodicals whose publishers know they must please advertisers to survive. The first casualty of this built-in chilling effect is, necessarily, the sustained commitment of a periodical to a genuinely radical point of view, one that goes against the societal grain.

Thus *The Real Paper* can publish—as it did regularly for several years—a radical journalist such as Andrew Kopkind. But, surrounded by ads for waterbeds and wines, Kopkind's work did not appear in a radical context. It was an intriguing but isolated element in the *The Real Paper*'s editorial mix, one that was made more palatable to the paper's Republican editor and publisher by the fact that Kopkind is well known. The commitment of *The Real Paper*, as a paper, to points of view comparable to Kopkind's was not forthcoming.

Tim Patterson, a freelance writer in Boston who has written for *The Guardian* and other leftist periodicals, analyzed the *Phoenix*'s and *The Real Paper*'s political reportage:

> They encourage political movements, they smile at them, but they don't get involved. And they don't exercise a leadership function in those areas. Clearly, one of the key, continuing political and social struggles in Boston has to do with racism, which is especially evident with the busing crisis. And neither of those papers [has] played a vanguard role. When outrages come up, they get covered. When there are community protests, they get covered. But the papers don't put themselves out on a limb. And busing is a constant, throbbing issue in Boston.

Rather than advocate fundamental social change, then, the alternative weeklies give sympathetic coverage to those who do—such as the Clamshell Alliance, an antinuclear coalition covered extensively by both Boston weeklies in the middle and late seventies. The alternative weeklies reserve their enthusiasm for electoral politics, which they cover as a particularly racy sport and which they equate with colorful individuals whose indiscretions make good copy. The implicit message in coverage of this kind is that the establishment is corrupt, and frequently ridiculous, but it's probably here to stay, and, while fundamental social change might be nice, actively advocating it is a bit like tilting at windmills.

Mainstream politicians have come to appreciate the importance of city weeklies, as shown by the four-year tenure (from 1975 to 1979) of Martin Linsky, the former state legislator, as editor of *The Real Paper*. Other alternative papers have been bought outright by local and state politicians. The *Austin* (Texas) *Sun* and *New Times Weekly* in Phoenix were both purchased in the late seventies by socially prominent people active in Democratic Party politics. The *Maui* (Hawaii) *Sun* is owned by the president of the local Rotary Club.

Their reluctance to advocate basic political change led the urban weeklies into heavy coverage of arts and entertainment. In the early and middle seventies, that made them unique. The local dailies were often out of touch with the social mores and activities of young readers. By providing cultural coverage, the alternative weeklies did much to give encouragement and definition to local cultural scenes, which, in turn, provided the weeklies with readers and a financial base of support. By the late seventies, daily newspapers were beginning to duplicate this coverage, however, sometimes successfully.

Said Tim Patterson about the *Phoenix* and *The Real Paper*, "Alternative cultural criticism no longer crusades about the politics of culture, except in the area of a very diluted pro-feminist critique of sexism. Which can also be found in the *Globe* at about the same level of political intensity." The *Globe* also copies the format of the Boston weeklies from time to time, naming long-running features—such as its annual "Summerguide" listings—after similar features that appeared first in the weeklies.

Perhaps the most literal-minded copy of alternative publishing appeared briefly in Chicago, when the daily *Chicago Sun-Times* published a special section called "Sidetracks." "Sidetracks" attempted to duplicate the *Reader*'s soft features and guides—and wean young consumers from the *Reader* to the *Sun-Times*. The *Sun-Times* promoted "Sidetracks" as "the alternative section within an establishment newspaper." The experiment failed—evidently the *Reader*'s loyal legions were able to recognize a good copy—but it showed the urban weeklies that they face the possibility of losing the main distinction between the dailies and themselves: their listings and reviews. One city weekly, *Willamette Week*, in Portland, Oregon, is owned outright by the daily *Eugene Register-Guard*, whose publishers decided to deal themselves in on the action.

There is already a symbiosis between some daily newspapers and weeklies that are supposedly alternatives to them. In Boston, the *Phoenix* and *The Real Paper* regard the *Globe* as a beat; they delight in exposing the bigger paper's foibles and failures. "They'd both be out of business if they didn't have us to kick around," snorted *Globe* editor Tom Winship. The Boston dailies and weeklies also exchange key personnel. When *Phoenix* editor Bill Miller left the paper, he was hired to edit the Metro section of the *Globe*. The *Phoenix*'s media columnist, Dave O'Brian, is a former reporter for the daily *Boston Herald*.

The media columnist is an increasingly popular feature of alternative papers, but media columnists are rarely media critics. Usually they restrict themselves to doing stories about stories and announcing that the weather forecaster at Channel 6 is about to cross the street to Channel 7.

Such writing combines the features of a trade journal and a gossip sheet, creating much heat but shedding little light on the nature of media. Journalists are elevated to the status of celebrities, and their trade is glamorized—part of a trend in the wake of Watergate and "Woodstein" that can only be called self-serving.

Alternative journalists of the variety described above view themselves as professional colleagues of the mass-media journalists about whom they write and whose jobs they covet. This is in sharp contrast to radical journalists, who see themselves as political activists and outsiders and who find symbiosis with an adversary culture.

Alexander Cockburn told the 1979 conference of the National Association of Alternative Newsweeklies, "Without an alternative culture, there can be no alternative press. It should be our self-interested aim to foster new ideas. Without challenging the reader and making him think . . . we lose the vision that we started our papers for."

Rather than challenge readers, many urban weeklies of the seventies settled for soothing them. In the process, they helped neutralize large segments of America's most activist generation and blunted their own ability to present an authentic alternative vision.

IS THIS THE FACE OF A PRESIDENT?

INTELLIGENCE

DESPAIR

WARM-HEARTEDNESS

SEXUAL VITALITY

FATIGUE

VACILLATION

STAMINA

and *the Candidates*

East West Journal *engages readers with occasional diagnoses of well-known people by macrobiotic healers who study the face for clues to health. (Courtesy of* East West Journal.*)*

thirteen

Aquarian Enterprise

The Van der Horst Curve of Media Visibility
How to Deal with Despair ☐ The Family Bed

NewAge

June 1979 $1.50
Foreign $1.75

HARRISBURG
Will it really make a difference?

CLOSED for
RETHINKING

WHEN JOANNA ROGERS MACY published an article on "despair work" in the monthly magazine *New Age*, she did so with the idea of lifting the cloud of despair—despair over the apparently bleak fate of the planet Earth, despair for the future of her own family, herself, and her readers. Macy suggested using meditation exercises, dream-readings, and group discussions to confront despair, name it, and live through the dark night of the soul so that one might join with others to combat the conditions that cause despair—e.g., war, nuclear power, and pollution. "In the synergy of sharing," she wrote, "comes power."

Immediately after Macy's article appeared, she was inundated with letters from *New Age* readers who identified with her bouts with despair and shared her determination to do something about them. Invitations to speak at conferences and seminars arrived. Macy, a Buddhist scholar and a veteran of the antiwar movement, had struck a responsive chord.

"How to Deal With Despair," published in the June 1979 issue of *New Age*, was fairly representative of Aquarian Age media. The article was written in a warm, personal style; Macy confronted a problem and suggested a way out; her argument rested on the assumption that social change is desirable and possible and that it begins with the individual.

Some Aquarian argonauts have tempered esoteric pursuits with a renewed surge of whole-earth activism. (Courtesy of New Age.*)*

Moreover, her story appeared in a publication dedicated to putting people in touch with one another to effect change, and it was given an initial boost when *New Age* encouraged readers to write Macy and listed an address so they could do so.

Aquarian enterprises such as *New Age*—"Aquarian Age" and "New Age" are used interchangeably to describe the resurgence of mystical religions and humanistic psychologies in the seventies—are direct descendants of the countercultural media of the sixties. To the New Age media, the sixties underground bequeathed an abiding interest in mind-expansion, deep affinity with nature, and the belief that real, lasting change comes from changing one's self. The main difference between New Age and sixties counterculture media is the former's promotion of spiritual disciplines in place of drugs as agents of growth.

The deepest roots of New Age media go back considerably further than the sixties, of course. Leafing through New Age periodicals, one is reminded of the sporadic "Great Awakenings" and philosophical movements that have marked American history and the media they produced, such as the Transcendentalist magazine *The Dial* (1840–1844). In *New Age* and other Aquarian media can be heard echoes of these earlier eras: their study of humanity's relationship to God and nature, their attraction to charismatic leaders, their disaffection from the material world and the sins of the past.

Modern Aquarian media directly assist what might be called the latest American awakening. They interview and profile gurus, promote spiritual gatherings and therapeutic retreats, and advocate the application of spiritual principles in everyday life. Sufis, "born-again" Christians, "Jews for Jesus," Transcendental Mediators, "Moonies," Hare Krishna acolytes, Tibetan Buddhists, Native American shamans, and many more are represented in Aquarian media—seekers of universal standards in a time of cultural dissonance.

New Age media are alternative in the sense that they promote a type of religiosity—deep, mystical experience—and political engagement—environmentalism—that go against the societal grain. Many also attempt, with varying degrees of success, to exemplify in their own operations the fluid, cooperative workstyles championed by the sixties counterculture. Some, such as the collectively produced magazine *Rain*, are nonprofit and nonhierarchical; others, such as *East West Journal*, take the familiar path of advocating alternative values while they themselves operate with traditional corporate structure, complete with top-down management.

Regardless of their internal structure, New Age media largely eschew the propaganda of commodities one finds in the pages of *High Times* and the urban weeklies to promote lives of spiritual and psychological fulfillment. In their belief that social change begins with the individual, New Age media activists are not unlike mainstream American media and their celebrations of the self. Here, however, New Age media also depart from mainstream media, for they do not promote individualism based on personal achievement and private acquisition, but rather a type of self-realization in which personal growth is enhanced by working with others to pursue common social goals. New Age media advocate sharing the wealth, peacefully and voluntarily, in a steady-state economy which they pose as an alternative to rapacious industrialization.

Politically, New Age media share characteristics of both the left and the right. However, New Age media lean somewhat more to the left in their unanimous commitment to environmentalism, as the ecology movement—in its most radical sense—directly challenges the notion of progress through industrial development. Indeed, the ecology movement, like many Aquarian media, challenges the concept underlying industrialization—Western materialism itself.

In 1971, Japanese-born Michio Kushi was in America on a mission. His goal: to introduce Americans to the inner truths of yin and yang, the complementary opposites of Eastern philosophy. His version of Eastern wisdom was called the philosophy of macrobiotics.

One of Kushi's first acts was to establish a periodical, a herald of macrobiotics in the United States. From his Boston headquarters, Kushi, with the help of a few students, published a twelve-page tabloid newspaper called *East West Journal*. The *Journal* carried articles on the simple diet of brown rice, vegetables, seeds, and nuts followed by students of macrobiotics; listings of recipes; parables illustrating proper ethical conduct; and Kushi's theories, learned from the late Japanese master of macrobiotics, Georges Oshawa.

The philosophy that *East West Journal* was founded to herald in the West holds that the two basic principles of existence, yin (the passive) and yang (the active), are physically manifested in foods. By balancing one's diet between yin and yang, Kushi held, one is able to attune oneself to the energy of the universe and evolve as a spiritual being. Thus, macrobiotic cooking is far more than simply making sure one gets three square meals a day; it is a spiritual discipline. *East West Journal* differed from most earlier countercultural publications by advocating the assiduous study of this discipline in place of what Kushi considered the ultimate dead ends of psychedelic shortcuts.

In the years since its founding, *East West Journal* (*EWJ*) has grown into a 96-page monthly magazine, printed on inexpensive newsprint but with attractively designed, slick, four-color covers, complete with a universal price code required for sales in supermarkets. The magazine claims a paid circulation of 65,000 and a pass-along readership of a quarter million. According to editor Alex Jack, only about twenty percent of *EWJ*'s readers follow the macrobiotic diet, so articles of broader spiritual interest are included for the other 80 percent. *EWJ* has the largest circulation of any New Age periodical and is among the most frequently quoted.

"We're trying to provide practical information for people to regain their health," Jack explained, "which we see as square number one. Individual health is the key to personal change, and that's the key to social change. You change the world by changing yourself." Continued Jack, "We do not take confrontational approaches to things. We stay away from those kinds of judgments."

While they do not advocate political confrontation, articles in *East West Journal* are informed by a point of view. *EWJ* is critical of much of modern—and especially Western—culture, such as chemical additives in food and the use of high-technology equipment to cure disease; *EWJ* urges readers to adopt natural-food diets as a means of preventing disease instead. While some of the writing has a breathless, "gee-whiz" quality, cover stories and important features are generally well written and documented. Unlike mainstream reporters, many *EWJ* contributors participate in the activities they write about. Yoga teachers write about yoga, gardeners about gardening. A few have credentials as professional journalists.

EWJ has surprisingly strong reporting. Alex Jack was a reporter in Vietnam. Frequent contributor Peter Barry Chowka has written for the *Washington Post*. In 1977, Chowka wrote an exhaustive three-part series on the politics of cancer that ripped the American medical establishment with charges of ineffectiveness and profiteering. Scoring food additives and carcinogens in the environment, Chowka also blasted what he called "the pharmaceutical-medical complex":

Founded in 1847 to raise standards of medical practice in the U.S., the AMA [American Medical Association] presently derives half of its $20 million yearly income from advertising in its prestigious *Journal*. Most of the advertisements are placed by members of the Pharmaceutical Manufacturers Association. UPI [United Press International] reported on June 23, 1973, that $10 million of the AMA's retirement fund is invested in drug companies. In 1972, the AMA's own Council on Drugs concluded that the large income the AMA derives from drug manufacturers had made the organization "a captive arm and beholden to the pharmaceutical industry." The AMA responded by disbanding the Council on Drugs.

Chowka's reporting was accompanied by a short article by Kushi, who blamed the high incidence of cancer in modern society on dietary imbalances, and by a roster of practitioners of drugless cancer therapies, complete with their addresses.

Since then, *EWJ* has published several testimonials from persons who claim to have cured themselves of cancer and other serious diseases by adopting a macrobiotic diet. The most spectacular testimonial was that of a Philadelphia medical doctor and hospital administrator who now swears by macrobiotics. By publishing accounts of supposed cures and thorough reporting such as Chowka's, *EWJ* actively encourages alternative paths of healing and changes of lifestyle.

EWJ shares nutritional advice freely with whomever asks—advice which medical science usually considers unproven at best, quackery at worst, but which an increasing number of people follow, thanks to *EWJ*. "Sties on the upper eyelid," wrote publisher Leonard Jacobs in one issue, "are caused by overconsumption of eggs. On the lower eyelid, the cause is excessive intake of dairy food."

Although *EWJ*'s views on nutrition and medicine seem radical, the magazine can be quite conservative on some issues. Explained Alex Jack, "We tend to find value in the past, in the ancient ages, in all kinds of people in all countries, and especially in the family structure." *EWJ* made its regard for tradition concrete in 1980, when most of an issue was devoted to dissecting what its editors called "the myth of overpopulation" and to advocating large, traditional nuclear families. *EWJ* also editorialized against birth control nd abortion, asserting that the dangers to health and spirituality inherent in both were great.

Another area in which *EWJ* is conservative is its coverage of labor. Erewhon, a natural foods company affiliated with Kushi's macrobiotic community, was unionized in 1979 by workers who charged that management was distant and unresponsive. *EWJ* avoided mention of the union for a year after the organizing drive, even though Erewhon executives are often interviewed for stories in the magazine, and its pages routinely carry ads for Erewhon products.

EWJ's silence on the union seemed all the more, well, Old Age when *New Age*—another Aquarian publication—published a cover story on the subject. In the course of the *New Age* account, it was reported that Kushi had suggested to union activists that they were unhappy because their personal health was bad, not because working conditions were inadequate. Kushi's comment illustrates a limitation of the Aquarian precepts that *EWJ* advocates: namely, a reluctance to admit that anything outside oneself can be a source of problems.

In a round-table discussion on the alternative radio series "New Dimensions," Michael Rossman, a veteran of the Free Speech Movement and now an Aquarian commentator, observed:

> If you alone are responsible for what happens to you, then you aren't responsible for what happens to anyone else, because if they're responsible for their reality, and you're responsible for yours, then nothing you do basically can infringe in any fashion on their essential freedom. So the self is given a kind of license, an absolute license, to fulfill itself in existence. This is the ideology that's necessary to sustain the capitalistic system. It goes, "If you are only responsible for your own problems, they're only your problems. You've got nobody to blame for them. What should you do about them? You should try as best you can in your own way to make your condition better, but don't kick about the power structure of the universe or of society. There is an order: you have a place in the order. Do the best you can."

That *East West Journal* and the macrobiotic community of which it is a part subscribe to that ideology is made plain by the name Erewhon, drawn from Samuel Butler's 1872 novel *Erehwon* (but spelled slight different), in which people get sick only because they have committed crimes. In the book, sick people go to jail.

But while *EWJ* is reluctant to criticize its immediate "family," the magazine has published occasional critiques of the Aquarian culture—some of them quite perceptive. The most notable was a 1976 cover story entitled "Perils of Counterculture." Written by John de Graaf and originally published in a Minnesota alternative paper, *North Country Anvil*, the piece compared devotees of America's New Age with the nature-loving, guitar-playing *wandervogel* of pre-Hitler Germany.

De Graaf drew parallels between Charles Reich's *The Greening of*

America and a book published in Germany in 1923 which sang the praises of apolitical German counterculturists. He went on to detail the co-optation of that movement by the Nazis, writing, "Hitler's talk of a mystical community, the 'Volksgemeinschaft,' appealed to the yearnings of an alienated youth and won over large numbers of the young, who had no memory of the horrors of World War I."

De Graaf closed by calling for a synthesis of New Age insights into personal and spiritual life and radical analyses of political and economic structures to provide "thoughtful alternatives to the economic and psychic chaos about us." It was an exemplary piece of scholarship on de Graaf's part, and publishing it took some courage on the part of *EWJ*, whose editors must have known the piece would shake some of their readers. Most readers who wrote published letters to the editors did so to praise the piece, but that could have been as much a response to peer-group pressure as genuine agreement. Unlike, say, the letters pages of the *Village Voice*, where readers enmeshed in New York's personal and literary feuds are expected to take passionate issue with the writers of articles and each other, strong disagreement in the New Age movement and media is generally considered disruptive of harmony, and therefore bad form. Readers who disagreed with de Graaf's challenging piece may thus have kept their disagreement to themselves.

EWJ's utility to readers is not only intellectual but practical. The magazine publishes regular columns on gardening, cooking, and preventive medicine, plus "Sundial"—a section of "resources for natural living" that gives names, addresses, and prices for items such as wood-burning stoves and solar food-driers. The magazine also sells natural foods to readers via mail order and hawks utensils such as bamboo tea strainers and vegetable brushes. A lengthy calendar of classes and workshops and several pages of readers' classifieds help round out every issue, as do frequent ads offering books on macrobiotics that the magazine also sells by mail.

Characteristically, the macrobiotic journalists at *EWJ* maintain that change begins at home. "When we put out a really terrific issue," said Alex Jack, "it usually happens because all the staff have been particularly healthy that month."

EWJ has raised the number of American macrobiotic eaters from practically none to several tens of thousands in less than a decade and has served as an inspiration to other Aquarian media. Nevertheless, *EWJ*, like macrobiotics, is an acquired taste, as not everyone enjoys reading about forty-seven ways to barbecue a tofu-burger. The editors realize this and say they are looking for ways to broaden the magazine's appeal. Said Jack:

> We're trying to reach Middle America, and this is a matter of finding expressions that will really reach them, rather than using one's own esoteric jargon. This has been somewhat of a difficulty with alternative publications in general.
>
> We have our own vocabulary, too, particularly with "yin" and "yang" and "tao," terms that originated in the Far East, and that's an automatic turn-off to large numbers of Americans. But we try to talk to people in terms that they're used to. We're not crazy and we're not a religious cult. Macrobiotics is just common sense that everyone has inside themselves.

In 1974, several staff members of *East West Journal* left that pioneering publication, weary of following the demanding macrobiotic diet and set on publishing a general-interest magazine for Aquarian readers. In October of that year, they published the first issue of *New Age Journal* (now known simply as *New Age*), a newsprint magazine that has grown to a circulation of 35,000, with monthly issues of nearly a hundred pages.

Where *EWJ* saw the world through the lens of macrobiotic philosophy, *NAJ* threw open its pages to participants in the human potential movement—a grab bag of psychologies, diets, spiritualism, physical therapies, and back-to-the-land lifestyles, all aimed at producing personal growth and well-being in the midst of a competitive, materialistic society. *New Age Journal* shared with *East West Journal* the concept of a magazine as a tool. Beginning with issue number one, *NAJ* provided readers with news they could use. That focus has sharpened over the years. A typical issue of *New Age* offers recipes, gardening tips, yoga instructions, news of conferences and spiritual retreats, plus photo-essays and book and record reviews, to go with in-depth feature stories on the New Age groundswell. *New Age* also pays frequent attention to other alternative media efforts, publishing a regular column on independent film and video and running features on community radio. A regular section called "Tools for Living" lists organizations, publications, businesses, and other sources of information, complete with addresses, related to a variety of topics. And nearly all *New Age* articles, on whatever topic, end with a section on "access" that tells readers how to follow up on what they've just read about.

Peggy Taylor, who has edited *New Age* since its third month of existence, explained, "The magazine serves a networking function, putting people in touch with one another." She continued:

We always try to offer options for articles, for doing something about it. Our basic position is we all have a lot more participation in the world available to us than we are aware of, or that we use. And the reason we don't use it, most likely, is because we're not really aware of it.

The basic idea of the magazine is to empower people, to live more fully in the world, and take their high ideals—about just being loving, caring people and wanting to see things work out on the planet—and actually not just sit off in a closet somewhere and hope, but actually live it.

New Age projects a worldly mysticism that impels readers toward engagement and does not stop short of tweaking the noses of well-known spiritual leaders if it seems called for. At times, the magazine's desire to treat gurus like just plain folks shades over into cosmic gossip. A cover story in 1976 reported a split between Ram Dass and Joya—two popular American teachers—in loving detail, revolving around whether the two had broken their vows of celibacy with each other. "Look, I didn't fuck Ram Dass," reporter Stephen Diamond quoted Joya as saying, "but if I had, you'd better believe he'd stay fucked. My Sal—that's my [presumably former] husband and lover of twenty years—he tells me I'm the best in the world."

If *New Age* sometimes descends to earthly triviality, it more often clears the way for readers to become involved in whole-earth activism. *New Age* has covered the antinuclear movement since 1976, when eighteen activists peacefully occupied the construction site of a nuclear power plant at Seabrook, New Hampshire. Since then, the magazine has published frequent reports from Harvey Wasserman and opened its pages to strategy sessions for the likes of the Clamshell Alliance.

The June 1979 issue of *New Age* was devoted to discussing the future of the antinuclear movement, a growing groundswell that traces its philosophical roots to Gandhi and Thoreau and, more recently, to pacifists who opposed the Vietnam war. Feature articles by Wasserman and fellow Clamshell Alliance member Catherine Wolffe kept intact *New Age*'s reputation for participatory journalism. Unlike sixties underground media, however, the rhetoric of imminent Armageddon was tempered by hope, and police and utility company officials were seen as unenlightened opponents rather than deadly enemies. An earlier cover story included a "demonstrator's guide" to antinuclear groups around the country and outlined plans for further demonstrations at Seabrook.

In addition to its frequent antinuclear stories, *New Age* has published popular issues on personal relationships, health, and money. While *New Age* has a broader scope than *East West Journal*, the staff lacks *EWJ*'s grounding in a particular philosophy. As a result, *New Age* frequently flies off in pursuit of its staff's fancy of the moment. One of the subjects in which *New Age* has been keenly interested is money—"prosperity consciousness," in Aquarian terminology.

Prosperity consciousness is the notion that commerce can serve as a vehicle for spiritual realization, that seekers who have long felt guilty about making money can "give themselves permission" to be rich, and that this is consistent with the Buddhist ideal of Right Livelihood. The *Berkeley Monthly*, for one, was founded and operated on this basis. The idea was proposed most enthusiastically in a *New Age* interview with Robert Schwartz, headlined "American Business Needs You," in 1976. Response to the interview was so favorable that Schwartz was asked to write a column for *New Age*, which he did.

Effused Schwartz: "I'm getting increasingly excited about the idea of the marketplace and the domain of business and entrepreneurship as valid places to explore our growing personal awareness." He went on to quote one Jim Nixon, "a Californian distantly related to ex-President Nixon," on the virtues of commerce: "'Let me say first off that business, as a concept, has attracted too many attackers. It's currently popular to describe business as greedy and manipulative and overly competitive. In some cases, this is true; in other cases, not. I can find only one constant in all successful businesspeople. All successful businesspeople are businesslike—and that is *very* Zen.' Wow."

Schwartz, a former consultant at Time, Inc., and a multimillionaire director of a school for executives in Tarrytown, New York, helped *New Age* accelerate and legitimize a desire in some Aquarian circles to make money. Through his column in *New Age*, Schwartz became a latter-day Dale Carnegie. He told eager readers that making money could make them better people, that they were all right to want to enjoy the material plane, and that their spiritual growth would proceed apace with the growth of their bank accounts.

New Age published other features on business-as-spirituality, including a special issue on Right Livelihood that further encouraged that trend. *New Age* endorsed the apparent contradiction of making money as a way of spiritual realization by emphasizing the degree of self-involvement business takes and divorcing the reality of acting in a commercial context from its consequences: the accumulation of material goods and the triumph of some individuals over other, evidently less

Denise Levertov | Birth News: | Medical Watergate
On the Natural Guard | Infant Bonding | Part 3

NewAge

SEPTEMBER 1978 $1.50
FOREIGN $1.75

Right Livelihood

The New Economic Spirit
How to Have Less
and Be More

A spirited discussion of spiritual evolution versus materialistic greed served as the theme of this special issue on "Right Livelihood." (Courtesy of New Age.)

realized souls. While appearing to be new, this is essentially a restate-
ment of Calvinism—one's inner grace can be measured by the degree to
which God has rewarded one's works on earth. This current of New Age
thought is not so new, after all.

Despite the professed altruism of New Age periodicals, materialism
sometimes rears its indulgent head in their pages. Ads for expensive
weekend seminars and workshops, as well as meditation pillows and
pyramid kits (to "increase the psychic abilities within you!"), share the
pages of periodicals such as *New Age* with articles on how to escape this
mundane material plane altogether. Ads for herbal elixirs to regrow hair
and restore sexual vigor are also common, linking some New Age media
with another American tradition: that of the snake-oil seller.

A variety of highly specialized commercial journals also "target"
markets of vegetarians and yoga students. Several general health magazines, such as *Prevention* (circulation: two million), *Let's Live*, and *Bestways*
saturate the health-food market with news of nostrums and cures, but
they are distinguishable from New Age media by their reliance on food
supplement advertising, their lack of articulated spiritual values, and
their almost total lack of critical perspective. Practitioners of good-
vibration journalism, the health-food magazines do not publish a dis-
couraging word—unless it is about government attempts to regulate the
wide-open health-food industry.

New Age has continued to weigh acquisition and entrepreneurship as a
vehicle for self-actualization, but the magazine has backed off from some
of the more blatant moneymaking schemes that have made the rounds in
New Age circles. *New Age* devoted a cover story in 1979 to statements
from Aquarian heavyweights such as author George Leonard (*The Silent
Pulse*) who were generally critical of a chain letter called "The Circle of
Gold" which promised profits and the knowledge of higher realities to
the winners.

In the pages of *New Age*, one can read many such debates about ethics
and the direction of New Age thinking which give fascinating glimpses
of a movement very much in progress. Its contradictions notwithstanding, *New Age* is an interesting magazine. Its experiments are open to
public inspection, its commitment to a nonviolent and intensely felt
environmental activism is unflagging, and it serves as a useful guide to a
still small, but vital, current in American life.

CoEvolution Quarterly is a hybrid periodical born of the fusion of the
tradition of the independent inventor and the field of humanistic science.

Add to that the lysergic-acid visions of its creator, Stewart Brand, and you have a unique publication that either is or is not an Aquarian periodical, depending on which issue—even which page—one is reading at any given time.

If that sounds confusing, it's because *CoEvolution Quarterly (CQ)* is extremely, deliberately eclectic. "The *Whole Earth Catalog* was published to meet needs people were expressing," Brand explained. "*CQ* is more self-indulgent. Basically, we print what excites us."

Brand started *CQ* in 1974, three years after he ended the *Whole Earth Catalog*, as an intellectual sequel to that immensely popular publication. *CQ* sells an average of 40,000 copies of its 150-page issues, is nonprofit, and takes the unusual step of publishing a detailed breakdown of its finances in every issue. It does not carry paid advertising. While its paid circulation is modest, *CQ* is read by scientists, scholars, government officials, engineers, and assorted varieties of Aquarian argonauts, giving the magazine influence out of proportion to its circulation.

The editorial grab bag at *CQ* in a given issue is likely to contain summaries of scientific reports such as those of the ecology-minded Worldwatch Institute; reviews of books (C. G. Jung's *Word and Image*, Norman Cousins' *Anatomy of an Illness*, Tom Wolfe's *The Right Stuff*, reviewed by ex-astronaut Russell Schweickart); poetry; fiction; instructions on how to install "appropriate" small-scale technology, such as solar panels for the home; and long, speculative pieces on politics, culture, or science, often in the form of open letters and debates on such subjects as "voluntary simplicity" and orbiting space colonies.

CQ's articles are often written by readers, sometimes by well-known contributors, sometimes by both. Poet Gary Snyder, California Governor Jerry Brown, essayist and farmer Wendell Berry, the late economist E. F. Schumacher, the loquacious inventor Buckminster Fuller, media visionary Gene Youngblood, satirists Paul Krassner and Dan O'Neill, the late anthropologist Gregory Bateson, and underground cartoonist R. Crumb have all contributed at one time or another. The magazine also prints numerous letters from readers, which Brand, in an almost unheard-of move, pays for. "I figure they put some effort into writing them," he said, "and they contribute to the magazine, so they should be paid."

CoEvolution Quarterly is a New Age publication in the sense that it is extremely ecology-conscious and a strong advocate of holistic lifestyles. But, following Brand himself, *CQ* is scientific and rational, too, and not given to the kind of emotional "touchy-feely" quality that informs many

Aquarian média. In a (favorable) review of a feminist magazine—*CQ*
reviews other magazines—Brand wrote, "Whenever I hear the word
'share' I would reach for a gun if I had one. 'Share' is frequently followed
by 'feelings,' and I have enough of my own, thank you; please do us both
a favor and repress yours."

Brand's personality is indelibly imprinted on *CoEvolution Quarterly*, as
is his writing style. Short, pithy sentences and the use of paradox and
surprise abound in the magazine's copy. Simply put, Brand is the boss at
CQ. He oversees a staff of fifteen—"about enough for two volleyball
teams"—in a functional building on the shores of San Francisco Bay.
Brand and company frequently break for volleyball in the middle of a
workday; volleyball is one of Brand's favorite pastimes.

Brand indulges his intellectual passions in the pages of *CQ*. In recent
years, these have included a fascination with massive, orbiting space
colonies; voluntary simplicity; flirtations with conservative thinkers
such as economist Milton Friedman and futurist Herman Kahn; and a
close political alliance with Jerry Brown.

Brand touched off a long-simmering controversy in 1975, when he
invited Princeton professor Gerard O'Neill to expound upon his theories
on space colonies in the pages of *CQ*. The colonies—giant floating
structures that would orbit the earth—would relieve overpopulation on
terra firma, O'Neill argued, strengthen humanity's spirit of adventure,
and beam solar energy down to an energy-starved earth. Brand heartily
concurred.

It seemed a strange endorsement to be coming from a person who had
long encouraged a return to the land, simplicity of form, and small-scale
enterprise. But Brand was nonplussed, quoting his intellectual mentor,
Gregory Bateson, on "the necessary paradox." Said Bateson, "A paradox
is a contradiction in which you take sides—both sides."

The space colonies detractors saw the "paradox" as something rather
less elegant: a contradiction, plain and simple, in which taking both sides
is schizophrenic at best, dishonest at worst. Megacorporations and the
military would control any space colonies, they warned, and interstellar
expansionism is even less desirable than the earthly kind.

Brand's endorsement of space colonies was consistent, however, with
his love of technology—evident in even the earliest issues of the *Whole
Earth Catalog*. His ardor was matched by officials of the National Aero-
nautics and Space Administration (NASA), who expressed increased
interest in O'Neill's ideas after they were aired in *CQ*. NASA is one of
Brand's favorite organizations. He has published many photos and arti-

cles on space (the photograph of the earth on the cover of the *Whole Earth Catalog* was a NASA photo) and hired ex-astronaut Schweickart to write about space for *CQ*.

The *Quarterly* also sparked a fascinating debate on the virtues of voluntary simplicity—doing more with less to spare the earth the agonies of the throwaway economy. Brand saw poetic elegance in the idea, and he cooperated in marketing research on the concept by publishing in *CQ* a lengthy questionnaire from the Stanford Research Institute (SRI) which asked readers what they ate, wore, read, watched, earned, and thought about a variety of things, both philosophic and pragmatic. SRI sold a report based on the responses to corporations interested in penetrating a new and growing market for durable, high-quality, expensive products. It was the most popular report in SRI history and sparked business interest in *CQ* as a trend-setting publication.

Again Brand was flooded with letters, and again many were critical, arguing that he had betrayed the *CQ* community by acting as a shill for big business and that the idea of promoting voluntary simplicity in an age of monopolies was an illusion anyway. One of the letter writers, Sherry Thomas of *Country Women* magazine, observed: "It's easy to romanticize both self-reliance and material simplicity. . . . Taxation policies, subsidies to agribusiness, monopoly control of feed and equipment companies, land speculation, ecological destruction by local corporations—these are not incidental to our little 'voluntarily simple' farms—they are part of a careful web to insure that the small farmer won't survive. And, short of major social changes, many of us won't."

As many critics also pointed out, voluntary simplicity is most easily practiced by persons with financial options—people who can afford to be poor. Content to live on the margins of society, protected by savings, inheritances, advanced education, or skills acquired earlier as members in good standing of mainstream society, they can opt out of the "rat race" and read *CoEvolution Quarterly* by the fire.

Thomas' criticism also cut to the heart of objections to Brand's editorial perspective in *CQ*—specifically, the complaint that he ignores the political context in which decisions are made. Brand proposes a type of benign technocracy to cure society's ills, largely ignoring questions of who will work the controls.

In *CoEvolution Quarterly*, Brand follows a very American policy of "pragmatism" and open-endedness in which the refusal to take a consistent position is cited as evidence of flexibility. In line with this, Brand has had kind words for Milton Friedman—whose economic policies, adopted by Chile's military junta, resulted in slashed social services and a sharp rise in inflation and unemployment—and Herman Kahn—the futurist who once asserted that nuclear war is thinkable and winnable. Kahn was tape-recorded in a late-night discussion in Jerry Brown's office, and the resulting transcript was published in *CQ*, where it occupied thirty-two pages of the Spring 1977 issue. Kahn inveighed against what he called "The New Class"—educated liberals and radicals whom Kahn accused of stymieing progress with their effete challenges to industry's plans to rework the landscape for greater efficiency. "I'll run the Mississippi backwards," Kahn announced at one point, outlining a hypothetical scenario for development.

"When it comes to political, social, military, or economic analysis," Brand wrote in his introduction to the discussion, "there is no view I'm more interested in than Kahn's." Does this make Brand a closet conservative? Not necessarily. The discussion with Kahn was punctuated by comments from Amory Lovins, a classic New Class thinker and an advocate of "soft," renewable energy, who was also present in Brown's office that night, and whose remarks counterpointed Kahn's. That same issue carried an essay by Wendell Berry on the virtues of the small family farm and an article by a communist trade-union leader on cooperation between workers and environmentalists in Australia. Politically, *CQ* is a grab bag.

The politician who most resembles *CQ*'s zigzagging political line is Jerry Brown, whom Brand served as a paid, part-time advisor for several years. Brand's job was to act as an intellectual catalyst and organizer of special events for Brown. His biggest project was the organization of Space Day, a statewide celebration of space exploration held in 1978. In Space Day, Brand's intellectual passion for space coincided—not incidentally, one assumes—with Brown's passion for revitalizing the aerospace industry, which is concentrated in California. During the same timespan in which Brand worked for Brown, the Governor served as an unpaid contributing editor to *CQ*, where he "lent" other key advisors—space and communications aide Schweickart, environmental resources secretary Huey Johnson, state architect Sim van der Ryn—to *CQ*. As a result, the Brown administration policies, particularly on environmental matters, were previewed and discussed in *CQ*, which acted as an intellectual laboratory for policy decisions. In his way Brand, a quintessential outsider in the sixties as a hippie publisher, became an insider in the government of the nation's richest and most populous state.

CoEvolution Quarterly, in turn, has become a party line on which government and business leaders eavesdrop—when they're not talking themselves—on the bright young technicians of the counterculture.

Books from both mainstream and alternative publishers have long been important to New Age devotees. Hesse, Castaneda, Watts, Leary, Huxley, and practical visionaries like Buckminster Fuller and E. F. Schumacher—the late author of *Small is Beautiful*—have heavily influenced counterculturists. New Age publishers have produced quite a few books of their own as well, several of which sold extraordinarily well through word-of-mouth and advertising in alternative media.

Most successful New Age books are practical volumes that show readers how to manifest their visions in concrete ways in daily life. Growing and preparing one's own natural food is one way in which New Age seekers attempt to take control over their lives and health. Shambala Publishing Company issued several spiritual books in the seventies that sold moderately well, but their biggest seller (400,000 copies sold) was a cookbook, the *Tassajara Bread Book*, which emerged from a Zen center in California where the students made their own bread with natural ingredients. Another cookbook, this one for vegetarians, did nearly as well. Nilgiri Press' *Laurel's Kitchen*, written by a group of women concerned with healthy food, sold 80,000 copies as a $15 small-press hardbound book before Bantam Books issued an expanded paperback version that went into several large printings. New Age bestsellers also reflected the growing fascination with things Eastern. Bill Shurtleff and Akiko Aoyagi's *The Book of Tofu* sold 90,000 copies as a small-press book. By buying such books, New Age readers were doing more than expressing curiosity about new, easy-to-prepare dishes; they were working with the ingredients of their lives.

Even the most popular spiritual book, Ram Dass' *Be Here Now*, published by New Mexico's Lama Foundation, was a type of religious cookbook that combined the author's cosmic tales with techniques for achieving meditational bliss. A pie-chart came as part of the book to show how income from *Be Here Now* was used by the Lama Foundation and to explain the reasoning that went into setting the cover price: an easy-to-remember $3.33.

The do-it-yourself spirit also moved Mark Satin—a young American draft resister living in Canada—to write, design, and even typeset his own book, *New Age Politics: The Emerging New Alternative to Marxism and Liberalism*. The book sold 10,000 copies, which Satin mailed from his basement before he sold reprint rights to a mainstream publisher—to secure, he explained apologetically, more money and wider distribution for his work.

Like Jerry Rubin, Rennie Davis, and many other ex-New Leftists, Satin was a born-again activist who found new hope for social change in religion and humanistic psychology. He propounded a "transmaterial" basis for politics that emphasized the spiritual and psychological dimensions of life an established the correlation between the consciousness of individuals of individuals and the quality of life in society. Satin found in a convergence of feminism, environmentalism, and the appropriate technology movement the basis for his new politics. "Should We Look to the Proletarat," read one of Satin's chapter titles, "or to All Who Love Life?"

Satin closed *New Age Politics* with a resource directory which listed New Age periodicals and groups—even his own address, so that readers could reach him personally. Like other New Age books, Satin's volume was meant to put people in touch with themselves and each other.

All of the media discussed thus far serve a valuable networking function in the farflung Aquarian community. That is, they link like-minded people, not only with inspirational messages, but also with concrete information people can use in their daily lives.

Some alternative media efforts appear irregularly, shine briefly, and then flicker out, their limited purposes achieved. *The Briarpatch Review*, a newsletter that links three hundred Bay Area countercultural businesses, appears only when the membership perceives a need for publication. A Berkeley bakery called Uprisings puts printed messages of upcoming events in its packages of bread. The medium—bread—is highly perishable. So are the time-dated messages. But the medium and the message become one in a most unique Uprisings network.

Such publications are useful ephemera, links in quickly shifting communities of interest. Other networking publications are carefully written, dense with information, and meant to be digested slowly. Two examples are *Brain/Mind Bulletin* and *Rain*.

Brain/Mind Bulletin, a four-page newsletter published in Los Angeles by author-journalist Marilyn Ferguson, offers concise summaries of research into human potential in a number of areas. The language of the *Bulletin* is calm and lucid, but the discoveries Ferguson reports are startling. Essentially, they verify scientifically the mystical insights into the human condition that Eastern and native cultures have been propounding for years.

Reported a 1979 issue of the *Bulletin*, "A statistical study published in the *British Journal of Social and Clinical Psychology* (18:71–75) revealed a stunning correlation between the planetary configurations at the birth of more than 70,000 Frenchmen and whether they later proved to be introverts or extroverts. The odds against such correlations occurring by chance are 10,000 to one, according to the report by Michel and Francoise Gauguelin and S. B. G. Eysenck."

Published since 1975, the *Bulletin* has found a receptive constituency among scientists, teachers, physicians, and others who rely on its reporting to keep up-to-date in a rapidly changing field. Some of the readers also contribute items to the *Bulletin*, closing the communications loop. Ferguson's biweekly effort has a paid circulation of nearly 8,000, with subscribers in thirty-eight countries. In 1980 Ferguson started a similar newsletter, *Leading Edge*, to report on "social transformation" in education, business, communication, and other fields inspired by New Age adherents.

Rain, a monthly magazine published in Portland, Oregon, performs a similar function for the community of interest that coalesced around E. F. Schumacher's ideas about safe, locally controlled, appropriate technology. *Rain* joins overviews of the effects of technology on culture with blueprints on how to construct solar water heaters, wind-driven generators, and the like. The collectively owned and produced magazine also operates a lending library in Portland and serves as a valuable source of information about energy, locally and nationally.

"Just yesterday we were interviewing people at a collective theatre here in Portland," said *Rain* coeditor Carlotta Collette in an interview, "and they were saying that they used *Rain* extensively in planning a children's show they were doing on energy, and got all the back issues of *Rain* in order to compile the information."

Not only is *Rain* strong on clear, usable how-to features, but it also includes the type of social/political overviews of technology that *CoEvolution Quarterly* often downplays or overlooks. In *Rain*'s January 1980 issue, for example, readers found excerpts from Ray Reece's book *The Sun Betrayed*. Published by the collectively operated South End Press, *The Sun Betrayed* argues that large corporations, with the support of the federal government, have deliberately brought up patents on solar technology and delayed its implementation to protect their investments in nuclear power and fossil fuels. Added Collette, "I think that *Rain*'s contribution is really significant in terms of defining alternative technology as more than just equipment. The best technology is a good society."

Aquarian networks are not limited to print media. Indeed, the instantaneous nature of electronic media make them particularly well suited to impromptu networking. On May 6, 1979, shortly after the accident at the Three Mile Island nuclear power plant, an ad hoc group of videomakers joined forces to produce a live, three-hour program on a massive antinuclear march on Washington. The Public Interest Video Coalition, as they called themselves, put the program together in only ten days and with virtually no money. After managing to secure access to a communications satellite for a minimal fee, the coalition beamed its program over twenty public television stations.

"Nuclear Power: The Public Reaction" included live interviews with demonstrators and commentary by mainstream journalists and pronuclear figures invited to appear on the show. The program won a 15 percent share of the audience on San Francisco's KQED—considerably more than that station normally snares. Rather than focusing on the mobilization's stars, such as Jane Fonda and Jerry Brown, as did the limited commercial coverage of the event, the coalition provided an all-important context for understanding the demonstration: the hows and whys and human emotions that were part of the rally.

There is also a great deal of interest in New Age circles in forging ongoing computer networks to share and store information. One of the first such community computer networks was set up in San Francisco in the early seventies, when a group of "computer freaks" calling themselves Resource One picked up, free of charge, an outmoded computer from the TransAmerica corporation. After refurbishing the machine, Resource One set up shop as a grassroots computer project.

The brainchild of Pam Hart, a computer programmer who wanted to make computers "serve the people," Resource One devised information retrieval systems for San Francisco's free medical clinics and community switchboards. Later, the ten-person group helped speed research projects for the National Lawyers Guild, Aid for the Aged, and the Institute for the Study of Non-Violence. They also installed a computer terminal in a cooperatively operated, nonprofit record store in which people could program games and poems or retrieve the names of people who shared their interests in, say, recycling used materials. Resource One ended in the middle seventies when staffers departed to do other things, most of them computer-related.

Computer networking is not exclusively New Age, of course. Conventional businesses have used computers for networking throughout the seventies. However, New Age media activists—with their intense commitment to decentralization, person-to-person communication, and humanistic use of technology—are making increasing use of computers to convey Aquarian ideals. As part of nonprofit projects with minimal (or no) user's fees, they are almost pure process, and thus almost pure alternative media.

Aquarian media activists have also made imaginative use of radio technology. Perhaps their most noteworthy success is the nonprofit New Dimensions Foundation. Founded in 1973 by Michael and Justine Toms, New Dimensions specializes in interviews with leading New Age thinkers. From its beginning as a half-hour program every other week on San Francisco's public radio station KQED, the program expanded to a weekly, four-hour format that incorporated live interviews with listeners' calls.

"We did the show for four hours every Saturday night for four years," recalled Michael Toms. "And we learned to fill that expansive space. All the walls start to break down when you talk that long, there's not four hours of prepared talk, you get down to the nitty-gritty where communication begins. Now we know how to do that in less time." The program is now one hour long and is syndicated weekly to sixty stations, nearly all of them noncommercial.

Michael Toms, who does most of the interviews himself, has talked with a Who's Who of Aquarian Age celebrities: Buckminster Fuller, Linus Pauling, Stewart Brand, Patricia Sun, Werner Erhard, Ram Dass, Charles Reich, Theodore Roszak, John Lilly, Dane Rudhyar. All told, New Dimensions has produced nearly 3,000 hours of interviews, with the express purpose of becoming what Toms terms "transformational media."

Toms believes that mass media are fixated on bad news. "You watch the six o'clock news and you wonder how much worse things can get. After three minutes, you're depressed." New Dimensions, Toms said, tries to "enliven, enable, and empower" listeners: "There are people out there who want to hear about other possibilities. We are able to give people other ways to look at the world. When you listen to someone who looks at the world in a different way, your own mind is expanded; you find a lot of confirmation, and realize you're not alone. New Dimensions provides a support system to this underground of people."

Toms believes New Dimensions has been successful, both in marketing itself and in changing people's lives—the first step, he believes, along with other Aquarian activists, in changing society. To maximize its impact, New Dimensions sent its tapes free of charge to any radio station that asked for them until 1979, when the foundation almost went broke. New Dimensions now charges a modest fee for its programs, as well as selling audio tapes of its most popular shows to individuals via direct mail. "We've got files full of letters from people saying, 'I heard your show on healing cancer or on transactional analysis or whatever, and it changed my life.' "

In the spring of 1980, New Dimensions programs were accepted for satellite broadcast to the 207 National Public Radio stations, which are free to pick up the programming or bypass it. "In a sense, we've done what we've done so far in the closet," Toms said. "Satellite broadcasting will enable us to do it outfront."

Most New Dimensions programs are intimate, conversational, and upbeat. Toms interviews people he respects and tries to "make them feel at home, to become themselves." At their best, New Dimensions programs are warm and informative; at other times, their obsessive optimism casts Toms as a New Age Norman Vincent Peale.

New Dimensions' sometimes ethereal radio is complemented by the down-to-earth environmental reporting of the listener-sponsored Pacifica stations. New York's WBAI began coverage of the nuclear power issue from a strongly antinuclear point of view in 1974, when Sam Lovejoy knocked down the weather observation tower of the proposed nuclear power plant near Montague, Massachusetts. Shortly thereafter, reporter Jon Kalish started the first regularly scheduled antinuclear program in American radio. While WBAI is more of a leftist station than a New Age outlet, the station's antinuclear coverage dovetails with Aquarian concerns about the wayward atom.

WBAI's Pacifica counterpart in Berkeley, KPFA, devoted live, nearly round-the-clock coverage to the Three Mile Island accident for several days after news of the mishap broke. Interviews with utility officials and Nuclear Regulatory Commission spokespeople, as well as antinuclear activists, gave Bay Area residents with relatives in Pennsylvania the disquieting feeling that they knew more about the innards of the crippled plant—and the feverish political maneuvering going on outside it—than did their families in Harrisburg, who relied on mass-media coverage.

The Three Mile Island near-disaster was dramatic enough on its own, of course, but the eerie timing of the release of *The China Syndrome* made it all the more compelling. *The China Syndrome* was written by an independent filmmaker from Chicago named Michael Gray, who had won plaudits in the early seventies with his documentary on the death of a Black

Panther leader, *The Murder of Fred Hampton*. *The China Syndrome* made an effective antinuclear statement, but it was only one film, eventually to be withdrawn from circulation. For a sustained cinematic study of the nuclear power issue, one must look not to Hollywood, but to the rolling hills of rural New England.

America's leading antinuclear and pro-ecology filmmakers, by the late seventies, were four New Age media activists who operated a collectively run, nonprofit company called Green Mountain Post Films (GMPF). The young filmmakers, led by Charles Light and Dan Keller, were old alternative media hands, part of the circle of friends that clustered around the influential Marshall Bloom, who co-founded Liberation News Service and inspired the farm branch of LNS. They were also friends of Sam Lovejoy's. So, when Lovejoy committed his act of civil disobedience, it seemed natural for GMPF to make *Lovejoy's Nuclear War* (see Chapter Nine).

In the early seventies, most of GMPF's output was spiritual and introspective. (GMPF's first film was about a trance medium.) But when plans to build the Montague nuclear power plant were made public, the group ended its withdrawal from politics. The years on the land had changed them in certain ways, however. Said Charles Light:

> It gave us a really good foundation, just a different sense of values than what people had been dealing with in the sixties. Just by living close to the land, getting away from the cities and that kind of tension and getting some degree of feeling of self-reliance and being able to handle the world, the physical elements of it.
>
> Obviously, you don't learn much about how to operate a camera, a tape recorder, or an editing machine just by living on a farm. But you do in a way, because you're operating a tractor, and that gives you an understanding about the way things work.

Angry confrontation was not on their agenda. Rather, attempts to persuade viewers to work together—voluntarily and peacefully—for shared goals formed the heart of Green Mountain Post's films. The revitalized activists turned out films carefully balanced between personal interviews that give a feeling for the human dimension of things and points of information that give the films a grounding in science. Green Mountain Post Films, in short, dropped the agitation that New Left groups had included as an integral part of their agitprop films, while retaining the propaganda.

Those elements of style were skillfully blended in GMPF's second energy film, *The Last Resort*, a 60-minute documentary on the occupation of the Seabrook construction site by nonviolent protestors. The film also explores the impact of the plant on the town of Seabrook. Says one townsperson, also a demonstrator, "Today, we'll be going and breaking a law, but it will be answering a higher law. We've got to do it, because we're locals." The film's title is a quote from candidate Jimmy Carter, who described nuclear power as "the last resort" while campaigning in New Hampshire in 1976. The film includes footage of Carter making the statement to a reporter.

Selected highlights of *The Last Resort*, along with clips from a 1979 ecology action film by GMPF called *Save the Planet*, were incorporated into a feature-length 1980 release titled *No Nukes*. *No Nukes*, an independent production that drew on the talents of Haskell Wexler and Barbara Kopple, as well as Green Mountain Post filmmakers, was a glossy documentary of antinuclear benefit rock concerts, made to raise money and consciousness for the movement. A somnambulistic if well-intended film, *No Nukes* benefited immensely from GMPF footage which, among other things, showed a heartbreaking interview with an Army veteran suffering from leukemia, which he believed he developed by being ordered to witness an atomic bomb test in the 1950s.

From antinuclear documentaries, GMPF has branched out to make and distribute films on other environmental issues: strip mining, pesticide use, conservation of the wilderness. The company, which describes itself as "a nonprofit educational cooperative specializing in films on energy," also imported several European documentaries on nuclear power for American distribution. GMPF has made five films of its own and distributes another twenty. Workstyles in the group are fluid, according to cooperative member Hedy Sherman: "Nobody is above anybody. We each have our areas of interest, but everybody can do everything."

GMPF has become an international clearinghouse for films on the environment. In return, GMPF's own films have been shown north of the border by the Canadian National Film Board and by West German national television. One of GMPF's imports—a rough 8-millimeter home movie of a German nuclear power plant occupation—was blown up by GMPF to 16 millimeters and used as a training film in nonviolent tactics by the Seabrook demonstrators. GMPF's films are designed to stimulate that kind of social change. Said Light, "We work primarily through antinuke, solar energy, safe energy, and other political-type groups. They'll organize a meeting around one of our films. They'll have film showings and they have speakers, and the film serves as a way to get people who aren't familiar with the issues familiar with them in a hurry."

Asked if this was of a piece with the sixties activism members of the group experienced, Light replied, "Oh, sure. For several years, until about 1973, our energy was directed inward, getting close to the land. The nuclear plant served as an impetus to get us to come full circle."

Except for the sales of the *Whole Earth Catalog* at its peak, and other countercultural "how-to" books, Aquarian media have remained small. As with most creative enterprises, however, their influence cannot be wholly measured by their size. To New Age media goes much of the credit for introducing meditation, yoga, and futuristic techniques such as biofeedback and for reintroducing traditional diets of unadulterated foods. They have also boosted the popularity of unconventional health practitioners such as naturopaths, acupuncturists, and herbalists as alternatives to allopathic medical doctors.

Gradually, holistic health—working with the whole person and letting the body heal itself with a minimum use of intrusive drugs or surgery—has seeped into American life. So have countercultural ideas about nutrition and preventive medicine. New Age media hailed a highly publicized Senate report in 1978 which urged Americans to cut down on sweets, fats, and salt and increase their intake of fresh fruit, produce, and whole grains; it was what many of them had been proposing for years.

The lifestyle sections of mainstream periodicals reflect and widely disseminate attitudes aired earlier in alternative media. Articles on natural childbirth, visualization exercises, vegetarian diets, and drugless methods of reducing stress are far more common than they were twenty or even ten years ago. Popular—and often unorthodox—nutritionists such as Paavo Airola and Carlton Fredricks, who, several years ago, would have been given hearings mainly in countercultural media or health-food magazines, now hold forth on television talk shows and commercial radio broadcasts.

Despite their considerable impact, New Age media are a long way from their announced goal of transforming America. Their appeal, like that of the movement whose principles they articulate, is still largely to white middle- and upper-class persons, individuals with education and skills and the ability to move easily in society—even downward, if they choose. This is an anomaly in a society in which most people are still trying to move up. The rejection of materialism promoted in New Age media is not likely to have sustained appeal to the working class and the poor. Aquarian lifestyles, like the sixties counterculture that gave them early impetus, are largely products of affluence.

But if Aquarian media have not transformed America, they *have* influenced it. New Age media have submitted fresh evidence that material possessions, per se, do not guarantee health or happiness. They have argued persuasively for transplanting Eastern spiritual traditions to American soil as part of the rich compost of Jeffersonian and Transcendental thought that has long ennobled American life. And they have unearthed new information—fundamental, personal, usable—with which a small but significant number of Americans have changed their lives.

NOVEMBER 1976   A MAGAZINE FOR THE REST OF US   ONE DOLLAR

M O T H E R
JONES

HERZOG: WORLD'S BEST FILMMAKER?

ROCK REMEDIES

TIMOTHY LEARY'S SPACE COLONIES

FEMINISTS ON MOTHERHOOD

THE NEXT SIX WARS

IS THIS DEVICE THE NEW THALIDOMIDE?

Its story is clearly (cont. p. 36)

fourteen

The New Muckrakers

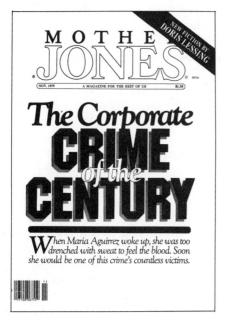

MOTHER JONES NEW FICTION BY DORIS LESSING

NOV. 1979   A MAGAZINE FOR THE REST OF US $1.50

The Corporate CRIME of the CENTURY

When Maria Aguirrez woke up, she was too drenched with sweat to feel the blood. Soon she would be one of this crime's countless victims.

IN NOVEMBER OF 1976, reporters Mark Dowie and Tracy Johnston published a story in *Mother Jones* magazine about the dangers of the Dalkon Shield, an interuterine device that sickened and even killed some women. Going over manufacturers' data a year later, Dowie noticed that a full million of the contraceptive devices were unaccounted for. They hadn't been sold to American women, and they weren't in storage in the United States either. Intrigued, Dowie started digging.

The result of his investigation, carried out with the help of several other reporters, was an anthology of articles collectively titled "The Corporate Crime of the Century." Published in the November 1979 issue of *Mother Jones*, the articles detailed the "dumping" of harmful, banned substances—pesticides, drugs, Dalkon Shields—in developing countries by multinational United States corporations. The exposé caused a firestorm of controversy in the Third World, sparked proposed legislation, and won *Mother Jones* a coveted National Magazine Award for excellence in reporting.

On February 25, 1980—four months after the *Mother Jones* issue appeared—the *Washington Post* ran a front-page story on corporate dumping that substantially confirmed what Dowie and company had un-

Mother Jones's investigation of the "dumping"
of hazardous substances in Third World nations
sparked reform legislation and won a National
Magazine Award. (Courtesy of Mother Jones.)

earthed. Unlike *Mother Jones*, the *Post* stopped short of calling dumping a crime. "One of the weak points of American journalism is that they will struggle and struggle for 'objectivity'," snorted Dowie. "Our position is simple. We think dumping is evil, and we want to stop it."

Although the corporate dumping exposé was a major story, it was not revealed in what most people think of as a major magazine. This is not an unusual pattern for major stories in American journalism. According to Carl Jensen—the head of Project Censored, a program that records the fate of important investigative stories—alternative media "cover the stories that the mass media should be doing. Sometimes those stories are later given wider currency in the commercial media, sometimes not."

Jensen, a sociology professor at Sonoma (California) State University, organized Project Censored in 1977. With the aid of his students and a panel of media professionals including syndicated columnist Mary McGrory, former FCC commissioner Nicholas Johnson, press critic Ben Bagdikian, and CBS reporter Mike Wallace, Jensen cites ten stories every year which receive little or no attention in the mass media. The nominees include exposures that were broken in mass-media outlets and then dropped. In 1979, six of Project Censored's ten selected stories originated in the alternative media, with another two coming to light in liberal outlets such as *The Nation*.

Why don't the mainstream media give more attention to major exposés—or, better yet, break the reports themselves? Jensen believes that the mass media generally avoid handling complex, long-term topics, such as the dangers of low-level radiation, because such investigations require specialized knowledge which most journalists lack; because analysis simply doesn't "play" as well as action in the dominant electronic media; and because "let's face it, the first priority of the commercial media is to make a profit and these kinds of stories step on a lot of toes."

Jensen's first two points, true as far as they go, are probably secondary. *Mother Jones* employed generalist editors and freelance writers to break its dumping story. Pacifica radio stations make skillful use of actuality (live or taped voices of persons other than the newscasters) but work tough-minded reporting and analysis into the news by dispensing with commercial interruption and allotting forty-five minutes to nightly newscasts. Lack of motivation—rather than a lack of capability—in the mainstream media seems to be the main reason why *Mother Jones* and *The Progressive*, and not the *Washington Post* and CBS news, served as the leading sources of major investigative reports in Project Censored's first three years.

Alternative media differ from the mainstream media not only by producing more muckraking—the exposure of wrongdoing in public life as a prelude to effecting progressive reform—but also by producing a different kind of muckraking. "A lot of periodicals tell you about the illegal stuff, the guy with his hand in the till and so on," said Mark Dowie. "That's all well and good, those stories need to be done. But our tendency is to focus on practices that are perfectly legal. By exposing them, we may be able to inspire legislation and other changes."

Muckraking, as practiced by *Mother Jones* and other alternative media outlets, differs from pure documentary in that it doesn't passively present a set of facts or outline a problem, but advocates a solution. Muckraking can shade over into political analysis, but, unlike pure analysis, it depends on the revelation of new information to galvanize the reader/listener/viewer into action. Muckraking also differs from sensationalistic "yellow journalism" by advocating a political solution to social problems rather than reveling in the gory details of tragedy and scandal. Muckraking is purposeful, political, moralistic reporting.

Muckraking began just after the turn of the century. Journalists such as Lincoln Steffens, Ida Tarbell, Ray Stannard Baker, and Upton Sinclair were media moralists who sought to bring Christian conscience and scientific principles of management to the business trusts and corrupt political machines that controlled American politics. The muckrakers helped install reforms such as the direct election of senators, professional city managers, antitrust laws, pure-food-and-drug legislation, and democratic voting procedures such as the initiative, the referendum, and the recall.

The most popular muckrakers appeared in the mass-circulation magazine *McClure's*. But when S. S. McClure, the magazine's owner and namesake, announced plans to reach out, octopus-like, into other businesses, *McClure's* leading writers—Steffens, Tarbell, Baker—left in 1906 to take over an ailing periodical called the *American Magazine*. The group ownership and consensus-editing policies of their *American* anticipated the cooperative structure of alternative magazines such as the *Ramparts* and *Mother Jones*.

The term muckraker was originally pejorative. It was popularized by Theodore Roosevelt, who, quoting John Bunyan's *Pilgrim's Progress*, likened crusading journalists to "the man with the muckrake." Bunyan's muckraker was a metaphor for one who coveted earthly treasures. Crusading journalists, of course, led attacks on the pursuit and accumu-

lation of wealth, but that did not faze Roosevelt. By labeling the reporters as persons obsessed with the seamy side of life, Roosevelt stood Bunyan on his head and shrewdly took the initiative from his critics in the press.

Over the years, the word muckraker became a term of honor among many journalists, but the tradition of muckraking was honored more in the breach than in the observance by the mass media. Newsletters such as George Seldes' *In Fact* and *I. F. Stone's Weekly* carried on the muckraking tradition in the forties and fifties. But it wasn't until the ascendance of *Ramparts* in the middle sixties that a new generation of media activists brought muckraking back to broad public attention.

To even a casual reader of periodicals, *Ramparts* was omnipresent in the sixties. Full-page ads trumpeting scoops on the CIA and the Vietnam war engaged the eyes of readers in the *New York Times*, flashy magazine covers grabbed them at newsstands, and followups to major *Ramparts* newsbeats—such as its exposure of the CIA's secret funding of the National Student Association—cropped up on the front pages of daily newspapers around the country.

Ramparts had not always been a muckraking sensation. Founded in 1962 as an intellectual Roman Catholic journal by millionaire Edward Keating, the publication had a woebegone circulation of 2,000 in 1964, after Keating had poured a cool million dollars into what seemed like a bottomless pit. In desperation, Keating turned to Warren Hinckle, a large, manic, one-eyed reporter for the *San Francisco Chronicle*, who promised to revitalize the magazine.

Hinckle did more than revitalize *Ramparts*—he transformed it. Gone was the dull, dusty quarterly format. Shortly after Hinckle took the helm of the slowly sinking Good Ship *Ramparts*, the magazine became a monthly, printed on slick paper, with an arresting, contemporary design. Advertising maverick Howard Gossage, who had popularized Beethoven sweatshirts and been an early booster of Marshall McLuhan, signed on as an advisor. Earnest considerations of papal encyclicals gave way to the powerful, provocative investigative reporting that was to become the magazine's trademark. Hinckle designed *Ramparts* to compete with the mass-circulation magazines *Time, Life,* the *Saturday Evening Post,* not to stay moored in the quiet waters of respectable left-liberal intellectual publishing. He called the new style "radical slick." *Ramparts* still lost money, but it began to move editorially under its own power.

Along with its Vietnam stories, *Ramparts'* biggest scoop was its expo-

Warren Hinckle: the large, manic, one-eyed enfant terrible of Ramparts *in its muckraking hey-day, at ease in 1980. (Photo by Chester Simpson.)*

sure, in March of 1967, of the long-time funding and control of the National Student Association (NSA)—an organization of college student governments—by the CIA. The whistle was blown by a participant in the scandal, one Michael Wood, a disenchanted NSA fundraiser. With Wood's help, *Ramparts* nailed down the story by tracing CIA money to the NSA through shadowy foundations.

Ramparts' means of getting a story proved fully as controversial as the contents of the stories it printed. Describing radical reporters as "guerrilla journalists" without the clout and contacts of established "access journalists," *Ramparts* managing editor Robert Scheer recalled, "Guerrilla journalism came about because we didn't want to be part of access journalism. We hung out at parties and eavesdropped and stole memos and every other damn thing to crash through." Remembering his role in breaking the NSA story, Scheer told *(MORE)*, a now-defunct journalism review:

> At *Ramparts*, we printed plenty of documents that had been pilfered. When you feel a story is important and there is no other means to get it . . . you use certain means. For example, we were going after the NSA-CIA connection. . . . We could not prove that the international organization they belonged to had received funds from the San Jacinto Foundation, which we knew was a CIA front. So I went to Leiden Holland, to the offices of the San Jacinto Foundation, and I got into that office by cajoling and by flattering and by everything else. . . . And I would do it again.

Although Scheer's "confession" shocked some mainstream journalists, it was de rigueur to be shocking at *Ramparts*, inside and outside its pages. One cover photograph pictured the editors holding aloft their burning draft cards. A pet monkey named Henry Luce cavorted in the official *Ramparts* office, while in the unofficial office—Cookie Picetti's Star Buffet—Hinckle scattered notes on the bar, planned upcoming issues, and feverishly wrote headlines.

Ramparts, with Hinckle as editor and Scheer as managing editor, was a mass of contradictions: a leftist magazine that depended on capitalist millionaires to pay the bills; a magazine of serious-as-a-heart-attack reporting that was not above using a flippant cover line or a teasing photo to grab attention; an advocate of a communal society that was run strictly along hierarchical lines, edited by two hard-driving, hard-nosed young who who drove their underpaid writers and staff as hard as they drove themselves and barely noticed when some less hardy soul fell by the wayside. A mass of contradictions—but people read it.

Hinckle's profligate ways sent the magazine into bankruptcy in 1969. Reorganized as a less flamboyant, collectively run magazine, *Ramparts* continued to publish, but without its earlier impact. Its exposés had not been for naught, however. Jessica Mitford, herself a formidable muckraker, cited *Ramparts* and its writers as key factors in the downfall of two Presidents. "In the cases of both Johnson and Nixon," she said, "young, energetic muckrakers lighted the flame. Robert Scheer's pamphlet on how we got involved in Vietnam [see Chapter Four] triggered the move to end that war. That started the chain that led to Bernstein and Woodward and the ouster of Nixon."

Watergate made investigative reporting—as muckraking came to be called—popular, for a time, in the mass media. Unlike the early muckrakers, however, the reporting that helped bring down the Nixon administration did not go beyond the exposure of "bad guys" to a structural analysis of social and economic conditions that made "dirty tricks" and secrecy possible.

Instead, mass-media reporters inveighed against the checkered careers of key individuals and rushed into print with breathless accounts of midnight trysts of the Tidal Basin. A not illogical consequence of this emphasis on personalities was the glamorization of journalists themselves—who they were, how they got that way, how they got the big story, what they thought about it. Journalists began appearing in *People* magazine as subjects, not contributors. As the larger implications of Watergate—the whys as well as the whos and hows—faded into the background, the image of the journalist as superstar grew brighter.

In late 1973, a new magazine, optimistically called *New Times*, arrived to package circumscribed investigative reporting with the glossy writing of the New Journalism. *New Times* was the creation of former Time-Life executive George Hirsch, who bankrolled the magazine with money from Chase Manhattan, the Bank of America, and American Express— exactly the type of institutions at which the original muckrakers had aimed their blows. It was a sign that investigative reporting had arrived—and was considered harmless by its proper targets.

New Times did publish some notable exposures, including a devastating piece in 1977 on poisons in drinking water, articles spotlighting corruption in the drug industry, and a report of antiblack jokes by Secretary of Agriculture Earl Butz which cost Butz his job. These stories were paired with run-of-the-mill reviews and lifestyle features on fads such as skateboarding. Written in a bright, upbeat style, *New Times* kept its distance from political movements that could have sustained the magazine, and, as liberalism declined as a social force in the late seventies, the magazine stagnated. In November 1978 Hirsch killed *New Times* in favor of a magazine on running.

Clearly, from an alternative journalistic and political view, something else was needed—a vehicle for hard-hitting reporting that would go beyond the superficiality of *New Times*, the trendiness of *People*, the internal contradictions that helped cripple *Ramparts*. In the early months of 1976, that magazine arrived, and within a year or two it became perhaps the most important alternative periodical in America.

Named after the pioneering socialist organizer Mary "Mother" Jones (1830–1930), *Mother Jones*, a ten-times-yearly magazine with a circulation of 250,000, is the largest left-of-center periodical in the United States. Its circulation matches that of *Ramparts* at its peak, and its leading exposures—of dangerous contraceptive devices, exploding cars, and the dumping of toxic substances abroad—equal *Ramparts'* best. *Mother Jones'* biggest stories have been reprinted in mainstream periodicals, including the *Boston Globe*, *Washington Star*, and *London Sunday Times*.

Mother Jones is a lineal descendant of *Ramparts*, founded by former *Ramparts* editors and writers Paul Jacobs, Adam Hochschild, and Richard Parker. All three were activists as well as journalists. Jacobs was a former organizer and supporter of a variety of left and liberal causes. Hochschild was a veteran of the antiwar movement and an heir to the Amex mining fortune. Parker, also an antiwar vet, is the great-great-great-great grandson of the commander of the Minutemen at Lexington.

Jacobs, Hochschild, and Parker left *Ramparts* in 1974 after a short stint, determined to start their own magazine. "We couldn't get along with the other people in the *Ramparts* collective," Parker remembered, "and it became total war." Hochschild echoed Parker's epigrammatic assessment, telling ruefully of the time a tie vote on what story would go on a *Ramparts* cover was broken by the mail clerk, a person Hochschild felt had no editorial expertise.

The disaffected trio wanted a magazine like *Ramparts*, only different: activist but introspective; socialist but viable; democratic but business-like. They set up shop in San Francisco, where *Ramparts* also made its home. In 1975, after its second bankruptcy and interminable staff splits, *Ramparts* called it quits, clearing the way for the new publication.

Some of the tumult endemic to *Ramparts* marked *Mother Jones'* early days. In June 1976, six months after *Mother Jones* began publication, a group of feminist writers and editors, angered by what they saw as antifeminist bias in *Mother Jones'* pages and on its staff, met with the magazine's founders. They demanded that *Mother Jones* live up to its slogan—"a magazine for the rest of us"—by including radical feminists in its constituency. They also proposed that *Mother Jones* turn over an issue to feminists to edit and demanded that the magazine publish women writers on a regular basis and employ feminist editors to ensure a follow-through on commitments. In the meantime, feminists would avoid buying or writing for *Mother Jones*, on the rare occasions when their work was solicited. Marge Piercy, Robin Morgan, Alix Kates Shulman, Rita Mae Brown, Susan Griffin, and other leading feminist writers endorsed the boycott.

Mother Jones' editors refused to turn over the magazine for the proposed issue, but they did hire a female editor, Amanda Spake. They also published a special ten-year celebration of the women's movement in the August 1977 issue, at which time the boycott of *Mother Jones* was called off. A feminist influence showed in many of *Mother Jones'* subsequent articles, including several of its most successful muckraking efforts.

Mother Jones also exhibited a strong environmentalist influence. Its first issue, dated February/March 1976, carried an investigative article by Paul Jacobs which documented safety failures in an atomic reactor built in India with U.S. aid. The story drew wide attention in the mass media and resulted in a Congressional cutoff of U.S. aid to India. (Aid was restored in 1980 by the Carter administration.)

That first issue set the tone for *Mother Jones*. Although the magazine tried, from the beginning, to illuminate personal life in its pages, its efforts were generally weak. (A powerfully written memoir of the communist entry into Peking in 1949 by Li-li Ch'en, which won a National Magazine Award, was an exception.) Correctly perceiving that left-of-center publications generally suffer from a lack of humor, *Mother Jones* also set out to provide a few chuckles, with even less success. The magazine's stabs at humor consisted mostly of coy plays on the word *mother* and flippant filler that could have appeared anywhere. Muckraking was what *Mother Jones* did best, and it was with muckraking that the magazine made its mark.

Mother Jones made an editorial splash with a story entitled "A Case of Corporate Malpractice," published in the November 1976 issue. Written by Mark Dowie and Tracy Johnston, the article detailed the misleading marketing of the Dalkon Shield. With the aid of confidential corporate memos, Dowie and Johnston showed how a Johns Hopkins medical doctor who invented the device published exaggerated claims of its effectiveness in a prestigious medical journal—without informing readers that he stood to make a bundle if the shield sold. Thanks in large part to the doctored test results, it did.

Almost immediately, however, reports came in to A. D. Robins, the company which marketed the Dalkon Shield, that many women who used it suffered serious medical side-effects, including nausea, bleeding, and infection. Company memos showed that the questions of a female physician about the safety of the Dalkon Shield were brushed aside. Seventeen women died of complications arising from its use before the shield was quietly taken off the market in 1975.

The *Mother Jones* report included a chart estimating that the Dalkon Shield's physician-inventor, Dr. Hugh Davis, made over $700,000 on his creation. Spliced into the narrative in italicized type was the true personal story of a woman who used the device and subsequently nearly died from infection, eventually submitting to a complete hysterectomy to save her life.

The story, which exemplified the approach *Mother Jones* takes to muckraking, was thoroughly documented; marked by a sense of understated, tightly focused anger; and grounded in personal anecdote and description that made the human costs of the medical policies under examination all the more vivid. The piece incorporated a directory labeled "If You Need Help," which gave readers the address of an activist group established to protect the medical rights of women.

Dowie and Johnston concluded their piece with a brief but pointed statement of *Mother Jones'* philosophy:

> As long as there is a free market for medical products, that's the way business will be done. Indeed, though there have been civil lawsuits aplenty as a result of the Dalkon Shield, the whole affair has been considered so normal a way of conducting free-enterprise medicine that Johns Hopkins took no action against Davis, state medical authorities censured neither Davis nor [Thad Earl, a key salesperson], and the government left the A. D. Robins Company alone.

That statement—not included until the cumulative weight of the authors' evidence had presumably touched the reader—established *Mother Jones* as socialistic in a subtle way. In comparison to the rambunctiousness of *Ramparts* and the abrasive frontal attacks of underground media, *Mother Jones* is restrained, almost quiet. But unlike the underground media, *Mother Jones* addresses movements, not a unified Movement. And unlike the sixties radicals who inspired *Mother Jones*, the magazine speaks primarily to readers who may be curious but not committed, people just edging into activism and not yet ready to heed the bugle call to the ramparts of the revolution. *Mother Jones'* political stance is one of gradual, peaceful reform, fueled by moral indignation. That indignation is fed, in turn, by assessing the human costs of deprivation and inequality.

Another of *Mother Jones'* highly publicized muckraking efforts was a cover story, published in the September/October 1977 issue, which detailed the propensity of Ford Pinto subcompact cars to explode and burn in rear-end collisions—for want, author Mark Dowie contended, of an $11 part to protect the gas tank. Dowie's report, based in part on internal Ford memos never intended for publication, charged that Ford knew the car would explode and burn—and coldly went ahead with production of the Pinto anyway.

Observed Dowie acidly, "Burning Pintos have become such an embarrassment to Ford that its advertising agency, J. Walter Thompson, dropped a line from the end of a radio spot that read, 'Pinto leaves you with that warm feeling.'" Concluded Dowie, "Ford knows the Pinto is a firetrap, yet it has paid out millions to settle damage suits out of court, and it is prepared to spend millions more lobbying against safety standards."

The *Mother Jones* story caught fire as soon as it was released. Ford was forced by government order to recall over a million Pintos. And in a landmark case in 1978 the company was sued for corporate liability in the deaths of three teenagers who were rear-ended in a Pinto. *Mother Jones* had a hand in the suit too. The Indiana state trooper who arrived at the scene of the accident was a *Mother Jones* reader who gave the prosecuting attorney copies of Dowie's story.

In March 1980, after spending a reported $1 million for its defense, Ford was acquitted by an Indiana jury. Despite the not-guilty verdict, Dowie claimed a partial victory for consumers. The Indiana law that permitted charges of corporate liability for homicide "has been tested and found workable," Dowie wrote, despite the exclusion of 250 items of evidence by the trial judge. Dowie attributed the acquittal to "the brilliant legal maneuverings of Ford's . . . defense team, which included a Watergate prosecutor and a lawyer who shared offices with the trial judge for twenty-two years."

The Pinto story won a National Magazine Award for public service in 1978.

Mother Jones examined profitable wrongdoing in another blockbuster issue, published in November 1979, on the corporate dumping of lethal

FREE

VALLEY Advocate

AMHERST/NORTHAMPTON/GREENFIELD

THE ALTERNATIVE IN THE PIONEER VALLEY
VOL.VII NO.45 JUNE 25, 1980   40 PAGES

Wasting Away

The Advocate's series on hazardous chemical waste in the Pioneer Valley looks at what the government knows and doesn't know about poisons that have been piling up for years.

Page 10

L.A. WEEKLY

The Publication of News, People, Entertainment, Art and Emotions in Los Angeles

Free

Volume 2, Number 46   October 17-23, 1980

SMOG
THE INSIDE AND UNTOLD STORY
WHY IT'S GETTING WORSE
WHO'S TO BLAME

A Special Investigative Report on the Real Causes and Politics of Bad Air by a Team of L.A. Weekly Researchers Led by Rian Malan

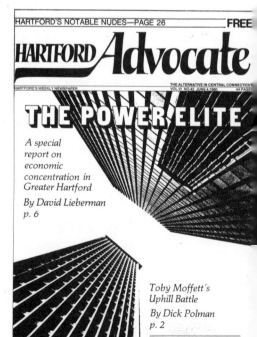

FREE

HARTFORD Advocate

HARTFORD'S WEEKLY NEWSPAPER

THE ALTERNATIVE IN CENTRAL CONNECTICUT
VOL.VI NO.42 JUNE 4,1980   44 PAGES

THE POWER ELITE

A special report on economic concentration in Greater Hartford

By David Lieberman
p. 6

Toby Moffett's Uphill Battle

By Dick Polman
p. 2

Hartford's Investments In Apartheid

By Bruce Kauffman
p. 10

products abroad. In keeping with *Mother Jones'* tone and style, the four-article package did not begin with a polemic against capitalism, but with cover lines evoking the agony of a Third World woman who died from complications of an unsafe IUD such as the Dalkon Shield, now banned in the U.S. but still used in some countries.

An exhaustive 25-page special section showed: how corporations label products with warnings where warnings are required and omit them where they're not; how they use third countries to route dangerous products to nations with laws against importing items that are banned from sale in their country of manufacture; how dangerous drugs are sold under other names.

Again, the magazine didn't stop with describing the problem, but provided a prescription for change. Names and addresses of activist organizations accompanied the stories, and copies of the magazine were hand-delivered to every foreign embassy in Washington. At this writing, legislation inspired by the story is pending in Malaysia and the Philippines as well as in the U.S., where a proposed law would require that Third World governments be fully informed about what they are importing and that those substances be duly labeled with warnings in the local language.

Mother Jones readers were also galvanized. According to Adam Hochschild, the magazine filled 20,000 requests for reprints—"four times as many as we ever thought we'd need."

Dowie, who doubled as a writer and *Mother Jones'* publisher from early 1978 until the summer of 1980 (when he was replaced by Jacques Marchand), was understandably proud of the story. "It's what I think investigative reporting should be. Investigations should be long-term. They should be deep. They should be politically motivated. They should be advocacy journalism."

Where does *Mother Jones* get the money to conduct those complex, time-consuming investigations? According to Hochschild, only about 5 percent of *Mother Jones'* revenue comes from advertising. That's partly because the magazine has tried to avoid relying on advertising (it gets by on subscriptions, donations, and newsstand sales) and partly because major advertisers, fearing they may be next to be muckraked, avoid *Mother Jones.*

Mother Jones began life on the basis of grants and gifts from a number of donors—some of them, such as Burt Lancaster and producer Jennings Lang, members of the Hollywood film community. After a hugely successful mailing, *Mother Jones* started publishing in 1976 with 80,000

Alternative weeklies published exposures of environmental hazards and political wheeling and dealing. (Covers courtesy of respective periodicals.)

subscribers. The magazine now takes in $3 million a year in revenue, nearly enough to break even and enough to leave its original quarters over a McDonald's to occupy *Rolling Stone*'s spacious old San Francisco office. The airy room where Jann Wenner once held forth is now a library.

In addition to subscribing to *Mother Jones*, one can belong to the Foundation for National Progress, the nonprofit foundation that publishes the magazine. The Foundation for National Progress is designed as a research center for radical scholarship, hosting visiting and permanent fellows and issuing reports. It also operates the New School for Democratic Management, a business school for cooperative enterprises organized loosely along the "decentralized, humanist, democratic socialist" lines which the foundation and *Mother Jones* identify as their underlying philosophy.

Mother Jones appears to have worked through some of the internal problems that plagued its early years—and destroyed other left-leaning media enterprises such as the redoubtable *Ramparts*. The paper's twelve full-time business employees elect their publisher every year, and a six-person editorial board—evenly divided between women and men—selects the managing editor, who makes day-to-day decisions.

"The set-up is a compromise between a radical collective and a traditional business structure," Hochschild explained. "It's not a pure democracy, but it is democratic. We operate on the assumption that six heads are better than one."

Mother Jones is not without continuing stress, however. Cofounder Paul Jacobs was fired in 1976, supposedly for not giving the magazine his full attention. (Jacobs died in January of 1978, after writing for *Newsday* and other publications and helping to make the powerful film *Paul Jacobs and the Nuclear Gang*, examined later in this chapter.) Richard Parker left *Mother Jones* in 1978 to begin a leftist direct-mail firm. "I clashed with the people there," Parker admits candidly, "and I wanted to use what I learned on the business side at *Mother Jones* for the entire left." Of the three cofounders, only Adam Hochschild remains.

The departure of original staffers has made room for new talent, however, such as feminist writer Deirdre English, who joined the magazine as a full-time editor in 1979. English's influence is evident in the increased number of feminist contributors to *Mother Jones* and in issues such as the April 1980 special on "Sex, Porn, and Male Rage," in which she wrote an even-handed and perceptive commentary on pornography.

In its brief publication life, *Mother Jones* has also developed several excellent writers with personal voices, such as Parker, a keen, trained economist who analyzes the world economy; Dr. Hugh Drummond, a medical doctor whose biting, impassioned examinations of the American health-care system have provided the magazine with some of the muscle it often lacks between exposures; and Jeffrey Klein, a coeditor and former creative writing teacher whose self-critical looks at the left and deft, naturalistic narratives provide *Mother Jones* with a model of good storytelling.

Muckraking remains the magazine's strong point—and the favorite of readers, according to readership surveys. *Mother Jones'* most popular subscription premium was a booklet called *Raising Hell: A Citizens' Guide to the Fine Art of Investigation*. Written by Dan Noyes of the Center for Investigative Reporting, the booklet is a mother lode of information on how to dig up data. "The readers loved it," smiled Noyes. "It addressed them as doers, not simply observers."

Because of the popularity of muckraking in *Mother Jones*, the Foundation for National Progress established a special Investigative Fund, financed by readers' donations. "Like the social change it can trigger, top-notch investigative journalism doesn't just happen," *Mother Jones* explained to its readers. It takes time and effort, like the nine months Mark Dowie spent researching the Pinto story, the hundred interviews he conducted, the dozen books he read, and the 23,000 miles he traveled to complete the research.

It also takes money. that's where the Investigative Fund comes in. For a story on pesticides in the special corporate dumping issue, *Mother Jones* funded writers at the Center for Investigative Reporting. The resourceful journalists at the center also secured funding from the independent Fund for Investigative Journalism, based in Washington, D.C. In this way, three alternative media organizations joined forces to produce a muckraking classic of worldwide significance.

While *Mother Jones* has been cracking investigative stories and garnering deserved publicity, scores of alternative periodicals, most of them rooted in the new provincialism of the seventies, have been breaking news on local and regional levels. Some of those publications, such as the *Hartford* (Connecticut) *Advocate*, a weekly with a circulation of 100,000, are relatively large, prosperous, and respected. Others, like the small, struggling *Rochester* (New York) *Patriot*, labor in obscurity, often unable to pay the reporters who scoop entrenched local dailies.

The triweekly *Patriot*, founded in 1973, has made a habit of beating the daily *Democrat* and *Chronicle* to the punch on important local stories.

In one instance, the Rochester Port Authority announced plans to build oil storage tanks which many community residents didn't want. Checking into the plan, the *Patriot* found that the Port Authority was illegally constituted. Moreover, local business leaders told the *Patriot*, they didn't want the tanks, supposedly being built for their benefit. Under the glare of publicity generated by the *Patriot*, the Port Authority scrapped its plans.

In another instance, sources in New York State's prison system told the *Patriot* that prison inmates—some of them active in prison reform—were being subjected to behavior modification. The state Department of Corrections branded the story a lie and threatened to sue the *Patriot*. The planned suit was dropped, however, when the *Patriot* quoted from the behavior modification program handbook, which the paper had acquired. Citing "adverse publicity," state officials dropped that program too.

The *Patriot* produced these and other stories on a shoestring budget financed by community residents who set up the paper as a subscriber-owned enterprise. The *Patriot* also describes itself as "subscriber-run," meaning that volunteers—up to forty at a time—join five part-time, paid employees to put out the paper. According to *Patriot* staffers, the local Gannett-owned daily papers took out eight subscriptions to the *Patriot*, frequently running their own versions of *Patriot* stories, nearly always without attribution.

In keeping with the seventies' new provincialism, when local alternative papers turn their attention to national and international issues, they like to give them a local twist. Thus, when the *Hartford Advocate* wrote about South African apartheid in July 1978, the paper did so by working its criticisms into a muckraking story about the Hartford city employees' pension funds invested in corporations—such as General Motors and Dow Chemical—which do extensive business in South Africa. In addition to asking whether such investment was morally justifiable, *Advocate* reporter Bruce Kauffman asked whether the money couldn't be better spent by investing in programs to revitalize Hartford's declining neighborhoods.

According to *Hartford Advocate* managing editor Dick Polman, the daily *Hartford Courant* did not cover the issue until hearings on divestiture were held by city authorities as a result of the *Advocate* story. "When the hearings were held," said Polman, "we got out only mention in the *Courant* in five years." Continued Polman, "The article was up for a

Business Journalism Award sponsored by the Connecticut Chamber of Commerce." It lost, according to Polman, "because the story wasn't 'objective'. It had a point of view. The writer stepped out and asked the critical moral questions."

Polman's comment illustrates another fact of life in American journalism. With the rare exception of a story as big as *Mother Jones'* corporate dumping expose, new is not really news to the general public until it is "validated" by the mainstream media. Alternative media are simply too small (and are still often considered barely respectable) to break a story by themselves. Thus, as the results of Project Censored's surveys show, alternative journalists often act as pathfinders, developing stories that may or may not later be confirmed and disseminated by the mainstream media.

In one such instance, the husband-and-wife team of Paul Shinoff, a former carpenter, and Mary Shinoff, a former nurse, published detailed accounts of the dangers of asbestos to San Francisco area shipyard workers. The stories, which appeared in the December 1975 and March 1976 issues of the Shinoffs' alternative monthly, *Labor Pulse*, were inspired by a one-inch item in the *San Francisco Chronicle* noting a successful lawsuit against his employers by a worker sickened by asbestos.

As part of their six-month investigation, the Shinoffs contacted hundreds of workers normally exposed to asbestos. They found thirty-five workers who turned out to have asbestos-related disease. (Exposure to airborne asbestos fibers can cause asbestosis, a lung disease, and several kinds of cancer—a fact known to scientists since the 1930s, but withheld from workers by company doctors. Four out of ten asbestos workers exposed to the substance die from their exposure.)

The *Chronicle* failed to break this significant story, *Chronicle* science writer David Perlman told the *Columbia Journalism Review (CJR)*, because "there's so little asbestos here [in California]." In fact, as *CJR* writer Betty Medsger showed, California supplies two-thirds of the asbestos produced in the U.S. The state rock, serpentine, is a source of commercial-grade asbestos.

On March 13, 1976, the *Chronicle* finally began a series of stories about asbestos-related occupational hazards—four months after the Shinoffs' first piece appeared. The Shinoffs won a Robert Kennedy Journalism Award for their work. *Labor Pulse* slowed to a halt in 1976. Two years later, however, largely as a result of the *Labor Pulse* stories and their validation in the *Chronicle*, shipyard workers in the Bay Area were screened in a mobile X-ray unit, and health and safety standards for California workers coming into contact with asbestos were put under review.

Occupational safety, along with power relations in the workplace, has long been a topic of concern in the American leftist press. While a glance at leftist periodicals shows many to be awash in imprecise rhetoric, several left publications provide consistently good sources for investigative news.

The Progressive, the largest (circulation 40,000) of the older left-leaning periodicals, has published since 1909 and is still based in founder Robert LaFollette's home state of Wisconsin. *The Progressive* is known for its left-liberal political analysis, but its muckraking accomplishments are at least as impressive. The magazine placed three of the top ten stories of 1978 on Project Censored's list:

> A REPORT which showed that large-scale organic farming is producing large, high-quality crops in Europe, and even, quietly, in America— despite the disparagement of chemical manufacturers, who stand to profit from continued sales of chemical fertilizers and pesticides.
>
> AN ACCOUNT—based on a review of recent, little-publicized data— concluding that there is a connection between poor nutrition and mental imbalance.
>
> A REPORT debunking the myth of American upward mobility. The story showed that the top 1 percent of the population owned 24 percent of America's net worth in 1860 and 25 percent in 1977.

Moreover, in recent years, *The Progressive* has published an account of sweatshops in American cities which prompted two network TV documentaries and brought to public attention the plight of American GIs now suffering from radiation-induced illness who participated in the cleanup of Nagasaki. *The Progressive*'s battle against prior restraint (see Chapter Six) for its probe of secrecy surrounding the nuclear weapons program was also an outgrowth of the magazine's muckraking.

Militant leftist publications such as the *Guardian* (circulation 20,000) show that ideology and investigation are not necessarily incompatible. Indeed, a commitment to covering a subject can result in informative stories that other papers may have missed because they didn't know enough, or care enough, to develop the stories themselves. The *Guard-*

ian's contacts with foreign revolutionaries and its knowledge of international issues at times helped the paper produce extraordinarily prescient reports.

In 1954, the paper warned that "Guatemala is Dulles' next target" and reported on "how Washington moves to crush popular rule"—two weeks before a U.S.-backed coup overthrew the leftist government of that country.

In 1961, the *Guardian* claimed: "The events of the first two weeks of April have made it crystal clear that the government of the United States is harboring on its soil a counterrevolutionary movement whose purpose is to overthrow by force the legitimate government of Cuba." A week later, the U.S.-backed Bay of Pigs invasion took place.

In December of 1963, the *Guardian* published an article by Mark Lane, called "A Brief for Lee Harvey Oswald," which punched the first holes in official explanations of John F. Kennedy's murder. After the story was mentioned in the *New York Times*, the *Guardian* received 50,000 orders for reprints of the story.

In the middle and late sixties, Wilfred Burchett's wartime scoops gave *Guardian* readers an inside look at Southeast Asia (see Chapter Four). A decade later, the paper commissioned Sara Rodrigues as the only Western correspondent stationed permanently in Angola while that country was embroiled in a civil war that drew global attention. Her reports gave *Guardian* readers a weekly diet of information on guerrilla efforts, ultimately successful, to end the Portuguese colonial empire in central Africa.

A score of organizationally sponsored "party papers" are also published by leftist groups. Many are turgidly written, with militant posturing that makes them almost parodies of radical periodicals. Occasionally, however, their closeness and commitment to a particular issue or event will serve as the basis for sound reporting.

Workers' Viewpoint, the weekly organ of the Communist Workers Party (CWP), published a penetrating account of the shooting deaths of five CWP members at the hands of Ku Klux Klan and Nazi Party members in Greensboro, North Carolina, on November 3, 1979. Alleging a police conspiracy with the Klan to murder CWP leaders, *Workers' Viewpoint* identified inconsistencies in police accounts and collated reports from other media, enriched by on-the-spot accounts by CWP members. The CWP's interest in the events in Greensboro was evident, but their paper's disturbing report warranted a followup by other media.

No followup came, in any substantial form, until the *Village Voice* ran a cover story on May 26, 1980, corroborating all the important points in *Workers' Viewpoint*. The mass media remained silent.

Starting in the mid-sixties, several organizations devoted to research and funding of investigative journalism with a liberal or radical slant appeared. The first was the North American Congress on Latin America (NACLA), a group of leftist scholars who banded together in 1966. Shortly thereafter, NACLA published a popular booklet called "Who Rules Columbia?" detailing the interests of the university's trustees and their extensive business ties to corporations engaged in defense contracting at the height of the Vietnam war. Columbia students used the information to develop their critique of the wealthy, bureaucratic "multiversity" as part and parcel of the American establishment—not, as university officials would have it, a nonpolitical oasis of pure reason.

NACLA also inaugurated publication of a quarterly magazine called *Report on the Americas*. The *Report*, which is still published, illuminates the power structure of Latin American countries and the role of U.S. multinational corporations in the region's politics. NACLA's *Report* detailed, for example, the exodus of U.S. textile mills from Texas directly across the border to Mexico, where environmental safeguards are lax and wages are low.

In 1973, NACLA showed a burst of imagination by publishing a muckraking comic book. *The Incredible Rocky* told the story of the Rockefeller business empire from John D. Rockefeller on: the ruination of the family's rail competitors; the expansion into vast, horizontally integrated corporations; the enormous holdings and influence-peddling in Third World countries. *The Incredible Rocky*, drawn and researched by Joel Andreas, a 17-year-old high-school student, sold over 100,000 copies.

In 1978, the New York-based NACLA split into two groups. A West Coast offshoot, headquartered in Oakland, opened a library for radical scholars called the Data Center. Stuffed with books, periodicals, and files of clippings on leading corporations, and augmented by the personal papers of reporters such as the late Paul Jacobs, the Data Center is an open text for muckrakers.

What radical muckrakers need more than research material, however, is money. The *Mother Jones* Investigative Fund finances only articles destined for publication in that magazine. But the Fund for Investigative Journalism, founded in 1969, awards grants of up to $2,000 to

Joel Andreas's comic book investigation of the Rockefellers was both accurate and funny. (Courtesy of North American Congress on Latin America.)

underwrite the cost of research for a variety of media outlets. Many of the fund's grants go to alternative journalists. According to Howard Bray, the fund's executive director, "The airing of information that investigative journalism provides is essential under our form of government. Investigative reporting is now in vogue, but serious journalists were committed to it before Watergate. And there will be a need for it for a long time to come."

The Fund for Investigative Journalism, which is itself funded by foundation grants and private donors, has underwritten hundreds of articles and several dozen books. Its list of credits includes a grant to Seymour Hersh for the My Lai story. The fund also helped back Jessica Mitford's exposé of prison conditions, *Kind and Usual Punishment*. For another story, the fund financed a writer who had been squirreling away material for three years in shoeboxes, researching abuses in New York City's court system. "That's what we're here for," said Bray, "to sustain a writer on a project that might be long term, might not be done adequately without our help, or might not be done at all."

As mentioned previously, the fund also helped finance the corporate dumping story for *Mother Jones*, prepared by David Weir and Mark Shapiro of the Center for Investigative Reporting (CIR). Located in a rococo, triangular-shaped building five blocks from the Data Center in Oakland, the nonprofit CIR was formed in 1977 "to demystify investigative reporting," according to cofounder Lowell Bergman. Said Bergman: "We're trying to break down some of the competition and ego problems that separate one isolated writer from another by collaborating among ourselves and with other reporters on long-term projects. We also act as consultants to community groups that want to learn how to research, say, their town's power structure, but don't know how to go about it."

Bergman practiced what he preached. In 1976, after discovering the foreign ownership of a hotel slated for demolition in San Francisco, Bergman turned over his files to hotel residents who were resisting eviction. Bergman, whose workstyle was formed in the commune that put out the *San Diego Street Journal*, saw the CIR's cooperative structure as a philosophical extension of his earlier work. Beset by legal expenses incurred in defending himself against a libel suit by alleged Mafia figures for an article he coauthored in *Penthouse* magazine, Bergman left the CIR in 1978 to take a well-paying job with ABC television's "20/20."

The CIR now does occasional stories for ABC, such as a report on the effects of atomic testing on U.S. service veterans, which CIR reporters picked up from *Enlisted Times*. In addition to *ABC*, the CIR does stories for alternative news organization such as *Mother Jones* and Pacific News Service.

"We're trying to become more activist," said Mark Shapiro, who joined cofounders Weir and Dan Noyes and lawyer-journalist Becky O'Malley at the CIR in 1979; "The Center is alternative in our vision of investigative reporting." Echoing Mark Dowie, Shapiro said, "The typical investigative piece in daily newspapers is looking into scandals on the local water board. That's OK, they're out there doing it, but it doesn't get beyond the scandal, about who has the power and how those structures work. What really needs to be talked about is corporate domination of the economy."

And that takes not only perceptive issue and trend analysis, but skilled sleuthing by journalists who are committed to doing it. Much of this type of reporting comes from alternative news services. Since alternative services—small and poor compared to the wire services and the news services of major dailies—can't compete in timeliness or volume with the majors, they try to do them one better by providing more in-depth coverage.

The two most comprehensive and important alternative services are Liberation News Service (LNS) and Pacific News Service (PNS). LNS is still closely tied to the radical left movements, while PNS has grown spectacularly from its original antiwar constituency and now circulates material with a left-liberal slant to daily newspapers. Both services emphasize analysis as well as reporting, but, in their sustained scrutiny of government and business, LNS and PNS have produced notable exposures.

LNS' identification with victims of society led the news service to develop some of the first reports of the dangers of Agent Orange, a deadly herbicide—used as a defoliant in Vietnam—which has been found to cause birth defects and cancer. These and other reports went out to some 360 subscribers, about one-fourth of which are outside the U.S. However, the service's radical perspective keeps its material out of culturally oriented alternative papers, and LNS' work is little known outside the alternative media.

Pacific News Service, by way of contrast, managed to do what no other alternative news service has done: have its material accepted for publication by daily newspapers, including the *Los Angeles Times* and the *Boston Globe*. Branching out from its base of alternative periodicals, PNS more than doubled its number of subscribers (to 250) between 1977 and 1979.

In 1977, PNS uncovered plans to build a large, coal-fired power plant

just across the border in Mexico to avoid California's stringent environmental laws. It also illuminated a seemingly senseless killing in San
Francisco's Chinatown by revealing that organized crime enlisted youth
gangs to carry out its dirty work. The PNS report was helped in no small
measure by the fact that managing editor Sandy Close and fellow PNS
editor Franz Schurmann speak Cantonese and have contacts in the
Chinese community normally off limits to outside journalists.

Moreover, PNS has emphasized the analytic skills of scholar-writers
to turn seemingly routine data into a form of intellectual muckraking. In
1978, for example, PNS associate editor Martin Brown successfully
challenged a RAND Corporation report that announced a narrowing of
the income gap between white and black Americans. Brown, a research
economist, obtained the original data from RAND, ran them through a
computer, and showed that RAND's study had used only data on black
males in the labor force. When the increasing number of unemployed
black males was included, results showed that the income gap had
widened. Brown's futuristic detective work was printed in dailies such as
the *Milwaukee Journal* and black papers such as the *Jackson* (Mississippi)
Advocate, where it countered the optimistic RAND report with a very
different picture of American reality.

While alternative media activists were using print media to bring to life
information about society's shortcomings and abuses, independent
filmmakers were developing an investigative cinema. One such
filmmaker was Haskell Wexler, an Academy Award-winning cinema-
tograper who used his earnings from TV commercials and conventional
films to bankroll his own projects. Offered Wexler, "When you work, as
I do, in the mainstream . . . the mainstream is polluted. And if you stay
in that pollution, you too, whether you know it or not, get that way."

Wexler began as a radical cinematographer, shooting films for the
left-wing United Electrical Workers Union and secretely processing
footage of *Salt of the Earth*, the 1956 labor docu-drama, at night in a
Chicago film lab. After doing commercial film work in he fifties, Wexler
turned to making his own films. His first effort was *Medium Cool*, a
fictional story of a TV camera operator who learns he cannot remain
aloof from the political tumult swirling around him (the film was set
during the 1968 Chicago convention). After *Medium Cool*, Wexler teamed
with a group of Chilean filmmakers to make *Brazil: A Report on Torture*.
Released in 1971, the film exposed the widespread torture and imprisonment of dissidents in Brazil, carried out by police trained and
armed by the United States.

The film "was seen by the whole U.S. Senate at one time," Wexler said, "and subsequently, they cut the military appropriations for Brazil. That was very important." On a more somber note, Wexler added, "There were twenty-seven people connected with that film, and three of us are alive now. They were killed when the junta took power [in 1973] in Chile."

Newsreel, the erstwhile New Left filmmaking group, also added muckraking films to its repertoire in the seventies. Their best-realized effort, *Controlling Interest* (1978), was an exposure of multinational corporations. The film calculates the cost of runaway shops on an aging New England town abandoned by globe-trotting multinationals. It presents effective interviews with corporate executives who speak frankly about their decision to leave the community with which their industry had a historic association in favor of cheap labor abroad. Where a print journalism would merely describe what the loss of jobs meant to the town, the film dramatizes it by showing angry faces and empty factories. The following year, when *The Nation* did a similar story about the loss of a manufacturing plant in Chicago, Project Censored (which does not monitor film) tapped the story as one of 1979's top "ignored " reports.

The most sobering of all the independent muckraking films, *Paul Jacobs and the Nuclear Gang* (1979), digs out the tragic life stories of civilian victims of nuclear testing in the fifties. The story began in 1957, when Linus Pauling told Jacobs—the future *Mother Jones* editor—that isolated communities in Utah and Nevada had been exposed to high levels of radioactive fallout from atmospheric nuclear testing. Jacobs did a series of articles on the radiation victims, who had been assured by the government that the tests would not harm them.

Twenty years later, with the film crew following him, Jacobs, terminally ill with cancer, returned to Utah. Most of the people he had talked to in the fifties were dead from cancer. During the filming, Jacobs deteriorated shockingly. A powerfully built man with a shaved head that made him look formidable indeed, Jacobs wasted away before the cameras and finally expired. He was convinced his illness had been caused by exposure to radiation while investigating the effects of fallout in the fifties.

Paul Jacobs and the Nuclear Gang is a powerful, controversial film. Many stations refused to show it when public television bought the film from its producers, Jack Willis and Saul Landau. Nevertheless, the film won an Emmy for best program in 1980. It also won the George Polk Award for Investigative Journalism, and it is an understandably popular choice for use in antinuclear organizing.

Mother Jones' Pinto recall and jury trial; the *Rochester Patriot*'s torpedo-ing of prison behavior modification; the Fund for Investigative Journalism's underwriting of the My Lai story; Pacific News Service's dissection of the cheery RAND Corporation report; Haskell Wexler's blow against aid to torturers—these stories and others illustrate the impact of alternative muckrakers on public opinion and public policy.

Their influence—especially in reference to their resources—is considerable. And yet, for radical activists who desire to transform society, muckraking has very real limitations. It inspires piecemeal reform, not transformation, and reforms can be rolled back. In the radical view, muckraking helps the establishment recognize its weaknesses and make cosmetic changes as a means of avoiding substantial change. Upton Sinclair's *The Jungle* spurred pure-food laws for the meat-packing industry, but not the revolution in productive relationships it was meant to trigger. "I aimed at the public's heart," Sinclair groaned, "and by accident, I hit it in the stomach."

Sinclair's complaint illustrates a limitation of media as vehicles of social change: However much media shape and color social and political action, they cannot maintain it themselves. "Without an on-going movement of people," remarked Jessica Mitford, "no amount or ranting and writing is going to help very much. You see, you must have the people behind you."

Thus the dilemma of the alternative muckrakers—having revived the muckraking tradition and honed their skills to equal those of the best reporters, they have just begun their work.

fifteen

Alternative Media In the Eighties

THERE IS A TWO-PANELED illustration in the June 1978 issue of *Mother Jones* that conveys a great deal about the past and future of the alternative media culture. In a panel depicting the political climate of 1968, a long-haired young man in bell-bottom jeans, wearing a peace symbol on his bodyshirt, single-handedly wrestles two businessmen in suits and ties—the he-man of radical machismo fantasies in action. In the panel depicting 1978, a group of activist women, wearing expressions of controlled anger, look to the future. One holds a sign that reads "No Nukes." Overhead soars a balloon adorned with the symbol of women's liberation. The only man in the picture sits, disabled, in a wheelchair, holding a sign that reads "Environment."

The drawing dramatically illustrates the evolution of the alternative movements and media, not only from 1968 to 1978, but also from the

A transition from fiery confrontation to the slow, patient building of alternatives characterized the seventies. What will the future hold for the alternative media culture: continued growth in an era of aggressive patriotism? (Illustration by Lucinda Colwell; poster by James Montgomery Flagg.)

early sixties to the early eighties. Allowing for some exaggeration—activist men are not all helpless onlookers—the drawing vividly expresses the belief of most alternative media activists that the scenario of immediate, violent revolution has been played out and replaced by the peaceful but militant long-term struggles of feminism, environmentalism, and grassroots community and factory organizing. While the drawing represents a lowering of expectations, it also conveys hope for the future, tempered by the knowledge that remaking America is a lifetime commitment.

In the text accompanying the illustration, Adam Hochschild characterized the guerrilla fantasies of *Mother Jones'* predecessor, *Ramparts*, as almost comically inflated, while allowing that:

> It is all too easy to poke fun at the illusions of ten years ago; all of us who were around then were to some extent naive. The overwhelming horror of Vietnam made all political choices seem urgent and simple. In retrospect, one unspoken assumption seems to lie behind many of the [*Ramparts*] articles. It was that the whole system we were fighting was so weak that a few shouts, kicks, and a good hard shove would bring it all crashing down. It didn't, but at least now we're wiser in the knowledge of what a slow and cooperative job real change is going to have to be.

What brought about this change in the attitudes of alternative media activists? Surely the kamikaze attacks of the Weather Underground, the failed theatricality of the media guerrillas in Chicago, the co-optation of once radical-sounding ideals into commercial formulae all had much to do with it. So, too, did the recognition that, by the late seventies, many of the progressive social changes advocated by the alternative and underground media were under attack. Abortion rights were being curtailed. The ERA appeared stalled. The defense budget was spiraling upward. Anticommunism was back in vogue. Draft registration had been restored. In short, America had entered a period of backlash, encouraged by conservative commentators in the mass media such as syndicated columnist Ronald Reagan and television commentator Phyllis Schlafly.

As earlier chapters have shown, political backlash has often swelled into institutionalized repression of the radical media themselves, derailing movements for social change and forcing the next generation of activists to reinvent the wheel. One thinks of the government suppression of *The Masses* and *Appeal to Reason* in the early twenties, the harassment of the *National Guardian* and Pacifica radio in the early fifties, the secret war against the underground media in the late sixties and early seventies, and the disastrous effects of such repression on the radical movements of those years.

Speaking to alternative media activists at the beginning of a new decade, one is struck by both their apprehensiveness that radical media and movements could again be forced into hibernation and their determination to prevent that from happening. In an interview in the *Mother Jones* office in the spring of 1980, shortly before Mark Dowie resigned as publisher to turn to full-time writing, he proclaimed that the purpose of that muckraking monthly was to "get the center to move more to the left and the left to talk to the center. We're trying to keep people in the political center from becoming fascists in the eighties. I think the magazine can be a revolutionary weapon," Dowie asserted, comparing his colleagues at *Mother Jones* to the revolutionary pamphleteers of the colonial era.

Not all alternative media activists share Dowie's vision of a leftist revolution nor his fear that America is on the verge of fascism, as it has been known historically in Europe and Japan. But they do share Dowie's intention to use the alternative media as political instruments to hold and, if possible, enlarge the territory they have staked as their own.

For the alternative media to expand their influence, they must first enlarge their constituencies. Despite the sweeping nature of their world views, alternative media still appeal mainly to white, well-educated, middle-class people under forty. Recognizing this, many alternative activists have made expanding their journalistic and political base a top priority in the eighties. Writes Adam Hochschild in the article quoted earlier, "If you asked the twenty people who work at *Mother Jones* for their visions of this country's future, you'd get thirty different answers. But one thing we'd probably all agree on is that any American movement for social change that really gets off the ground must include a range of people far broader than the middle-class group of men and women who read this magazine."

In order to broaden *Mother Jones'* appeal, Hochschild continued, the magazine has expanded traditional leftist notions of what is political:

[In the sixties] if you had suggested that sexual harassment at the office (p. 21 of this issue), or the exploitation of secretaries (p. 19) [was political] . . . all but a handful of women's movement pioneers would have laughed.

Similarly, a Movement heavy would probably have found light-weight an issue like the computerization of food buying, which Amanda Spake discusses on p. 38, and just plain oddball the discoveries of John Ott (p. 49) on the ill effects of artificial light. What would Lenin think? Best to leave all that consumer stuff to Ralph Nader.

Perhaps it is basically a question of whether you believe the Revolution imminent, or whether you believe that radiation, computers, light pollution, and the rest may kill us all before it arrives. And that changing *every* way human beings are exploited, whether the sacred texts happen to mention them or not, is what any meaningful revolution must be about.

Mother Jones' revised agenda follows logically from developments in alternative media in the early seventies, which emphasized the political dimensions of personal life and the nuts-and-bolts practicality of changing one's life here and now. It also draws on the pioneering work of *Our Bodies, Ourselves*, and the *Whole Earth Catalog*, in that persons not already members in good standing of the alternative media culture are viewed, not as adversaries, but as potential allies in a broad-based movement to change American society.

Both the inclusiveness and the practicality of alternative media efforts of the early eighties can be seen in a film called *The Life and Times of Rosie the Riveter*, completed by independent filmmaker Connie Field in 1980. A 60-minute documentary that juxtaposes interviews with women who worked in the factories and shipyards of World War II with vintage footage, Field's film highlights both the contributions that women workers made to the war effort and the propaganda campaign by government and industry at the end of the war to move them out of "men's jobs." After Field finished *Rosie*, she worked closely with organizations such as the National Association of Neighborhood Women and the Council of Labor Union Women to develop written study guides to go with the film.

Unlike the agitprop films of the sixties, *Rosie the Riveter* was developed to appeal to a large audience of feminists, working people, leftists, and older men and women, including former "Rosies" eager to see their history recorded and interpreted on screen. This inclusiveness, along with a glossy technical finish that contrasts with the grainy immediacy of sixties cinema, sets *Rosie* (and the maturing genre of independently made political documentaries) apart from earlier films by Newsreel and other politically radical filmmakers.

"I worked in Boston Newsreel, where I learned how not to make films," Field told *In these Times'* Pat Aufderheide. "Most of our films were useful at the time, but most did not have longevity. We don't have the same kind of movement now, to sustain films like that. Now you need a film that can reach a mass audience. You need technical quality. People watch TV and go to feature movies, and they expect a lot."

Most of the alternative media enterprises that show signs of prospering in the eighties share Field's concern for high technical quality and broad appeal, as well as her film's reclamation of history. Beginning with the books and articles on "lost women" in the feminist press in the early seventies, activists have shown an abiding interest in recovering the history of radical movements and reinterpreting American history from an activist perspective. Regard for history was rarely manifested in the sixties underground media; when the issues of the day—particularly the war—seemed so pressing, activists had little time for contemplating the past. Today, however, alternative media activists record and study history, not out of simple nostalgia, but to discover clues to unlock the problems of the present.

Mother Jones, among others, publishes radical analyses of the past, including features on its predecessors in the leftist press, such as *The Masses, Appeal to Reason*, and, of course, *Ramparts*. The magazine's slick paper and professional design are geared toward attracting a mass audience, and the enticement appears to be working. In 1980, some stores in the Safeway supermarket chain began selling *Mother Jones* right next to the checkout counters, where the muckraking monthly competes with the *National Enquirer*'s latest scoops on Elvis Presley and Jackie Onassis. According to Hochschild, supermarket sales have been good, although they are still a small percentage of *Mother Jones'* sales; 90 percent of the magazine's circulation comes from paid subscriptions.

Like other healthy alternative enterprises, *Mother Jones* has established a continuing symbiosis with its constituents. *Mother Jones'* special Investigative Fund, for example, is not only largely funded by readers' donations, it is also an outgrowth of reader input. "In our first year [1976], we carried a lot of lifestyle features, stories on backpacking, the circus, and so on," said Hochschild, "on the mistaken assumption that we had to soft-pedal our politics. Well, the readers told us in no uncertain terms that they could get that kind of material elsewhere." It was in response to a readership survey that *Mother Jones* decided to emphasize the political muckraking that has become its trademark.

That kind of intimate, intense relationship marks other continuing success stories such as that of Persephone Press, a lesbian-feminist publishing house in Boston, whose books have demonstrated appeal both inside and outside the feminist community. Persephone Press has published titles such as *Coming Out Stories*, a collection of personal histories of lesbians who decided to publicly acknowledge their homosexuality; Sally Gearhart and Susan Rennie's exploration of female spirituality, *A Feminist Tarot*; and Gearhart's futuristic novel, *The Wanderground*. Several of Persephone's books have attracted the attention of mainstream publishers in search of reprint rights, but Persephone has chosen to work with alternative distributors rather than sign over their titles to commercial houses.

Publishers like Persephone maintain their independence so that they can present undiluted feminist writing—a rarity outside the alternative publishing world, as even popular writers such as Marge Piercy have discovered. Discussing her novel *The High Cost of Living* (published by Harper & Row in 1978), Piercy said that "the New York marketplace" responded tepidly to her decision to make the main character in the book a lesbian. "But lesbianism is not what it's about," Piercy protested. "Leslie is a lesbian like she has red hair; it was only one part of her character. I thought you could do that now, but the cultural dragons assumed no one was going to be interested in the fabric of the relationships except other lesbians."

Feminist publishers such as Booklegger Press' Valerie Wheat seconded Piercy, observing that, ". . . if it seems that women's books are 'accepted' now, that equal numbers will be published and reviewed, that's not the point. Only certain forms have received the imprimatur: the housewife-in-revolt novel, the how-to-get-yours guide for the woman executive, history or biography of women that is not too radical. But the men at the top make the decisions." Such limitations on the free circulation of unconventional ideas help explain why alternative media—continuing in their role as creative critics of the dominant culture—continue to exist and why disenfranchised people—recognizing media that speak to, for, and with themselves—support media alternatives.

Media outlets that inspire the most intense identification from constituents are usually those that welcome community participation in more than a token sense. Popular enterprises such as the National Federation of Community Broadcasters (NFCB) stations draw staff members chiefly from among their listeners. The resulting community response has helped the stations grow in size, influence, and number. "Our vital signs are all up," said NFCB associate Randy Thoms. "We have more applications for membership than we had members [twenty-five] five years ago."

Moreover, the stations' open-door policies have allowed them to assemble staffs which are broadly representative of the population as a whole. When the NFCB surveyed its members in 1979, the organization found that 17 percent of station staffers were minority persons—roughly the percentage of nonwhites in the national population. The average staffer earned just over $8,000 a year, putting the alternative broadcasters among the poor and working-class listeners at whom most community stations beam their programming. Women comprised 37 percent of the staffs, well below the percentage of females in the populace; however, community stations did not generally shunt women into menial jobs. Females constituted 35 percent of the station managers and 27 percent of the program directors. The average age of the NFCB staffers was a fairly young 28, reflecting most of the stations' distance from a portion of the public invisible to all varieties of American media: the elderly.

At the marginally alternative urban weeklies that comprise the majority of members of the National Association of Alternative Newsweeklies (NAAN), alienation from the old and poor is not viewed as a limitation, but as a marketing advantage. Most NAAN papers have a near-obsession with bombarding the postwar Baby Boom generation with products, especially the affluent young whites who compose the most desirable consumers in that generation. This, of course, is not accidental. Before the *Advocate* newspapers were started in 1973, their cofounders studied *The Statistical Abstract of the United States* to find the most lucrative market for their embryonic enterprise. Targeting—and staying with—the Baby Boom was the smart thing to do for young entrepreneurs.

The result of many NAAN papers' preoccupation with the postwar generation has resulted in their near-total avoidance of the old, the poor, and the nonwhite. That fact does not go unnoticed within the organization itself. At a panel discussion at the 1980 NAAN convention, Dick Clever, the managing editor of *Willamette Week*, remarked that, "As I look around this room, I see a perfect profile of the power structure. There are no nonwhite faces here and there have been very few women on any of the panels." At another session, Bob Roth, editor and publisher of the *Chicago Reader*, allowed as how his paper had only two black workers among a staff of twenty-six "in a city that is fifty percent black. We try to attract blacks," Roth went on. "We print listings of events on

Chicago's south and west sides, where our readers would never dare to go. But blacks seem totally uninterested in our papers." There followed a discussion in which nearly all the NAAN papers acknowledged that they had few black readers or workers—and that those black staffers they did have were nearly all confined to menial jobs.

The NAAN journalists are not malicious racists who keep out racial minorities because they fear and despise nonwhites. Their papers have little appeal to minorities for a simple reason: nearly all the articles and ads are tailored for affluent consumers, and most of them are white. Although many urban weeklies recognize running articles about minorities and the poor as part of their journalistic responsibility, few direct their papers at such readers or work with them to produce papers with broad-based constituencies. *Advocate* copublisher Ed Matys opined that the distance most urban weeklies keep from minorities and the poor— who, after all, comprise an increasing proportion of the population of American cities—could be combined with a type of socially conscious reporting. "I think the role that the alternative press can play in the eighties is that of being an agency that explains what the needs are at the bottom to the new privileged class, to show them that being conversant with the problems is in their self-interest."

More authentic forms of alternative journalism are produced with, or even by, minorities and the poor (such as the minority-owned and run KPOO radio in San Francisco); they don't merely convey information about suffering people, at beneficent remove, to a "new privileged class." However, the commercial corporate structure itself—which presupposes a top-down management structure and a need to maximize profits by directing a media product at consumers with enough money to support advertisers in high style—almost guarantees that conventionally operated media will remain remote from disenfranchised people, minimizing their potential for empowerment and maximizing their dependence on the advertising supplements, guides, and articles on "coping" discussed in Chapter Twelve.

Journalists such as *San Francisco Bay Guardian* editor-publisher Bruce Brugmann embrace such editorial policies not only because they bring in advertising dollars, but because they can, he said, be considered as a useful form of information. Brugmann told the 1980 NAAN convention that lifestyle guides for coping in a recessionary economy were one way to score points with media consumers in the eighties. "We find it useful to say, 'Yes, there are problems, and here are ways to deal with them, to keep on enjoying the good life in hard times.'"

Everyone likes to save money, of course, and there is nothing wrong with publishing budget guides per se. But such material usually begs important questions. *Why* are we experiencing hard times? Who's to blame and who can help? What can we do to resolve—not just survive—a time of crisis? When budget guides largely supplant hard-hitting reporting and analysis in an era of worldwide convulsions, such material seems trivial, even cynical. Media outlets that follow the ten-great-places-to-find-croissants-after-midnight path to success have exchanged the windows on the world they could provide for mirrors.

Some alternative media may mirror the mass media in another important respect if a phenomenon of the late seventies turns into a trend—namely, the growth of alternative newspaper chains. The *Boston Phoenix*'s Stephen Mindich tried, and failed, to start successful papers outside his home city. So did Ken Simon of the *Syracuse New Times*, whose unsuccessful spinoff weeklies in Buffalo and Ithaca, New York, nearly bankrupted his original paper. By the end of the decade, however, the Amherst-based *Advocate* had four newspapers in New England and one in upstate New York—the *New Times*, ironically, which Simon was forced to sell in early 1979 because of debts incurred in his unsuccessful expansion. The combined circulation of the *Advocate* papers is 350,000, or three times that of the runnerup *Phoenix*.

Sensitive to the charges of press critics that the centralization of mass media reduces journalistic diversity, *Advocate* co-owner Ed Matys defended the chain concept among urban weeklies, claiming that the papers can be tailored to reflect their respective localities. Matys also said that constantly escalating publishing costs—for newsprint, postage, labor—may prevent new papers from getting off the ground in the eighties and may even drive some established papers out of existence. He concluded that effective out-of-town ownership could benefit affected communities, pointing to the *Advocate*'s purchase of the *New Times* as an example. "We saved a dying newspaper," Matys said.

Fair enough. But Matys and his partners could administer euthanasia to the *New Times* if the paper lost money or otherwise displeased them. The *New Times*' employees—not to mention its readers—would have nothing to say about it. This mode of operation is identical to that of the Newhouse chain of daily papers, with which the *Advocate* competes in Syracuse. The *Advocate* papers are not to be dismissed as alternative outlets. They publish sometimes excellent local reporting—the *Hartford Advocate*'s exposé of city pension funds in corporations that do business with South Africa, for example. And their arts coverage is usually much stronger than that of their daily competitors. But the *Advocate* chain is strictly conventional in structure. More thoroughgoing alternatives, such as *Mother Jones*, cannot be shut down by executive fiat.

Fortunately, centralized ownership is still an unusual state of affairs in the alternative media, where the new provincialism of the seventies continues to flourish. The trend to localism has spawned papers with strong community roots not only in major media centers, but in industrial centers like Baltimore and Flint, Michigan, small towns like Chico, California, and Eugene, Oregon, and Sun Belt communities such as Tucson, Arizona. If recessionary setbacks to small local papers prove as serious as Matys predicts, however, they could stunt the growth of genuinely local papers, since a publication controlled from afar cannot be truly local.

One journalist who has come to this conclusion is Ken Simon, the former *New Times* owner and chain publisher. Emphasizing that he was not criticizing his former *Advocate* partners as individuals, Simon allowed, "The concept of an alternative chain is somewhat at odds with itself. It can be a profitable ego-gratification to the owner. But the problem is, if there's any money to be made, it's being taken out of the city and put into acquiring other properties." An alternative chain, in sum, is a contradiction in terms.

But if conventional business structures blunt the alternative thrust of media enterprises that use them, finding a financially viable means of operation that is also alternative in nature can be extremely difficult. One means of staying alive in troubled times is by seeking out government and foundation grants. This approach is nothing new for alternative media; as Chapter Three showed, it was a timely Ford Foundation grant that put KPFA radio back on the air in 1951 after the station had nearly expired from lack of funds. Today, KPFA receives 30 percent of its annual budget from grants, most of them federal monies. Many small presses are also underwritten by government, often through state arts councils and the National Endowment for the Arts. The Bay Area Video Coalition—an expanding association of San Francisco videomakers—is supported, in part, by the Rockefeller Foundation. *Harrisburg*—a monthly alternative magazine in Pennsylvania's capital city—gets by with CETA money.

Such arrangements put the American power structure in the intriguing and advantageous position of subsidizing its critics. Alternative journalists so funded, sensitive to the likes and dislikes of their patrons, can hardly help being susceptible to self-censorship—the withholding of the vital fact, the softening of the critical phrase—in an attempt to hold onto their funding. Should subsidized crusaders strike establishment targets too hard, they run the risk of being suppressed by outside agencies. When *Harrisburg* argered Metropolitan Edison Company, operator of the Three Mile Island nuclear power plant, with its antinuclear reporting in 1978, officials of the company wrote Washington to demand that *Harrisburg*'s CETA funding be cancelled. The government declined to slash the magazine's funds that time, but one suspects that in a time of intensified political repression, *Harrisburg* would not have been so fortunate.

The solicitation of large private donors—wealthy individuals believed to be sympathetic to alternative ideals—for vital operating funds carries a similar risk. One remembers Louis Schweitzer's threat to withhold support from WBAI because of Chris Koch's documentaries on North Vietnam in 1965, and the resulting staff split and cancelled subscriptions that dispute occasioned. In such dependency relationships, powerful patrons can mute or even silence the trumpets to arms sounded by alternative media activists simply by stopping payment on their checks.

Instructive experiences like the Koch-Schweitzer fight and the *Harrisburg*-Metropolitan Edison dispute lead one to conclude that soliciting gifts and grants, while desirable and perhaps essential as a short-term strategy for survival, is hardly conducive to long-term independence for alternative media. In Europe, radical daily newspapers sell for the equivalent of a dollar. European readers buy their paper because they identify with and support its point of view. The paper is not subsidized by government handouts, nor is it fat with compromising advertising. In America, as in Europe, the only way to be fully alternative is to be financially self-sufficient.

Of course, attaining financial self-sufficiency is more easily said than done. Alternative periodicals such as *Chrysalis*, the feminist journal of politics and art, and *Seven Days*, launched as an alternative to *Time* and *Newsweek*, both folded in 1980 after failing to bring in enough money to meet expenses. *Chrysalis* coeditor Kirsten Grimstad reported difficulty in attracting and keeping staffers with business skills with the modest salaries that *Chrysalis* could afford to pay, adding that emergency projects such as programs for battered women and rape victims attracted more of the feminist community's limited financial resources than did the feminist media. *Seven Days* editor Dave Dellinger, the long-time pacifist journalist, attributed that magazine's demise to its initial undercapitalization and the frantic game of catch-up its publishers were forced to play after beginning publication in 1975.

Some alternative periodicals, however, have entered the eighties with modestly successful financial game plans. *In These Times (ITT)*, a leftist newsweekly with a circulation of 20,000, finances its operations by working closely with a network of readers who contribute money (and information) to the paper beyond their normal subscription fees. This not only helps the paper in a specifically financial sense, it also lays the groundwork for political associations that help make it a more effective organizing tool.

Founded in 1976 by James Weinstein, a historian of the American left, *ITT* was established along the lines of the old *Appeal to Reason*, whose readers—the "Appeal Army"—supported that paper with grassroots subscription drives and donations. Weinstein started *ITT*, he said, to supersede "a left counterculture" that he felt talked mostly to itself. Since then, *ITT*, which advocates a gradual, reformist path to socialism, has forged links with the left wing of the Democratic Party and with liberal unions such as the Machinists, which buy subscriptions for members, helping to finance the newspaper. This style of operation makes *In These Times* considerably more than a propaganda sheet aimed at passive consumers; it makes readers into coworkers.

While *In These Times* employs a model rooted in the past to build an effective political organization, some alternative media activists view the eighties as a time to make use of the latest technological innovations to increase their clout. "Rather than be enslaved by satellites and other new technologies," said KPFA news director Alan Snitow, "we'll need to use them to achieve our aims as community [journalists] by improving local service, exchanging information, sharing resources, and presenting alternative visions."

To this end, the Pacifica radio network plans to inaugurate a national newscast from production facilities in Washington, D.C., beamed to over two hundred noncommercial stations around the country via communications satellite. The program is scheduled to begin in late 1981. According to Snitow, the half-hour newscast will differ from the taped feature format of National Public Radio's popular "All Things Considered" by being a mostly live program with an accent on hard news, presented from a stronger left-liberal perspective than that advanced by cautious NPR journalists. The bulk of the news is expected to be gathered by local reporters at subscribing stations.

While Snitow and the other journalists planning the newscast hope to produce a good program, they are, Snitow said, equally interested in freeing subscribers' small news departments to concentrate on local coverage. "Our purpose," said Snitow, "is to build up those local resources so we're really building up a network that has community roots"—a network that can help shape the country politically as well as journalistically.

The kind of grassroots involvement which the Pacifica newscast is intended to further on a national scale, through the use of space technology, is also a goal of earthbound projects in specific localities. Berkeley's Community Memory project, a user-controlled computer network that flourished briefly in the early seventies, is scheduled to return to operation in late 1981 as an expanded electronic "bulletin board" and index into which users will type messages and donate and retrieve information. A dozen small computers are expected to be connected to larger terminals, forming a network utterly without centralized direction. If the project unfolds according to plan, the terminals will be overseen by neighborhood groups which can rent or buy them outright to help pay for maintenance. As in the original version of Community Memory, the keywords will be chosen by the users so that no arbitrarily selected categories will predetermine the way the community communicates with itself.

Community Memory is the handiwork of media activists who believe—as did early alternative visionaries such as Michael Shamberg—that easy-access, decentralized technology, deployed in a noncommercial context, can help create a media democracy in which everyone has access to information and to the means of communicating with everyone else. This view contrasts with that of mainstream pundits such as Marshall McLuhan, who predicted that the dissemination of modern media technology would, in itself, bring us together in a democratic global village.

The world didn't have to wait until the recent, long-awaited appearance of video cassettes and discs, home computers, two-way television, and other inventions to see the false optimism of McLuhan's view. The telephone, for example, has been with us for a century, and, while it is an unquestionably useful device, the telephone did not make America significantly more democratic. Phone users who call one another to commiserate about the bland sameness of Presidential candidates move no closer to controlling the political process that produces those candidates by talking on marvelous equipment rented from a monopolistic utility. It is the social context in which media are used that gives them a political character, which can be, by turns, either alternative or conventional.

In Columbus, Ohio, an ambitious commercial cable television project called Qube employs computerized attachments to TV screens to record viewers' yes and no votes about which celebrity interviews they want to see, what prizes they want to compete for from televised game shows, what sponsors' products they would like to know more about. A computer printout, recording consumers' requests for information about, say, Ford Pintos, is then punched up and forwarded to Ford. The viewers have nothing to say about the questions they are given to decide in this "participatory" system. Instead of being a communications medium through which participants exchange information that they themselves choose, Qube is a distribution system that delivers consumers to advertisers.

This contrasts sharply with projects such as Community Memory, where alternative media activists—which place modern media technology in a decentralized, noncommercial context—create a system that comes close to pure process and true democracy. Sandy Emerson, a Community Memory staffer and coeditor of the *Journal of Community Communications*, writes:

> We believe that free-flowing, non-hierarchical and interactive communication is a style of information exchange which may empower people, not by giving them a "vote" on issues not of their own choosing, but by giving them direct control over the content of the information they receive. This implies increased ability (and responsibility) for ascertaining the truth and usefulness of the information. By encouraging self-reliance rather than reliance on "experts," this communications style may encourage cooperatives and collective effort in and among communities. The communities concerned may be neighborhoods or associations of interest-groups sharing common goals.

Media, then, offer social and political alternatives to the powers that be when they are embedded in, and controlled by, communities of human beings—the way Community Memory is planned to be, the way the most authentic expressions of the underground press were.

Without the many manifestations of alternative media, the progressive social and political movements of the last fifteen years would have had but a fraction of the success they did in strengthening the humanistic features of American society. The influence of the alternative media on sexual mores, spirituality, health, and all manner of things political has been impressive, all the more so given their chronic lack of resources. From the alternative media came the first courageous reporters who worked against the Vietnam war and exposed its atrocities to public view; environmentalists who helped show Americans how to respect and care for the natural world; feminists who clarified the radical vision by challenging myopia within the movement and its media; muckrakers who kindled public outrage and inspired reform legislation; artists and visionaries who explored the farthest reaches of literature, audio, and video documentary art.

Taken together, the alternative media have been the unacknowledged cutting edge of American communications—media where new and unconventional ideas are introduced, where journalistic and political risks are taken. With risk, of course, comes the possibility of loss, as the crusading journalists in the underground discovered when they suffered the illegal attacks of a repressive government; as *The Progressive* demonstrated when that magazine was hit with the first use of prior restraint in American history, in violation of the publication's First Amendment rights. Contemporary assaults against what are, in many ways, America's most innovative media should give Americans pause, for they link our time with the crudest violations of press freedom of the past.

Like the repression alternative media have suffered, the contributions they have made have been a critical part of American life since before the Revolutionary War. Modern alternative media activists are irreducibly joined with the risk-taking journalists we celebrate at a distance: the pamphleteers, abolitionists, suffragists, socialists, muckrakers and other radicals who sought to dig to the root of the American experience to uncover an authentically democratic creed.

Today's alternative media are rooted in that tradition. Thus, when Mark Dowie compares his colleagues to the revolutionary pamphleteers, he is not speaking in airy metaphors, but invoking a concrete historical tradition. We overlook or thoughtlessly revise that tradition at the risk of denying our past, misapprehending our present, and limiting our future.

As they have done in the past, the alternative media will change in response to the political climate, help change that climate by their activist character, and, having done so, change again. As always, they will leave their mark on our national life in surprising ways—essential tools in the continuing task of reinventing America.

Sources

Chapter One. *Catalysts of Change*

Written sources of material, other than those cited in the chapter, include Eric S. Foner's *Tom Paine and Revolutionary America.* James Monaco's *Media Culture* was a source for the holdings of Time, Inc. The March 4, 1980 issue of the *Boston Phoenix* explained how the Ayatollah Khomeini used tape cassettes to take power in Iran. Ben H. Bagdikian's article "The Media Manipulators" in the June 1978 issue of *The Progressive* cited the number of American newspapers and radio and TV stations. The April 2, 1979, *San Francisco Chronicle* supplied the news that half of the United States Gross National Product comes from the production and dissemination of information. Jim Motavalli's article in the March 26, 1980, *Syracuse New Times* provides background material on the Christian Broadcasting Network. The *High Country News'* struggle for survival was detailed in the November 4, 1980, *San Francisco Examiner.*

Chapter Two. *Rise of the Underground Press*

In addition to material cited in the text, sources include: Robert J. Glessing's book *The Underground Press in America,* for figures on the number of underground newspapers. Frank Luther Mott's studies *American Journalism: A History* and *A History of American Magazines* provided much of the information on early American periodicals, as did John Tebbel's *The Media in America.* Roland E. Wolseley's *The Black Press, USA* offered valuable information on black periodicals. Sidney E. Ahlestrom's *A Religious History of the American People* served as a source on spiritualist and Theosophist periodicals, as did Paul Kagan's *New World Utopias.* Marion Marzolf's *Up From the Footnote: A History of Women Journalists* is an informative history of feminist journalism. Karl Marx's comment on working for the *New York Tribune* was cited in the Winter 1979–1980 issue of *Journalism History.* Background on *The Masses* came mainly from William L. O'Neill's *Echoes of Revolt;* O'Neill's book supplied much of the information on legalistic supression of *The Masses* and other magazines during and after World War I, as did Everette E. Dennis and Melvin E. Dennis' article "100 Years of Political Cartooning" in the Summer 1974 issue of *Journalism*

Quarterly. The definitive history of the *National Guardian* is former coeditor Cecil Belfrage and James Aronson's book *Something to Guard.* The history of *I. F. Stone's Weekly* is summarized in Neil Middleton's introduction to *The I. F. Stone's Weekly Reader,* Andrew Kopkind's profile of Stone in *Ramparts* in 1974, and Jerry Bruck's film *I. F. Stone's Weekly.* Kevin Michael McAuliffe's *The Great American Newspaper* is an exhaustive history of the *Village Voice.* Information on *The Realist* came from a profile of Paul Krassner in the August 3, 1964, *Newsweek,* while Krassner's "silly putty" quote was taken from a 1968 feature in *Life.* Lawrence Leamer's book *The Paper Revolutionaries* is an excellent source on the underground press, as is John Burks' lengthly article in *Rolling Stone,* October, 1969; in addition, representative selections from the underground press were reprinted in book-length anthologies, such as Jesse Kornbluth's *Notes From the New Underground,* Tom Forcade's *Underground Press Anthology,* and Allan Katzman's *Our Time;* Richard Neville's *Play Power* is another in-depth source on the underground press. The tenth anniversary issue of *The Black Panther,* dated April 19, 1977, supplied basic information on that paper's early days; a diagram of a Molotov Cocktail appeared in August 1967 in the *New York Review of Books.* Paul Krassner's "purient interest" quote in the section on the underground's attitude toward sex is taken from his book *How a Satirical Editor Became A Yippie Conspirator in Ten Easy Years.*

Chapter Three. *The New Media Environment*

The history of the Workers Film and Photo League, including the influence of Soviet filmmakers on Americans, was drawn mainly from an article by Russell Campbell, Campbell's interview with Leo Seltzer, and Tony Safford's interview with Samuel Brody, published in Issue No. 14 of *Jumpcut* magazine in 1977. Background on *Salt of the Earth* came mainly from Deborah Silverton Rosenfelt's introduction to the shooting script, published in book form in 1978. Emile de Antonio's filmmaking career was detailed in an article and interview with de Antonio in *Jumpcut* No. 10–11, published in 1976; de Antonio's quote on *Millhouse* is from an interview with Bernard Weiner in the November 28, 1977 issue of the *San Francisco Chronicle*. The recent history of American radical documentary film was covered by John Hess in *Jumpcut* No. 22, published in 1980. The early history of video art and documentary is drawn from several books, including Gene Youngblood's *Expanded Cinema*, Jonathon Price's *Video Visions*, and Michael Murray's *The Videotape Book*. The early history of KPFA-FM and the Pacifica network was outlined in KPFA's April 1979 *Folio* magazine, Padreign McGillicuddy's overview in the April 1979 issue of the *Berkeley Monthly*, Gene Marine's retrospective in the April 15, 1979, *San Francisco Examiner and Chronicle*, and Chris Koch's article in the February 1972 KPFA Folio; WBAI radio and Bob Fass were viewed in Steve Post's book *Playing in the FM Band*; Post's quote on Fass appeared in the May 31, 1978 issue of *The Aquarian Weekly*. Lorenzo Milam's financial dealings were outlined in the September 3, 1973 issue of *Broadcasting*. The origin of FM rock radio on KMPX and KSAN-FM were remembered in day-long broadcasts on KSAN on May 21, 1978, from which quotes attributed to Bob McClay, the Congress of Wonders, Tom Donahue, and Scoop Nisker were drawn. In addition to Glessing and Leamer, sources on the graphic innovations of underground newspapers include articles by Steve Kraus and Charlie Frick in *Alternative Media* magazine in 1979. Mark James Estren's *History of Underground Comics* is the leading history of that artistic form. Len Fulton's reminiscence in the *Publish-It-Yourself Handbook*, edited by Bill Henderson, outlined the founding of the Committee of Small Magazine Editors and Publishers; the same volume recalled Barbara Garson's self-publication of *MacBird* and Stewart Brand's early days with the *Whole Earth Catalog*. Lawrence Ferlinghetti remembered City Lights' publication of *Howl* in a 1978 interview with Michael Helm in *City Miner* magazine. Ellen Ferber's assessment of the impact of resource guides on the small-press publishing movement came from her introduction to the 15th edition of the *International Directory of Little Magazines and Small Presses*.

Chapter Four. *What Rough Beast*

Wilfred Burchett was profiled unsympathetically in the February 27, 1967 issue of *U.S. News & World Report*, the June 1, 1967 issue of *The Reporter*, the June 15, 1971 issue of the *National Review*, the April 11, 1975 *National Review*, and the March 17, 1978 issue of the same magazine. Belfrage and Aronson write sympathetically of Burchett in *Something to Guard*. Background information on the Gulf of Tonkin incident was drawn from Anthony Austin's book *The President's War*. Burchett's books, *Vietnam: Inside Story of the Guerrilla War* and *Vietnam Will Win*, are largely collections of his *Guardian* pieces. The dispute between Chris Koch and Louis Schweitzer over Koch's Vietnam documentaries was detailed in the November 20, 1965, *National Guardian*. The story of

Robert Scheer and "The Vietnam Lobby" article in *Ramparts* was told in Warren Hinckle's book of memoirs, *If You Have a Lemon, Make Lemonade*, as are the stories behind the Green Beret and Michigan State exposés. Harrison Salisbury's travels were recounted in his book *Behind the Lines*, as well as the Winter 1966–1967 issue of the *Columbia Journalism Review*, and Phillip Knightly's study of war reportage, *The First Casualty*. George Cavelletto's piece for LNS was published in the October 2, 1969, *San Francisco Good Times*. *Amex-Canada*'s history was recorded in a tenth anniversary issue of the magazine, published in Toronto in 1978. The history and impact of underground GI papers was told by Glessing, as well as Aronson in his book *Deadline for the Media*, plus Andy Stapp's *Up Against the Brass*. Seymour Hersh's story about his My Lai exposé was told in his book *My Lai 4*; Knightly and Robert Cirino, in his book *Don't Blame the People*, also recount the development of the My Lai story.

Chapter Five. *The Media Guerrillas*

Paul Krassner recalled the founding of the Yippies in his book *How a Satirical Editor. . . .* The theory and practice of the Yippies at the Pentagon and Chicago demonstrations was examined by Abbie Hoffman in *Revolution for the Hell of It* and *Woodstock Nation*, and Jerry Rubin in *Do It!*, *We Are Everywhere*, and *Growing (Up) at 37*. A report on the Hinckle-Scheer split was published in the March 27, 1969 issue of the *San Francisco Bay Guardian*. The Chicago Conspiracy Trial was detailed in Rubin and Hoffman's books, as well as Dave Dellinger's *Contempt* and Jason Epstein's *The Great Conspiracy Trial*.

Chapter Six. *The Secret War*

Mott and Tebbel wrote about the suppression of *Publick Occurrences*. Fred J. Cook's *The FBI Nobody Knows* tracked the career of J. Edgar Hoover, including the controversy over Jack Levine's criticism of the bureau on WBAI in 1962. Nelson Blackstock's *Cointelpro* gave an overview of covert surveillance and disruption of radical movements. Background on the repression of *The Black Panther* was published in that paper's tenth anniversary issue in 1977. Richard Nixon's attempt to cut off funding for the Public Broadcasting Service was detailed in the February 2, 1979, *San Francisco Chronicle*. The CIA's "Project Resistance" was disclosed in the April 5, 1978 *Boston Phoenix*. CIA surveillance of Phillip Agee was recounted in Chip Berlet's article in the Fall 1978 issue of *Alternative Media*. The FBI's infiltration of underground papers was revealed in a series of articles in the *New York Times* in December 1977. The CIA's offensive against *CounterSpy* magazine was covered in the July 10, 1978 issue of *Inquiry* magazine. The bombing of KPFT radio's transmitter was explored in the *Rolling Stone* of February 18, 1971. Local police surveillance of *View From the Bottom* was uncovered in the April 1, 1979, *New Haven Advocate*. Lawrence Leamer told the story of printer Bill Schanen's life and death relationship with underground papers. Warren Hinckle told reporter Michael Goldberg about his problems printing the "Guerrilla War, USA" issue of *Scanlan's* in a 1980 interview in *Boulevard*s magazine. The Mark Knops case was reviewed in the Fall 1970 issue of the *Columbia Journalism Review*. The legal difficulties of KPFA and KPFK with underground communiques were reviewed in the March 1978 KPFA *Folio*. The FBI's harrassment of the makers of the film *Underground* was detailed in the November 5, 1975, *Rolling Stone*. The ransacking of *Big Mama Rag* and Diana Press was retold in the March 28, 1978, *Daily Californian*. Tom Forcade's quote on government repression was taken from Kornbluth's underground anthology.

Chapter Seven. *The Selling of the Counterculture*

Stewart Ewen's *Captains of Consciousness* provided a study of the development and underlying assumptions of advertising, as well as its social consequences; Susan Krieger's *Hip Capitalism* demonstrated those consequences concretely, using KSAN-FM as a case study. Gay Talese's *Thy Neighbor's Wife* recounted the early days of *Screw*; Neville's *Play Power* tracked the evolution of pornzines from the underground press. The rise of rock journalism was chronicled by Steve Chapple and Reebee Garofalo in their book *Rock'n Roll is Here to Pay*. The quote from Paul Williams was taken from the May 30, 1978, *Chicago Reader*. John Sinclair's rock and revolt philosophy was spelled out in his book *Guitar Army*. John Lennon's statement in *Black Dwarf* was reprinted in the May 5, 1969, *Rolling Stone*. The rise of *Rolling Stone* was charted in the April 25, 1969 issue of *Time*, the January/February 1969 number of the *Columbia Journalism Review*, the December 1974 issue of *(MORE)*, by Chapple and Garofalo, and in a two-part article by Robert Sam Anson in *New Times* in 1976; the figures on *Rolling Stone's* sale and number of staff were taken from the April 19, 1978 issue of the *San Francisco Chronicle*, reprinted from the *Washington Post*.

Chapter Eight. *A Time of Transition*

Differences between underground and alternative journalism were explored in Daniel Ben-Horin's article "Journalism As a Way of Life" in *The Nation*, February 19, 1973. Stephen Diamond's quote on getting back to the land is from his book *What the Trees Said: Life on a New Age Farm*. The quote and retrospective on Robert Kramer's filmmaking career are from J. N. Thomas' interview with Kramer in the January 27, 1978 *Berkeley Barb*. John Shuttleworth explained the philosophy of *Mother Earth News* in interviews in the January 1975 and January 1980 issues

of that magazine and in the August 1978 issue of *Free Enterprise*.

Chapter Nine. *The New Provincials*

Gurney Norman's term "the new provincialism" appeared in a 1971 issue of *Place* magazine. The early days of the Boston weeklies were treated in the July 1972 issue of *(MORE)* and in the book *Co-Ops, Communes, and Collectives*, edited by John Case and Rosemary C. R. Taylor; the quote from Ted Gross came from Andrew Kopkind's piece in *Co-ops*, etc. Brian Livingston wrote about the origin and purpose of the Cascadian Regional Library in *New Age* in 1977. Susan Lyne outlined the success story of *Ectopia* for *New Times*, April 29, 1977. Richard and Suzi McClear discussed their radio station KAXE in the *Village Voice* of July 5, 1976; George Stoney of the Alternative Media Center talked about community radio in the same piece. Don Wood wrote about the National Federation of Community Broadcasters in the January 17, 1978 issue of the Lincoln, Nebraska, *Gazette*. Rob Nilsson's quote about *Northern Lights* was taken from the *San Francisco Examiner* of September 25, 1979. Amanda Spake also wrote about the making of the motion picture in the January 1979 *Mother Jones*.

Chapter Ten. *Sexual Politics*

Casey Hayden and Mary King's "memo" was quoted in a special "Women in the South" issue of *Southern Exposure*, published in 1977. The background on Nanette Rainone's WBAI radio program came from Post's *Playing in the FM Band*. The women's takeover of *Rat* was memorialized in Robin Morgan's *Going Too Far*. Marilyn Webb's memories of the early days of *off our backs* was taken from the paper's tenth anniversary issue, published in February 1980. The various means by which feminist staffers produce newspapers was explained in an article in *Big Mama Rag*, dated June 1978. Julia Reichert and Jim Klein were interviewed in the October-December 1975 issue of *Jumpcut* (No. 10). A history of *Our Bodies, Ourselves*, written by Bev Eaton, appeared in the September-October 1979 issue of *New Roots*. *Wimmen's Comix*, The Feminist Press, and numerous feminist periodicals were reviewed in *The New Women's Survival Catalog* and *Sourcebook*, edited by Kirsten Grimstad and Susan Rennie. The history and philosophy of *Ms.* was laid out in "Personal Reports" in the magazine's June 1974, November 1974, and November 1979 issues; additional history and political criticism were found in Redstockings' book *Feminist Revolution*, including Ellen Willis' article "The Conservatism of *Ms.*" Filmmaker Will Roberts was interviewed about *Men's Lives* in the February 21, 1980 issue of *The Advocate*. Baird Searles' program on WBAI was recounted by Post. A history of gay male periodicals was included in the tenth anniversary issue of *Gay*

Sunshine, published in 1980. Articles reviewing the political and commercial clout of the gay culture and gay press appeared in the February 1977 *(MORE)*, the August 28, 1977, *San Francisco Examiner*, the November 25, 1978 *San Francisco Chronicle*, and the *Boston Phoenix* of July 8, 1980.

Chapter Eleven. *The High Society*

Tom Forcade was interviewed by Gabrielle Schang for the April 1979 issue of *Overthrow*, wherein Forcade described himself as "a social architect," estimated the volume of the paraphernalia industry, and recalled the founding of *High Times* after a nitrous oxide party. Forcade's life and death were reviewed in the November 23, 1978 *Soho Weekly News*, where friend Michael Antonoff recalled Forcade's "who hasn't dealt?" remark, the *Village Voice* of November 27, 1978, where another friend, A. J. Weberman, recounted Forcade's depression over an associate's death and his subsequent drug use, and the Spring 1979 issue of *Alternative Media*, wherein Chip Berlet wrote that Forcade ran *High Times*, for a time, from a telephone booth. Information on the size of the marijuana trade in Hawaii was taken from the *San Francisco Examiner*, in northern California from the Associated Press, in Colombia from the *New York Times*, all in 1978. Violence in the dope trade was discussed in the August 19, 1978, *San Francisco Chronicle* and the March 19, 1978, *New York Times*. The ad copy for *Dealer* magazine was quoted in Abe Peck's survey of the paraphernalia industry in the January 27, 1977, *Rolling Stone*. Gabrielle Schang's statement about *High Times* becoming "the cultural magazine of the eighties" was drawn from the October 29, 1979, *San Francisco Chronicle*. Demographics of the *High Times* readership were taken from the *Los Angeles Times*, November 5, 1979.

Chapter Twelve. *Ten Great Places to Find Croissants After Midnight*

The social and journalistic influences on the urban weekly newspapers were detailed in articles on the National Association of Alternative Newsweeklies, including David Shaw's story in the *Los Angeles Times*, May 30, 1978; Steve McNamara's piece in the *Pacific Sun*, May 4, 1979; and Martin Linsky's article in *The Real Paper*, April 1, 1978. The sale of the collectively operated *Real Paper* to private investors was examined in the March 1975 issue of *(MORE)* and *The Real Paper's* fifth anniversary issue, published July 30, 1977. The Boston weeklies were profiled in Michael VerMeulin's feature "Alternatives, Inc." in the November 1979 *TWA Ambassador;* statistics on the *Boston Phoenix's* demographics were taken from Ira Kamin's story in the July 27, 1980 issue of *California Living* magazine. The early history of the *Chicago Reader* was recounted in the *Chicago Tribune* of November 23, 1975 and the August 1972 *Chicago*

Journalism Review; the *Reader's* demographics were taken from the *Wall Street Journal*, October 17, 1979. Barbara Kravitz's comment on the negative impact of free-circulation periodicals on political community papers comes from the February 2, 1980, *Real Paper*. I. F. Stone and Alexander Cockburn's criticisms of the NAAN papers were reported in the March 31, 1979 issue of *Editor and Publisher*. *Creative Loafing* described itself as "America's most unique newspaper" in its June 7, 1978 issue. The sale of the *Maui Sun* to the local Rotary Club president was announced in the *Sun* in April 1979. Background on the gentrification of American cities by affluent young professionals was taken from Tim Patterson's article in the *Guardian*, November 11, 1978, Thomas Bron's Pacific News Service piece in the *Willamette Valley Observer*, July 6, 1979, and Katy Butler's stories in the *San Francisco Chronicle*, September 1, 1979. Tom Winship's remarks about the Boston weeklies was taken from Dan Wakefield's piece on the *Phoenix* and *The Real Paper* in the *New York Times Magazine*, February 15, 1976. Andrew Kopkind wrote critically of "hip capitalism" in the *Boston Phoenix*, August 8, 1972.

Chapter Thirteen. *Aquarian Enterprise*

Ahestrom's *A Religious History of the American People* provided background on the historic "Great Awakenings". Michael Rossman's *New Age Blues* is a critical study of Aquarian authoritarianism and its materialistic offshoots, such as "prosperity consciousness." Tim Patterson wrote critically of prosperity consciousness in the *Guardian*, February 7, 1979. Robert Schwartz was profiled in the October 16, 1977, *San Francisco Examiner and Chronicle*. Gregory Bateson's "paradox" quote was taken from Stewart Brand's *Two Cybernetic Frontiers*. Peter Barry Chowka's story in *New Age* in 1979 detailed the Public Interest Video Network's broadcast of an antinuclear rally in the wake of the Three Mile Island accident. Brand wrote about Resource One in *Two Cybernetic Frontiers*. The March 17, 1980, *Village Voice* identified Jon Kalish's show on WBAI as the first regularly scheduled antinuclear program in American radio.

Chapter Fourteen. *The New Muckrakers*

Justin Kaplan's biography, *Lincoln Steffens*, provided background information on the historical origins of muckraking. Warren Hinckle's *If You Have A Lemon . . .* told the story of the early *Ramparts*. Jessica Mitford's quotes on *Ramparts* and muckraking were taken from the *East Bay Express*, March 9, 1979. Adam Hochchild also remembered Hinckle and *Ramparts* in the Summer 1975 issue of the San Francisco journalism review, *Feedback*. Tim Patterson reviewed the brief heyday of *New Times* in the January 10, 1979, *Guardian*. Mark Dowie's "Pinto trial" quote came from a Pacific News Service piece

Dowie wrote, released in March 1980. Background on the *Guardian's* top stories was published in the paper's thirtieth anniversary issue in October 1978, and in Belfrage and Aronson's *Something to Guard*. Details of Pacific News Service's muckraking were published in David Armstrong's piece in the September/October 1978 *Columbia Journalism Review*. Upton Sinclair's quote on muckraking came from Kaplan's biography of Steffens.

Chapter Fifteen. *Alternative Media in the Eighties*

Connie Field's quote on Newsreel came from an interview with Pat Aufderheide in *In These Times*, October 15, 1980. Marge Piercy's comments on the difficulty of using a lesbian protagonist in her novel *The High Cost of Living* was taken from the *Boston Phoenix*, April 11, 1978. Valerie Wheat's observation on feminist publishing comes from a book she coau-

thored with Celeste West, *The Passionate Perils of Publishing*. The Bay Area Video Corporation's sources of funding were listed in the organization's newsletter *Video Networks* in 1980. *Harrisburg's* threatened loss of CETA money was covered in the April 4, 1979 *Washington Post*. *In These Times* outlined its financial structure in the paper's October 8, 1980 issue. The National Federation of Community Broadcasters published the results of its membership survey in its *Newsletter*, March 4, 1980. The social impact of the home computer boom was critically assessed in *In These Times*, January 31, 1979 and *New West*, April 10, 1978, and viewed optimistically in Alvin Toffler's *Future Shock*. The Qube system was profiled in the July 7, 1978 issue of *New Times*. Sandy Emerson and Lee Felsenstein explained the principle of the Community Memory system in the Fall 1978 *Journal of Community Communications*.

Chronology

1776—Thomas Paine's *Common Sense* published.

1827—Birth of *Freedom's Journal*, first black-owned, black-run abolitionist newspaper.

1831—Founding of William Lloyd Garrison's *The Liberator*, the leading white-run abolitionist journal.

1843—Publication in the Transcendentalist magazine *The Dial* of Margaret Fuller's "The Great Lawsuit," leading intellectual contribution to Women's Rights convention at Seneca Falls in 1848.

1851–1852—Serialization, prior to its publication in book form, of Harriet Beecher Stowe's *Uncle Tom's Cabin* in the abolitionist paper *National Era*.

1868–1972—Susan B. Anthony and Elizabeth Cady Stanton issue *The Revolution*, leading nineteenth century feminist journal.

1895–1917—Publication of the weekly *Appeal to Reason*, whose circulation of 760,000 in 1912 was the largest of any American radical periodical before or since.

1905—Serialization, before its publication in book form, of Upton Sinclair's muckraking classic, *The Jungle*, by *Appeal to Reason*.

1911–1971—Max Eastman edits *The Masses*, whose eclecticism anticipates the underground media of the 1960s.

1917—Supression of *The Masses* and other radical periodicals under the federal Espionage Act.

1924–1958—Publication of the Communist Party's *Daily Worker*, featuring columnist Woody Guthrie.

1930–1936—Workers Film and Photo League turns out catalytic prolabor documentaries in depths of the Depression.

1949—KPFA-FM founded in Berkeley as first listener-sponsored radio station in the United States.

1953–1917—Publication of *I. F. Stone's Weekly*, leading source of news and analysis for anti-Vietnam War movement.

1955—Dan Wolf, Ed Fancher, and Norman Mailer found the *Village Voice*, which strongly influences later underground and alternative papers.

1956—*Salt of the Earth*, independent prolabor and profeminist film made under wraps by blacklisted Hollywood leftists.

1956–1972—*The Ladder*, influential early lesbian periodical, published.

1958—City Lights Press publishes Allen Ginsberg's *Howl*, selling 800,000 copies and challenging conventional ideas about obscenity and madness.

1958–1974—Paul Krassner issues *The Realist*, a satirical fusion of fact and fantasy that inspires underground papers.

1963—Emile de Antonio releases *Point of Order*, an anti-McCarthy film that inspires spate of radical documentaries.

1963—*National Guardian* publishes Mark Lane's "A Brief for Lee Harvey Oswald," is beseiged by 50,000 requests for reprints.

1964—Bob Fass popularizes freeform radio on New York's WBAI-FM.

May 1964—Premiere issue of *Los Angeles Free Press*, first underground paper, founded by Art Kunkin.

January 1965—Wilfred Burchett's stories in the *National Guardian*, filed from National Liberation Front-held areas of South Vietnam, challenge Pentagon's characterization of the war.

July 1965—Publication of "The Vietnam Lobby" in *Ramparts* reveals roots of U.S. involvement in Southeast Asia.

1965—Barbara Garson's self-published *MacBird* ridicules Lyndon Johnson's war policies, sells 400,000 copies.

1966—Paul Williams publishes *Crawdaddy*, first magazine of serious rock music criticism.

1966—Underground Press Syndicate founded.

1966—First issues of *San Francisco Bay Guardian* and *Boston After Dark*, early liberal consumer newspapers that anticipate seventies urban weeklies.

January 1967—*San Francisco Oracle* sponsors first Human Be-In, held in Golden State Park.

March 1967—*Ramparts* exposes CIA funding of National Student Association.

April 1967—Tom Donahue initiates freeform rock radio on San Francisco's KMPX-FM.

June 1967—Monterey Pop Festival, publicized mainly through the underground press, is held in California, focusing international attention on the market for rock music and related lifestyles.

October 1967—Liberation News Service founded to service underground and aboveground media with radical journalism.

November 7, 1967—First issue of *Rolling Stone*.

December 1967—Underground media activists found Youth International Party (Yippies), plan demonstrations at 1968 Democratic Convention in Chicago.

1967—First issue of *Zap*, first underground comic book, published by cartoonist Robert Crumb.

1967—First issue of *The Bond*, leading antiwar GI paper.

January 1968—Antiwar documentary filmmaking organization Newsreel founded.

May 1968—Small-press activists form Committee of Small Magazine Editors and Publishers to coordinate nationwide activities.

October 1968—First issue of *Whole Earth Catalog*.

November 5, 1968—J. Edgar Hoover issues directive to FBI field offices ordering surveillance of underground newspapers, kicking off a secret war of governmental repression.

November 1968—First issue of *Screw*, sex tabloid that steals thunder (and advertising) from sex-oriented underground papers.

April 1969—Baird Searles launches "The New Symposium," first show for gays in American radio, on WBAI.

November 13, 1969—Dispatch News Service releases Seymour Hersh's story on the massacre of Vietnamese civilians at My Lai by U.S. troops.

1969—Raindance Corporation, alternative video group, formed.

1969—Cartoonist Ron Cobb designs ecology symbol.

January 1970—First issue of *Mother Earth News* and early feminist newspaper *It Ain't Me Babe;* women seize underground paper *Rat*.

December 1970—Boston Women's Health Collective's *Our Bodies, Ourselves* published, sells two million copies in fourteen languages, catalyzes women's health movement.

1970—Houston alternative station KPFT blown off the air twice by powerful bombs.

1971—Michio Kushi founds *East West Journal*, leading New Age periodical, in Boston.

1971—Julia Reichert and Jim Klein release *Growing Up Female*, influential early feminist film.

1971—Susan Griffin's essay on rape in *Ramparts* helps change perception of rape from crime of passion to act of control.

January 1972—Rita Mae Brown, Charlotte Bunch, and other activists start *The Furies*, pioneering journal of lesbian feminism.

July 1972—First issue of *Ms.*

1973—Underground Press Syndicate changes name to Alternative Press Syndicate.

1973—Michael and Justine Toms start "New Dimensions," leading New Age syndicated radio program.

September 1973—First issue of *Valley Advocate*, eventual flagship of 350,000-circulation *Advocate* newspaper chain.

1974—KVST, nation's first viewer-sponsored television station, broadcasts in Los Angeles for year and a half.

1974—First issue of *High Times*, published by Tom Forcade.

1974—Stewart Brand starts *CoEvolution Quarterly*, magazine successor to the *Whole Earth Catalog*.

1975—National Federation of Community Broadcasters founded to unite local community stations.

1975—*Ramparts* folds.

1975—Independently produced antiwar documentary *Hearts and Minds* wins Academy Award.

1975—Ernest Callenbach self-publishes *Ectopia*, novelistic herald of small-is-beautiful self-sufficiency.

1976—Former underground cartoonist Tony Auth wins Pulitzer Prize with *Philadelphia Inquirer*.

1976—Independently produced men's liberation film *Men's Lives* wins Academy Award.

1977—*Harlan County USA* wins Academy Award.

1977—Joan Micklin Silver's independently produced film *Between the Lines* portrays life at alternative newspapers spoiled by success.

September 1977—Mark Dowie's article in *Mother Jones* forces recall of Ford Pintos on safety grounds.

February 1978—Larry Flynt, new owner of the *Los Angeles Free Press*, folds pioneering underground paper after fourteen years of publication.

April 1978—National Association of (Alternative) Newsweeklies founded in Seattle.

November 17, 1978—UPS and *High Times* impressario Tom Forcade dies of self-inflicted gunshot wounds in New York City.

1979—Film *Paul Jacobs and the Nuclear Gang*, shown on public television, wins Emmy.

1979—*The Progressive* magazine suffers first case of judicial prior restraint in U.S. press history for attempting to publish a story on the H-Bomb.

1980—*Mother Jones* story on "corporate dumping" wins National Magazine Award, is corroborated four months after publication by *Washington Post*.

1980—Independent filmmakers Haskell Wexler, Barbara Kopple, and Green Mountain Post Films collaborate on *No Nukes*, first feature-length antinuclear movie.

October 1980—Publication of *The Next Whole Earth Catalog*.

Bibliography

Ahlestrom, Sydney E. *A Religious History of the American People*. New Haven, Conn.: Yale University Press, 1972.

Aronson, James. *Deadline for the Media: Today's Challenges to Press, TV & Radio*. Indianapolis: Bobbs-Merrill, 1972.

Austin, Anthony. *The President's War: The Story of the Tonkin Gulf Resolution and How the Nation Was Trapped in Vietnam*. Philadelphia: Lippencott, 1971.

Barrett, Marvin. *Rich News, Poor News: Alfred I. DuPont-Columbia University Survey of Broadcast Journalism*. New York: Columbia University Press, 1978.

Belfrage, Cedric, and Aronson, James. *Something to Guard: The Stormy Life of the National Guardian, 1948–1967*. New York: Columbia University Press, 1978.

Blackstock, Nelson. *Cointelpro: The FBI's Secret War on Political Freedom*. New York: Vintage, 1976.

Blavatsky, H. P. *An Abridgement of The Secret Doctrine*. Humphreys, Christmas, and Preston, Elizabeth, eds. Wheaton, Ill.: Theosophical Publishing House, 1967.

Brand, Stewart. *Two Cybernetic Frontiers*. New York: Random House, 1974.

————. ed. *Space Colonies*. New York: Random House, 1977.

Burchett, Wilfred G. *Vietnam: Inside Story of the Guerrilla War*. New York: International Publishers, 1966.

————. *Vietnam Will Win*. New York: Guardian Books, 1968.

————. *Grasshoppers and Elephants: Why Vietnam Fell*. New York: Urizen, 1977.

Callenbach, Ernest. *Ectopia*. New York: Bantam, 1977.

Cantor, Milton. *The Divided Left: American Radicalism, 1900–1975*. New York: Hill and Wang, 1978.

Carnahan, Don, ed. *Guide to Alternative Periodicals*. St. Petersburg, Fla.: Sunspark Press, 1977.

Case, John, and Taylor, Rosemary C. R., eds. *Co-ops, Communes & Collectives: Experiments in Social Change in the 1960s and 1970s*. New York: Pantheon, 1979.

Catledge, Turner. *My Life and the Times*. New York: Harper & Row, 1971.

Chapple, Steve, and Garofalo, Reebee. *Rock 'n' Roll is Here to Pay: The History and Politics of the Music Industry*. Chicago: Nelson-Hall, 1977.

Cirino, Robert. *Don't Blame the People*. New York: Random House, 1972.

Conlin, Joseph R., ed. *The American Radical Press, 1880–1960*. Westport Conn.: Greenwood Press, 1974.

Cook, Fred J. *The FBI Nobody Knows*. New York: Macmillan, 1964.

————. *Citizens Media Directory*. Washington, D.C.: National Citizens Committee for Broadcasting, 1977.

Dean, John. *Blind Ambition*. New York: Simon and Schuster, 1976.

Dellinger, David. *Contempt: Transcript of the Contempt Citations, Sentenes, and Responses of the Chicago Conspiracy 10*. Chicago: Swallow Press, 1970.

Dennis, Everette E., and Rivers, Wiliam L. *Other Voices: The New Journalism in America*. San Francisco: Canfield Press, 1974.

Diamond, Stephen. *What the Trees Said: Life on a New Age Farm*. New York: Delacorte Press, 1971.

Dickstein, Morris. *Gates of Eden: American Culture in the Sixties*. New York: Basic Books, 1977.

Didion, Joan. *Slouching Toward Bethlehem*. New York: Delta, 1968.

DiPrima, Diane. *Revolutionary letters, Etc., 1966–1978*. San Francisco: City Lights, 1979.

Downie, Leonard, Jr. *The New Muckrakers*. Washington, D.C.: New Republic Books, 1976.

Ellison, Harlan. *The Glass Teat*. New York: Ace, 1969.

Enzensberger, Hans Magnus. *The Consciousness Industry: On Literature, Politics & the Media*. New York: Seabury Press, 1974.

Epstein, Jason. *The Great Conspiracy Trial: An Essay on Law, Liberty, and the Constitution*. New York: Random House, 1970.

Eshenaur, Ruth Marie. "Censorship of the Alternative Press: A Descriptive Study of the Social and Political Control of Radical Periodicals (1964–1973)." PhD dissertation. Carbondale, Ill.: Southern Illinois University, 1975.

Estren, Mark James. *A History of Underground Comics*. San Francisco: Straight Arrow, 1974.

Ewen, Stuart. *Captains of Consciousness: Advertising and the Social Roots of the Consumer Culture*. New York: McGraw-Hill, 1976.

Farber, Jerry. *The Student as Nigger*. North Hollywood, Calif.: Contact Books, 1969.

Ferguson, Marilyn. *The Aquarian Conspiracy*. Los Angeles: J. P. Tarcher, 1980.

Foner, Eric S. *Tom Paine and Revolutionary America*. New York: Oxford University Press, 1976.

Forcade, Thomas King, ed. *Underground Press Anthology*. New York: Ace, 1972.

Fried, Alert. *Socialism in America: From the Shakers to the Third International*. Garden City, N.Y.: Doubleday, 1970.

Fulton, Len, and Ferber, Ellen, eds. *International Directory of Little Magazines and Small Presses*, 15th Ed. Paradise, Calif.: Dustbooks, 1979.

Gans, Herbert. *Deciding What's News: A Study of CBS Evening News, NBC Nightly News, Newsweek, and Time*. New York: Pantheon, 1979.

Georgakas, Dan, ed. *Left Face: A Sourcebook of Radical Magazines, Presses, and Collectives Actively Involved in the Arts*. New York: Cineaste and Smyrna Press, 1978.

Gitlin, Todd. *The Whole World is Watching; Mass Media in the Making and Unmaking of the New Left*. Berkeley and Los Angeles: University of California Press, 1980.

Glessing, Robert J. *The Underground Press in America*. Bloomington, Ind.: Indiana University Press, 1970.

Goldstein, Joseph; Marshall, Burke; and Schwartz, Jack. *The My Lai Massacre and its Coverup: Beyond the Reach of Law?* New York: Free Press, 1976.

Grimstad, Kirsten, and Rennie, Susan, eds. *The New Women's Survival Catalog*. New York: Knopf, 1973.

_____. *The New Women's Survival Sourcebook*. New York: Knopf, 1975.

Halberstam, David. *The Powers That Be*. New York: Knopf, 1979.

Henderson, Bill, Ed. *The Publish-It-Yourself-Handbook: Literary Tradition and How-To*. Yonkers, N.Y.: Pushcart Press, 1973.

Hersh, Seymour, M. *My Lai 4: A Report on the Massacre and its Aftermath*. New York: Random House, 1970.

Hinckle, Warren. *If You Have A Lemon, Make Lemonade*. New York: Putnam, 1974.

Hoffman, Abbie. *Revolution for the Hell of It*. New York: Dial Press, 1968.

_____. *Woodstock Nation: A Talk-Rock Album*. New York: Vintage, 1969.

Hollowell, John. *Fact & Fiction: The New Journalism and the Nonfiction Novel*. Chapel Hill, N.C.: University of North Carolina Press, 1977.

_____. *Hip Culture: Six Essays on its Revolutionary Potential*. New York: Times Change Press, 1970.

Joan, Polly, and Chessman, Andrea. *Guide to Women's Publishing*. Paradise, Calif.: Dustbooks, 1978.

Kagan, Paul. *New World Utopias: A Photographic History of the Search for Community*. New York: Penguin, 1975.

Kaplan, Justin. *Lincoln Steffens: A Biography*. New York: Simon and Schuster, 1974.

Katzman, Allen, ed. *Our Time: Interviews from the East Village Other*. New York: Dial Press, 1972.

Knightly, Phillip. *The First Casualty: From the Crimea to Vietnam: The War Correspondent as Hero, Propagandist, and Myth Maker*. New York: Harcourt Brace Jovanovich, 1975.

Kornbluth, Jesse, ed. *Notes from the New Underground: An Anthology*. New York: Viking, 1968.

Krassner, Paul. *How a Satirical Editor Became a Yippie Conspirator in Ten Easy Years*. New York: Putnam, 1971.

Krieger, Susan. *Hip Capitalism*. Beverly Hills: Sage, 1979.

Lasch, Christopher. *The Culture of Narcissism: American Life in an Age of Diminishing Expectations*. New York: Norton, 1978.

Leamer, Lawrence. *The Paper Revolutionaries: Rise of the Underground Press*. New York: Simon and Schuster, 1972.

Legge, Nancy. *Access. Film and Video Equipment: A Directory*. Washington, D.C.: American Film Institute, 1978.

Leibling, A. J. *The Press*. New York: Ballantine, 1961.

Lewis, Roger. *Outlaws of America: The Underground Press and its Context*. New York: Penguin, 1972.

McAuliffe, Kevin Michael. *The Great American Newspaper: The Rise and Fall of the Village Voice*. New York: Scribner's, 1978.

McLuhan, Marshall. *Understanding Media: The Extensions of Man*. New York: McGraw-Hill, 1964.

——————. *The Medium is the Massage.* New York: Bantam, 1967.

McWilliams, Carey. *The Education of Carey McWilliams.* New York: Simon and Schuster, 1977.

Mailer, Norman. *The Armies of the Night: History as a Novel, the Novel as History.* New York: New American Library, 1968.

Marzolf, Marian. *Up from the Footnote: A History of Women Journalists.* New York: Hastings House, 1977.

Middleton, Neil, ed. *The I. F. Stone's Weekly Reader.* New York: Random House, 1973.

Milam, Lorenzo W. *Sex and Broadcasting: A Handbook on Starting a Radio Station for the Community.* Los Gatos, Calif.: Dildo Press, 1975.

Monaco, James. *Media Culture.* New York: Delta, 1978.

Morgan, Robin. *Going Too Far: The Personal Chronicle of a Feminist.* New York: Random House, 1977.

Mott, Frank Luther. *A History of American Magazines,* Vols. 1–5. Cambridge, Mass.: Harvard University Press, 1938.

——————. *American Journalism. A History: 1690–1960.* New York: MacMillan, 1962.

Mungo, Raymond. *Famous Long Ago: My Life and Hard Times with Liberation News Service.* Boston: Beacon Press, 1970.

——————. *Total Loss Farm: A Year in the Life.* New York: E. P. Dutton, 1970.

Murray, Michael. *The Videotape Book.* New York Bantam, 1974.

Neville, Richard. *Play Power: Exploring the International Underground.* New York: Random House, 1970.

Novak, William. *High Culture: Marijuana in the Lives of Americans.* New York: Knopf, 1980.

Obst, Lynda Rosen, ed. *The Sixties.* New York: Random House, 1977.

O'Neill, William L. *Echoes of Revolt: The Masses, 1911–1917.* New York: Quadrangle, 1966.

Passman, Arnie. *The Deejays.* New York: MacMillan, 1973.

Petrusenko, Vitaly. *The Monopoly Press.* Prague: International Organization of Journalists, 1976.

Post, Steve. *Playing in the FM Band: A Personal Account of Free Radio.* New York: Viking, 1974.

Price, Jonathan. *Video Visions: A Medium Discovers Itself.* New York: American Library, 1977.

Rabbit, Peter. *Drop City.* New York, Olympia Press, 1970.

Redstockings. *Feminist Revolution.* New York: Random House, 1978.

Reich, Charles A. *The Greening of America.* New York: Random House, 1970.

Renan, Sheldon. *An Introduction to the American Underground Film.* New York: Dutton, 1967.

Rossman, Michael. *New Age Blues: On the Politics of Consciousness.* New York: Dutton, 1979.

Roszak, Theodore. *The Making of a Counter Culture.* Garden City, N.Y.: Doubleday, 1968.

Rubin, Jerry. *Do It! Scenarios of the Revolution.* New York: Ballantine, 1970.

——————. *We Are Everywhere.* New York: Harper Colophone, 1971.

——————. *Growing (Up) at 37.* New York: M. Evans, 1976.

Sale, Kirkpatrick. *SDS.* New York: Random House, 1973.

Salisbury, Harrison E. *Behind the Lines: Hanoi, December 23, 1966.* New York: Harper & Row, 1967.

——————. *Without Fear or Favor: The New York Times and its Time.* New York: Times Books, 1980.

Satin, Mark. *New Age Politics; Healing Self and Society.* New York: Delta, 1979.

Scanlon, Paul, ed. *Reporting: The Rolling Stone Style.* Garden City, N.Y.: Anchor/Doubleday, 1977.

Schiller, Herbert I. *The Mind Managers.* Boston: Beacon Press, 1973.

Schudson, Michael. *Discovering the News: A Social History of American Newspapers.* New York: Basic Books, 1978.

Shamberg, Michael, and Raindance Corporation. *Guerrilla Television.* New York: Holt, Rinehart, and Winston, 1971.

Shepperd, Walt. *Conjuring a Counter Culture.* Paradise, Calif.: Dustbooks, 1973.

Silber, Irwin. *The Cultural Revolution: A Marxist Perspective.* New York: Times Change Press, 1970.

Sinclair, John. *Guitar Army.* New York: Douglas, 1972.

Stapp, Andy. *Up Against the Brass.* New York: Simon and Schuster, 1970.

Talbot, David, and Zheutin, Barbara. *Creative Differences: Profiles of Hollywood Dissidents.* Boston: South End Press, 1978.

Talese, Gay. *Thy Neighbor's Wife.* Garden City, N.Y.: Doubleday, 1980.

Tebbell, John. *The Media in America.* New York: Crowell, 1974.

Teodoro, Massimo, ed. *The New Left: A Documentary History.* Indianapolis: Bobbs-Merrill, 1969.

Toffler, Alvin. *Future Shock.* New York: Random House, 1970.

Tuchman, Gaye. *Making News: A Study in the Construction of Reality.* New York: Free Press, 1978.

Vidal, Gore. *1876: A Novel.* New York: Ballantine, 1976.

Walker, Daniel. *Rights in Conflict: Convention Week in Chicago, August 25–29, 1968: A Report.* New York: Dutton, 1968.

Weber, Ronald, ed. *The Reporter as Artist: A Look at the New Journalism Controversy.* New York: Hastings House, 1970.

West, Celeste, and Wheat, Valerie. *The Passionate Perils of Publishing.* San Francisco: Booklegger Press, 1978.

Wilson, Michael. *Salt of the Earth* (screenplay). Commentary by Rosenfelt, Deborah Silverton. Old Westbury, N.Y.: The Feminist Press, 1978.

Wolseley, Roland E. *The Black Press, USA.* Ames, Iowa: Iowa State University Press, 1971.

Youngblood, Gene. *Expanded Cinema.* New York: Dutton, 1970.

Index